DISRUPTIONS

DISRUPTIONS

Constitutional Struggles,
from the Charter to Meech Lake

ALAN C. CAIRNS

Edited by Douglas E. Williams

Canadian Cataloguing in Publication Data

Cairns, Alan C.
  Disruptions : constitutional struggles, from the Charter to Meech Lake

Includes bibliographical references.
ISBN 0-7710-1874-6

1. Canada – Constitutional history. 2. Canada –
Politics and government. 3. Canada – Constitutional
law. I. Williams, Douglas E., 1949–   . II. Title.

JL31.C35 1991   320.971   C90-094947-3

73891

Printed and bound in Canada by John Deyell Company

McClelland & Stewart Inc.
The Canadian Publishers
481 University Avenue
Toronto, Ontario
M5G 2E9

Contents

Editor's Preface

Constitutional issues above all, of course, are those which implicate a
common general interest and are testing-grounds of unity.
                                        – J.A. Corry, *My Life and Work*

. . . they had not thought their way through the conditions which limit
and determine any definition of the national interest.
                    – Frank H. Underhill, *In Search of Canadian Liberalism*

These essays by one of Canada's most eminent political scientists provide
students of Canadian politics, law, and society with much needed historical perspective on our recent constitutional turmoil. Spanning nearly
two decades of intense socio-political and constitutional transformation
– from the electoral victory of the Parti Québécois to the recent death of
the Meech Lake/Langevin Constitutional Accord – the essays gathered
here probe both the substance and the process of the Constitution Act of
1982, with particular emphasis on the far-reaching implications of the
Charter of Rights and Freedoms, the hotly contested implications of the
Meech Lake Accord, and the intellectual and political impediments that
jeopardize the overall health of Canadian constitutional development.

The essays – several of which appear here for the first time and most of
which have yet to receive widespread exposure – are organized chronolog-
ically in the order of their composition. This, in turn, reflects the evolving challenges as well as political and academic responses to the
increasingly unstable, leftover business of Canada's constitutional past.
In Professor Cairns's introduction, written especially for this volume, as
well as in Chapters One and Two, the sources of and tensions within the

increasingly self-conscious constitutional discourse that has come to characterize our times are explored in the context of a number of recently emergent social and political forces. Most notable among these are the emergence of a broadly based nationalist movement in Quebec, the growth of strong provincializing tendencies in Canadian federalism as a whole, former Prime Minister Trudeau's deep commitment to a pan-Canadianizing and entrenched Charter of Rights and Freedoms, and various attempts to overcome and respond to the crisis in national unity that characterized the late seventies, the most notable of which was the Pepin-Robarts Report of the Task Force on Canadian Unity.

The author's introduction also draws attention to the profound transformation to Canadian constitutionalism represented by the addition of an entrenched Charter of Rights and Freedoms. The Charter, he observed in 1981, is not merely "playing around with the externals of our existence." On the contrary, he characteristically argued, "over time the cumulative results of its application will reach deeply into our innermost being, manipulating our psyche, and transforming our self-image." Our children, he goes on to contend, "will be very different people because of this Charter." Such a dynamic, social-psychological view of the Charter on Cairns's part is but the most recent instalment of his ongoing attempt to disabuse Canadians of the all-too-common tendency to think of constitutions as merely formal, instrumental arrangements of the machinery of government and the division of powers.

As he observed some two decades ago in "The Living Canadian Constitution," an essay that is emblematic of his thought as a whole, a functioning constitution for an historic people such as Canadians "is also a set of internalized rules and norms that structures the behaviour of citizens and office holders." It embodies, he goes on to observe, "conceptions of community that help mould citizen identities, and it makes a potent contribution to the symbolic order from which Canadians seek recognition and affirmation of their various identities and values."[1] In one fashion or another, virtually all of the essays in this volume underscore the extent to which the Constitution Act of 1982, especially its Charter of Rights and Freedoms, represents a profoundly different relationship between Canadians and their governments than the constitutional arrangements it replaced. More specifically, Chapters Three, Four, and Seven underscore the extent to and terms under which the constitutional settlement of 1982 was a true, but extremely unstable political compromise. It was riddled with largely unanticipated contradictions, the resolution of which eluded us as a national political community during the Meech Lake/Langevin rounds of constitutional negotiations.

While the Charter underlined our rights as Canadians, thereby strengthening the national community within the federation as a whole, the amending formula of the 1982 constitution reaffirmed the primacy of governments and an enhanced role for the provinces in all subsequent constitutional change. In the essays that follow, Cairns outlines the extent to which this fundamental contradiction was exacerbated by the terms agreed to by the federal government and the provinces during the initial negotiations that led to the Meech Lake Accord. In the wake of the 1982 Constitution, federal and provincial governments confronted a profoundly different citizenry than that of the pre-Charter era, a citizenry deeply involved in and differentially affected by the future of constitutional change. Whereas earlier discussions of constitutional renewal had almost exclusively concerned themselves with problems stemming from one or another aspect of federalism – reconciling the aspirations of the French- and English-speaking "founding" peoples, or those of the territorially based provincial communities and the federal government, for example – the post-1982 period witnessed the emergence of a host of newly chartered constituencies, each with a niche and vested interest in both the process and substance of all further modifications to the constitution.

In his recent Corry Lecture at Queen's University, Cairns described this change in Canadian constitutional culture as one of "constitutional minoritarianism." The constitutional changes of 1982 – above all the Charter – literally brought a host of new groups and their identities into the constitution in an historically unprecedented manner. The inclusion of Section 27, for example, with its explicit reference to the multicultural heritage of Canadians, "inevitably generates a specific debate on the relevance of ethnicity for how we treat each other in the public domain, and how we view ourselves as a people."[2] In Chapter Seven below, Cairns explores some of the complexities of this emergent ethnic dimension in our constitutional culture, as well as some of the intellectual barriers (especially among political scientists and lawyers) that stand in the way of our full appreciation of its significance and volatility.

The 1982 Constitution Act similarly provided a new site of contestation and the positional struggle over relative status and tangible rewards for the male-female cleavage and gender disputes by virtue of Sections 28 and 15, for aboriginal peoples through Section 25 of the Charter, Section 35 of the Constitution Act, and Section 91 (24) of the BNA Act, which grant them a special constitutional identity, and for a host of "disadvantaged individuals and groups" – including those defined in terms of "race, national or ethnic origin, colour, religion, sex, age or mental or physical disability" – by virtue of Section 15 (1 and 2). Such a proliferation of constitutional vantage points and identities poses a severe challenge to scholars, politicians, bureaucrats, citizens, lawyers, and judges alike as their inherited mind-sets previously had inclined them to approach the constitution almost exclusively in terms of the traditional languages of federalism and parliamentary government.

In Chapters Eight and Nine, Professor Cairns delicately explores some of the more debilitating sources of intellectual and disciplinary reluctance to adjust to the emergence of this new constitutional culture. Prominent among these, as just noted, are the hegemony among political scientists and many constitutional experts of the traditional languages of parliamentary government and federalism, as well as a long-standing neglect among political scientists of questions of race, ethnicity, and the symbolic allocation of status, and the inability of English Canadians to define themselves as a truly national community in the way that the Francophone Québécois have increasingly managed to do. Students of Cairns's earlier work will be familiar with his long-held view that such studies in the sociology of our knowledge and ignorance are integral moments in both the life of a discipline such as political science and the world it strives to comprehend and help to understand itself. For those engaging his ideas for the first time, I would heartily reiterate one of Cairns's favorite acronyms, FRIN – further research is necessary; save in this instance, the research in question is mere reading and, therefore, a great deal easier than original archival work since Cairns's essays on such matters are readily available and their context pellucidly clear.[3]

The most critical essays in this volume concern the process and substance of the recently defeated Meech Lake/Langevin Accord. Chapter Four analyses the growing rift between the less deferential, more participatory attitude of the post-1982 constitutional chartered groups and their elites, on the one hand, and the more typical attempt of both levels of government to frustrate such an emergent culture of participation, on the other. During the Meech Lake fiasco, both the federal and provincial governments drastically underestimated and sought to bypass the complexities that flow from having brought the citizenry into the constitution through the Charter in the manner suggested above. Given such enormous changes in Canada's constitutional culture, and the contradiction at the heart of the 1982 Constitution Act, Cairns contends here that "Canadians have stumbled into a constitutional game without having agreed on the rules to govern the competition or the norms that the results are to serve." Chapters Six and Seven explore the dynamics by which the so-called "Quebec round" of constitutional negotiations that led to the initial Meech Lake/Langevin Accord quickly became, in fact, an unprecedented provincializing exercise in constitutional change at the grave expense of any sustained concern for or defence of the national interest as a whole.

The author's conclusion, written especially for this collection, is above all concerned – as its title suggests – with passing judgement on the demise of the Meech Lake/Langevin constitutional accord. After a detailed consideration of the question of whether or not Quebec was "betrayed" by the process of constitutional patriation and renewal in 1982, the author goes on to build upon the earlier reflections of J.A. Corry concerning the necessity of developing an ethos of constitutional morality to preserve the national political community in the face of powerful tendencies currently at play threatening its very survival. At this point in history, citizens, politicians, and scholars alike desperately are in need of an extension of the sort of civility that Corry argued on behalf of in the constitutional relations between the two competing orders of governance in his time. Not only do we need a more democratized amending process of the constitution than the one devised in 1982, Cairns argues, but we also require a far more extensive public debate of the substance of reform than was possible in the Meech Lake process, including all the supports that such a debate requires (such as principled government position papers, an open, public process of consultation, and a scholarly commentary sensitive to the dramatically changed nature of Canada's constitutional culture).

In his earlier attempt at an intellectual autobiography, Alan Cairns tellingly remarked that "one of the most difficult challenges for an academic is to bring an authentic, personal voice to the collective disciplinary task of research and writing."[4] The degrees of difficulty in rising to such challenges increase enormously during times of political crisis and constitutional turmoil – times when even the most "objective" of scholars feel their most cherished values and communities eroding beneath their most recent footnotes, reflections, and hopes. It is a great tribute to the personal as well as professional character of the author that these essays keep both sets of obligations and interests fully in sight – in understanding, in principled reflection, and in sympathy with the viewpoints and constituencies with which he disagrees. Were our political elites and fellow students of Canada's recent constitutional malaise to do the same, there *might* just be some hope that our future, whatever its manifest imperfections, would be a shared adventure as opposed to the currently disastrous dead end it seems headed toward.

Author's Introduction: The Growth of Constitutional Self-Consciousness

These occasional essays, spread over a dozen years, are one person's attempt to make sense of Canada's tumultuous history from the Parti Québécois victory to the rise and fall of the Meech Lake Accord. They focus on the concluding half of the most acrimonious period of constitutional struggle since Confederation. That period, which began in 1960 with the victory of the Lesage Liberals in Quebec, culminated in a frenetic decade and a half that included the 1976 election of the Parti Québécois, the 1980 Quebec referendum, the 1982 Constitution Act, and finally, the drama of the Meech Lake Accord.

With Meech Lake behind us, an era of constitutional challenge and response that began with the breakdown of the post-World War Two constitutional consensus is now history. More generally, if more speculatively, the Canada that was born in 1867, for which provincehood was the essential vehicle for accommodating Francophone Quebec, appears also to be passing into history. The attempts in recent years to patch up traditional Canada have failed, and the calm and confident voices emanating from Quebec as these words are being written (early July, 1990) unhesitatingly assert that yesterday's Canada is just that, that an extensive disentanglement of Quebec from Canada is on the short-term horizon. The Meech Lake debate makes clear that behind the linguistic division between Francophone Quebec and English Canada lie two constitutional solitudes, whose containment within the same country appears increasingly problematic. In that debate, the inability of English Canada to appreciate the significance of the Accord for Quebec was paralleled by the insensitivity of Francophone Quebecers to pan-Canadian values.[1]

13

The sources of the breakdown in constitutional consensus that became visible in the sixties are more complex and diverse than is commonly believed. The most potent challenge came from the politicized state-centred Québécois nationalism that emerged in the early sixties, gained a passionate advocate in the Parti Québécois, and gave credibility to the possibility that a Quebec outside of or loosely associated with Canada was realistic. While demands for constitutional change spread to the other provinces, those from Quebec had a unique gravity, for only Quebec could plausibly threaten to fracture Canada.

Clearly, the constitutional aggressiveness of the western Canadian provinces, and of Newfoundland in the Brian Peckford era, was more than free-rider exploitation of the constitutional fissure carved out by Quebec, but their demands were not driven by ethnic nationalism, by the memories of a former conquest, or by the impressive population figures and diversified economy that were inescapably part of Quebec's threatening bargaining power. That qualification aside, the constitutional provincialism of the other provinces was not a paper tiger, but was the constitutional expression of an impressive array of province-building measures. If the more extreme provincial demands were more passionately espoused by governing provincial elites than by the provincial residents for whom they claimed to speak (see Chapter Two), those elites wielded weighty fiscal, bureaucratic, and jurisdictional resources that made their voices count. Based on their official status, provincial premiers and cabinet ministers came together with their federal counterparts in the executive federalism arena in which the rolling adjustments to a managed federalism were worked out. As constitutional crises and conferences succeeded each other, both orders of government devoted increasing bureaucratic resources to manipulating a constitutional order that in more normal times was simply taken for granted. As Canada lurched toward possible disintegration, a shrewd constitutional self-consciousness, fluctuating between aggressive self-interest and a diffuse concern for the overall constitutional order, became part of the habitual mind-set of first ministers, ministers of intergovernmental affairs, and their advisers.

By themselves, the challenges posed by Quebec and the other provinces to the constitution under which they claimed to be groaning would have generated much of the constitutional activity explored in the following essays. Government domination of the constitutional order, however, was not unchallenged. From the sixties to the eighties, a mushrooming battery of society-driven demands vied for the attention of constitutional policy-makers.

These constitutional pressures from below, which were especially strong in English Canada, were mutually reinforcing. They all contested the dominance of governments as power centres in the constitutional order, the centrality of federalism as the key constitutional organizing variable, and the assumption that the English- and French-speaking founding or charter peoples were privileged social categories to which the constitution and public policy should be inordinately sensitive. European ethnic groups, particularly the Ukrainians, disputed the premise behind the Royal Commission on Bilingualism and Biculturalism by resisting the second-class status accorded to them by its title and terms of reference. As a result, the official policy of multiculturalism announced in 1971, following on the earlier Official Languages Act of 1969, separated language and culture in Canadian policy. Canada, as a consequence, was to have two official languages but no official cultures.

The ethnic challenge to French-English hegemony was not restricted to later immigrants whose ancestors had not met on the Plains of Abraham. Canada, along with other settler countries, confronted an unexpected revival and aggressiveness of its aboriginal populations. Status Indians received the federal franchise in 1960, successfully resisted the assimilationist objectives of the federal government's 1969 White Paper on Indian Policy, and along with the Métis and non-status Indians rapidly acquired a remarkable political visibility. The latter two groups struggled to gain (or regain) some of the recognition and services that their status brethren received. Indian women, who had lost their status on marriage to non-status men, fought and regained that status in 1985. In 1982, the Métis made a major symbolic breakthrough when they were identified in the Constitution Act as one of the aboriginal peoples of Canada. The Inuit, previously labelled Eskimos, emerged from their long obscurity as one of Canada's forgotten peoples, and by the eighties they were key participants in the constitutional conferences exploring self-government possibilities for aboriginal peoples.

Sex joined ethnicity as a politicized social category following on the report of the Royal Commission on the Status of Women (1970), formed in response to feminist pressures. The women's movement, as it came to be called, received institutional recognition in various ministries and bureaus at federal and provincial levels, developed its own organizations and leadership, and turned its attention to the constitutional arena in the late seventies. Its aggressive lobbying led to the sex equality clause (Section 28) of the Charter and a wording in the Section 15 equality clause that was sensitive to many of the demands of women's groups. By the late eighties, the women's movement in English Canada, although seriously weakened and upset by its constitutional disagreement with its Québécois counterpart, was one of the most vigorous opponents of the Meech Lake Accord, fearing that it would weaken the sex equality rights of the Charter.

Politicization also spread to visible minorities, a new social category (and a new label) that crystallized following the more relaxed immigration requirements of the mid-sixties that opened Canada to immigrants from Africa, Asia, the Pacific islands, and the West Indies. Finally, as a result of the 1982 Charter, official-language minorities – Francophones outside and Anglophones inside Quebec – acquired constitutional entitlements in education that singled them out from the general provincial populations in whose midst they resided.

The political and constitutional emergence of the preceding groups was stimulated by the diffusion of an anti-majoritarian ideology of rights that on the one hand generated pressure for protection from discrimination, and on the other hand led to claims in appropriate circumstances for affirmative action for particular groups. At the legislative level, the policy response to rights demands was a proliferation of human rights commissions across the federal system and the progressive expansion of their mandates. In constitutional terms, the first significant response was the 1960 Diefenbaker Bill of Rights that, in spite of its many weaknesses, including the fact that it was only an ordinary statute of Parliament, injected a hesitant citizen-state discourse into the constitutional arena. As this rights-oriented discourse gathered strength it became a helpful political resource for the later Trudeau federal governments that saw a strong Charter as a potent instrument of Canadian unity.

The multiplication of self-conscious minorities in an increasingly heterogeneous society challenged the post-war constitutional world with its taken-for-granteds of federalism and parliamentary government, of a version of founding peoples dualism in which the British were more equal than the French but both were more equal than the others, of a quiescent and relatively invisible native population, and of a sexual division of labour and prestige in which the public sphere of politics and state affairs was *de facto* if not *de jure* reserved for men. Unlike Quebec nationalism and the aggressive provincialism of English Canada that challenged the constitutional order on, so to speak, its own traditional terms, these new or reinvigorated socio-political movements threatened many of the basic, often implicit, social assumptions on which the constitutional order had rested.

Perhaps appropriately, the massive decline in the deference accorded to men by women, to Anglophones by Francophones, to the rest of Canadians by aboriginal peoples, and to the French and the English by those who came later coincided with the attenuation and then virtual disappearance of the political and emotional significance of the formerly potent British connection. The traditional elitism of the constitution was no longer legitimated by its now fading British imperial roots. After the domestication of the amending formula in the 1982 Constitution Act, Canadians could no longer avoid the self-examination and the self-responsibility for their constitutional identity and evolution that had been possible as long as major constitutional amendments required the passage of legislation by the British Parliament. Belatedly, more than a century after Confederation, Canadians were on their own, freed from the external (if only symbolic) authority that had previously acted as a mild restraint on centrifugal pressures. For example, after the passage of the 1982 Constitution Act, status Indians, who could no longer look to the British Crown as the protector of their treaty and other rights, became much more politically aggressive.

As the British past became more memory than living reality the explicit language of rights displaced the implicit trust in authorities and the related hierarchical community assumptions formerly fostered by a monarchical tradition. Concurrently, as Canadians moved toward final control of their constitutional future, their domestic heterogeneity was both more pronounced and its component parts more politicized than previously. Consequently, the voyage of constitutional self-discovery on which Canadians embarked went far beyond the federal-provincial dimensions of their existence to the exploration of the political consequences and constitutional significance of sex, race, ethnicity, language, and other cleavages of contemporary Canadian society.

In spite of the preceding stress on societal pluralism, it is not wildly inappropriate to examine the constitutional history of the 1960-90 period in federalist terms, as the era of the titanic struggle between federal and provincial governments, especially Quebec, to shape the future of Canadian federalism. The centralized federalism of the first decade and a half after World War Two did not survive into the sixties and seventies when challenged by centrifugal pressures channeled into the constitutional arena by provincial governments. Thus, the first three chapters dealing with the period up to the proclaiming of the 1982 Constitution Act focus mainly on the concerns and actions of governments and political parties, on the premise that they were the leading actors in this period of constitutional change.

That premise was sustained in this early bout of constitution-making by the absence of a Charter, which was later to draw Canadians directly into the constitutional order, and by a complementary definition of the constitutional issue as federal and thus to be resolved by rearranging the relations among governments. Admittedly, the elitism to which this led was no longer sacrosanct. Quebec appealed to its electorate in a referendum on its future relations with Canada in 1980. From the mid-seventies onward, the federal government carefully prepared itself for a possible unilateral appeal to Westminster for patriation and constitutional changes that would bypass provincial governments, and would have to rest on popular support. Further, the major constitutional change consistently sought by the federal government from the late sixties was a Charter, in the struggle for which its presumed beneficiaries, an emerging civil rights constituency, played a strong supporting role.

Since the Charter's arrival, it is no longer possible to think of the constitution almost exclusively in terms of federalism and parliamentary government, the institutional arrangements in which executive dominance flourishes – in the former by the practices of executive federalism that bring governments together to manage their inescapable interdependence, and in the latter by the theory of responsible government and the instrument of the disciplined majority party on which it is normally based. The Charter selectively challenges executive dominance in both of these arenas – in the former by affixing a taint of illegitimacy to the practice of first ministers deciding on the substance of constitutional amendments in secret, which they then announce as a *fait accompli* to citizens viewed as spectators, and in the latter by giving individuals and litigation lobby groups the capacity to challenge government legislation in the courts.

By the time of the Meech Lake Accord, the traditional dominance of governments in formal constitutional change no longer appeared legitimate to the representatives of the numerous groups that challenged its substance and process. It is depressingly evident that the leading actors in the governments that structured the Meech Lake process drastically underestimated the Charter's impact on the constitutional culture of Canadians, especially in English Canada. Clearly, the constitution was no longer a concern only of governments. On the contrary, women, visible minorities, the disabled, and others felt that they, too, now had stakes in the constitution, and they inevitably assumed that changes in the constitution that might weaken their rights were by definition not matters to be decided by governments alone. Thus, one of the most dramatic developments of the seventies and eighties was the enlarging of the cast of would-be constitutional actors.

Our understanding of the new reality produced by the emergence of these new players is hampered by the too-easy availability of the traditional inherited language of federalism and by the natural tendency of governments to justify their constitutional objectives as being no more than readjustments of federalism that properly concerned them alone; thus the early tendency of governments to discuss, explain, and justify the Meech Lake Accord in the federalism terms of bringing Quebec back into the constitutional family, as if that task could be pursued without any repercussions on the aboriginal peoples and the various interests that cluster around the Charter. Feminist groups, aboriginal elites, a vast array of ethnic organizations, Charter activists, and others bluntly denied that such a segregation of their concerns and those of governments was possible. They were convinced that their constitutional rights and agenda were or might be threatened by the Meech Lake Accord. By both words and actions they denied the hegemony of federalism issues, the leadership role that governments assumed flowed from such issues, and the implicit claims by governments that the constitutional management of federalism could be neatly compartmentalized from the concerns of these emergent constitutional clienteles.

The Charter also challenged the belief that the representation of territorially bounded populations by the leaders of the governments of Canadian federalism was an adequate response to the representational requirements of constitutional bargaining. With the Charter in place, it was now a criticism, not simply an observation, to note that, unlike first ministers, not all Canadians are "white, male, able-bodied, middle-aged, and Christian." Further, those who accusingly proffered these observations had few doubts that their constitutional concerns would be overlooked if one of their own was not at the table.[2]

The unwillingness of various groups that formerly could be excluded or ignored to accept any longer their sideline status is a remarkable constitutional development. It reflects the convergence of several interrelated factors. The new aggressiveness of women, aboriginals, and others and the rhetoric of rights that they wielded were in broad terms supported by changes in the international environment. The idea of rights was vigorously championed by the United Nations in its Charter, in the 1948 Universal Declaration of Human Rights, and in an ever-growing list of rights covenants that were frequently followed by consciousness-raising ventures, such as International Women's Year in 1975 and the Decade of Disabled Persons (1983-1992), to stimulate positive state action. The ending of European imperialisms and the delegitimation of the racial hierarchies on which they had been based made an independent contribution to the attack on ethnically or racially based inequalities within Western states. This cultural shift was of special significance in Canada because of the profound ethnic and racial transformation of Canadian society from the mid-sixties to the present.

Concurrently, a positive self-consciousness developed among various formerly marginalized groups, epitomized by the phrase "coming out" that gays and lesbians employed as they left their closets, and this self-consciousness insisted on respect for their "difference." "Coming out," or perhaps more appropriately "becoming visible," can also be applied to women, aboriginals, the disabled, racial minorities, and others. Formerly peripheral, isolated, and ignored groups came out of the background and replaced their former deference and quiescence with a demanding, sometimes shrill behaviour suggestive of the insecurities that accompanied the transition from passivity to a more public posture.

In the Canadian case, the opening up of the constitution stimulated a specific constitutional self-consciousness in the innumerable groups that paraded before the hearings of task forces and federal and provincial constitutional committees that were a pervasive feature of the seventies and eighties. Inevitably, the participants came to see the constitution not as a permanent, unchanging part of the institutional landscape but rather both as a potential policy instrument for their particular goals and as making the most fundamental statement that a society can about who counts, and how much.

The impact of the preceding developments, international as well as domestic and cultural as well as explicitly constitutional, would have been much less had it not been for the simultaneous explosive emergence of interest groups to speak for these new identities and ambitions. According to a recent Canadian survey, over three-quarters of citizens' groups dealing with environmental, multicultural, native, and women's issues have been founded since 1960. Their rapid growth, including a capacity to prepare briefs and appear before legislative committees, was immensely aided by extensive government subsidization. From the survey just noted, nearly half of the groups' revenues came from government sources, rising to over 80 per cent for native groups.[3] This funding assistance accelerated the build-up of expertise and self-confidence and gave group organizations the resources to maintain visibility and contact with their clientele.

The most important political stimulus to citizen constitutional participation, at least in English Canada, came from the Charter, and for aboriginals from the clauses that defined "aboriginal," protected their rights, and guaranteed them constitutional conferences at which their rights were to be defined.[4]

The federal government viewed the Charter positively as a nation-building instrument. Many of the provincial governments viewed it apprehensively and with hostility as province-weakening. For many of the citizen groups, however, it was profoundly status-enhancing. For the first time they had a major place in the constitutional order. The constitution spoke to them generally in the language of rights, and often specifically to particular groups by individual clauses that pertained especially to them. The sense of entitlement and recognition held by such groups was enhanced by their almost universal belief that their particular clauses had been only reluctantly granted in 1980-82 by at least some of the governments, rather than graciously awarded. Thus women, the disabled, and aboriginals, for example, came to feel that particular constitutional clauses or phrases belonged to them, that they had hard-earned niches in the constitution and possessed constitutional stakes, indeed had constitutional identities.[5] Accordingly, it was only to be expected that they would come to think of themselves as constitutional actors, especially if formal constitutional change looked as if it might weaken what they had already won or, in the case of aboriginals, was necessary to add constitutional specificity to the abstract recognitions they had received.

In sum, a dramatic diffusion of a constitutional self-consciousness occurred, especially among the elites and organizational representatives of the various social categories that had been brought into the constitution in 1982, mainly but not exclusively via the Charter. They had attained an admittedly precarious place or recognition in the constitution, partly as a result of their access to the process of constitution-making in 1980-81. That recognition logically and psychologically supported the assumption that their constitutional participant role would be enhanced, not reduced, in constitution-making processes that occurred after they gained constitutional status. The magnitude and significance of this transformation in constitutional culture was not appreciated by the political managers of Meech Lake.

In the aftermath of the 1982 Constitution Act several basic leftover constitutional tasks confronted Canadians. The first, which was viewed as a discrete task, was to identify and define the rights of the aboriginal peoples in a series of constitutional conferences. This effort failed after four conferences, mainly devoted to aboriginal self-government. This failure generated a deep disillusionment in aboriginal leaders that was aggravated by the apparent success of the Meech Lake private sessions in returning Quebec to the constitutional family. The second, and politically the most important, task was to gain the formal allegiance of the Quebec government to the new constitutional order when the time was ripe, presumably by some response to constitutional aspirations that had not been addressed in the 1982 settlement. The third was to integrate the Charter, the newly emerged rights-possessing citizenry, and the specific groups given particular recognition into a revamped constitutional order whose sensitivities could no longer be monopolized by the values of federalism and parliamentary government. That integration could not be confined to the judicial arena in which private actors could challenge government legislation on Charter grounds; nor, as it turned out, could aboriginals be siphoned off into a series of constitutional conferences whose ultimate failure to specify their rights could be considered only an unfortunate sideshow from the real constitutional business of bringing Quebec back in. To put it differently, the constitutional family to which Quebec was to return with honour and enthusiasm was not just the family of the governments of the federal system but a constitutional family that included aboriginal Canadians, as well as the various groups that had been catalysed into constitutional self-consciousness by the Charter.

This was the constitutional context within which the most prominent shortcoming of the 1982 Act, the unwillingness of the Quebec government to agree to its terms, had to be addressed. As the Quebec government had been the prime contributor to the previous quarter of a century of constitutional introspection, Quebec's official alienation was not a minor defect but a major flaw. This political truth was not invalidated by the fact that Quebec's exclusion from the immediate post-referendum intergovernmental consensus on constitutional change had been almost inevitable, given the antipathy of the then-governing Parti Québécois to federalism and the direction of constitutional change congenial to Trudeau. (See Chapter Ten for a discussion of the "betrayal" of Quebec.) Quebec's exclusion was undeniably a serious constitutional weakness that prudent leaders of governments would seek to correct in propitious circumstances.

Theoretically, the healing passage of time, including the socialization of Québécois to the Charter, might have incrementally and almost subconsciously brought Quebec back into the fold, for Quebec's exclusion was not technical or legal – in law the constitution applied to Quebec – but moral, political, and symbolic. There is, in fact, some evidence, admittedly thin, that Quebec's adhesion to the Charter was strengthening at the time of the Meech Lake Accord. Prior to his 1985 election victory, Bourassa had spoken favourably of the Charter.[6] After the election, the new Liberal government stopped the automatic application of the notwithstanding clause to all new legislation. Gil Rémillard, the constitutional scholar and Quebec's Minister for Canadian Intergovernmental Affairs, indicated Quebec's willingness to give the federal Charter priority over Quebec's Charter.[7] He subsequently referred to the Charter as a "document of which we as Quebecers and Canadians can be proud. . . . We want Quebecers to have the same rights as other Canadians."[8] Further, Anglophones and allophones in Quebec, like minorities elsewhere, saw the Charter as a protective instrument.

The Quebec Liberal sympathy for the Charter was not surprising. The 1980 constitutional proposals of the Quebec Liberal Party had argued strongly for a Canadian Charter that would be "at the very heart of the social consensus which must bind all the people of a country."[9] No mention of a notwithstanding clause was made in this proposal. However, the theoretical possibility that a developing Quebec allegiance to the Charter might transform it into the instrument of pan-Canadian unity desired by Trudeau was greatly reduced by several political factors. Quebec's constitutional exclusion was a valuable political resource to various political actors, a resource that was not to be incrementally and casually dissipated when Quebec's exclusion could be the occasion for constitutional gains for Quebec and political rewards to those who could gain credit for this breakthrough. Further, the depth of that exclusion was most readily underlined, especially by the Parti Québécois, by identifying the Charter as an instrument that reduced the powers of the Quebec government. That perception had been fed by the unwillingness of Trudeau, when the Charter was being fashioned, to extend the notwithstanding clause to minority language rights, especially dealing with the language of education in the provinces.

For the Parti Québécois, this had been a crucial reason for rejecting the agreement that became the 1982 Constitution Act. "[N]o self-respecting Quebec government," asserted Lévesque before the Quebec National Assembly, "could ever abandon the smallest fraction of this absolutely fundamental right to protect the only French island in the English-speaking sea of the North American continent."[10] The Quebec government's deeply and passionately felt sense of exclusion, which was simultaneously a beneficial political asset that could be wielded in the next round of constitutional bargaining, generated a comprehensive response. The government and the nationalist intellectual elite of the province succeeded brilliantly in portraying the 1982 Act as a betrayal of Quebec. The government refused to participate in constitutional conferences and generally reduced its participation in the intergovernmental arena. The Parti Québécois further underlined its constitutional alienation by an across-the-board application of the Section 33 notwithstanding clause, a stratagem they could employ because the Charter's language of education clauses facilitated the portrayal of "the Canadian Charter as merely the latest in a long series of alien regimes imposed on Quebec by *les Anglais* [and made] . . . it politically easy to pass a blanket *non obstante* provision applicable to all existing Quebec legislation."[11] Lévesque's attitude to the Charter was summed up in his pithy comment that the government would "make it as . . . difficult as we can for . . . that bloody Charter to be applied to Quebec."[12]

Weiler's apt summary of the Charter's early years in Quebec is cogent: "By taking the initiative immediately, before the Charter had time to put down roots in Quebec political life, and by making the use of the *non obstante* formula a matter of legislative routine, the Parti Québécois was able to remove all the political hazard of invoking the formula for particular laws, thus frustrating the entire scheme of the Charter."[13] The negative Parti Québécois attitude to the Charter coloured its response to Mulroney's indicated willingness to reach an accord with Quebec. In 1985 the Parti Québécois government proposed that Quebec be exempted from all but the democratic rights (Sections 3-5) of the Canadian Charter and that the primary rights protection for Québécois should be found in the Quebec Charter of Human Rights and Freedoms.[14] The Charter's negative image in Quebec was subsequently sustained by the fact that up until 1989 Quebec had had more statutes struck down (five) than any other province, and these had tended to be major statutes dealing with language and education.[15]

Thus, while the early responses of the new Bourassa government were relatively sympathetic to the Charter, its reception in Quebec was always more conditional than elsewhere in Canada. In particular, the Parti Québécois, initially as a government (1976-85) and subsequently as a major opposition party, was deeply concerned "about entrenchment of individual rights in the area of language, since such rights could alter the social and cultural priorities reflected in collective rights in that area."[16] Also, the Parti Québécois gave the use of the notwithstanding clause against the Charter a certain nationalist legitimacy in Quebec that it lacked in other provinces.[17] Nevertheless, the Meech Lake Accord would have signalled an official Quebec government acceptance of the Charter. This would have removed the stigma of its inclusion in what the nationalists viewed as the imposed Constitution Act of 1982. That acceptance, however, required that the Charter and indeed the entire

"Constitution of Canada shall be interpreted in a manner consistent with . . . the recognition that Quebec constitutes within Canada a distinct society" – the Meech Lake response to one of Quebec's five conditions for its allegiance to the constitution.[18]

The positive response of the Conservative Mulroney government to Quebec's five conditions emerged from the history of competition between Liberals and Conservatives for the Quebec federal vote. For nearly two decades, the federal Liberals under Trudeau had battled Québécois nationalism in all its guises. With the at least temporary return of the independence-seeking nationalists to the federalist game after the referendum, there was an obvious mutuality of interest between the federal Conservatives seeking a breakthrough in Quebec and the chastened nationalist forces seeking to expand Quebec's power within federalism. Since this led to a strongly nationalist Quebec group in the caucus of Mulroney's victorious Conservatives after the 1984 election, there were strong political pressures in both Quebec and Ottawa for a Meech Lake type of response to Quebec's exclusion. Thus, it was almost inevitable that the Conservative government would make common cause with the Quebec nationalists, including the Bourassa Liberal government, in highlighting the major flaw of 1982, the exclusion (or betrayal) of Quebec. Both the provincial Liberals and the federal Conservatives would gain politically from a successful effort to repair the damage.

This scenario's attractiveness was enhanced by the fact that Mulroney was a bilingual Quebecer who appeared to be personally driven by a powerful antipathy to Trudeau, and by a personal desire to surpass him in the history books.[19] Further, the 1982 Constitution Act and particularly the Charter were much less valued by the Tories, who had obstructed its legislative passage prior to the September, 1981, Supreme Court decision, than by the Liberals, for whom the Charter was a crowning achievement. This eroded the resistance of the Progressive Conservative Party to a profitable alliance with the Quebec nationalists to rectify what they both described as the constitutional immorality of the Trudeau Liberals in proceeding without Quebec in 1982.[20]

In reality, such a Conservative alliance with Quebec nationalists had much deeper roots than the particular setting of party competition in the mid-eighties. Diefenbaker had benefited from an electoral alliance with the Union Nationale of Duplessis in 1958; Stanfield had espoused a two-nations philosophy in 1968; and Joe Clark had brought Quebec nationalists into the party and shown sympathy for the nationalist demands of Quebec. In all cases, the structure of federal party competition in Quebec inevitably left federal Conservative leaders with little choice but to align themselves with the Quebec nationalist cause. The Conservatives were desperately trying to escape from an historic condition of inferiority in Quebec that had nineteenth-century roots. This was clearly indicated by Lowell Murray after the apparently successful constitutional bargaining at Meech Lake and Langevin House, when he proudly asserted that the Conservative Party "has been waiting for an achievement like this since the day Louis Riel was hanged."[21]

In spite of the Quebec origins of Meech Lake, as the pieces fell into place it became clear that the Quebec round would be a provincial round, that the bulk of the concessions to Quebec would be extended to the remaining nine provinces as a response to the principle of the equality of the provinces. This is one of the themes, somewhat acerbically presented, of Chapters Five and Six. They make clear that the self-restraint the other provinces agreed to apply to their own distinctive constitutional demands would be generously compensated. Thus, getting the other provincial governments initially on side was not as difficult as might appear from the "Quebec round" label (inaccurately) applied to this constitutional package. It remains surprising, however, how little comment has been devoted to the fact that seven provincial governments, all but Ontario and New Brunswick, that had deserted Quebec in 1981-82, and thus shared the responsibility for Quebec's "betrayal," were also to benefit handsomely from the attempt to repair the constitutional damage for which they had been at least guilty accomplices.

Chapters Four and Seven, like Chapters Five and Six, written while Meech Lake was still an ongoing saga, exploit the Meech Lake materials to make particular points about the kind of constitutional people Canadians are becoming. The former portrays the emerging cast of would-be constitutional actors – women, aboriginals, the disabled, etc. – and documents their fury, prior to the breakthroughs in the Manitoba and New Brunswick hearings, at a constitutional amendment process that occasionally allowed them to speak at legislative hearings, with the proviso that the seamless Meech Lake web was to be immune from their criticisms.

The message of Chapter Four, which has subsequently been echoed by nearly all of the badly bruised first ministers emerging from the Meech Lake failure, is that closed sessions of executive federalism are no longer legitimate vehicles from which *ex cathedra* pronouncements of proposed constitutional changes can be issued to the subservient faithful. Chapter Seven underlines the point that needs no underlining to a Vancouverite, that the shrinking proportion of Canadians of French and British background is no longer capable of sustaining a "two founding peoples" definition of Canada. Aboriginal leaders pointedly add that if founding people status is to be taken seriously, the claims of their people are sufficiently superior that the British and French should be regarded as recent immigrants still settling in. From the opposite end of the time scale, the new arrivals decreasingly drawn from Europe and disproportionately concentrated in the three metropolitan centres of Vancouver, Montreal, and Toronto are resistant to a constitutional order that, as in Meech Lake, and aboriginals excepted, appears to equate constitutional significance to the length of one's ancestral line in Canada.

At the most general level, the Meech Lake failure was due to the inability of the old federalism, defined as an affair of governments, to beat back the new constitutional forces stimulated by the Charter and by the scattering of aboriginal clauses in various parts of the constitution. Defence of the Charter and the new constitutional order it symbolized against the encroachments of the Accord was the dominant theme of the Accord's critics before legislative committees. There was also a certain symbolic appropriateness that the filibuster that made it impossible for the Manitoba legislature to meet the June 23 deadline was led by an aboriginal MLA, Elijah Harper, whose cousin had been shot by a Winnipeg policeman in an incident that led to a provincial native justice inquiry. The Manitoba Chiefs' organization that backed him made it clear that their objective was to kill the Accord. The analysis of the Accord as the setting for a confrontation between newer and older versions of the constitution is a major theme of Chapter Ten, written especially for this volume.

The rise and fall of the Meech Lake Accord will become one of the most intensely examined episodes in Canadian history. In an overworked phrase, Meech Lake, in spite of its name, is a watershed.

We know with some confidence what is behind us, and we can make plausible, if contestable, statements about what caused the Meech Lake failure. The future is more of a question mark, although it is reasonably certain that the Quebec/rest-of-Canada relationship will be much looser than was true of the first century and a quarter of our common existence. Each increment of prediction beyond that generalization is a hostage to fortune and testimony to an unjustified academic self-confidence.

When asked what he thought of the French Revolution, Chou En-lai reportedly said, "It's too soon to tell." [22] Of the Meech Lake Accord and the preceding decades of constitutional activity, it is almost too soon to frame the questions, let alone proffer confident answers. Social scientists have been routinely taken aback recently by futures they did not predict. Thus a paroxysm of laryngitis would appear as a divine blessing to any scholar asked to read aloud the message about the Canadian future to be extracted from the entrails of our constitutional experience.

In large part, the answer the entrails give will depend on whose behalf the question is being asked. The disagreement between Quebec and the rest of Canada over the desirability of the Meech Lake Accord will be repeated in divergent answers to many of the retrospective questions that can be addressed to that searing experience. Meech Lake will join the Durham Report, Confederation, the hanging of Riel, and conscription in two world wars as key historical events whose competing interpretations underline the perennial French-English dualism of Canadian life.

According to a major post-Meech poll, taken shortly after the official demise, two out of three Quebec residents stated the Accord should have been ratified, while two out of three in the rest of Canada were opposed; only 34 per cent of Quebec residents said Quebec should remain a province as now, while in the rest of Canada 81 per cent supported that status for Quebec. Responsibility for the failure of the Accord is apportioned differently in Quebec and the rest of Canada, with Mulroney more strongly blamed outside of Quebec and the reverse being true for Newfoundland Premier Clyde Wells.[23] If the country breaks up, what will initially be seen by many Québécois as an escape into freedom will be experienced very differently as a defeat in English Canada. The latter's identity and *raison d'être* have always been much more bound up with Canada as a coast-to-coast nation, and with a strong central government, than has been true of Francophone Quebecers. It is possible, of course, that English Canada, digesting its lengthy education in a failed attempt to patch up the existing constitutional order, may come to see an independent Quebec more as a blessing than a defeat.

Uncertainty about the future of English Canada, that ambiguous entity that Quebec with its solid Francophone majority defines as the other national partner, is compounded by its lack of cohesion. English Canada is geographically fractured by the massive presence of Quebec sprawling astride the St. Lawrence and separating Atlantic Canada from the five provinces to the west of Quebec. Further, English Canada is no longer British, and its future will be even more multiracial and multicultural than is already the case. The remarkable contemporary experiment in the mixing of peoples that is occurring in many Western states is far advanced in English Canada. While a similar future awaits Quebec, its impact so far is less pronounced in that province. Thus, English Canada is called upon to redefine itself vis-à-vis Quebec while its own ethnic demography is unstable.

An effective response is further hindered by English Canada's political fragmentation into nine provinces and two territories, with an additional substantial minority within Quebec. A provincial premier can speak only for the provincial dimension of the local citizenry. The authoritative voices of provincialism reduce the English Canada for which they imperfectly speak to, at best, an aggregation of friendly rivals. Obviously, the Anglophone and allophone minorities in Quebec do not see their provincial government as a plausible constitutional advocate for their constitutional concerns. The small city-size mixed populations of the northern territories are marginalized by numerical weakness and further reduced in constitutional visibility by the fact that their government leaders lack official status at constitutional conferences. The multiple provincial and territorial voices portray English Canada as a discordant babble.

While from the perspective of a Québécois nationalist this diaspora-like fragmentation may appear to be counterbalanced by English Canada's control of the federal government, this, too, is an illusion. The federal government cannot speak for English Canada as such. Its inescapable mandate as long as Canada survives is to represent all of Canada, which necessarily includes both Quebec and Francophones outside of Quebec. So demanding is that imperative that Canada has had prime ministers from Quebec for all but twelve of the more than forty years since St. Laurent assumed office in November, 1948.

Thus, the structure of the federal system deprives English Canada of any single official actor or centre of power to articulate its concerns. By contrast, the Quebec Francophone population is singularly privileged by its decisive majority status within Quebec and its numerical weakness elsewhere in the country. Premier Lévesque used to complain about how federalism divided Quebecers by pitting their federal against their provincial selves. English Canada is subject to far more profound and disabling divisions, mute testimony to which is offered by the absence of an English-Canadian counterpart to the Quebec Premier to address the problem in English Canada. The divisions in English Canada are not a problem to any government, and that is the problem. Hence, the requirement for English Canada to inform Quebec "what English Canada wants" is a far more difficult task than its reciprocal.

Further, English Canada in some ways has fewer intellectual or psychological resources on which to build a more independent future than does Quebec. Quebec, ever sensitive to its minority condition, is not thinking of independence, sovereignty-association, or a distinct status for Quebec in federalism for the first time. For Quebec, the politics of disentanglement posit an exciting goal, one that builds on an historic and continuing strand in Quebec political thought. Canada-outside-of-Quebec has no such intellectual heritage or minority ambitions on which it can build. As a complacent majority, English Canada has historically been committed to the whole and has not seen the country's break-up as probable or desirable. Should the Quebec response to the perceived Meech Lake rebuff lead to demands for an extensive constitutional separateness of or sovereignty for Quebec, English Canada is unprepared by disposition, by its past pan-Canadian identity, and by the virtual absence of a helpful intellectual heritage for the unsought goal of virtual *de jure* independence for itself.

To some extent, the Charter strengthens the civic identity of English Canada. It has generated a much greater sense of connection to the constitution for English Canadians than formerly prevailed, a recognition that the constitution is not a distant, detached arrangement of supreme indifference to daily life, but on the contrary is the expression of the normative order by which Canadians are supposed to live and by which they define themselves. On the other hand, that consciousness of a constitutional connection is often highly particularistic, stronger at the level of women, ethnic groups, and aboriginals (although their linkage is not primarily with the Charter) than at the level of English Canada as such. In any event, as long as Canada survives, the Charter applies to all of Canada, not just English Canada. Also, although the Charter may constitute a cultural base for an English-Canadian identity, it does not solve the institutional problem that English Canada is headless.

So, as preparations proceed in Quebec for the post-Meech Lake round, English Canada is in a paradoxical and deeply frustrating situation. On the one hand, the constitutional culture of English Canada is newly suffused with a participant ethic and a sense of connection to and identification with the constitution. On the other hand, no vehicle exists to tap and mobilize those participant impulses behind officeholders with a right to speak for English Canada, or the rest of Canada, or Canada-outside-of-Quebec – the available labels are many and equally unsatisfactory – as a potential political community.

Accordingly, the emergence of various forms of constitutional self-consciousness that has been the organizing theme for this introduction applies only weakly to an English Canada considered as a discrete actor that might have an autonomous future thrust upon it. In the next few years, the inchoate character of English Canada and the political difficulty of articulating its constitutional concerns will almost certainly emerge as one of the key impediments to a rational reconstruction of the constitutional future of Canadians. While the existential trauma of the possible break-up of Canada will stimulate efforts to overcome English Canada's lack of voice, they may be inadequate. The manner of disentangling Quebec from Canada may generate a sense of English-Canadian cohesion capable of sustaining a new state of English Canada linked to Quebec, but such a beneficial outcome is not inherent in the nature of things. If that cohesion crystallizes, it will be the result of human will, leadership, and effort overcoming the structural barriers to its emergence. In the fashioning of new constitutional arrangements, the numerical strength of English Canada may not compensate for the political difficulties capable of thwarting the development of coherent options for a meaningful English-Canadian constitutional future. A more elaborate analysis of the difficulty of giving voice to English Canada is presented in Chapter Eight.

These essays do not speak with a single unvarying voice, although they are produced by a single author. The changing constitutional scene they explored was subject to such profound fluctuations from year to year that a total consistency could only have been achieved by a deliberate insulation from the buffeting world outside. Further, in writing them I have been made only too aware that constitutional discussion is an emotional minefield, to be avoided by those who wish to keep their cool.

The constitution is no longer a prosaic document that instrumentally only packages government jurisdictions in separate federal and provincial boxes. It now makes the most authoritative statements available to free societies about the relative status of the various major categories into which the citizens can be divided. Consequently, it taps deep emotions of identity and concerns for status and recognition. Thus, those who are satisfied or dissatisfied with their constitutional treatment employ the language of honour, shame, and betrayal. Mulroney's consistently reiterated goal was to get Quebec to return to the constitutional family with "honour and enthusiasm." Elijah Harper, the aboriginal MLA who thwarted legislative discussion of the Accord in Manitoba, did so in order "to symbolize that aboriginal people are not being recognized as the first people of this country and not being recognized as founders of this country."[24] The vice-chief of the Assembly of First Nations, Ovide Mercredi, asserted that Prime Minister Mulroney had "insulted and hurt aboriginal people by [prematurely] praising Meech Lake as a victory for all Canadians." He added: "The Prime Minister does not understand this country. We had no alternative but to take direct political action [to block the Accord] to defend our integrity and our honor."[25]

This emotional language of identity, hurt, self-esteem, and indignity powerfully indicates how the constitution and our psyches have become intertwined. It underlines the difficulty of constitutional change. One can split the differences in dollars and powers, but pride and dignity are less easily divided.

I have been at public conferences in which panelists have lost their temper and English-Canadian members of the audience have been in tears as they tried to voice their apprehensions that they might outlive their country – the reciprocal of the separatist tears at the time of the 1980 referendum defeat, occasioned by the wounding recognition that the country they were imprisoned in would outlast them.

In such circumstances, dispassion and clinical objectivity are not easily attained by academic and other commentators. The importance of constitutional talk to our future explains both the need for clarity and candour and the impediments that stand in their way. Chapter Nine explores some of the taboos and biases among which we manoeuvre with difficulty as we try to communicate "truth," while hedged in with constraints. Readers of these essays may pick up additional evidence of bias, founded on my sympathy for the Charter, that may inhibit the kind of appreciation of the nationalist realities of Quebec that is natural to Québécois political scientists.[26]

I sympathize with the author who introduced a recent collection of her essays with the remark, "I disagree with myself in this book, and I find in myself both severe and tender feelings toward the [person] I have been, whose thoughts I find here."[27] I offer no apologies for the perhaps too thinly veiled passion and commitment that lie behind these essays, nor for the contradictions an attentive reader will undoubtedly find. Scholars of the contemporary must pay the price of a certain inconsistency as they respond to the refutations offered by a turbulent, unfeeling world to the guiding assumptions of last month's, let alone last decade's, analyses. If there were no contradictions I would despair over my inability to grow and to learn.

Repetitions may outnumber contradictions, for like a dog worrying a bone I have been seized, perhaps obsessed, with certain themes to which I have returned. Although the publisher's editor has removed some of the repetition, some remains. One justification for surviving repetitions was offered by G.K. Chesterton with the laconic observation that no one had listened the first time. A second is that later repetitions, at least in intention, are more subtle and refined. Like other observers and participants in the constitutional game, I have tried to profit from what Canadians have gone through, to the end that nuance might displace unwarranted early simplifications.

My response to the dramatic events through which Canadians have lived is intimately linked to my attitude to Canada, the state and its people that have been the patients of so many recent constitutional doctors. Trudeau was fond of quoting Thucydides, who attributed greatness to Themistocles, a man who could dispassionately accept that Athens was not immortal.[28] To an all-seeing god, who has observed so many Ninevehs and Tyres reduced from greatness to dust, the future of the little Canadian experiment may scarcely deserve an entry in the divine logbook that spans millennia. Even three Canadian historians taking the long view recently averred that if Canada "were to disintegrate Canadians would probably continue to live in much the same way as they do now. And it is the lives of persons, not nations, that really matter."[29]

For most of the professoriate, however, who are neither gods, historians, nor Themistocles, such divine disinterestedness or insouciance is neither what we feel nor seek to attain when our own country is our subject. The Canada that is being left behind was not, in spite of many scars and blemishes, a place and a time for which Canadians need be ashamed. If the comparison is not with utopias eternally waiting to be born but with real-world countries, the Canadian past will deserve a modestly honourable place in the annals of humanity's efforts to create civil polities. At a minimum, a "B+" would probably be awarded by impartial judges.

Chapter One

Recent Federalist Constitutional Proposals

"[I]n Canada constitutional analysis and review is a highly developed science and a widely practised art."[1] Unfortunately, the rejection of constitutional proposals is even more highly developed and widely practised. However, like suitors trying to marry the king's daughter, there is no shortage of candidates for the role of new Founding Fathers.

This commentary will focus mainly on the two most prominent contenders of the last year: (1) the Trudeau federal government position as expressed in the Constitutional Amendment Bill, the supporting white paper *A Time for Action*, and a miscellany of specific position papers, and (2) the three volumes of the Task Force on Canadian Unity, particularly *A Future Together*.[2] A summary of the fragmentary propositions of the Conservatives and the NDP is included.[3] There is much more available to illustrate the present state of constitutional thinking in Canada, in particular the constitutional proposals of the governments of Alberta and British Columbia, *Towards a New Canada* by the Committee on the Constitution of the Canadian Bar Association, the Canada West publication *Alternatives: Towards the Development of an Effective Federal System for Canada*, the First and Second Reports of the Advisory Committee on Confederation of the government of Ontario, the Proceedings of the Special Committee of the Senate on the Constitution, the Proceedings of the Special Joint Committee of the Senate and the House of Commons on the Constitution of Canada, and the working document of the Quebec Liberal Party, *Choose Québec and Canada*. More is yet to come, especially from the contending political forces in Quebec and from the recently elected minority Conservative government.

Preliminary Observations

Several preliminary observations will set the constitutional debate in context.

(1) In the midst of the pressures for change and the reiterated assertions of the need for urgency in constitutional revision, various spokesmen for governments and parties indicate a high degree of satisfaction with the existing constitution.[4] There is general acceptance that a largely unchanged system of parliamentary government, and the monarchy, untouched at least for the moment,[5] should continue as basic features in the new constitutional arrangements.

(2) The Supreme Court is very much on the agenda of reformers. It has recently encountered a barrage of criticism from the provinces very similar in tone and in accusations of bias to the earlier criticisms by the federal government, and its nationalist supporters, of the Judicial Committee of the Privy Council. Thus its entrenchment in the constitution and changes in composition and in appointing procedure to enhance its legitimacy as umpire of the federal system are ubiquitous in reform proposals.

(3) Somewhat surprisingly, Senate reform in membership and function has emerged as one of the centrepieces of various proposals for constitutional change to make Ottawa more sensitive to the regional diversities of the country. Both the British Columbia government and the Task Force on Canadian Unity recommend a second chamber appointed entirely by provincial governments, and view the revised Senate as one, if not the key instrument of a renovated federalism. The whole British Columbia package hinges on "major Senate reform . . . [as] the main feature of the overall reform of federal institutions . . . . It is in creative and far-reaching reform of the Senate that our main hope for better decision-making in the country lies."[6]

(4) The themes of provincialism, regionalism, dualism, and alienation are seldom absent from the contemporary literature of constitutional revision. The regions, the provinces, and the provincial governments are almost universally described as unhappy with the outlets provided by the existing system. The response to their alienation is either a decentralization of power to the provinces, a greater provincial role at the centre, or a mixture of both.

Although significant restrictions on provincial autonomy would flow from the implementation of the proposed federal Charter of Rights and Freedoms, and of the various recommendations, especially of the Task Force on Canadian Unity, to minimize provincial barriers to the movement of goods, capital, and labour, the provinces are only a distant, secondary target of reformers. The dominant emphasis is on the central government as the site for reform. The original Confederation settlement was based on a major premise that the flow of intergovernmental influence in the federal system should spring from a central government capacity to make provincial governments more amenable to Ottawa's leadership. As the second century of Confederation unfolds, the leaders and the led have changed places, and the general tenor of proposed reforms is overwhelmingly directed to making Ottawa more sensitive to provincial pressures.[7]

In addition to Senate and Supreme Court reform to enhance sensitivity to regional diversity, a direct provincial role on various boards, commissions, and agencies at the federal level, or in the procedures for appointments of members, is a commonplace of reform suggestions. Further, various federal government capacities – declaratory power, spending power, and emergency power – are to be tightly controlled. Others, such as disallowance and reservation, are to be eliminated.

Contemporary supporters of centralization no longer see themselves as in the vanguard of progressive constitutional change, riding the current of favourable historical forces, as did the English-speaking critics of the depression federalism of the thirties. They do not have the luxury of regarding the provinces with contempt as did that previous generation. Thus, with the partial exception of the NDP, there is no advocacy of old-fashioned centralization in which strong federal powers are wielded in response to Ottawa's definition of the national interest. Contemporary centralists fight a rearguard action to limit how much they have to give away, and to restrict the amount of provincial input into federal institutions to the unavoidable.

(5) The search for a new constitution may not succeed in its objective, but it is markedly extending the comparative perspectives of students and practitioners of Canadian politics to Switzerland, Germany, Australia, and the United States. There is very little looking to Great Britain for answers. The Pepin-Robarts Task Force report informs us we should emulate the Swiss in our appreciation of diversity, favourably draws our attention to the Swiss principle of linguistic territoriality, recommends a limited form of proportional representation hitherto regarded as suspect and alien, and advocates a Canadian version of the Bundesrat to incorporate the provincial governments into central government decision-making. Indeed, if references to Germany, especially to the Bundesrat, continue to proliferate, Germany will soon qualify as a Mother country. Finally, the Charter of Rights and Freedoms proposed by the former Liberal government clearly derived some support from the American

model, not least in its language of putting citizens before institutions, and from the various international instruments that have emanated from the United Nations.

This internationalization of perspective is a very recent phenomenon. It is related to a developing experimentalism, a willingness to depart from tradition, which is edging from the fringes to the centre of the debate. The possible utility of proportional representation and of referenda is indicative of this emerging tendency.

(6) The post-November, 1976, constitutional debate is not lacking in bizarre features. While the precipitant was clearly the election victory of the Parti Québécois and the threat thus posed to Canadian unity, *A Time for Action*, the federal government's rationale for its constitutional amendment bill, could not bring itself to mention the factors behind the renewed urgency for constitutional reform. In twenty-six lucid pages there was passing mention of "the separatist movement," and a cryptic allusion to unspecified "events in Quebec [that] were making the task of constitutional renewal more important and more urgent than ever," and nothing more.[8] The official proposals of the governments of Alberta and British Columbia, the only two provincial governments to publish their positions in extensive form, display less interest in Quebec than in a reconstructed Canadian federalism more appropriate to their provincial visions. Further, the government of Quebec has been a bystander in the constitutional discussions triggered off by its attainment of office in 1976.

In a sense the constitutional debate up until the recent federal election has been a form of shadow-boxing pending the referendum and the crystallization and clarification of the official demands of the Quebec government. The real debate between Quebec, Ottawa, and the other nine provincial governments has not yet been joined.

The Progressive Conservative Party

The position of the new Conservative government on constitutional reform will be affected by the party's election promises, its minority government status, the existence of Conservative governments in seven of the ten provinces – including Alberta and the pronounced provincialism of the Lougheed administration[9] – the striking weakness of the party in Quebec, the developing play of political forces in the country, and the constitutional predispositions developed by the party in opposition.

The election outcome gives a powerful nudge to dualistic thinking as a Conservative government based on English Canada confronts a PQ government committed to independence. Neither of the two contending parties possesses significant representation from the minority community in its electorate. This strengthens the PQ claim to be the sole legitimate government spokesman for the Québécois and makes it difficult for the federal government to avoid being cast in the unacceptable role of spokesman for English Canada. In other countries such a crisis situation would exert pressure for a coalition government of national unity, an unlikely development in the Canadian case.

The election results also give a significant impetus to the cause of electoral reform. Conservative Party discussion papers and speeches suggest a willingness to consider proportional representation in order to overcome the alienation of regions whose party vote is not fairly reflected in the caucus membership of the major national parties.[10] The interaction between the regionalization of the national party system and the coming Quebec-Ottawa confrontation combines with partisan self-interest to increase the attractiveness of a partial proportional representation system for which the recommendation of the Pepin-Robarts Report could serve as a starting point for discussion.

Pre-election Conservative proposals are scattered through party discussion papers, several speeches by Flora MacDonald, the Kingston Communiqué, and speeches by the party leader. As befits an opposition party their position is less clear cut, more tentative, and less fully elaborated than that of the former Liberal government.

The basic Conservative analysis is that the "national government has somehow lost the ability to reflect within itself Canada's regional diversity," and that this shortcoming can be rectified either by major decentralization or by the creation of "national institutions which are truly federal, not just central."[11] The former is rejected on the ground that the existing constitution is already decentralized to the point of jeopardizing the national government's capacity to pursue national goals. Hence, the party recommends federalizing national institutions by direct provincial participation in a newly constructed House of the Provinces, the majority of whose members are to be delegates of provincial governments sitting with a small number of central government delegates, and by a provincial role in appointments to the Supreme Court and to federal agencies and commissions whose policies have a significant impact on provincial interests.

The revised House of the Provinces, which is the keystone of Conservative thinking, is designed to ensure that national policies are subjected to scrutiny by the delegates of provincial government for their regional impact. The Conservatives also advocate provincial control of offshore resources, tight controls on the federal spending power and the federal declaratory power, and an expansion of concurrent jurisdiction to include cultural development. Minority language education is to be handled by the provinces "since education is exclusively a matter of provincial jurisdiction."[12]

The thrust of the Conservative proposals dealing with provincial input into central institutions is closer to the Pepin-Robarts Report than to the constitutional posture of the former Liberal government. However, the underlying Conservative constitutional philosophy possesses an explicit national orientation closer to the Liberal definition of Canada than to the heavy stress on dualism and regionalism found in Pepin-Robarts. In the words of the discussion paper *The Constitution and National Unity*, the "central government has a breadth of vision and an overall concern that is greater than the sum of the provincial views."[13] This belief will certainly be strengthened by the possession of office.

The NDP

The NDP position on the constitution, as reflected in recent speeches and party resolutions, merits brief analysis as an indication of the social democratic interpretation of our present problems. Further, the minority government situation created by the May 22 election may give the NDP constitutional analysis a practical importance it formerly lacked.

Briefly put, the NDP considers the existing constitution to be fundamentally sound. Like Sir John A. Macdonald, the party believes that a flourishing economy can attenuate regional divisions. What is needed to restore the legitimacy of Ottawa is decisive national leadership and effective national policies. The "basic concerns of French-speaking and English-speaking Canadians at this point in our history," according to the party leader, "have almost no connection with constitutional matters."[14] The crisis in our affairs is primarily economic, not constitutional, and reflects the failure of economic and cultural leadership by Ottawa. Further decentralization in a system considered already excessively decentralized is rejected as it contradicts "the reality . . . that we need an active and effective national government to hold us together."[15] Special status for Quebec is unnecessary as the existing constitution provides adequate powers for the people of Quebec through their government to control "their own destinies in most of life's central concerns."[16] A Charter of Rights, including minority language rights, should be entrenched in the constitution as a matter of justice, but such a Charter is essentially irrelevant to Québécois nationalism, a diversion from the real issue that, accordingly, will do little "to lead in the future to the generation of feelings of unity toward Canada by the Quebecois."[17] Further, the particular Liberal Charter proposed in Bill C-60 is castigated as ridden with loopholes, and our judges are considered too timorous to give credence to the stated seriousness of the government's intentions.[18]

The party agrees with the desirability of a provincial say in the selecting of Supreme Court judges. However, the proposed Liberal House of the Federation is an "abomination" to be rejected out of hand,[19] "a perfect example of how absurdity emerges when intelligent men allow creativity to triumph over reason."[20] The proposed House would "act effectively as a check on democracy, ... on the will of the people of Canada expressed in a federal election to elect the House of Commons."[21] The resultant deadlocks, from the NDP perspective, would foster regional discontent and alienation from federal politics.

A much better method of generating effective regional input into central political institutions would be by a modified system of proportional representation that would add approximately 100 members to the House of Commons, "20 from each of our regions distributed among the parties on the basis of the proportionate share of the regional vote obtained by each party."[22] The implementation of such a change would provide the alienated peripheries of Atlantic Canada and western Canada an enhanced capacity to exert influence "in the power structure of Ottawa." All national parties would become more regionally representative. The meeting of regional criteria for cabinet appointments would be facilitated by the larger pool of regional representatives from which ministers would be selected. Further, the quality of regional representation would improve because "the regionally elected members would come from lists announced by the parties in the course of the election campaign [and] the inevitable tendency would be for each party to prepare a list of distinguished men and women." A byproduct of generating more effective regional input into the House of Commons would be the obsolescence of the poorly played regional representation role of the Senate and the abolition of the latter "as a mere anti-democratic hindrance."[23]

The most striking aspect of the NDP position is the paucity of constitutional change considered necessary. There is no talk of provincial societies, and although Quebec nationalism is welcomed, Québécois apparently do not need any more power at the provincial level. The stress is on the needs of Canadians for jobs, housing, and economic growth to be attained by federal leadership that recognizes the necessity of economic planning. The way to restore Ottawa is to employ the powers that already exist, eliminate anti-democratic anachronisms such as the Senate, and contribute to greater regional sensitivity in the only place where it matters, the House of Commons, by supplementing the existing House membership by additional members selected on a regional basis by proportional representation.

Little remains of the NDP flirtation with the two nations of the sixties. The traditional stance in favour of central authority is reaffirmed. In spite of their criticisms of the then governing Liberal Party's constitutional proposals, the NDP position is much closer to that of Trudeau than to the position of the Task Force on Canadian Unity or to the proposals emanating from the provincial governments of Alberta and British Columbia. The party's response to the strident provincialism of the contemporary debate is neither decentralization of powers to the provinces nor a significant provincial government input into the decision-making machinery of Ottawa. No more is proposed than the "delegating [of] much administrative authority to the provinces."[24] The reform of the electoral system and the abolition of the Senate, the two institutional changes of most importance to the party, are designed to strengthen the federal government and enhance its democratic character.

The Position of the Former Liberal Government

The overall rationale for the constitutional proposals of the former Trudeau government is contained in *A Time for Action*, supplemented by various official statements and speeches by Trudeau and other cabinet ministers, especially Marc Lalonde and Otto Lang. Justifications for particular proposals contained in Bill C-60 are found in separate position papers on *The House of the Federation*, *The Supreme Court of Canada*, *The Canadian Charter of Rights and Freedoms*, and *The Canadian Constitution and Constitutional Amendment*. In addition, of course, there are Bill C-60 itself, the Explanatory Document that accompanied it, and the discussions before the Joint Committee and the Senate Committee.

Bill C-60 quickly got caught up in the competing meat grinders of the Joint Committee and the separate Senate Committee, the latter not looking kindly on those who sought its radical transformation. As a result, and also because of some infelicitous wording pertaining to the monarchy and the Governor General, along with other indications of hasty drafting, the federal position drowned in the detail of its own bill before it could gather support.

The federal package referred to phase I only, constitutional changes that Ottawa claimed were within the unilateral amending power of the central government. Hence, the division of powers was excluded, and the federal proposals were unavoidably seriously incomplete. However, it is clear that Ottawa did not foresee "any massive shift of powers from the federal government to the provinces."[25]

The constitutional reconstruction proposed in phase I was an attempt to modify the relations between the governments and peoples of Canada in such a way as to enhance federal legitimacy, strengthen the national community, and increase Ottawa's sensitivity by a very selective regional input into federal institutions. The federal bill covered the following: (1) a new preamble and statement of aims in the constitution; (2) a Charter of Rights and Freedoms, including linguistic guarantees; (3) a new House of Federation to replace the Senate and provide more effective regional representation in Ottawa; (4) modifications to the Supreme Court to enhance its legitimacy; (5) a miscellany of other clauses pertaining to the Governor General, the Prime Minister and cabinet, and the institutionalization of the First Ministers Conference. In addition, the federal government released a white paper on constitutional amendment that, although it stated no government position, indicated a certain appreciation of the virtues of referenda, in clearly defined situations, as instruments for bypassing the need for provincial government approval of constitutional amendments.

In marked contrast to the Task Force publication *A Future Together*, *A Time for Action* stressed a common Canadianness, a national identity, and a unity that "must transcend the identification Canadians have with provinces, regions and linguistic and other differences."[26] This document and the federal policy it expressed were concerned with the cultivation and fostering of Canadians. "Canada has made us what we are today and it has made us more alike than we may think. We share a history, a vast territory, a North American spirit, a sense of national solidarity, and the same democratic values."[27] Given the appropriate "transcendent loyalty" Canada can be more than the sum of its parts and a new constitution can provide Canadians "with an enlightened basis for patriotism."[28]

A basic vehicle for attaining that transcendent loyalty was the proposed Canadian Charter of Rights and Freedoms. The proposal for an entrenched Charter binding on both levels of government, and as comprehensive as possible, was an attempt to move in an American direction and thereby "confirm the preeminence of citizens over institutions . . . and ensure that . . . rights and freedoms are inalienable." At a more profound political level it was an attempt to enhance and extend the meaning of being Canadian and thus to strengthen identification with the national community on which Ottawa ultimately depends for support. The Charter would establish "new rights for Canadian citizens to live and work wherever they wish in Canada."[29]

So central was the Charter to the federal strategy that one of the two federal conditions for constitutional renewal was its inclusion in the constitution and its application to both levels of government. The resultant rights and freedoms were to be country-wide in scope, enforced by a national supreme court, and entrenched in a national constitution beyond the reach of fleeting legislative majorities at either level of government. The consequence, and one very clear purpose, was to set limits to the diversities of treatment of Canadian citizens by provincial governments, and thus to strengthen Canadian as against provincial identities. Rights must "not be dependent on the particular place where an individual chooses to reside." [30]

Ottawa was trying to construct by constitutional engineering a national community defined by the rights its citizenry possessed. The Charter would set limits to the capacities of provincial governments to build distinctive provincial communities based on separate bundles of rights or their denial specific to particular provinces. The complete attainment of this objective required entrenchment, which in turn required unanimous provincial consent. In the interim, the Charter would only have enjoyed the status of an ordinary statute, with its coverage of matters under provincial jurisdiction restricted to the agreeing provinces.

The same nationalizing purpose ran through the language proposals of the Charter, to minimize the salience of geography and province of residence for the availability of schooling in either official language and for the receipt of provincial government services. This was simply the latest expression of the basic federal strategy of the last fifteen years to minimize differences between Francophones within and without Quebec, and thus to resist the priority role as the defender of the French language sought by the government of Quebec. The federal objective was "to ensure throughout Canada equal respect" for the French and English languages.[31] The existing "inadequacy of the language rights guaranteed by the Constitution . . . has jeopardized the progress of the French-speaking people of Canada, led them to withdraw in spirit into Quebec and added strength to the separatist movement in that province." [32]

On the one hand the federal government tried to create from the heterogeneity of Canadian society a national legal community of possessors of rights, and thus indirectly to provide a particular kind of community base for its own support. On the other hand, it was equally concerned with establishing particular definitions of the nature of provincial communities and their relation to provincial governments. Although A Time for Action (p. 11) refers to "strong provincial identities," the more fundamental federal tendency was to stress the variegated diversities, cultural, partisan, and ethnic, within each province and thus undermine the claim of provincial governments to speak for a homogeneous provincial interest. Equally noticeable was the consistent tendency to stress the extent to which the major linguistic communities overlap provincial boundaries. Thus the French-language community was carefully defined so as to diminish any exclusive or special role for the government of Quebec. The "geographic area of each language community" contains "significant minorities of the other." [33] The Statement of Aims of the proposed federal constitutional bill referred to "a permanent national commitment to the endurance and self-fulfilment of the Canadian French-speaking society centred in but not limited to Quebec." [34] It is also notable that the proposed double majority provisions in the House of the Federation with respect to linguistic issues did not give "special status" to MPs from Quebec. The Francophone side of the double majority was to include French-speaking MPs from outside Quebec and was to "help to protect the language of the French-speaking Canadians from all provinces." [35]

The federal position was based on a desire to facilitate the exit of French Canadians from Quebec to viable French-Canadian communities elsewhere in the larger homeland of Canada. This would diminish the Quebec government's control of its population and weaken the incentives for provincial patriotism to push identification with Ottawa to the fringes of the Québécois psyche. The Quebec government position of the PQ, by contrast, will be designed to maximize Quebec government control over the lives and identities of Quebecers. To the PQ not only is the federal system a threat, for as Morin observes it "divides Quebeckers against themselves," [36] but the federal strategy of making the central government itself sensitive to French Canadians and facilitating the survival of French-Canadian communities outside of Quebec is in principle unacceptable, and doubly so if feasible. The success of such a strategy, by facilitating exit, would loosen the ties between French-speaking Quebecers and their provincial government, which Lévesque wishes to tighten. Federalist Quebecers, as Lévesque revealingly remarked recently, are "foreigners." [37]

The Trudeau philosophy has long been hostile to having the boundaries of political systems coterminous with the boundaries of nationality. This antipathy is now extended to claims for a homogeneous provincial interest. This orientation, which leads to a stress on intra-provincial diversities, was strikingly evident in the criteria proposed for the selection of the members of the new House of the Federation. The House, as critics have pointed out, would have been a veritable smorgasbord of parties. Half the membership from each province was to be chosen by the

House of Commons following each federal election, proportional to the popular vote in that province for parties in the House. The remaining half of the provincial membership was to be selected by the separate provincial legislative assemblies after each provincial election, proportional to the popular vote for the parties in the assembly.

The federal position paper on the House of the Federation positively gloried in the free expression of political views its diverse membership would stimulate. Majorities would be difficult to create because of "the multiplicity of federal and provincial parties represented in the new chamber, all of whom will have different allegiances and objectives." Further, the multiple party system of the revamped upper house would have the advantage "that interregional 'cleavages' or hostility could be softened by the formation, with regard to different specific issues, of different inter-party alliances which cross regional boundaries."[38] The Bundesrat solution, explicitly espoused by the Task Force, was opposed because it would not facilitate the expression of intra-regional diversities.[39] Provincial governments, it was pointedly observed, often represent only a minority of the electorate and members appointed by provincial governments therefore could not adequately convey the rich diversities of provincial political life with the accuracy of the complex system of proportional representation proposed by Ottawa.

The House of the Federation was an attempt to undermine the developing tendency for provincial governments to set themselves up as spokesmen for their provinces even in matters under federal jurisdiction. It was designed to facilitate the expression of regional views by other than provincial government spokesmen. This federal strategy makes clear what is often overlooked, that there are two very different ways of federalizing national institutions, with very different purposes in mind. The federalist Trudeau version, which is designed to bypass the provincial governments, is intended to make Ottawa more sensitive to regionalism, but not to provincial governments as such.[40] Federal strategy and purpose are therefore diametrically opposed to the alternative version espoused by the Task Force on Canadian Unity, the government of British Columbia, and others, which is designed to build in provincial government power at the centre.[41]

An additional indication of the Trudeau government's desire to bypass provincial governments was the suggestion that referenda be seriously considered as mechanisms for obtaining approval for constitutional amendments when governments are opposed.[42] While the developing practice of referenda in the United Kingdom is often considered a device by politicians to escape from the contradictory pressures in their own electorate and from division within government itself, the federal government suggestions were designed to bypass anticipated obstruction coming from self-interested provincial governments by appealing to the common sense of provincial electorates.

The Liberal government's constitutional proposals just described were not well served by the scattering of publications in which they were contained and defended. Spread over several months, emanating from various departments, and appearing in such diverse forms as the turgid legal prose of a draft parliamentary bill and the shaky eloquence of *A Time for Action*, the federal position never got off the ground. No big picture emerged to capture the imagination.

Yet the federal position was a serious, if overly complicated attempt to create a defensible, durable justification for a strong central government and a Canadian community. The Trudeau response to the pressures of dualism and regionalism represented a logical, intellectually coherent strategy to harness and tame these dynamic forces within a Canada-wide community, and within the central government itself in the House of the Federation. The corollary of the preceding, easily discerned although nowhere given comprehensive expression, was the desire to keep provincial governments in their place, create new spokesmen for provincial interests, and undermine the ability of provincial governments to stray from their proper role as spokesmen on provincial matters to spokesmen on federal matters.

Inevitably this was a high-risk strategy, for it defied the political ambitions of provincial premiers and was out of tune with the prevailing intellectual opinion sympathetic to "small is beautiful" and captivated by province-building. It turned a blind eye to the overwhelming assimilationist pressure on French-language communities outside of Quebec, New Brunswick, and northeastern Ontario, and, as Landry observes, responded only marginally to the historic claims of Quebec.[43] A more sensible mix of vision and reality, a little less cleverness, and a more adroit introduction of its proposals would have better served the federal cause.

The Pepin-Robarts Report

The report of the Task Force on Canadian Unity, *A Future Together*, has had the signal experience of being warmly received on both sides of the language divide. It is well written, even eloquent, and at least temporarily filled the vacuum in our constitutional discussions left by the assault on Bill C-60. Its positive reception was facilitated by its compactness and a certain vagueness about details that were to be filled in by subsequent bargaining.[44]

The great strength and profound weakness of the report both spring from the simplicity of its major organizing principles. The commissioners' response to the crisis that called them into existence is based on their interpretation of the contemporary Canadian reality, which, they feel, no longer fits the constitutional system that has incrementally evolved since 1867.

> In our judgement, the first and foremost challenge facing the country is to create an environment in which duality might flourish; the second is to provide a fresher and fuller expression of the forces of regionalism in Canada's constitutional system and power structure. . . . it is in the context of the *present* crisis that we assign priority to these two, and we do so for a very simple reason. Each, if ignored or left unsatisfied, has the power to break the country, and each must accept the other if a new period of harmony is to be achieved.[45]

In their discussion of duality the commissioners hammer home one brutal, fundamental point – not only is the great divide between French and English Canada a crucial reality – indeed the crucial reality – but the French side of that divide is represented by the people, the province, and most importantly, by the government of Quebec. The report has declared a winner in the intense intergovernmental struggle between Quebec and Ottawa that has gone on for a decade and a half over the locus of a homeland for the Francophone community. The Task Force sides with the position of successive Quebec governments in stating that the main question raised by duality is "the status of Quebec and its people in the Canada of tomorrow." The report notes and accepts what it views as "a growing linguistic territorial concentration which is rendering Quebec increasingly French and the rest of the country, excluding New Brunswick, increasingly English."[46] Outside the bilingual belt that "extends from northeast New Brunswick, through Quebec, into adjacent parts of Ontario," the trend to linguistic assimilation of the French-speaking minorities is so strong as to be virtually irresistible.[47]

The Francophone side of duality, therefore, is no longer the community, or communities, of French Canada from the Atlantic to the Pacific, as it is in the Trudeau formulation, but French Canada in Quebec, speaking through the provincial government, and increasingly self-defined not as French Canadians who belong to Canada, but as Québécois, citizens of a French-language state in the making. To this fact the constitutional structure of Canada must adapt.

With commendable realism the Task Force's discussion of language policy recognizes the sociological facts in language retention and the political unwillingness of some provincial governments to give constitutional sanction to policies doomed to failure.[48] The commissioners wisely assert that "For good and compelling social and political reasons, each of the eleven governments must be free to respond to its unique situation." They do not, therefore, "brandish the club of the constitution." Instead, they appeal to the intelligence and fairness of the provincial majorities in the hope that minority language education will be made available and sustained by provincial statutes.[49]

The second socio-political fact to which a revised constitution must adapt is the growing regionalism of Canada, which the commissioners feel has transformed the country since the mid-sixties. They adopt a particular political definition of regionalism, which leads them to view the provinces and the northern territories as the

basic building blocks of Canadian society and the ... political frameworks through which the various regional communities express and will continue to express themselves. ... The provincial political institutions are the primary frameworks through which regional populations can organize and express themselves, and their existence serves in turn to develop the social networks and interests based on them, thus reinforcing the provincial focus of regionalism.[50]

The last paragraph of the report sums up the commissioners' basic conviction that duality and regionalism, which find their major expression through the provincial governments of Quebec and English Canada, with the additional criterion of "the sharing of benefits and power form the Canadian trilogy of our collective saga."[51] Duality and regionalism, which "lie at the heart of the Confederation crisis," will be employed as yardsticks in the examination of existing institutions and behaviour and for evaluating proposed reforms.

Where an existing practice or institution is being reviewed, or a new one being suggested, we will ask: To what extent and in what sense does it usefully advance the recognition of duality (or regionalism)? We believe that any general reform effort, however well intended, which fails to enhance duality or which offends the principle of regionalism is unlikely to increase harmony and unity in Canada. Our criterion to determine what constitutes enhanced recognition is the principle of sharing, more particularly power sharing and the equitable distribution of benefits.[52]

Consistent with the provincial focus that emerges from the primacy accorded duality and regionalism, the handling of the national dimension of the country's existence is characterized by hesitation and embarrassment. The report caricatures the kinds of unity it opposes, the identified alternatives to its own vision, as (1) "the submersion of diversity into one homogeneous mass"; (2) "an image of artificial, government-induced flag-waving, and 'patriotic' celebrations which do not spring from any natural emotional source"; and (3) a "pan-Canadian nationalism" that denies both regionalism and dualism.[53]

The tendency of the Task Force is to avoid any implication that a national community exists that might have rights against the lesser communities of which the country is composed:

Canadian unity is ... the sum of conditions upon which the various communities and governments of Canada agree to support and sustain the Canadian state. As such, it endows each of the parts with something it would not have if it stood alone. It is, then, a just union of constituent elements, or, as one dictionary puts it, a harmonious combination of parts.[54]

The essence of the Task Force position appears, somewhat curiously, in a section on the "enhancement of the Canadian dimension." The Canada to which we are to feel loyalty is simply "the association" that respects the particular identities and various communities that are important to us. The overriding stress on what divides us, on why we have provinces, and on the small worlds in which we live undermines the credibility of the occasional reference to common interest, common purpose, and common will and thus provides little sociological or psychological justification for a strong, autonomous central government role.[55]

The Task Force report lacks the subtlety necessary to handle the complexities of an identity which, earlier, for English Canadians could accommodate elements of Canadianness and Britishness and now allows the great majority of Canadians, even in Quebec,[56] to live comfortably with both provincial and Canadian identities and loyalties. This lack of subtlety is partly the product of an ahistorical approach that denies the commissioners adequate insight into the admittedly complex and uneven distributions of a Canadian identity and loyalty. That there was some lurking concept of Canadianism sustaining a degree of participation in World War One that resulted in more Canadians being killed than Americans, and that in both world wars contributed to a relatively unchallenged major reduction in the utilization of provincial government powers, would not be comprehensible to the readers of the report. The commissioners, possibly due to the great haste with which they worked, have produced a tract for the times, whose incompleteness and inconsistencies undermine its aspiration to be an adequate base for constitutional renewal.

Unfortunately for the logical coherence of the report the commissioners stray from their declared yardsticks of dualism and regionalism. In a short section on "the objectives of constitutional reform," the first objective is "to preserve and reinforce the ability of the central institutions to serve as the legitimate focus for the common interests of all Canadians." Elsewhere, the "essential role and responsibilities of the central government" include "to sustain, encourage and symbolize a Canadian identity and pride." [57] While these objectives are laudable, they are unrelated to the report's own yardsticks for evaluating the direction of change, and they fly in the face of the report's sociology with its overwhelming focus on provincial communities based on regionalism and dualism as the primary communities in which Canadians live. The belated insertion into the discussion of the national role suggested above is not sustained by a sociological and psychological recognition of a national community, or of any concept of a Canadian identity forged in the previous century of our existence.

The suspicion that the appearance of a possibly not insignificant role for Ottawa, seemingly unrelated to the criteria of dualism, regionalism, and sharing that constitute the report's most frequently employed criteria for assessing change, portends a smorgasbord of conflicting criteria for constitutional transformation, is well-based. When the report discusses the distribution of powers additional criteria appear, including efficiency, effectiveness, "political responsiveness, sensitivity, and closeness to the concerns of the individual citizen," and "the overall balance of responsibilities which each order of government will have." [58] The elaboration of criteria to guide constitution makers becomes even more confusing when "the allocation of specific powers within policy areas" is discussed. The negotiators of our constitutional future are now advised to "adopt a systematic functional approach," including the allocation of "specific responsibilities within a given general domain exclusively or concurrently to the order of government best suited to carry them out." [59]

There may be some silken thread of consistency capable of tying together the proliferation of criteria, or guiding principles, from (1) duality, regionalism, and power-sharing to (2) the central government task of sustaining Canadian identity and pride and (3) the employment of a "systematic functional approach" for the allocation of specific powers, but if so, it is not readily apparent. Constitution makers who express agreement with the report will quickly find that they are on opposing sides of the contradictions these shifting criteria conceal from those who read the report quickly. The Task Force is to be commended for leaving an area of flexibility and ambiguity to those with the responsibility of injecting substance into the many nooks and crannies characteristic of a detailed working constitutional document, but when that flexibility and ambiguity are inadequately constrained by a clear sense of limits then the report's contribution to constitutional problem-solving is seriously reduced.

The report's recommendations exploit the diversity of criteria at its disposal. The trilogy of dualism, regionalism, and power and benefit-sharing, which constitutes the fundamental theme of the report,[60] is reflected in its recommendations for a binational Supreme Court with five civil law members of the enlarged eleven-member court, a new Council of the Federation composed of provincial government appointees, the recognition of the key role of the government of Quebec with respect to the French-Canadian nation, and a provincial role in appointments to various boards and commissions. Further, the priority that both dualism and regionalism give to the provinces is manifest in restrictions on the federal emergency power, the declaratory power, and the spending power, in the elimination of the federal powers of disallowance and reservation, in the allocation of the residual power to the provinces, in the suggestion for the appointment of judges to all provincial courts by provincial governments, in the transfer of recommendations for appointment of the Lieutenant Governor to the provinces, in enhanced provincial taxing powers in the area of indirect taxation, and in giving basic control of language policy to the provincial level. Further, it is suggested as a guide that the provinces should be given

> the main responsibility for the social and cultural well-being and development of their communities, for the development of their economies and the exploitation of their natural resources, and for property and civil rights. This implies exclusive (or occasionally concurrent) jurisdiction over matters pertaining to culture, education, health, social services,

marriage and divorce, immigration, manpower and training, the administration of justice, natural resources including fisheries, regional economic development, trade within the province, consumer and corporate affairs, urban affairs, housing and land use, and environment. It implies, as well, correspondingly adequate powers to tax. The provincial governments should also have the right, as long as they abide by Ottawa's overriding foreign policy, to establish some relations with foreign countries to sign treaties in matters coming under their jurisdiction.[61]

The complexity of the interaction between dualism, which is at the base of the report's recognition of the unique responsibilities of the government of Quebec, and regionalism, which provides the justification for powerful provincial governments in English Canada, is illustrated by the grappling with the question of what difference, if any, should exist between the powers of the government of Quebec and those of the remaining provincial governments.

The report avoids the use of "special status," "different status," and "particular status," correctly recognizing their political unpopularity outside of Quebec. It also attempts to provide a response that avoids the appearance of granting *de jure* special status to Quebec, while holding out the possibility of its *de facto* existence. "Let us put our conviction strongly: Quebec is distinctive and should, within a viable Canada, have the powers necessary to protect and develop its distinctive character; any political solution short of this would lead to the rupture of Canada." However, this necessary recognition of Quebec should not be achieved by the assigning to Quebec of "formal law-making powers, denied to other provinces, over such matters as culture, language, immigration, social policy, communications and some aspects of international affairs . . . . much the more preferable approach is to allot to all provinces powers in the areas needed by Quebec to maintain its distinctive culture and heritage, but to do so in a manner which would enable the other provinces, if they so wished, not to exercise these responsibilities and instead leave them to Ottawa."[62] This is to be done both by placing relevant matters under concurrent jurisdiction with provincial paramountcy, and thus letting each province decide whether or not to exercise its jurisdictional authority, and by providing constitutional procedures for delegation.

This strategy is capable of producing two antithetical outcomes at the opposite ends of the spectrum and a variety of possible temporary resting positions in between. If only Quebec employs the powers given to all provinces we have achieved the reality of special status imperfectly concealed by a uniformity of constitutional possibilities for all provinces. If this scenario of *de facto* dualism develops, the problem of the participation of Quebec MPs in the federal House of Commons, and of Quebec ministers in the federal cabinet, a constitutional problem of the first magnitude that has long concerned Trudeau, must be faced.

The Task Force offers no guidance. The question is not adequately answered or successfully avoided by the device of linking the possibility of a unique Quebec position with respect to the distribution of powers to "our traditions," which include for Quebec "a distinct status: in its civil law, in the recognition of French as an official language, and in the fact that three of the nine judges of the Supreme Court must come from that province."[63] These aspects of distinct status, as Ramsay Cook cogently argues, do not refer to the distribution of powers, and thus do not raise the question of the working of the Parliament of Canada.[64]

Alternatively, all provincial governments, and the choices will be made by governments, not the provincial electorates, may opt for the exercise of the powers that only Quebec needs, in which case a profound decentralizing impulse is injected into the workings of Canadian federalism. Here special status is avoided by the emasculation of the federal government. Even if this scenario does not immediately develop, the exercise of federal power in the affected areas will always be conditional on provincial governments not seizing the responsibilities and powers held out to them in perpetuity by the Pepin-Robarts constitution.

In all probability what would develop is a differential provincial response, shifting over time, which would produce an ever-changing mix in the exercise of federal and provincial power throughout the country. It is not self-evident that this is an outcome to be fostered by constitutional statecraft.

The apparent progression to a League of States to which the criteria of dualism, regionalism, and sharing seem to be tending is not checked by the scattered references to nation-building and the Canadian identity,[65] which leave the impression of being afterthoughts, survivals from a previous era. Unexpectedly, however, several recommendations provide sustenance for a national community.

The report recommends the entrenchment in the constitution of certain individual and collective rights binding on both levels of government. Here the report refers to Canadians and categorically states that differences in the treatment of the fundamental rights of individual Canadian citizens are unacceptable. The logical relation of this assertion, which posits a Canadianism, to the allegedly dominant criteria of dualism and regionalism, which provide support for provincial governments, is unclear. It would seem to be either in conflict with them or unrelated to them.[66]

The report also contains an imaginative proposal for a modified system of proportional representation to apply to about sixty additional House of Commons seats. This "electoral reform is urgent and of very high priority" to counteract the tendency for "party membership in the central parliament" to become "concentrated in regional blocks."[67] This proposal to make each national party in the House of Commons more representative of the Canadian people indirectly strengthens the central government and thus provides a countervailing pressure to the enhancement of the powers of provincial governments in central government institutions and in jurisdictional authority characteristic of much of the rest of the report.

The final element of support for Ottawa and the overall Canadian community is the strong argument concerning the benefits of economic integration, with the resultant attribution of the major voice in economic policy to the central government. Characteristically, the perspective on benefits and losses is primarily that of the regions or provinces, and only secondarily the benefits to individual Canadians. The extra wealth generated by economic integration can be transferred to the poorer provinces to facilitate their economic adjustment.[68] Further, the economic integration from which the economic surplus flows is ultimately limited by what the regions will allow.[69] Nevertheless, the Task Force constructs a cogent argument for removing the barriers to interprovincial trade, to the mobility of professionals and tradesmen, to the movement of capital, "especially with regard to corporate mergers and the purchase of land," and for reducing restraints on the "international and interprovincial exchange of professional and commercial services." Preferential provincial purchasing policies should be permitted only "to alleviate acute economic hardship." In addition, industrial strategy, "the main weapon for economic adjustment," must undergo a "further concentration of power in the central government," although that admittedly conflicts with the principles of regionalism and dualism.[70] These are all very significant limitations on the developing tendencies to autarchy in a multiplicity of provincial government policies and practices.

Although the commissioners are quick to point out that "a country is not a business deal" – in the context of a discussion about the economic costs and benefits of Confederation to Quebec[71] – their whole analysis belies their profession. The continued existence of a central government is justified overwhelmingly on the grounds that economic integration produces a surplus that can be used for the benefit of the regional parts of which the country is composed.[72] In that constant reshuffling of position by which rich provinces and poor provinces change places over time, Alberta becomes transformed from a recipient to a donor, and Ontario shows indications of moving in the opposite direction. There is, however, little in the report to induce us to be sharers when calculations of self-interest dictate the contrary. Thus, although the report attributes a significant economic role to Ottawa[73] – along with the responsibilities in defence and foreign policy – the justification for that role is fragile and subject to never-ending calculation. A role for the central government, no matter how extensive, is likely to be ephemeral if it is sustained only by the provincial/regional self-interest to which the report gives priority. Although there are scattered indications to the contrary, the basic constitutional philosophy of the Task Force is a modern version of the compact theory in which Ottawa exists on sufferance, and the federal government, as Premier Duplessis used to say, is the child or creature of the provinces.

Conclusion

We are, as the preceding discussion reveals, in a situation of profound constitutional malaise. In 1864-67 constitutional discussions took place with only four governments, P.E.I., Nova Scotia, New Brunswick, and the Province of Canada. They were grappling with serious internal problems for which federalism seemed an escape and a solution. Even so, Confederation was less the result of willing intergovernmental agreement, or the freely given assent of the separate electorates, than a grudging response that doubtless would not have been given without the heavy mix of persuasion and coercion applied by the British government through the agency of the colonial office and the colonial governors.

In the late seventies we have no external power able to intervene and help achieve by other means what cannot be achieved by consensus. We have, instead, ten provincial governments, several of which have populations larger than the population of the new Dominion of Canada in 1867, one of which is bent on escaping from the complexities of federalism to the complexities of sovereignty-association, a still powerful if battered central government, and an absence of agreement on the principles and procedures for comprehensive constitutional change.

The hurdles to be jumped before we reach the promised land are despairingly high and numerous, reflecting the powerful and self-seeking nature of the interests to be conciliated. It is little wonder that some look for escape routes by the devices of referenda and constituent assemblies. Perhaps Belloc is closer to the truth:

The Doctor smiled and took his fees,
There is no cure for this disease.

The patient, however, may stagger on in a kind of half-life for a long time to come. Not only is there yet no cure. There is also no easy way to die.

Chapter Two

An Overview of the Trudeau Constitutional Proposals

In February, 1981, the University of Alberta held a constitutional conference entitled "Beyond the B.N.A. Act." Several of the articles and accompanying commentaries were published in the Alberta Law Review, XIX, 3 (1981). *The following note was my response to Richard Simeon's published paper, "An Overview of the Trudeau Constitutional Proposals." (A.C.C.)*

The conventional response to Professor Simeon's paper would be to present a tightly organized analysis, to make intellectually coherent the chaotic events that pass for constitution-making in contemporary Canada. Since we should not unfairly castigate our politicians for having transformed the constitutional order of the fifties into the constitutional chaos of the seventies and eighties, it would be aesthetically appealing, a kind of one-upmanship, to impose an analytical order on their contributions to our disintegrating constitutional system. It has proved even more tempting, however, to describe chaos on its own terms, to respect the frantic *"ad hocery"* in Ottawa, the provincial capitals, and London by providing a series of seven disconnected observations. These may not constitute a McLuhan probe, or an Innisian kaleidoscope, but as fragmentary, somewhat random juxtapositions they may produce some insight.

I

The willing and unwilling participation of academics in the constitutional process should not be overlooked. Many of the academics at this conference have been involved in one way or another with the governments engaged in the pursuit of constitutional change. In my own case this has been restricted to a part-time involvement as a member of an academic advisory committee to the British Columbia Cabinet Committee on Confederation.

A striking, positive example of the academic role is that of Professor William Lederman of Queen's University, a frequently cited authority in the briefs prepared by the dissenting provinces for the United Kingdom Kershaw Committee and for the court challenges to the proposed federal Resolution. Before the earlier 1978 Special Joint Committee on the Constitution of Canada, Professor Lederman played a key part in setting in motion the political and judicial process that ultimately led to the Supreme Court reference on the Senate and to the court's finding that the Liberal government's Senate proposals in Bill C-60 were beyond the power of Ottawa.

Lederman has played his role as an academic, providing detached objective analysis, albeit as a very visible participant. At a different level there is the slow filtering of ideas from the academic community into the minds of political actors. The classic example here is the emergence from the obscurity of a 1971 academic article by Donald V. Smiley[1] of the concept of instrastate federalism, which has, in a decade, become little short of a new conventional wisdom to one school of constitutional reformers.

The boundaries between academic and political life are constantly being breached, in both directions. There are pervasive pressures and temptations for academics to take sides. In pursuit of their objectives politicians will exploit and manipulate academics as they seek to legitimize their constitutional positions. In these circumstances, academics have an obligation to seek objectivity, to avoid seeking cheap publicity, and to sit courageously on the fence where appropriate.

A horrifying example of the dangers posed to academic life by the constitutional crisis was recently provided by the public labelling of academics who appeared before the Joint Committee as Liberal, NDP, or Conservative experts – a deplorable departure from the previous assumption that scholars gave evidence as scholars.

II

The process of constitution-making was dramatically transformed by the migration of the constitutional discussions from the intergovernmental meetings in July, August, and September to the televised Joint Committee hearings from November, 1980, to February, 1981. Throughout the summer, the proceedings were dominated by governments claiming to speak for people and pursuing the interests of governments. As the scene shifted to the Joint Committee hearings profound changes in focus, style, and demands were immediately evident.

Part of the difference sprang from the reduction of the original summer agenda of twelve items to a more restricted package which, in its original form, included only patriation, an amending formula, equalization, and a Charter of Rights. The shift to the parliamentary forum and the Joint Committee had major consequences beyond the narrowing of subject matter. It gave the national parties a prominence they had lacked in the lengthy summer discussions between governments, and it deprived the provincial governments of a prominence they had enjoyed. Provincial interests were necessarily more visible in an intergovernmental bargaining context than in the federal Parliament with a Liberal majority and a supportive third party, the NDP, which had not entirely rejected the centralism of its founders. Provincial visibility was not helped by the strategy decision of most provinces not to appear before the Joint Committee but instead to try and block the federal package by resort to the courts and lobbying in the United Kingdom.

The opening up of the process brought in the public in the form of interest groups, particularly ethnic organizations and civil rights advocates. The cumulative effect of these factors was to make the concerns of provincial governments suddenly of much less importance. The Charter, which had received at best only a lukewarm reception from provincial governments all summer, was the focal point of most citizen groups. Not only were they overwhelmingly in favour of a Charter, but they exerted very strong pressure and lobbied skilfully to get a Charter much less respectful of parliamentary supremacy than the first version presented to the Joint Committee, and they succeeded to a truly remarkable extent.

III

The appearance of aggressive citizens' groups and civil rights proponents of entrenchment set the stage for a direct conflict between provincial governments and the vociferous advocates of a Charter with teeth in it. In fact, so smoothly and inexorably did the scenario unfold that it is difficult not to assume that it was all manipulated by the Federal-Provincial Relations Office. The sequence of events went like this: the federal government initially devised a Charter with an introductory clause[2] designed to placate those provinces, the majority in fact, which were opposed to anything more than a weak and limited charter. Inevitably, the Charter quickly became the centrepiece of the hearings. Equally inevitably, those most eager to appear as witnesses were not the concerned believers in the desirability of protecting parliamentary supremacy from the encroachments of the judiciary, but those concerned with protecting the citizen against the abuse of state power, or those seeking to carve out for themselves or their clients a special protected place in the constitution with, where possible, an invitation to affirmative action on their behalf. The federal government, finding that its originally weak Charter had not elicited any additional provincial government support, rationally concluded that its limited resources of political capital were better deployed in placating the voluble critics parading before the Joint Committee. This led to a much tougher Charter, one even less congenial to the unhappy provincial governments than its predecessor. Each manifestation of federal government sensitivity to the civil rights community was an insensitivity to those provincial governments opposed to a strong Charter.

By the end of the Committee hearings the federal government had boxed itself in, doubtless not without some recognition that its resultant lack of manoeuvrability was advantageous in its conflict with the provincial governments. The federal government, as Chrétien noted, had aroused public expectations it could not disappoint, even if, regrettably, this required more disappointments for provincial governments.

That this scenario was entirely planned by some manipulative genius is unlikely. That its advantages were glimpsed with increasing clarity as the process unfolded is undoubted. Those critics of the federal package who suggest at this stage (mid-February, 1981) that the Trudeau government should lop off the Charter and go to Britain for patriation and an interim amending formula requiring provincial unanimity for matters affecting the provinces are politically naive. To ask the federal government to drop the Charter is to ask them to give up the most popular part of their package, to betray and undermine their most vocal support base, to turn the federal NDP against them, and to damage the prospect of obtaining an amending formula falling short of a unanimity requirement. The basic federal hope, surely, must be that an amending formula with little provincial support and a Charter that most provinces oppose will both be sustained by popular support for the latter.

IV

If the Charter goes through in roughly the form in which it emerged from the Joint Committee, the long-run effect on Canada will be profound. Section 15 (2), for example, constitutes an open invitation for affirmative action programs aiming at "the amelioration of conditions of disadvantaged individuals or groups including those that are disadvantaged because of race, national or ethnic origin, colour, religion, sex, age or mental or physical disability." In this respect the new Canadian constitution will be more American than the American constitution.

Over time, the Charter will fundamentally change the Canadian political system and the very identity of the Canadian citizenry. There is an unfortunate tendency, a product of the domination by lawyers of this area of constitutional discussion, to argue the virtues or demerits of the Charter in terms of citizen/state relations, to debate the issue in terms of the best methods for protecting rights. In so doing, the American approach is contrasted with the British, leaving Canadians with the choice of being faithful to their receding imperial past or of following the practice of the giant to the south.

While these perspectives are not useless, they ignore the profound impact of the Charter on identity and community in Canada. The Charter is not playing around with the externals of our existence. Over time the cumulative results of its application will reach deeply into our innermost being, manipulating our psyche and transforming our self-image. Our children will be very different people because of this Charter. The Charter, by underlining our rights as Canadians, strengthens the national community against provincial communities.

The beneficial consequences from the federal government perspective will be most strikingly evident when the Charter is successfully applied against provincial governments, for in such a case a Canadian right is being protected against a provincial encroachment. But even if the Charter is successfully invoked against federal legislation there is still a gain to Ottawa. Every successful invocation of the Charter, even against the federal government itself, contributes to a sense of Canadianism. In the long run this can only strengthen the central government against the provinces.

V

Professor Simeon argues that:

> *How* we get a new constitution is as important as what it actually contains. Its legitimacy depends on the degree of consent it can command. This Resolution, opposed by most provinces, and apparently by a majority of public opinion, lacks sufficient consent. It splits and divides us more than it unites.[3]

That there is something in what Simeon says is undeniable. On the other hand, it is my own impression that his is an extreme interpretation, overly influenced by the climate of near hysteria and exaggeration that engulfs us now and works against the long view and the cool vision. To look briefly back to 1867 and the events leading up to it is to be somewhat reassured that constitutions not born in immaculate conception may still have a capacity for survival. There was little evidence of widespread popular support for the original BNA Act among those whose existence was being transformed by this elite-led drive to political union. That the people were not consulted was due not only to the belief that to do so would have been an Americanism, unworthy of an experiment whose *raison d'être* was to ward off American encroachments, but also for the very practical reason that it was not entirely clear that the people would have responded with even a weak "yes." That the black drapery and bunting on the streets of Halifax, Nova Scotia, on July 1, 1867, was not celebrating the new birth with joy but protesting a betrayal with anger is a commonplace in our introductory lectures in political science and history dealing with the Confederation period. Further proof was provided by the first federal elections in that province, which sent eighteen of nineteen Members of Parliament to Ottawa to repeal the BNA Act.

This earlier exercise in constitution-making was thus not without its blemishes if measured by the criteria applied by some critical observers of the present exercise. The manipulative role of British governors in Nova Scotia and New Brunswick was not irrelevant to the achievement of Confederation. More generally, the basically sympathetic support of the British government for the political regrouping of her British North American colonies was an immensely helpful external impetus to the creation of a new country. Yet in spite of all the shortfalls from perfection that accompanied its formation, the British North America Act, now in its 114th year, has some claim for inclusion in the Guinness Book of Constitutional Records.

The comparison between 1867 and the present should not be pushed too far. Contemporary circumstances are different. The strong opposition of powerful provincial governments to the Trudeau Resolution had no exact counterpart in the 1860s, partly of course because those most opposed did not then immediately join the new nation. Nevertheless, it is not impossible to look ten years down the road and see a Canada with an entrenched Charter, an amending formula very much like the one now proposed by Ottawa, a Canada with someone other than Trudeau at the helm, and a Canada in which the changes embodied in the Trudeau package have become part of the accepted fabric of Canadian political life.

VI

In the closing pages of his presentation Professor Simeon tellingly observes that most Canadians do not wish to choose between competing provincial and federal government visions of the country's future. We live easily with our dual loyalties at the grassroots level. "I doubt," he concludes, "that the polarization we see now between governments is shared by most citizens." This is a profound observation. It undermines the academic model of "consociational democracy" that has enjoyed some popularity in Canadian studies, and that suggests Canadians are a divided people held together by political elites who have stitched a thin fabric of consensus across the regional fissures and cleavages allegedly characteristic of the underlying society.

The opposite is more nearly true – that we are a united people divided by our governments. This, it can even be suggested, is in the very nature of contemporary Canadian federalism. In pursuing his objectives and responding to the self-interested cues emanating from the pyramid of political and bureaucratic power over which he presides in Ottawa, Mr. Trudeau is driven to exaggerate the Canadian component of our identities. He has no responsibility for our various provincial existences. Indeed, in some circumstances our provincial identities may be seen as a threat to his larger political goals. It is equally logical and natural for our provincial leaders to exaggerate the provincial components of our identity. They have no responsibility for our national identity although they cannot completely disregard it, as even Mr. Lévesque recently discovered. Thus, political leaders at the two levels, by the very nature of the roles they play, are driven to this exaggeration, to this one-sidedness. In the division of labour between governors and governed, the forces of unity are more deeply rooted in the underlying society than in the competing and governing elites of the federal system.

VII

Finally, let us enjoy the spectacle. We are being provided with brilliant spectator sport. The greatest juggler in the world could not keep so many balls in the air at once. Consider the following:

(a) Courts in three provinces, in a staggered sequence, ruled on the constitutional legality of the proposed federal Resolution. Offstage the Supreme Court awaited the final act of the judicial play in which it will be called upon to respond to the inevitable appeals from the provincial courts.

(b) The Joint Committee was elbowed off the stage after extending its time in the limelight from the original early December deadline to the middle of February. In the Joint Committee three parties from two Houses danced before the television cameras in that curiously mingled search for political advantage and the public good characteristic of partisan activity.

(c) The debate returns to the House of Commons and the Senate. The Senate, through its Joint Committee members, has already managed, by securing an appropriate amendment, to eliminate the threat to its survival contained in the original proposal, which gave it only a suspensive veto. The communication to the Liberal cabinet that the Resolution itself might encounter difficulties in the Senate should an absolute Senate veto not be restored had the desired effect.

(d) Meanwhile ten provincial premiers and ten provincial cabinets, in some cases supplemented by committee hearings or legislative debates, have been and are plotting their strategies for and against the federal proposal.

(e) Across the Atlantic, in the United Kingdom, the Kershaw Committee issued its first report recommending against automatic British compliance with any Canadian request.

(f) Shortly, the British Parliament – both the House of Commons and the House of Lords, who may disagree with each other – will be called upon to respond to the final version of the Resolution.

In the midst of all of this, the issue of "colonialism" is raised again, threats of referenda and elections to settle the issues are heard, leaked and filched secret documents have become almost a daily occurrence, the United Kingdom High Commissioner in Ottawa has indicated he will take early retirement, and the Canadian High Commission in London insinuates that the British government is tapping its phones.

I remember the Second World War when my parents wondered if there would be any more news after that great global conflagration ended. They need not have worried.

Indeed, when we are asked in the year 2000 where we were in the great constitutional crisis of the seventies and eighties, we can proudly say that we were there, every night – with Knowlton Nash.

Chapter Three

The Politics of Constitutional Renewal in Canada

The proclamation of the Canada Act in April, 1982, was the culmination of two decades of constitutional controversy. In the 1960s the basic challenge to the historic constitutional system deriving from Confederation in 1867 came from dynamic nationalist elites in the province of Quebec, who were frustrated by the constraints of the limited jurisdictional autonomy enjoyed by the provinces in the Canadian federal system. By the mid-1970s, when Quebec nationalism had installed in office a provincial government committed to independence, Quebec had been joined by other provincial governments, especially in western Canada, which were equally frustrated by the limitations the existing federal system imposed on their ambitions.

The centrifugal pressures deriving from provincial demands for constitutional restructuring were met by a central government that, in the last analysis, viewed constitutional change more as a vehicle for its own ambitions than as one attuned to provincial visions. The clash of competing versions of preferred constitutional futures, and profound disagreements over the procedures to be followed in bringing about constitutional change, embittered and complicated the constitutional agenda. The limited constitutional settlement that resulted was acclaimed more for its temporary closure of the constitutional debate than for its intrinsic qualities or its likely contribution to resolving the constitutional malaise of a disharmonious federal polity. Although the achievement was limited, in the politics of Canadian constitutional development even limited changes are rarities deserving scrutiny and analysis.

The following analysis is broken down into several major sections: the context of the Canadian search for constitutional change; the legal processes of constitutional change; the actors in the reform process; the arenas of conflict; the impact of constitutional reform; and concluding reflections. A chronology of the major events is available in the appendix to this chapter.

The Context of the Canadian Search for Constitutional Change

The drive for constitutional change cannot be understood without reference to the widespread ambivalent and contradictory attitudes to the Canadian constitution in recent decades. Castigated by one group of critics as an obsolescent relic of a time long ago and far away and hence no longer suited to contemporary requirements, the constitution was strongly defended by others as a still living instrument of government tested by a century of experience.

Between the critics and the defenders were the calculators, whose attitude to the constitution was based on a carefully balanced assessment of the likely consequences of constitutional change. The calculators, a large and shifting group, included those who preferred the security of the existing constitution, with its known imperfections, to a constitutional settlement they feared could only be achieved by a divisive process likely to poison the intergovernmental environment for years to come. Other calculators were not opposed to major constitutional change as such, but only to change detrimental to their interests. The status quo was their second choice, to which they gave a conditional allegiance in preference to the first choices of others.

Throughout the constitutional exercise of the 1960s and 1970s there was a recurring tendency to dismiss the issue as an irrelevance, a distracting sideshow that was clearly secondary to the economy, the energy crisis, or whatever appeared in the morning headlines. While much of this was simply the politicking of a free society, it reflected the essential consideration that the Canadian search for constitutional renewal was not a response to a complete constitutional breakdown. The alternative to constitutional change was not chaos. Even the most aggressive advocates of change recognized, on occasion, the relative attractiveness of the status quo. Prime Minister Trudeau, who was prepared to proceed unilaterally against widespread provincial government opposition in 1980-81, had earlier viewed the opening up of the constitutional issue as a "can of worms" best left alone. After the defeat in the Quebec referendum of the proposal for a qualified version of independence, Quebec Prime Minister Lévesque, Trudeau's major opponent, was reduced to a pragmatic and tactical defence of the existing constitution, which he had devoted years of his life to destroying, rather than see his opponent's proposals triumph.

Thus the status quo was not without its defenders, both principled and opportunist, throughout the whole period of constitutional turmoil. Nevertheless, since the mid-1960s there had been a pervasive concern about the capacity of the existing constitution to regulate relations between the federal and provincial governments. Occasional indications by governments that they might not respect Supreme Court rulings were symptomatic of a general decline in the legitimacy of the constitutional system. The 1960s and 1970s were a period of rapid expansion in the public sector at both levels of the federal system and governments did not appear to pay the same attention to jurisdictional boundaries as previously. Dicey's confident statement that federalism means legalism seemed of diminishing validity; constitutional allocations of legislative authority ceased to function as fences productive of good neighbours. Canadian federalism, accordingly, came to display greater policy overlap, an increased incidence of intergovernmental conflict, and a diminished capacity for its resolution. Thus, quite apart from the nationalist pressures from Quebec, the political system was stretched almost to the breaking point by the clashing ambitions of competing governments. This diffuse malaise made a supporting contribution to the pressures for constitutional renewal, but in itself it was insufficient to galvanize political elites to action.

An additional contributory factor was the legacy of unfinished business in the evolution of Canada from colony to independence. The fact that the most important component of the Canadian constitution, the British North America Act (BNA Act), was a statute of the British Parliament, and in important respects could only be amended by that Parliament, was a continuing irritant to nationalist-minded Canadian prime ministers. As part of the general post-Second World War spate of nation-building activity, which included the admission of Newfoundland as another province, the abolition of legal appeals to the Judicial Committee of the Privy Council in London, and the adoption of a Canadian flag, a succession of prime ministers – St. Laurent, Diefenbaker, and Pearson – attempted unsuccessfully to eliminate this embarrassing anachronism. However, severing this link with Britain through "patriation" of the constitution required agreement on a domestic amending formula and this had neither the urgency nor the intrinsic importance to compel the wholehearted attention of busy political leaders in the late 1960s and early 1970s. In and of themselves these issues were not central to the ongoing life of the country. Further, they were issues that, if past history could be trusted, would consume immense amounts of political energy, but with little prospect of resolution.

However, once other pressures propelled the constitution onto centre stage, the goal of patriating the constitution and the related search for a Canadian amending formula had a profound impact on the constitutional reform process. As unfinished constitutional business they inevitably demanded attention. The participants in the process simply could not avoid grappling with the amending procedure, an issue of high symbolism and great practical importance to the development of the federal system. Since the major participants in constitutional renewal were the very governments whose interests would be differentially affected by whatever amendment procedure was adopted, acrimonious disagreement was predictable. Worse still, the procedures by which the new amending formula was to be agreed were themselves unclear. The historic failure of Canadian governments to agree on a comprehensive domestic amending formula meant that obtaining one, and any other constitutional changes affecting the balance between the federal and provincial governments, required a resort to the British Parliament. When failure to obtain federal-provincial agreement on a new amending formula was again repeated in the summer of 1980, Ottawa indicated its intention to proceed unilaterally with a request to the United Kingdom Parliament for a limited package of constitutional change, including its own preferred amending formula. As we shall see, this threat of federal unilateralism produced deep and bitter disagreement on what law and convention dictated as the legally necessary and constitutionally proper procedures to be followed in Canada before a request could be transmitted to the United Kingdom Parliament. Accordingly, not only was an amending formula central as an issue in a revised constitution, but the absence of universally recognized and accepted procedures for constitutional change, which such a formula was designed to overcome for future generations, elicited a major dispute over the appropriate roles of the federal and provincial governments and the United Kingdom government in the reform process itself.

Somewhat paradoxically, therefore, the agenda items of patriation and an amending formula, leftover business from yesterday's failures, were crucial components of a constitutional reform process triggered by quite other considerations. The survival power of these two interdependent issues partly reflected particular nationalistic goals of the federal government, summed up in the phrase "the bringing 'home' of the constitution." More basically, it reflected the political undesirability if not technical impossibility of continual resort to the United Kingdom Parliament in the lengthy multi-stage process of ongoing constitutional reform envisaged by Ottawa and at least some of the provinces. The disappearing relevance of the British connection, even in English Canada, reinforced the need to end this embarrassing indication of constitutional inferiority.

While the broad constitutional malaise and Canada's unfinished constitutional business were critical background factors, the real catalyst that thrust constitutional reform to the top of the national agenda was clearly the explosion of Quebec nationalism after 1960. Quebec society and polity were being transformed in what came to be known as the Quiet Revolution, a sweeping economic and social modernization of what had long been a highly traditional community. This transformation was led by the Quebec government, which became the prime collective agent of the Quebec people's search for a new security compatible with an economic and social modernity they no longer shunned. This elicited seemingly insatiable demands from Quebec for funds and jurisdiction, and a long series of confrontations between Quebec City and Ottawa confirmed the demise of the centralist equilibrium that had prevailed since the onset of the Second World War. The intense interaction between political and intellectual life in Quebec put the services of much of the intellectual community at the disposal of the Quebec nationalist movement. Thus reinvigorated, it was no longer satisfied with the inadequate jurisdiction of a province. This nationalist explosion inevitably gave Quebec's demands a larger significance than was attached to the more conventional pressures for more funds and autonomy that simultaneously surfaced in the provinces of English Canada.

A special poignancy and inner tension were inseparable from the psychology of Québécois nationalism. The confidence derived from the exhilarating breakthrough of the Quiet Revolution with its rising new class of Francophone technocrats mingled uneasily with fear and pessimism based on the shrinking demographic weight of Quebec in Canadian federalism. For the Parti Québécois, formed in 1968, the rational response to these hopes and fears was to escape from Canadian federalism, where Quebec's minority status could only worsen, to the independence of a Francophone state headed by the new men of power.

In the 1960s, the nationalist pressures emanating from Quebec and the general decentralist pressures developing in English Canada encountered a weakened Ottawa, hampered by a succession of minority governments. An emerging conventional wisdom asserted that the post-war hegemony of Ottawa would have to give way to a looser system. The changes necessary to meet the demands of the English-Canadian provinces could probably have been handled by the pragmatic piecemeal adjustments that had characterized previous cycles of centralization and decentralization.

The passion and volatility of political life in Quebec, however, were much more threatening. Sporadic violence, culminating in the October Crisis of 1970,[1] when a terrorist group kidnapped a diplomat, murdered a Quebec cabinet minister, and the War Measures Act was proclaimed, confirmed that the constitutional times were seriously out of joint. A greater threat to the existing constitutional system was the steady drawing together of the diverse separatist tendencies in Quebec in the Parti Québécois, under the leadership of a charismatic former minister from a previous provincial Liberal government, René Lévesque.

These Quebec developments made clear the erosion of an historic constitutional consensus that had both sustained the central government and allowed it to be an instrument for predominantly English-Canadian purposes. The federal government, seeing its own survival threatened by the Quebec-based challenge, undertook countermeasures. To reduce the attraction of an inward-focused Quebec nationalism that attributed negligible psychological meaning to a country-wide national community, it assiduously and deliberately fostered a new political definition of Canada, based on a transformed pan-Canadian community in which French Canada would flourish, not just in Quebec, but from coast to coast.

The instruments of this new country-wide dualism, building on the reports of the Royal Commission on Bilingualism and Biculturalism, which had propagandized the urgent need for recognition of the French fact, included the Official Languages Act of 1969 and a proposed constitutional recognition of official minority language rights at the provincial level. Support for this new national community was also to come from a proposed Charter of Rights and Freedoms binding on both levels of government, which would add substance to the concept of Canadianism. Finally, the implementation of a domestic amending formula would end the humiliating trek to Westminster, signal the formal coming of age of Canada, and invigorate a national community no longer emotionally crippled by a lingering colonial dependency relationship with the United Kingdom.

This was the basic agenda of the federal government and particularly of Prime Minister Trudeau in the first serious effort at constitutional renewal since the onset of the Quiet Revolution. It culminated, after several years of intermittent constitutional discussions, in the Victoria constitutional conference of 1971 and the proposed Victoria Charter, which, in a limited way, would have nudged the federal system in the direction of Trudeau's vision of Canada.[2] This effort, however, ultimately foundered on the unwillingness of the Liberal government of Quebec to give its agreement to a constitutional package that was more a response to Ottawa's version of the Quebec problem than to the aspirations of political elites and nationalist groups in Quebec.

The failure of this initiative led to a return to what passes for constitutional normalcy in Canada. The workings of the electoral system in Quebec provincial politics masked the growth of the Parti Québécois, particularly in 1973 when the party's 30 per cent of the vote produced only six of 110 seats in the Quebec National Assembly. Concurrently, the focus of intergovernmental tension and controversy shifted to western Canada, especially oil-producing Alberta, as the OPEC price increases upset the balance of regional forces on which the federal system had been based and produced fundamental conflicts of interest over energy-pricing between producing and consuming provinces. Although this did not initially have constitutional repercussions, it subsequently had a critical impact when constitutional reform reappeared on the intergovernmental agenda.

The trigger for the re-emergence of the constitutional issue was the unexpected victory of the Parti Québécois in the 1976 Quebec provincial election. The party was committed to sovereignty-association, a combination of *political* independence and some form of *economic* association or union with Canada, and promised to hold a referendum on the proposal within the lifetime of its government. The election of a government in Quebec committed to holding such a referendum shocked political elites in Ottawa and the other provincial capitals and unleashed a plethora of political activity directed to constitutional reform or at least to the appearance of it. Ottawa established in 1977 a Task Force on Canadian Unity (the Pepin-Robarts inquiry), which reported in 1979. It presented its own constitutional proposals to Parliament in 1978, in an abortive attempt to achieve significant constitutional reform before the Quebec referendum and thus to prove to the Quebec electorate the responsiveness of the federal system to demands for change. Throughout the period Ottawa and Quebec engaged in guerrilla warfare whenever an issue appeared on which either side felt it could embarrass the other. Outside the governmental forum there was a virtual explosion of conferences, seminars, and publications on constitutional ailments and cures as the public-spirited and the self-seeking sought to get their views on record.

Constitutional activity, from the election of the Parti Québécois on November 15, 1976, to the Quebec referendum in May, 1980, was beset by paradox and irony. A significant and unexpected effect of the Parti Québécois victory was to mobilize centrifugal pressures in English Canada. The earlier attempts to achieve constitutional change had been primarily Ottawa-Quebec confrontations with the provinces of English

Canada pressing few constitutional demands of their own. They had participated with varying degrees of enthusiasm, but they were essentially supporting actors. However, after 1976 the regionalism of English Canada, which the Pepin-Robarts report had coupled with dualism as one of the two powerful socio-political forces capable of destroying the country, was given an almost unbridled expression by the other nine provincial governments.

Although this new round of constitutional introspection was a reaction to the Parti Québécois victory, the provincial governments of English Canada did not focus on a response to Quebec. There was a remarkable, even surprising, unanimity of official response declaring that sovereignty-association was unacceptable.[3] However, beyond making clear that the PQ goal was based on a complete misreading of the dictates of self-interest in a Canada without Quebec, the governments concerned made no attempt to address themselves to a renewed federalism especially adapted to the concerns of Quebec.

The parochialism of the constitutional response of most English-Canadian provincial governments is readily explicable. In the absence of a Quebec consensus on the desired direction and details of constitutional change it made little sense for the provinces of English Canada to try and address themselves to Quebec demands. The Parti Québécois was committed to independence, not reform of the existing federal system, and it had no desire to see such reforms accomplished before it could hold its referendum. The federalist forces within Quebec politics, led by the provincial Liberal Party, did have elaborate proposals for change within the federal framework, but their ideas had no formal status in intergovernmental negotiations as Liberals were relegated to the opposition benches in the Quebec National Assembly throughout the controversy. The government of Quebec was therefore officially uninterested in projects of constitutional reform that both conviction and strategy required it to portray as unattainable. Indeed, Quebec participation in the constitutional discussions of 1978 and 1979, following the unveiling of Ottawa's own constitutional proposals in Bill C-60, was perfunctory. There were no Quebec demands on the table to which other governments had to respond.

Further, although Ottawa was compelled to address its version of the Quebec problem, it had to do so in a particular way. Bill C-60 was an attempt at pre-emptive constitutional reform. In order to bypass the anticipated objection of the Quebec government to any constitutional change that required its consent, Ottawa decided to concentrate on a limited package of reforms in its own institutions, which it could claim, unsuccessfully as it turned out, were within its exclusive jurisdiction.[4] This claim had a dual effect. To the extent that it was accepted, it absolved the other provinces from having to come to grips with the place of either Quebec or French Canada in Canadian federalism, for their consent was likewise considered unnecessary. If denied, as it was by several provinces, it deflected the debate from substance to procedures, and thus shelved the Quebec problem.

More generally, outside Quebec, the provincial disposition – Ontario and New Brunswick somewhat excepted – was to assume a division of labour in which leadership in constitutionalizing relations between language communities and governments, and in the rethinking of the Quebec-Ottawa relationship, was primarily Ottawa's responsibility. Since the Parti Québécois government, for its own political reasons, played down the provincialism of English Canada and portrayed Ottawa as the government of the English-Canadian nation, it also contributed to this governmental division of labour. The political psychology of the pre-referendum period in Quebec made a clear distinction between Québécois exercising their right to determine their collective future and the rest of Canada, implicitly defined as outsiders and spectators. Thus the provincial governments of English Canada were further absolved of any obligation to address Quebec concerns. Aside from rhetorical support for the federalist side, they accepted their outsider role and quietly proceeded to work out their own self-interested constitutional demands.

The federal leadership, unhampered by any need to address specific reform proposals of the Quebec government, remained faithful to the Trudeau objective of a bilingual and bicultural Canada. Consequently, federal government pressure on the nine other provinces was directed to ensuring increasing recognition and fair treatment of French-Canadian minorities in the provincial school systems outside Quebec, and more generally as consumers of provincial services in the French language. As such the federal strategy was designed to undermine the claim of the Parti Québécois to speak for a Francophone nation imprisoned within provincial borders.

Thus the unwillingness of the Parti Québécois government to participate seriously in the process of constitutional reform occasioned by its winning of office gave special visibility in constitutional discussions to the Trudeau view of the desirable relationship between Anglophones and Francophones and between Quebec and the other governments of Canadian federalism. It simultaneously encouraged the provincial governments of English Canada to consult their own self-interest in their proposals for constitutional change. The high-risk PQ strategy was aimed

74

at a referendum success that never happened. In effect, therefore, the PQ election victory had the paradoxical effect of diminishing concern for the role of Quebec and its government in Canadian federalism from 1976 until the 1980 referendum.

In marked contrast, regional feelings in English Canada, particularly in the West, were given vigorous constitutional expression. This tendency was strengthened by the fact that, concurrently with the assertiveness of Quebec nationalism, the federal system was experiencing a fundamental structural disequilibrium: the relatively stable regional distribution of *political power* at the centre was challenged by significant shifts in the regional distribution of wealth and *economic power*.[5]

The federal House of Commons, based on majoritarianism and a relatively undiluted principle of "rep by pop," was still dominated by the big battalions from the central provinces, Ontario and Quebec, which elect over 60 per cent of its members. The shift of economic power to the western provinces, generally a response to the enhanced significance of resources, especially energy, was not accompanied by any equivalent increase of western political power in Ottawa. The western perception of exclusion was aggravated by the political weakness of the governing Liberals in western Canada; in 1980 they elected only two MPs from the entire four western provinces. This tension between economic power and political weakness dramatically complicated the general process of redistribution between rich and poor regions, which is part of the bedrock of the Canadian federation. The West, excluded from power, felt vulnerable and feared that its new-found wealth would be confiscated and its control over its rich resources stripped away. These fears were dramatically heightened by the National Energy Program, a major new energy policy initiated by the federal government at the same time as the constitutional battle. Western provinces became more determined than ever to strengthen their constitutional position.

More generally, Canadian experience suggests that a federal system can more easily accommodate and respond to discrepancies in per capita wealth and income when the large provinces are rich and the small provinces are poor than when the reverse is true. In the latter situation the redistributive practices of the central government, between individuals and between governments, require much larger per capita transfers out of the rich regions. Moreover, such redistribution can be easily portrayed as a systematic exploitation that would be less likely to occur, or not to the same degree, if the rich had numbers, and hence power at Ottawa, as well as wealth. Further, the tension between majoritarianism and federalism is obviously exacerbated as the *dirigiste* and redistributive roles of the central government increase. The resulting frustration is particularly pronounced in the governments and citizens of rich provinces with small populations, and is likely to be aggravated by relatively abrupt regional shifts in economic power, as occurred in Canada in the 1970s.

Accordingly, the three most western provinces, especially Alberta and British Columbia, which were "have" provinces in the Canadian scheme of equalization, developed clear constitutional positions. Each sought to strengthen its position, either by an unassailable constitutionally protected fortress of provincial rights in the case of Alberta, by enhanced provincial government bargaining power within the central government in the case of British Columbia, or by strengthening provincial jurisdiction over resources in the case of Saskatchewan. The strong constitutional voices of these three provinces contributed to the downplaying of concern for Quebec and French Canada. The ethnic background and social evolution of Saskatchewan and Alberta have not resulted in positive contemporary attitudes to any form of cultural dualism.[6] British Columbia, the province furthest removed from Quebec, with the second smallest Francophone population in percentage terms in the country and the highest rate of linguistic assimilation to English, possessed minimal empathy for the Quebec, Francophone side of Canada.[7] The positions of these and several other provinces of English Canada were forcefully articulated in intergovernmental sessions both before and after the Quebec referendum.

In marked contrast, the demands of the government of Quebec never made it to the bargaining table. Indeed, the most remarkable fact about the last half decade of constitutional activity in Canada was that although the major impetus for constitutional renewal came from Quebec, and particularly from the Parti Québécois, the Quebec government was never a principal actor in the real world of intergovernmental bargaining over constitutional change. From 1976 until the 1980 referendum the PQ government was more like a member of the audience than an actor on the intergovernmental constitutional stage. As we have seen, in this period its attention was almost exclusively directed to the forthcoming Quebec referendum, which it hoped would strengthen its bargaining hand with a mandate to negotiate sovereignty-association. In retrospect, this period was characterized by a remarkable discrepancy between appearance and reality. "While Quebec moves on towards its fateful rendezvous," wrote one shrewd English-Canadian commentator in 1979, "the partner it assumes will keep it company does not know of, and makes no preparations for, such an historic encounter."[8] It looked as if all the momentum was on the side of Quebec, with the other governments of the country waiting nervously on the sidelines while the people of Quebec decided if Canada was to have a future. The reality was otherwise. The real action was taking place in Ottawa and in the provincial capitals outside Quebec. The Quebec government was preparing for a constitutional confrontation on its own terms that never took place. On May 20, 1980, the Quebec referendum on sovereignty-association was defeated by a clear margin of 59.5 to 40.5 per cent. The basic strategy of the Parti Québécois had failed, and Lévesque and his colleagues were quite unprepared for serious constitutional discussions on reform within the federal context.

When the crucial round of inter-ministerial conferences began in the summer of 1980, followed by the First Ministers' Conference in September, 1980, the Parti Québécois government was demoralized, reeling from its defeat in the referendum, pummelled by a series of by-election losses, and devoid of plans for a renewed federalism it had never sought. No one spoke for either of the two major Quebec constitutional positions. Sovereignty-association had been rejected by the Quebec electorate, and the constitutional vision of the provincial Liberals led by Claude Ryan had no official status. The Quebec government, with no mandate to pursue its own goals, was an ineffective advocate of the 60 per cent referendum majority that had voted to stay in Canadian federalism. Thus Quebec was basically a defensive participant at this time, hoping to re-establish its credentials as a major actor in Canadian federalism by creating a provincial common front against the Trudeau version of constitutional change and the unilateralism by which he threatened to pursue it. Conversely, the weakened PQ condition, in conjunction with the sense of victory that pervaded post-referendum Ottawa, strengthened Trudeau's claim to speak for Quebec and encouraged him to flesh out and aggressively pursue the constitutional renewal he had promised, but not detailed, in his limited but effective participation on the federalist side in the referendum campaign.

The politics of eighteen months between the summer of 1980 and the dramatic outcome in November, 1981, were hectic, complex, and intense. Key turning points marked the way: the failure of the federal and provincial first ministers to agree on a reform package in September, 1980; the launching of the federal government's drive to amend the constitution unilaterally and the mobilization of provincial opposition in the months that followed; the complex judgement of the Supreme Court on September 28, 1981, which forced the two camps back to the bargaining table, but with new ground rules; the last-minute agreement fashioned in the middle of the night at the First Ministers' Conference in

November and the immediate and passionate rejection of the package by the government of Quebec. Between each of these major events were dozens – indeed hundreds – of minor events that cumulatively shaped the process. Clearly, a detailed account of this period is beyond the scope of this chapter (the reader is referred again to the appendix to this chapter). Rather, the following sections focus on four critical dimensions of the constitutional battle: the implications of the legal procedures; the major actors in the reform process; the importance of the differing arenas of conflict; and the impact of constitutional change.

The Legal Processes of Constitutional Change in Canada

Relative clarity existed in the two areas where the BNA Act already authorized the making of amendments within Canada.

Section 92 (1) gave the provincial legislatures the power to make laws with respect to the "Amendment from Time to Time . . . of the Constitution of the Province, except as regards the Office of Lieutenant Governor." This provincial amending capacity, because of its restricted scope, was essentially irrelevant to the constitutional renewal process.

Section 91 (1) gave the Parliament of Canada the power to amend the constitution of Canada with significant exceptions, most particularly matters assigned exclusively to the legislatures of the provinces, or rights or privileges granted or secured to the legislature or the government of a province.[9]

Outside the ambit of these two sections of the BNA Act, explicit constitutional change by amendment required resort to the United Kingdom. Two aspects of this awkward legacy of colonialism were not disputed. The final amending body was the British Parliament and the only body constitutionally competent to formulate a request for amendment was the Canadian Parliament. However, other crucial considerations in the complex relationships between the British government and the federal and provincial governments in Canada were beset by ambiguity, untidiness, and profound differences of opinion over what the relevant laws and conventions were.

Westminster's role continued not because of any British reluctance to give up the last relics of imperial power, but because Canadians had been unable to agree on a domestic amending formula to cover the matters formally amendable only in the United Kingdom. This situation was unsatisfactory not only or primarily because of the indignity of a mature federal country having to resort to the Parliament of another country for formal amendments to its constitutional system. More importantly, the use, or threatened use, of the process could generate violent domestic controversy if provincial unanimity had not been obtained before the submission of a request to the United Kingdom for an amendment detracting from provincial powers.

The Trudeau government's patriation package of 1980-81 clearly fell into the category of amendments requiring British parliamentary approval. The federal government argued that neither the law nor the traditions of the Canadian constitution necessitated provincial consent before a Joint Resolution of the Canadian Parliament was forwarded to the United Kingdom Parliament, and that the role of the latter was to rubber-stamp the Canadian request without any concern for the procedural proprieties within Canada. The dissenting provinces contested the federal government position before the Canadian public, before three provincial courts of appeal and the Supreme Court of Canada, and in the United Kingdom. They claimed that provincial consent was necessary before such a request could be constitutionally forwarded to the United Kingdom Parliament – seven of the eight indeed argued before the Supreme Court that unanimity was necessary – and that Great Britain had an inescapable trusteeship responsibility to protect the provinces against a constitutionally improper, unilateral federal request.

The uncertainty and controversy attending the process of constitutional change had a crucial impact on both the substance of proposed reforms and on the strategies of the competing governments. They threatened severe damage to the institutions caught up in the battles and to the traditions of civility, which could not cope with the passions unleashed. The consequences were major.

(1) While the uncertainties of the amending procedures were exploited by both sides, the gravity of the federal-provincial tensions that surfaced made it clear that this had to be the final resort to Great Britain. The inclusion in the federal package of a domestic amending formula for the future was thus unavoidable.[10] So imperative was the requirement to settle the amending formula issue that the provincial Constitutional Accord signed by the eight dissenting provinces, and proposed as an alternative to the federal package, was simply an amending formula, which would allow patriation of the constitution but included no other matters of substance.

(2) The anomaly of a continuing British role gave the federal government the opportunity to pursue by unilateral request a particular amending formula and a Charter of Rights that were clearly unattainable by the route of unanimous intergovernmental agreement. That the final outcome fell short of federal aspirations is evident. Nevertheless, the federal effort, based on an asserted right to unilateral action, was the catalyst

without which the conservatism and inertia of the system would once again have stifled change.

(3) The British role, and the controversy over the proper manner of its use, multiplied the forums in which the constitutional struggle was played out, in the United Kingdom as well as in Canada, and provoked a major debate over their relative importance and legitimacy. The multiplicity of forums also gave an advantage to the participants with the most extensive resources and contributed to the dominance of governments over non-governmental participants in the reform process. For example, with the exception of native groups,[11] the various supporters of a strong Charter of Rights who lobbied so effectively in Canada did not participate in the attempts to influence the British government and they played no role before the courts.

(4) The controversy over the constitutionality of the federal package deflected attention from the substance of change to the question of procedures and led to a confused intermingling of the issue of constitutionality with the separate question of desirability. Both sides deliberately manipulated this confusion to the detriment of a stimulating educational discussion of the future of Canadians as a people.

(5) The lack of consensus on the propriety of the federal unilateral attempt fostered acrimony and divisiveness between governments in Canada. It also involved the courts and threatened to tarnish the reputation of the judiciary, drawn into a dispute where passions were high. It was not predictable in advance that "legal" answers would convince the losers. Further, procedural conflict threatened to damage relations between the Canadian and United Kingdom governments, the latter a potentially innocent victim of the Canadian failure to devise a workable and acceptable domestic amending formula.

These dangers became clear after the failure of the first ministers to agree in September, 1980. The subsequent federal attempt to proceed with only limited provincial support encountered massive obstacles. There were the legal appeals by the dissenting premiers. The federal Conservatives engaged in a lengthy filibuster, which was only lifted when the Liberal government agreed to refer its constitutional package to the Supreme Court. The nine Supreme Court judges ultimately delivered a convoluted, fence-straddling decision that gave support to both sides. The Court held that unilateral action was legal, but that constitutional convention required a substantial measure of provincial support for such changes. However, the Court carefully avoided specifying the precise extent of the provincial consent required, other than implying that unanimity was not essential. Provincial officials and politicians lobbied extensively against the federal package in the United Kingdom. Had the Liberals proceeded unilaterally it was far from clear that Westminster would have acceded to Ottawa's request.[12] There was even an oblique indication that had the final constitutional conference in November, 1981, broken down irrevocably, the Governor General might have intervened and required the holding of an election to let the people decide.[13] Finally, throughout the closing stages of the process, there were thinly veiled suggestions by some of the provincial governments that they might not respect constitutional changes implemented without their approval.[14]

Even the most obtuse had been made aware that constitutional renewal was not a casual affair for a Sunday afternoon, a pleasant interlude between more demanding tasks. The political system was stretched almost to the breaking point by this exercise in constitution-making.

Whatever the shortcomings of the final outcome, it must be seen in the context of the titanic conflict of wills out of which it emerged and the massive impediments to change imposed by the overall conservatism of the constitutional system.[15] Part of that conservatism lay in the procedural uncertainties attending any resort to the British Parliament for amendments. At the same time those very uncertainties provided the opening for a determined federal administration to employ Gaullist tactics of unilateralism without which deadlock probably would have chalked up one more triumph.

The Actors in the Reform Process

GOVERNMENTS

Canada has never enjoyed a strong tradition of public participation in the formal process of constitutional change. Thus when constitutional reform became invested with high political priority, it was not surprising that it was added to the lengthy agenda of the First Ministers' Conference, the key institution of "executive federalism" that brings together the political leaders of the federal government and the ten provincial governments to grapple with problems of intergovernmental concern. By the 1960s the First Ministers' Conference had become the central process of a working federalism, which could no longer afford to adhere rigidly and literally to a nineteenth-century division of powers and fiscal resources. It was the natural vehicle to respond to issues so central to the interest of governments as constitutional reform. Thus the dominance of governments in the constitutional reform process was taken for granted when the first concentrated efforts began in the late 1960s.

However, the long search for constitutional renewal strained the capacity of executive federalism, led to widespread questioning of its suitability for resolving constitutional tensions, and precipitated a striking tendency for governments to explore the environment for additional resources, either to strengthen their bargaining power within executive federalism or to bypass it altogether. This tendency became so pronounced that the closed world of traditional federal-provincial bargaining was severely shaken. By the time the constitutional resolution passed through Parliament, the cast of relevant actors had greatly expanded. The executives of both orders of government were still central. They remained the key actors and possessed the most bargaining resources. But the aggressive competition between governments for the support of public opinion opened up the process, and the more open process acquired a life of its own. From the vantage point of Ottawa and the provincial capitals it became disorderly and somewhat out of control. Indeed, as we shall see, in the final weeks before the formal parliamentary adoption of the constitutional resolution to be forwarded to Westminster, federal and provincial governments, especially the latter, were to be overwhelmed by a frenzied lobbying of women's groups and Indian organizations without parallel in Canadian history.

THE PUBLIC

The most dramatic role for the public was in the Quebec referendum, a straightforward exercise in nationalist mobilization. The Quebec government sought to strengthen its bargaining hand in the negotiations for sovereignty-association with the legitimation of a popular mandate. The initial promise of a referendum was part of a conscious strategy to remove the independence issue from electoral politics. The voters could then support the PQ solely as an alternative to the provincial Liberal government without reference to the party's *raison d'être*. This PQ strategy was based on the assumption that the willingness to vote against the Liberals and for the Parti Québécois would be significantly increased if the price of throwing out one government was not a successor government committed to taking radical steps to obtain Quebec independence. By lowering the stakes for the voter the party could capitalize on the unpopularity of the incumbent administration, win power, and then use the possession of office to maximum advantage in the build-up to the referendum that would follow in good time.

The referendum question was remarkably "soft" and included a promise by the government to hold a second referendum following negotiations for sovereignty-association, and thus to assure the electorate that "no change in political status resulting from these negotiations will be effected without approval by the people through another referendum." The second referendum was intended to destroy any impression that the Quebec government might act rashly – in advance of or in defiance of public opinion. This incremental *étapisme* failed after an emotional campaign that polarized the Quebec community. The referendum consultation, however, had a profound effect on the constitutional review process, for it decisively repudiated the PQ option and was exploited by the federal Liberal government.

Direct public involvement in other aspects of the constitutional exercise was sporadic, including occasional bursts of concentrated activity. There was very extensive public input into the hearings of the Special Joint Committee of Parliament on the Constitution of Canada in 1970-72, the Pepin-Robarts Task Force hearings, and the 1980-81 Special Joint Committee hearings. Both the 1970-71 Joint Committee and the Pepin-Robarts Task Force travelled extensively around the country, received numerous briefs, and held large public meetings. Further, after the Parti Québécois election victory in November, 1976, a select portion of the public was extensively involved in the numerous conferences held by universities, interest groups, and research organizations such as the Canada West Foundation.

The most important public role, however, was that of an audience carefully monitored and manipulated by the government players. The audience's reactions, past and anticipated, markedly influenced the behaviour of the actors and occasionally led to switches of the cast or the appearance of a new player. The importance of the audience was magnified by the extensive television coverage of constitutional conferences from the 1960s on. The National Assembly debates in Quebec on the referendum question were also televised, as were the 1980-81 Special Joint Committee hearings of the Senate and House of Commons on the federal government's patriation resolution.

Governments energetically tried to get the people on their side, the better to prove their democratic responsiveness. After the Quebec referendum the federal government brilliantly employed a "people versus powers" antithesis to contrast what it sought – a Charter of Rights for the people – with the jurisdictional goals of provincial governments, which were portrayed as selfish aggrandizement. In the subsequent unilateralism stage Ottawa deliberately strengthened the Charter to mobilize public opinion on its side after it became clear that the dissenting provincial governments could not be won over by a weak Charter. Section 15, dealing with Equality Rights, "was developed primarily on public relation grounds as a means of co-opting highly visible and vocal interest groups into supporting the Trudeau government's unilateral constitutional restructuring."[16]

When a 1981 provincial premiers' conference released poll results indicating widespread public opposition to federal government unilateralism and other support for the provincial governments opposing Ottawa, the results were immediately criticized by a chorus of polling experts as biased and unreliable.[17] The Prime Minister and the provincial premiers tried to mobilize support in their respective national and provincial constituencies by prime-time television addresses and speaking tours. Mass mailings of provincial government constitutional stands to the provincial citizenry were a novel departure in the Canadian politics of plebiscitarian democracy. There was extensive television, radio, and newspaper advertising by the competing governments and by the occasional private group. Quebec was particularly active in mobilizing its citizenry against Ottawa's threatened unilateralism.

LEGISLATURES

The role of legislatures and elected representatives from both sides of the House varied from government to government and over time. At the provincial level, legislatures were primarily used by governments to legitimate their stands and to engage in perfunctory ritualistic debate.[18] Legislative committees to inquire into constitutional matters were set up in several provinces, including Prince Edward Island, Nova Scotia, New Brunswick, Quebec, Ontario, Manitoba, and Alberta. Their impact, if any, on the constitutional position of their respective governments has not been studied, but was almost certainly minor.

For the Ottawa and Quebec governments, however, legislatures were key resources in the pursuit of constitutional goals. The Quebec National Assembly was a prominent forum for the expression of government views on the constitutional future of Quebec. This was most strikingly the case in the televised National Assembly debate on the referendum question, which was successfully orchestrated by the PQ government to gain an initial advantage in the pending province-wide referendum.

The federal government's use of the Senate and of the House of Commons reflected a mix of necessity and strategy. The resort to draft legislation for its 1978 constitutional proposals, Bill C-60, inevitably elicited an influential role for the House of Commons and the Senate and for the separate Senate and joint committees to which draft legislation was sent. On the other hand, the amount of scarce time devoted by both houses of Parliament and by committees to constitutional issues was in most cases more than the government wished. This reflected the pressure from opposition MPs to modify or delay the government's constitutional proposals and their eagerness to exploit the limelight provided by such a highly visible issue. In the case of its 1980-81 patriation resolution, the federal government had to gain approval of both the Senate and House of Commons for the constitutional package it proposed to forward to the United Kingdom. The legal necessity was supplemented by political desire as the government sought to legitimate its proposed unilateral act by stressing the moral authority of the national Parliament, representative of Canadians from coast to coast, as the proper body to debate and determine the constitutional amending package. Ottawa thus tried to stand on its head one of the clichés of Canadian federalism, that executive federalism leads to a bypassing of Parliament and legislative bodies: now it was to use Parliament to bypass the provincial governments.

POLITICAL PARTIES

The role of political parties in the constitutional process is difficult to pin down with precision. Neither the extra-parliamentary nor parliamentary wings of Canadian parties have been noted for policy innovations. Government parties in parliaments and legislative assemblies normally accept cabinet leadership in policy formation, while opposition parties see their role as one of opposing rather than proposing. Consequently, only one – or arguably two – of the many systematic analyses of Canadian constitutional discontents and proposals for their alleviation came from a political party. In two elaborate publications the Quebec Liberal Party,[19] at the time in opposition, gave both a philosophic defence and analysis of federalism and presented an exceptionally, possibly excessively, detailed set of proposals for constitutional reform. The role of the Parti Québécois, as distinct from the role of the provincial government, in the formulation and development of the official Quebec government position, from November, 1976, to the present, was certainly of considerable importance because of the centrality of the independence issue to the very existence of the party and its practice of intra-party democracy. With these two exceptions, both from Quebec, the irrelevance of parties as policy formulators in constitutional matters was little short of astounding.

At the national level the parliamentary parties displayed negligible policy creativity but much *ad hoc* responding to whatever initiatives Prime Minister Trudeau was pursuing. From 1968 to the 1981 constitutional agreement the basic outlines of the federal Liberal government's policy on the constitution consistently reflected the Prime Minister's long-held theoretical approach to Canadian federalism. The role of the

Liberal Party in and out of Parliament was supportive and mildly constraining, rather than independently creative. The party provided the troops to be managed in the Prime Minister's pursuit of his constitutional vision.

The Progressive Conservatives, after being badly burned on the constitutional issue during the 1968 election, had no substantive policy on the constitution. The procedural uncertainties of the Canadian process of constitutional change allowed them to avoid substance by turning themselves into the guardians of procedural proprieties. An attack on procedures rather than goals was their primary response to both the major Liberal constitutional proposals, Bill C-60 in 1978 and the patriation package of 1980-81. This procedural focus kept the party relatively united but deprived it of a major impact on the content of the constitutional debate. It is a remarkable tribute to the capacity of politicians for evasive action that the second major party in the country survived the constitutional turmoil of 1976-81, including a brief period in office, without developing a visible, coherent constitutional position beyond the occasional discussion paper or, *ad hoc*, evolving policy suggestions dictated by the requirements of parliamentary strategy. While the vision of Canada as a community of communities articulated by the party leader, Joe Clark, clearly contrasted with the more centralist Trudeau orientation, the constitutional implications that flowed from it were not spelled out.[20]

The New Democratic Party initially saw the constitutional issue as a distraction and a smokescreen to veil the leadership failures of the government in other areas. However, it sided with the federal government after Trudeau's October decision to take unilateral action, though this support subsequently provoked deep regional splits within the parliamentary party and between the national party and the only NDP provincial government in office (in Saskatchewan). The party's overall policy contribution, however, was sketchy and fragmentary. As an NDP member from Toronto pointed out: "Social democrats have never dealt effectively with the politics of language and ethnicity. And so we have never spoken directly to what is going on in Quebec. . . . Talking about the constitution makes us uncomfortable."[21] The major policy advanced by its leader, Ed Broadbent – a recommendation for modified proportional representation – was subsequently repudiated by the 1981 NDP national convention.

However, both the Conservatives and the NDP at the national level did have a marked effect on the constitutional strategies and positions of successive Liberal governments. Bill C-60 was shelved partly because of the extremely rough treatment it received in 1978 from a Special Joint Parliamentary Committee and from a separate Senate committee, especially from their opposition members and also from Liberal senators privately in meetings of the parliamentary party.

In 1980, the very limited provincial government support for the federal package induced the Liberals to try and justify their proposed unilateral approach by identifying the national Parliament as the constitutional tribune of the people. This inevitably gave the opposition parties considerable influence, which they were not reluctant to employ. The Conservatives could justify a highly critical posture on the basis of the divisions in the country at large, including provincial government opposition, and on the general controversy surrounding the unilateral method Ottawa proposed to employ. They were thus given the powerful political resources of influential allies outside Parliament and a high-sounding principled position that could be employed as a rationale for obstructionist tactics. Given the oppositionist role assumed by the Conservatives, the NDP provided the only possible additional parliamentary support for the Liberals. Given the further facts that all four western provincial governments were opposed and the Liberals had no MPs west of Winnipeg, the support of the NDP, with its western members, was absolutely necessary if the Liberals were to refute allegations that the proposed constitutional changes lacked a broad national base of support.[22] NDP support was equally necessary to undermine suggestions that the proposed constitutional changes reflected purely partisan Liberal concerns.

Thus the interaction of a particular regional distribution of party support in the House of Commons with the intergovernmental divisions on the federal package, introduced by the Liberals in the autumn of 1980, delivered an open invitation to opposition parliamentarians to play a prominent role. Conservative delaying tactics slowed down the Liberal steamroller, brought the Supreme Court into the picture, and gave the dissenting provinces an opportunity to develop a limited alternative constitutional package. The NDP, with its western support, was instrumental in adding a resource section to the Constitution Act, and with its strong civil rights orientation strengthened the Charter.[23] That the Conservatives and the NDP did not do more reflected the policy dominance of the Liberal government on an issue it had made peculiarly its own, its majority status, the general tendency for opposition parties to react rather than to initiate, and, most of all, the fact that neither party had an overall constitutional position.

The role of the opposition parties was profoundly influenced by the complicated interactions between the parliamentary system at both levels, with its institutionalized adversary politics between government and opposition, and the federal system, with its patterns of agreement and disagreement between governments. The cross-pressures generated when these logically distinct systems of conflict and co-operation were pulled closer together by the constitutional issue produced serious tensions, especially in the national parties, but occasionally at the provincial level as well.

Such disagreements between opposition parties of the same name at both levels of government were infrequent and relatively manageable.[24] More frequent and serious were intra-party conflicts when one of the branches of the party constituted the government. In such a situation the party in government has an extra clout and legitimacy it can employ as leverage on its opposition namesake at the other level. The Conservative government of Ontario, which supported Trudeau's package, put considerable pressure on Conservative MPs from that province to break with their national leader, who was leading the opposition to the Trudeau initiative.[25] When it became clear in the winter of 1981 that a satisfactory constitutional compromise between Saskatchewan and Ottawa was not forthcoming, the NDP government of Saskatchewan put very strong pressure on NDP MPs from Saskatchewan to break ranks with their national party and oppose the Liberal resolution.[26]

In such situations, the tension is most profound within the opposition party, which lacks the cohesion that comes from the possession of power. The federal NDP had most difficulty with its MPs from Saskatchewan whereas the Saskatchewan government, publicly at least, was not equally torn. Similarly, the frequent differences between the governing federal Liberals and the opposition provincial Liberals in Quebec, who were more involved in constitutional politics than any other provincial opposition party in the country, were much more troublesome for the Quebec Liberals.[27] Further, the flight of the national Conservatives from substance to procedure was not only a product of leadership difficulties in the party,[28] but was also a shrewd response to the plethora of provincial Conservative governments with their sharply divergent constitutional goals.

Federal-provincial intra-party relations were a much more serious problem for the opposition Conservatives than for the governing Liberals. Had the Conservatives controlled the central government, the increased capacity for cohesion imposed by the discipline of power would have encountered the increased tensions resulting from the necessity of making a policy choice unavoidably offensive to several Conservative provincial governments. By contrast, the unity of the governing Liberal Party in the face of a profoundly hostile environment was immensely aided by the total absence of provincial governments of Liberal persuasion at the time. Liberal unity in the face of the opposition of the Parti Québécois would not have been duplicated had the Quebec government been controlled by the provincial Liberal Party. An Ottawa-Quebec constitutional agreement with a provincial Liberal government led by Claude Ryan would not have been easy to achieve, and the strains within the federal Liberal Party resulting from such a disagreement would almost certainly have been much greater.[29] The manoeuvrability and decisiveness of the federal Liberals were partly due to their lonely eminence as the only Liberal government in Canada by the end of the 1970s.

At the provincial level, government parties seem to have been primarily the instruments of premiers.[30] Only scattered information is readily available on the constitutional stances of the various provincial opposition parties.[31] Outside Quebec, they were not under a great deal of pressure to develop constitutional policies, and they were accordingly, along with provincial governing parties, much less subject to internal divisions and strains than their federal counterparts.[32]

In general, provincial opposition parties played a noticeably lesser role than did federal opposition parties. Provincial legislative assemblies, Quebec again excepted, were not forums for major debate concerning the constitutional positions of the provincial governments. Provincial executives are typically freer of legislative control than is the federal cabinet. Further, as we have seen, constitutional requirements and federal strategy on various occasions required a prominent and visible role for the federal Parliament. This gave federal opposition parties a public platform far surpassing any similar opportunity or responsibility available to provincial opposition parties, except in Quebec.

The parties in the eleven jurisdictions of the Canadian system of parliamentary federalism simultaneously had to juggle government-opposition party relations within their own jurisdictions and cross-jurisdictional relations with government and opposition parties in other jurisdictions. The most noticeable pattern was for provincial opposition parties to be somewhat closer to the constitutional position of the federal government than was the constitutional position of the government they encountered in their own provincial bailiwick.[33] The same tendency operated at the federal level, where during the period of greatest intergovernmental controversy in 1980-81, the opposition Conservative Party could aptly be described as the in-house advocate of the dissenting provincial governments.

The reason for this structurally induced tendency is the elementary political logic that the enemy of my enemy is my friend. This complex pattern of cross-level links and affinities between opposition parties and government parties at the two levels was most strikingly revealed in the brief, intense, and confused period of Quebec-Ottawa bargaining and politicking between the intergovernmental agreement of November 5, 1981, with Quebec dissenting, and the parliamentary approval of the constitutional resolution a month later. Now that the federal government had reached an agreement with seven of the eight provincial allies whose cause the Conservatives had espoused, the Conservatives faced the choice of siding with the ten governments now in agreement, which included the federal Liberal government they hoped to replace, or attacking the inadequacies of the agreement and developing links with the only provincial government still opposed to their parliamentary foe. They chose the latter course. The Conservatives denounced the agreement for its exclusion of Quebec and pursued a number of initiatives designed to bring Quebec into it and, in the process, to embarrass the federal Liberal government.[34] Concurrently with the federal Conservative courtship of the PQ government, the federal Liberals courted the Liberal opposition party in Quebec. Indeed, several changes were made in the agreement between Ottawa and the nine provinces in response to suggestions and proposals from Ryan.[35] While the sincerity of the efforts of the parties in these criss-crossing linkages need not be doubted, it is relevant to note the mutuality of partisan interest involved. Both the federal Conservatives and the PQ shared a desire to hurt the federal Liberals. Both federal and provincial Liberals had a common goal of weakening the PQ. The pursuit of the public interest has a special savour if one's partisan enemies can be damaged in the process.

The adversary relationship between government and opposition parties at each level induces the latter to resist having their individuality submerged in a too common front with the government opponent they seek to throw out of office.[36] When governments are in disagreement this leads, as has been shown, to a moderate tendency to convergence between government and opposition parties at different levels. For the federal system as a whole this has a modest unifying effect, as it generates some rapport and mutuality of interest across jurisdictional boundaries at a time of prevailing intergovernmental discord.

The Importance of Arenas of Conflict

Possibly the most striking feature of the diffuse constitutional review process was how shifts from one arena to another changed the agenda and the actors. This was dramatically evident in the contrast between the closed intergovernmental meetings in the summer of 1980 and the First

Ministers' Conference in September, on the one hand, and the hearings held by the Special Joint Committee of Parliament in the autumn and winter of 1980-81 on the other. At the former sessions, both open and closed, the concerns of government dominated the proceedings. In stark contrast, at the Joint Committee hearings, where numerous interest groups appeared, the concerns of provincial governments were conspicuously unimportant. The principled defence of parliamentary sovereignty against an encroaching Charter of Rights, which the provincial governments employed to protect their jurisdictional integrity, was an almost total irrelevance to the ethnic groups, civil rights organizations, and lobbies on behalf of Indians, women, the disabled, the unborn, and many others, which campaigned and argued vehemently for a stronger Charter. Indeed, by switching from the intergovernmental arena to the committee forum of Parliament, the federal government set the civil rights activists against the provincial defenders of the British tradition of parliamentary supremacy, generated a national constituency for its constitutional package, strengthened its own Charter, and put the dissenting provincial governments on the defensive.[37]

This indifference to provincial government concerns displayed by most witnesses before the Joint Committee was not present in two other arenas called into existence by the dissenting provinces. One of these, a truncated version of the provincial premiers' conference, quickly took form after Trudeau announced the federal government's intention of proceeding unilaterally. The "Gang of Eight," as it came to be called after Nova Scotia and Saskatchewan joined, was responsible for the basic provincial government strategy opposing the federal patriation plans. In addition to orchestrating a propaganda assault against the substance of the federal position, the dissenting premiers challenged the federal package before the provincial courts of appeal of Manitoba, Newfoundland, and Quebec. In the judicial arena, legal and constitutional arguments dominated. The merits and demerits of the Charter were irrelevant. Interest groups were relegated to the audience. Legal gladiators disputed complex questions of law and convention pertaining to the rights of provincial governments to have a definitive say prior to a formal federal government request for legislation by the British Parliament amending the Canadian constitution.

While these court proceedings were under way, the dissenting premiers worked on their own limited constitutional package restricted to patriation and an amending formula. Unlike federal-provincial constitutional conferences where there is usually a televised segment and where a battery of reporters feeds the public with a shifting mix of rumour and fact, the

Gang of Eight and their officials stayed out of the limelight and conducted their proceedings in closed sessions. In spite of the massive and
documented public support for the Charter, they simply left it out of
their modest package of constitutional renewal. They devoted themselves
to the task of devising an amending formula, and since there was no
spokesman for the national government at their meetings the guiding and
relatively uncontested principle of their deliberations was the protection
of provincial sovereignty.[38] The provincial amending formula, labelled
the Constitutional Accord and officially released at a televised press conference in Ottawa in April, 1981, was curtly rejected by the federal
government as a recipe for fragmentation.

However, when the Supreme Court found by a majority of seven to
two that the federal proposals were legal, but by a different majority of
six to three asserted that they were unconstitutional in terms of convention, as they lacked sufficient provincial consent, there was immense
pressure on both sides to return to the bargaining table. After a month of
competitive bluffing, posturing, and jockeying for position the eleven
governments returned for another attempt to get intergovernmental
agreement. The Supreme Court decision had weakened the federal ability
to act unilaterally, but the justices had also pointedly refused to support
the position of seven of the eight provinces that provincial unanimity was
constitutionally required before a resolution affecting provincial powers
was forwarded to Westminster. In these circumstances the pressures to
reach a political agreement were almost irresistible. The provincial premiers knew that the Supreme Court had given the federal government the
resource of legality, that Ottawa could proceed with the support of the
governments of Ontario and New Brunswick. On the other hand, the
legitimacy of unilateralism had been gravely weakened, thus making
Ottawa more amenable to compromise than previously.

The interests that went into the compromise, however, were the interests of the governments that participated in its formulation. In closed
bargaining the proposal for referenda as part of the amending procedure
favoured by Ottawa was dropped.[39] The federal amending formula, which
had allowed the possibility of an amendment being passed against the
wishes of up to two provinces in each of the western and Atlantic regions,
was replaced by a slightly modified version of the formula proposed by the
Gang of Eight. The Charter, which earlier had been strengthened before
the Joint Committee and in Parliament, where there were few defenders of
the provincial premiers' devotion to the British tradition of parliamentary
supremacy, was diluted again in closed intergovernmental bargaining
where there was no direct participation of the groups that had so success-

fully strengthened the originally weak federal Charter. Although the Charter survived the final bargaining sessions, it was significantly qualified by the addition of an override provision that would allow any provincial government or the federal government to have its legislation stand in spite of conflict with the Charter in certain areas.[40]

Although this penultimate stage in the constitutional process was dominated by governments, they were undoubtedly responding to an almost palpable public pressure for an agreement. This was particularly the case in English Canada, a fact that made the English-Canadian premiers, and doubtless also the federal cabinet, most reluctant to carry their disagreement to the stage of a pitched battle before the British public. This reluctance was much less evident in the Quebec delegation, which, for other reasons as well, was the least likely to sign an agreement. Consequently, the intergovernmental agreement was signed by nine provinces and the federal government, with Quebec alone dissenting and asserting betrayal.

Somewhat surprisingly, this solemn agreement of ten of eleven governments was not the end of this phase of constitution-making.[41] The agreement had to be put into suitable language and then returned to Parliament for final passage before submission to Westminster. As the recognition sank in that in closed intergovernmental bargaining many of the rights fashioned and refined in the Special Joint Committee and in the House of Commons had been diluted, a blizzard of angry protest emerged, particularly from women's groups and from various aboriginal organizations. The former were furious that the clause guaranteeing the Charter's rights and freedoms "equally to male and female persons" had been made subject to an override by a group of male first ministers in secret sessions. The latter were angry that a clause by which the "aboriginal and treaty rights of the aboriginal peoples of Canada are hereby recognized and affirmed" had been completely deleted.

In both cases the symbolism of what had been done made a greater contribution to mobilizing women and native peoples than did the practical consequences of the changes, which were far from clear. In any case, orchestrated political pressure without parallel in Canadian history completely overwhelmed the provincial premiers responsible for the changes. They were compelled to agree to the removal of the applicability of the override to the equal guarantee of the rights and freedoms of the Charter to men and women and to the reinstatement of a modified version of the aboriginal rights clause.

Given the general, albeit fluctuating, government domination of the constitutional reform process throughout Canadian history, this successful assault on executive federalism by organizations of women and aboriginal peoples was in itself an event of great constitutional significance. Admittedly, both groups were overtly encouraged by the federal government and opposition parties. Further, an alliance between the "people" and Ottawa against the provincial governments had been a long-standing objective of Trudeau. Nevertheless, this dramatic display of grassroots mobilization was an early indication and portent of the fundamental change in the practices and values of Canadian democracy that the Charter of Rights promised to bring in its wake.

To look back on the constitutional reform process is to be made depressingly aware of the intimate correlation between the substance of various constitutional packages and the interests present or absent at their creation.

(1) The interaction of civil libertarians, ethnic groups, and the federal government produced a strong Charter and negligible concern for the interests and views of provincial governments opposed to the Charter.[42] Further, the amending formula developed by Ottawa was insensitive to the interests of provincial governments, with its provision for a referendum exercise of the "national will" to override the objections of provincial governments.

(2) The meetings of the government spokesmen for the eight dissenting provinces, by contrast, produced a Constitutional Accord scrupulously respectful of provincial autonomy and parliamentary supremacy. The Accord was hostile to any idea that the national community or the national government had rights against a provincial government, hostile to any suggestion that a provincial electorate could be allowed to support a constitutional option opposed by its own government, and hostile to any limitations on executive action that would flow from a Charter giving the courts authority to protect citizens' rights and liberties against encroachment by government.

(3) When both levels of government got together after the Supreme Court decision the interests sacrificed were the interests not present or only weakly represented. The referendum was eliminated, the Charter eroded. Advocates of constitutionally entrenched rights learned the clear lesson: closed sessions dominated by government spokesmen were far from being optimum forums for the triumph of their cause. Only the commitment of Ottawa to the Charter's role in strengthening the public's identification with the national community as opposed to the provincial communities preserved it from further emasculation.

In addition to the biases built into the various constitution-making arenas noted above, the overall process excluded a direct confrontation between the Canadian people and the provincial governments over the evolving reform package, and specifically over the Charter. In the only significant exceptions to this overall tendency, the last-minute lobbying by women and aboriginal groups, the provincial governments were overwhelmed.

The logic that different arenas benefit and harm different interests was not lost on the political actors who manipulated arenas and tried to maximize the legitimacy of the arena in which their claims were most likely to prevail. Governments opposed to the Trudeau package employed the courts to test its legality, vigorously lobbied for a British trusteeship role, denigrated the parliamentary forum as illegitimate, advocated a return to the First Ministers' Conference, and displayed little enthusiasm for and much hostility to suggestions of a possible referendum. The federal government, by an equally obvious political logic, stressed the role of Parliament as the representative of the Canadian people, tried to avoid resort to the courts, decided to bypass the First Ministers' Conference after the failure of the September, 1980, conference, described the British role as that of a rubber stamp, and released frequent trial balloons suggesting the possible use of referenda to resolve the controversy between governments.

The recognition of the difference in outcomes that could be generated by the use of different arenas was also behind the recurring suggestion that the process of constitutional change should be removed from governments and handed over to a constituent assembly whose deliberations would not be dominated by the self-interested concerns of governments. Governments responded to these suggestions with an eloquent silence.[43]

The Impact of Constitutional Reform

The achievement of the Constitution Act is so recent, and the intergovernmental hostilities that accompanied its creation so deep, that confident predictions as to its impact are premature. Caution is doubly necessary given the abstention of the government of Quebec from the agreement and its efforts to frustrate the Constitution Act, especially the Charter, to the extent of its ability. Moreover, the difficulty of predicting long-range consequences is compounded by the fact that the actual effects of recent constitutional change will depend on the conscious political behaviour of various elites. The modified constitution, like the evolving constitution since 1867, provides a set of barriers and resources for the federal and provincial political entrepreneurs of the future, it reshuffles the relations between several key institutions, and it modifies the relations between the governments and the peoples of Canada. The working constitution of Canadian federalism now exists within a partially altered framework. Its evolution will be the product of the future play of political forces, which will be influenced but not determined by the modified constitutional setting for tomorrow's political activity.

Further, only the naive would suggest that the Constitution Act is a definitive response to the constitutional discontents of recent decades. French-English and Quebec-Ottawa relations cannot yet be put on the shelf as problems no longer requiring attention. The intergovernmental discord born of competing big governments at both levels, which has been such a debilitating characteristic of recent Canadian federalism, was not addressed by the Constitution Act. The inadequacies of regional representation in central institutions remain untouched. Thus, while the achievement of the Constitution Act is not trivial, its main effect will be to change the rules of the game that will govern the constitutional controversies of the future. The newly modified constitution will not have the luxury of shaking itself down and working out its accommodations with Canadian society in a serene atmosphere of normalcy.

New constitutions and changes to old constitutions are not neutral instruments. They are crafted with purposes in mind, and although they may fail to achieve them, they will then manifest other biases brought to the surface by the political battles of the future. In the Canadian case, the Constitution Act speaks in contradictory and somewhat hesitant tones about the nature of the Canada it envisages and is intended to create. Nationalism and provincialism are mixed in very different proportions in the amending formula and in the Charter. Further, some of the constitutional changes conflict with Canadian traditions. Four significant changes are clear, however.

(1) The Senate suffered both a symbolic and practical defeat in having its previous absolute veto in the amending process replaced by a six months' suspensive veto. This deprives the Senate of ultimate control over its own future composition and powers. While the Senate is not thereby entirely devoid of political resources, its probable impact on future Senate reform is immeasurably weakened. This will push the debate on Senate reform further in the direction of its federal role as a regional house to the relative detriment of its second chamber responsibilities as an institution of legislative review. The survival of the existing Senate now depends on the difficulty of obtaining federal and provincial agreement on the specifics of its reform, under a new amending formula that requires resolutions of the Senate and the House of Commons, or the latter alone after 180 days, and resolutions of the legislative assemblies of

at least two-thirds of the provinces that have at least 50 per cent of the population of the provinces.

(2) The Supreme Court and the overall judicial system have been given expanded parts to play. The Constitution Act provides the judiciary with an opportunity and a responsibility to preside over the interaction between the Charter of Rights and Freedoms and Canadian society. While the Supreme Court may not immediately, or ever, become the equivalent of the American Supreme Court as the "conscience of the people," it will be nudged in that direction. It must be assumed that some future court will avail itself of the new power it has been given, no matter how much that new role departs from the British tradition.[44]

The addition of the Charter to the Supreme Court's responsibilities will subtly change the criteria governing the appointment of judges. Every increase in the discretion of the Court directs attention to the judicial philosophy of its members and the basic values that inform their decision-making. Hence, the new Court role will give added salience to jurisprudential considerations in the appointment criteria. Representative considerations will also be affected. Regional criteria for selection, derivative of the Court's role as umpire of the federal system, will increasingly be supplemented by other representational considerations, such as sex and ethnic background, as the Court manoeuvres in the minefield of citizen-state relations with the Charter as its guide.

The impact of the Charter on the Supreme Court is simply a by-product of its intended impact on Canadian society. The Canadian Charter of Rights and Freedoms represents the partial fulfilment of a long-standing federal government goal simultaneously to foster a national community and to enhance the status of the Canadian people relative to their governments. The proposed version of the Charter that emerged from Parliament immediately prior to the Supreme Court hearings on the constitutionality of the unilateral Liberal patriation package[45] was an encroachment both on parliamentary supremacy and on federalism. The essential political meaning of the Charter is implicit in the fact that Ottawa has consistently been its sponsor, while its major opponents have been found among provincial governments. The logic of this contrasting response of the central and provincial governments was based on the relationship of the Charter to the federal system. The Charter is a federal government instrument to limit the balkanization of Canada as a moral community by the differential and inconsistent impacts of ten provincial governments on the Canadian citizenry. That this federal effort coincided with an intensification of the provincial governments' manipulation of the societies and economies under their jurisdiction was politically logical. The federal goal was the establishment of a minimum base of rights for a national citizenry that could not be eroded by provincial government policies. Ottawa sought to limit the ongoing provincialization of Canadian society. Thus the Charter's restrictions on parliamentary supremacy had a nation-building purpose that made their acceptance more attractive to Ottawa than to the provinces. The national community of individuals the Charter was to foster was a positive good for Ottawa, and a politically threatening development for some of the provincial governments, particularly Quebec.

The provincial opponents of the Charter were able to weaken its limitations on their autonomy by the insertion of an override clause that applies to fundamental freedoms, legal rights, and equality rights. The override clause unquestionably mutes somewhat the symbolism of the Charter as well as giving both Ottawa and the provincial governments the practical capacity to evade its restrictions on their authority. However, Quebec apart, the probability is that the override will not be frequently employed. Each declaration of an override ceases to have effect after five years and can only be renewed by an express declaration of Parliament or a provincial legislature. The existence of the Charter, even with the override, strengthens the arsenal of the defenders of rights against the arguments of political executives for a necessary flexibility in the choice of instruments for problem-solving.[46]

In a larger sense the Charter elevates the status of the Canadian people vis-à-vis their governments. It adds a potentially powerful rhetoric to the claims of citizens that in normal times their rights have priority over the goals of governments. The long-run impact of this transformation of the feeling side of citizenship is potentially considerable. The language of rights is a Canadian language, not a provincial language. If the Charter takes root over time, the psyche of the citizenry will be progressively Canadianized.

The probability that this development will be to the advantage of Ottawa is high. On the other hand, because of the greater probable use of the override by Quebec and the less responsive Quebec cultural and political milieu in which the Charter will operate, its effect may be to widen the gulf between Francophone Quebecers and Canadian citizens outside Quebec.

(3) The language provisions of the Charter constitute an analytically separate federal government attempt to strengthen the Canadian community.[47] These provisions have two major foci. First, they embed in the constitution the status of English and French as the official languages of

Canada and New Brunswick, and detail the particular rights in legislative bodies, courts established by Parliament and any courts of New Brunswick, and in communications with the governments of New Brunswick and Canada. The provincial governments of Quebec and Manitoba continue to be governed respectively by Section 133 of the BNA Act and Section 23 of the Manitoba Act. Second, the Charter provides minority language educational rights throughout Canada for the children of Canadian citizens, in specified circumstances, to receive primary and secondary school instruction in English or French. These rights, however, depend on there being enough children "to warrant the provision to them out of public funds of minority language instruction," and where "the number . . . warrants, the right to have them receive that instruction in minority language educational facilities provided out of public funds."[48]

The minority language education provisions of the Charter are an impressive political achievement for Ottawa. Their practical consequences, however, are problematic. Provincial compliance may not be forthcoming, or may be partial or niggardly. The criterion "where numbers warrant" will undoubtedly generate conflicts between parents and provincial governments that will end up in the courts.[49] Acrimony will be most intense if shrinking numbers induce future provincial governments to withdraw educational rights previously respected. Further, the right to a minority language education may be more symbolic than useful if the sociology of language interaction outside the school militates against minority language survival. Demographic projections of future language use indicate a seemingly irresistible tendency for French-language speakers to be concentrated in Quebec and for Quebec to become increasingly French.[50] Since these are the very tendencies against which the new constitutional provisions are directed, there is a very high probability that the minority language educational rights of the Charter will be ineffective in preserving meaningful opportunities for French-language communities to survive in the four western provinces and in Nova Scotia, Prince Edward Island, and Newfoundland, and over time these rights may have only limited success in the bilingual belt in Ontario and with the Acadian community in New Brunswick. The long-run effect of a constitutional symbolism backed by so little substance may not be positive.

(4) The Charter of Rights and Freedoms, including the language provisions, derives from federal government ambitions to strengthen and reinvigorate the national community. The amending formula, on the other hand, is based on a vision of Canada almost completely antithetical to the guiding vision behind the Charter. As we have seen, the amending formula, originally fashioned by Alberta, betrays its origins as a purely

provincial document. Worked on and agreed to by eight provincial governments, it was indifferent to the interests of the national government and the national community. Its provincialist view of Canada was dominated by a fortress mentality. The original Accord gave each province a capacity to opt out of amendments "derogating from the legislative powers, the proprietary rights, or any other rights or privileges of the Legislature or government of a Province" and also required that such provinces receive financial compensation so that opting out would be costless.

The guiding philosophy of the Accord was that all provinces are constitutionally equal, that Quebec is a province like the others, and that the only authoritative spokesman for a province in constitutional matters is the provincial government. Accordingly, no combination of governments could deprive any government of its powers, rights, or privileges against its will. Further, not only could no national referendum majority change the constitution against the wishes of a provincial government, but the provincial electorate was equally denied the opportunity to express a constitutional position opposed to that of its governing political elite. The Constitutional Accord was a recipe for rendering unchallengeable the constitutional position of each provincial government. The Canadian political system, from the perspective of the Accord, was viewed as an aggregation of governments united by coexistence in space and little else.[51]

In the final sessions that fashioned the Constitution Act the provincial amending formula was somewhat modified at the insistence of the federal government.[52] Further, the federal government retains a veto over amendments. Consequently, the chequerboard Canada that Ottawa suggested would follow from the adoption of the Accord is entirely within the power of Ottawa to prevent. Finally, constitutional amendments have been rare events in Canadian federalism, and the modified Alberta formula now in the constitution is unlikely to increase their frequency.

The practical effect of the amending formula is less likely to be found in the consequences of its utilization than in the fact that its existence will constitute a barrier to formal change and hence induce resort to other methods to attain constitutional flexibility. In terms of political symbolism, however, the amending formula of the Constitution Act is of considerable importance, and it was to the definition of Canada in the provincial Constitutional Accord that Trudeau took such strong objection.[53] Both the Accord and the final amending formula based on it define Canada as a country of governments and deny the possibility that a provincial government can be required to submit to a constitutional change not to its liking in areas of importance. This symbolizes not only the defeat of majoritarianism, either of governments or of electorates, but of any conception of a national will to which in some circumstances a provincial government could be required to submit.

The significance of the provincial amending formula, which found its way into the Constitution Act, resides as much in the major alternative proposal it defeated as in its own characteristics. The preferred federal amending formula, present in the federal patriation package from the beginning, slightly modified in its pilgrimage through Parliament, and only finally dropped at the last minute, was based on a philosophy congruent with the federal Charter and incompatible with the provincial Constitutional Accord. The federal amending formula was an ambitious, and in the Canadian setting even daring, attempt to create an alliance between the Canadian people and the central government that would possess the constitutional authority to bypass provincial governments and the provincialism they naturally defended. A slightly modified version of the Victoria Charter amending formula, with the important addition of a referendum option, it was designed to redefine the constituent units of the Canadian polity. The provincial governments would now be subject to "the ultimate sovereignty of the people."[54] The disappearance of the federal formula in the final horse-trading thus thwarted a significant symbolic reconstruction of the Canadian polity, and instead confirmed that as far as constitutional change is concerned Canada is a country of governments, not a country of citizens.

Concluding Reflections

Observation of the Canadian process of constitutional reform is more educational than edifying. The chaotic and unpredictable process was constantly buffeted by extraneous considerations. The simultaneous energy crisis, precipitated by events outside Canada, clearly hampered the search for constitutional reform. Throughout the whole exercise from the late 1960s to the present the results of recent elections and the anticipation of forthcoming elections, which rarely highlighted the constitutional issue, had a marked effect on the bargaining power and self-confidence of the political actors. In the closed and intense sessions of First Ministers' Conferences, bargaining was obviously affected by the chemistry of personal likes and dislikes, by the pressure of time, by physical exhaustion, and by intelligence and stupidity. The constitutional renewal process cannot be isolated from these and other factors, which may seem irrelevant to the real issues at stake.

It is necessary to resist the tendency to see the visible constitutional actors as puppets of underlying socio-economic forces, borne along on currents they cannot deflect to a predetermined destination. To look back on the ebb and flow of constitutional activity in the last two decades, on the rise and fall of constitutional options, the fluctuations in the cast of political actors, the frequency of unexpected happenings, and the undoubted significance of seemingly trivial events is to be unimpressed by any suggestion that Canadians were observing an inexorable process relentlessly working its way out to some inevitable constitutional outcome.

Instability and unpredictability more accurately describe the tortuous flow of events, especially in the two years from the defeat of the brief Conservative government in the winter of 1980 to the ending of the constitutional debate in the Canadian Parliament in December, 1981. The year 1980, which commenced with the build-up to the referendum designed to break up Canada, "ended with an expression of federal power unprecedented since World War Two."[55] The flavour of the eleven months from the referendum outcome to the commencement of the Supreme Court hearings on the constitutionality of the Trudeau package was graphically described by a leading journalist: "Since last summer when Trudeau began his Long March toward a new constitution, harried all the way by the guerrilla tactics of the dissident premiers and the Conservatives, the ebb and flow of political fortunes has been more extreme, more abrupt, and more extravagant than in recent memory."[56]

The tumultuous conditions of the 1960s and 1970s, which battered the existing constitution and the political elites who worked it, clearly and unquestionably put the constitutional issue on the public agenda, contributed to its staying power as an issue that would not go away, and influenced the manner in which constitutional reform was approached. The key actors, however, were not conditions moulding men and women to their dictates, but political entrepreneurs pursuing the various preferred and competing constitutional futures that the opening up of the constitution allowed them to glimpse as within their grasp, if they could only play the constitution-making game better than their opponents.

There was no agreement among political elites on the desired direction of constitutional change. The constitutional problems of a disintegrating political system were mirrored in a cacophony of self-interested proposals that shared in common a relative lack of concern for other than the proposer. The federal government tried to generate constitutional change that would shore up its weakened position. Ottawa, under Trudeau, as had been true of the original Fathers of Confederation, sought constitutional power in order to transform the society and economy of the country in defiance of centrifugal pressures and on behalf of a strengthened Canadianism. In pursuing these objectives the federal government clashed with the majority of the provinces, whose governments had alternative definitions of the public interest in which constitutional change would serve their provincial ambitions.

Thus the constitutional struggle of recent years in Canada cannot be understood without reference to the clashing wills, ambitions, and visions of that small group of political leaders who happened to be on the stage when the time came for Canadians to have their constitutional rendezvous with destiny they had so long avoided. The prerequisite conditions to the emergence of the constitutional issue did not determine the stances of the actors or the skills with which they performed. The conditions were both constraints and resources from which the leading actors derived purposes and devised policies to pursue them. These policies were the products of creative intellectual efforts by political elites and their advisers selecting goals and the means for their attainment. Between the policies of the elites and the outcome lay the process. The process was the arena, or more properly series of arenas, in which the policy divisions among the elites, with intermittent public involvement, were played out and transformed. The major source of difficulty in reaching agreement was not primarily due to socio-economic or other divisions in society that were then manifested in elite intransigence, but to political divisions between members of the federal and political elites themselves, as was most strikingly the case with respect to the Charter.

The process acquired a certain momentum of its own. It became self-sustaining and somewhat detached from its original *raison d'être*. The provincial governments of English Canada, which had participated in only a desultory fashion in the 1968-71 constitutional discussions, were much more active and demanding in the constitutional activity that followed the Parti Québécois victory in 1976.

The parliamentary process in the unilateralism stage clearly enhanced the psychic involvement of the public. The Charter struck a resonant chord in the Canadian community. Much of the enthusiasm for the Charter no doubt reflected the effective proselytizing of the federal government in the previous decade and the impact of the televised proceedings of the Special Joint Committee. Participation in discussions of the Charter had a catalytic effect, both psychologically and organizationally, especially among lobbies for aboriginal groups and women. For the former, the constitutional process from the late 1970s gave them a visibility and political prominence they had not previously experienced. For the latter, the constitutional process, especially in the last year, tremendously accelerated the emergence of women's organizations as a powerful political force.

Thus the process generated more actors and more demands. The agenda widened. More and more issues were defined by governments as requiring constitutional resolution. A veritable flood of constitutional proposals and prescriptions emerged from academics, journalists, and publicity seekers – not entirely discrete categories. The Charter was in danger of becoming a grab-bag for every group in the country delighted with the possibilities opened up by the new, hitherto almost un-Canadian language of rights.

The process had a centrifugal effect. There was no consensus on what was to be done. The "crisis" always seemed insufficiently grave to induce more than fleeting thoughts of self-sacrifice by the major participants. As noted earlier, the politics of the pre-referendum period had a centrifugal effect on the generation of demands. The referendum defeat of sovereignty-association produced only a momentary euphoria, quickly followed by a return to the normal state of the pursuit of constitutional advantage by each of the government participants.

The untidiness and ambiguities of the process put an extra premium on the skilful use of resources to seek preferred goals and block the attainment of others. Indeed, the complexity of the process and the multiplicity of roadblocks constituted a strong bias in favour of the status quo and thus necessitated Herculean efforts to achieve even a modicum of change. For the federal government, and particularly the Prime Minister,[57] in the post-referendum round of constitutional discussions, a profound exercise of will, determination, pride, and arrogance worked against retreat in the face of massive opposition. The desire not to lose face combined with a certain stubbornness and a perception that here was an historic moment, one that might not recur for decades, to produce a federal political leadership hostile to suggestions for caution or for dropping the issue.

The enlarging of the agenda was succeeded by its narrowing as the number of issues proved unmanageable and the realities of disagreement became evident. Some issues were sidetracked, while others, such as patriation and an amending formula, which were not directly derived from the substantive controversies agitating the federal system in the 1960s and 1970s, survived to the end.

The final outcome, therefore, is not predictable from the demands fed into the system. With so many actors, so many arenas, so many hurdles and barriers, and so many shifting alliances the constitutional process performed its own alchemy on the way to the final outcome. The miscellany of grievances, claims, and policies seeking recognition was not in any direct way the cause of the final outcome, but only the raw material for a process that, with minor modifications or different performances by several of the actors, could have produced a quite different constitutional product.

That the resulting Constitution Act did not bring unalloyed satisfaction to any participant is not surprising. Indeed, it is altogether probable that had the momentum not built up to such an extent that the constitutional status quo had to be symbolically rejected to avoid the appearance of failure, Quebec would not have been the only government preferring the hitherto existing system to its successor.

Appendix: Chronology of Events[58]

1968	Trudeau elected Liberal Prime Minister and a new round on constitutional negotiations begins.
June, 1971	Rejection of Victoria Charter by the Quebec Liberal government.
November, 1976	Election of a Parti Québécois government in Quebec.
July, 1977	Appointment by the federal government of the Task Force on Canadian Unity under the joint chairmanship of Jean-Luc Pepin and John Robarts.
April, 1978	Claude Ryan becomes leader of the Quebec Liberal Party.
July, 1978	Federal government reveals its constitutional reform proposals in the form of draft legislation (Bill C-60), which is considered by a Special Joint Committee of the Senate and the House of Commons and a Special Senate Committee on the Constitution.
September, 1978	Supreme Court asked to rule on Ottawa's power to reform the Senate.
January, 1979	Publication of the report of the Task Force on Canadian Unity, *A Future Together*.
May, 1979	Joe Clark and the Progressive Conservative Party win the federal election.
December, 1979	Supreme Court rules against Ottawa on the Senate reform proposal contained in Bill C-60.
February, 1980	Trudeau and the Liberal Party returned to power in another federal election.
May 20, 1980	Parti Québécois loses its referendum on sovereignty-association.

Summer, 1980	Extensive ministerial discussions on constitutional reform, followed by a First Ministers' Conference September 8-12; conference fails to produce agreement.
October 2, 1980	Trudeau announces unilateral patriation with a Charter, an amending formula, and other items.
October 6, 1980	Liberal government places its unilateral resolution before Parliament.
October 14, 1980	Five provinces – B.C., Alberta, Manitoba, Quebec, and Newfoundland – decide to challenge the legality of the Trudeau proposals in the courts of three provinces. P.E.I. joins later. Nova Scotia and Saskatchewan hold out. Ontario and New Brunswick are Trudeau's only provincial allies.
November 6, 1980	Hearings of the Special Joint Committee of Senate and House of Commons begin.
February 3, 1981	Manitoba Court of Appeal supports Ottawa by a majority of 3 to 2.
February 13, 1981	Special Joint Committee reports to Parliament.
February, 1981	Nova Scotia and Saskatchewan premiers join the dissenting premiers, who now become known as the "Gang of Eight."
March 31, 1981	Unanimous Newfoundland Court of Appeal decision against Ottawa.
April 8, 1981	Conservative MPs end a seven-day filibuster after an all-party agreement to withhold the final debate and vote on the patriation package until after the Supreme Court rules on its constitutionality.
April 13, 1981	Parti Québécois returned to power in a Quebec provincial election.
April 15, 1981	Quebec Court of Appeal supports Ottawa by a majority of 4 to 1.
April 16, 1981	Vote in Parliament on final amendments to the federal government's constitutional package.
April 16, 1981	Eight provincial premiers sign a Constitutional Accord in Ottawa.
April 28-May 4, 1981	Supreme Court hearings on the question of Ottawa's right to act unilaterally.

September 28, 1981   Supreme Court judgement that unilateralism of federal government is legal but contrary to long-standing tradition.

November 2-5, 1981   First Ministers' Conference on the constitution; agreement reached on constitutional changes with Quebec dissenting.

November 24, 26, 1981 House of Commons approves amendments pertaining to sexual equality and aboriginal rights after extensive lobbying.

December 2, 1981   House of Commons approves final constitutional resolution.

December 8, 1981   Senate approves final constitutional resolution.

April 17, 1982   Queen Elizabeth proclaims the Canada Act.

Chapter Four

Citizens (Outsiders) and Governments (Insiders) in Constitution-Making: The Case of Meech Lake

Preliminary Observations

Much of the debate over the Meech Lake Accord concentrates on its impact on federalism – how it affects the relative status and power of the two orders of government, what it does to the system of interdependence in which they are locked, and how it will modify the workings of such institutions as the Senate and the Supreme Court. Behind these institutional concerns are related issues of community and identity, including the Accord's likely effect on the self-conceptions of Canadians as members of provincial and national communities. As Meech Lake is publicly justified as the vehicle for bringing Quebec back into the constitutional family, and as the package also responds to (and strengthens) the principle of the equality of the provinces, these federalism concerns have to be central to any overall assessment.

Valuable as such a focus unquestionably is, it is not the concern of this interpretive essay. The public reactions to Meech Lake go beyond federalism and reveal fundamental disagreements over the very nature and purpose of the constitution. Two major perspectives are clearly visible – the first reflects the assumptions of the government actors who produced the Accord; the second lies behind the reactions of many of the citizen groups, especially in English Canada, who challenge both the process and substance of the Accord. The first perspective, with deep roots in Canadian history, views the (written) constitution as a document of federalism, and thus of concern primarily to the governments whose affairs it regulates. In competition with this view is a second perspective that took shape in the post-World War Two period and culminated in the 1982 Charter. Since appropriate labelling helps to highlight the differences between these two perspectives, I have identified them respectively as the governments' constitution and the citizens' constitution.[1]

The Charter brought new groups into the constitutional order or, as in the case of aboriginals, enhanced a pre-existing constitutional status. It bypassed governments and spoke directly to Canadians by defining them as bearers of rights, as well as by according specific constitutional recognition to women, aboriginals, official-language minority populations, ethnic groups through the vehicle of multiculturalism, and to those social categories explicitly listed in the equality rights section of the Charter. The Charter thus reduced the relative status of governments and strengthened that of the citizens who received constitutional encouragement to think of themselves as constitutional actors.

The citizens' constitution to which this leads co-exists uneasily with the governments' constitution, a tension highlighted by the amending formula. The employment of the government-dominated amending formula may deliberately or inadvertently affect those parts of the constitution, especially the Charter, to which the citizenry is most intimately linked. Accordingly, the amending formula will likely become the focal point for future attempts to reconcile these competing views of the constitution.[2] To whom does the constitution "belong," and who is entitled to participate, and in what ways, in formally amending it, are now issues on Canadians' constitutional agenda.

The constitutional compromise of 1982 is, accordingly, unstable, as government domination of the amending process is considered illegitimate by many Canadians. The main task of this essay is to explore the emergence and nature of the citizens' constitution that lies behind that view. The citizens' constitution is a new arrival on the stage of Canadian constitutional history and the Meech Lake process, particularly the public input – impotent though it may be – provides a rich resource for its examination.

An essay that sidesteps most of the federalism debate of concern to the big government battalions that dominate our lives (as well as the amending formula) may appear frivolous or whimsical. On the other hand, to succumb to the federalism debate is to be blinded to the emergent views of the many groups that now contest its hegemony and will increasingly do so in the future. In any event, Meech Lake confirms that federalism does not lack defenders.

The Constitutional Basis of Our Constitutional Incoherence

> . . . the constitutional development of Canada cannot proceed in this fashion, where 11 First Ministers – 11 men – get together in a room and come up with a constitutional deal which compromises the fundamental

rights of any particular group of Canadians . . . it is a completely inadequate way to advance ourselves as a nation.[3]

The incoherence at the heart of our constitutional existence derives from internal contradictions in the compromise that resulted in the 1982 Constitution Act. The misreading of our past that suggests that Meech Lake is a correction or balancing of a centralist victory in 1982 ignores the elementary fact that the 1982 Constitution Act was itself a compromise in which both orders of government, Quebec excepted, along with citizen groups interested in a stronger Charter, achieved some of their objectives but had to sacrifice others. Putting to one side the 1982 resources amendment, which was clearly a victory for the provinces,[4] the basic compromise was provincial government agreement to the Charter sought by Ottawa in return for federal government acceptance of an amending formula designed to serve (provincial) government interests, and thus to repudiate the federal government's proposed "referendum provision," which the eight-province Constitutional Accord of 1981 stated was "opposed by many as being inappropriate to the Canadian federal system."[5]

There were additional supplementary concessions on each side. The federal government conceded Section 33, the notwithstanding override clause of the Charter, and thus made limited obeisance to the historic constitutional principle of parliamentary supremacy. The "Gang of Eight" provincial governments, on the other hand, had the amending formula they had fashioned in the provincial Constitutional Accord of 1981 somewhat weakened to accommodate federal government concerns. The original provincial proposal provided that up to one-third of the provinces, with less than 50 per cent of the population of all the provinces, could opt out of an amendment "derogating from the legislative powers, the proprietary rights or any other rights or privileges of the Legislature or government of a province." Further, the government of a province dissenting from "an amendment conferring legislative jurisdiction on Parliament" was to receive "reasonable compensation" in all cases from the government of Canada.[6] This iron-clad provincial protection was weakened in the text of the 1982 Constitution Act as reasonable compensation to opting-out provinces was restricted to cases of transfers of jurisdiction to the federal government of "provincial legislative powers relating to education or other cultural matters."[7]

It is now clear that this compromise is in trouble. The two basic features of the 1982 Constitution Act, the Charter and the amending formula, differ on the proper relation of the constitution to society. The amending formula, admittedly with a limited concession to representative government with its requirement of authorizing resolutions from legislative assemblies and Parliament, is overwhelmingly an affair of governments. As the Meech Lake process emphatically suggests the 1982 amending formula allows a domination by government, in effect by eleven first ministers, that is the very acme of executive federalism.

With the benefit of hindsight it is evident that the scholarly concentration on the Charter as the major outcome of 1982 underestimates the significance of the amending formula, with its capacity to change the constitution by a collective *fait accompli* of governments and derisory public input. The falling by the wayside of the referendum aspect of the federal government's 1980-81 amending formula proposals eliminated the possibility of an amending formula congruent with the underlying philosophy of the Charter, the other side of the 1982 package. The fact that both the federal government and the citizen groups they mobilized on their side in 1980-81 were much less aggressive in struggling for citizen input in the amending formula than in battling for a stronger Charter has led to the present constitutional incoherence in which these two legacies of 1982 speak to Canadians with very different voices and contradictory messages.

The Charter is not only a rearrangement of the machinery of government to the advantage of courts and to the detriment of legislatures. It also enhances the status of citizenship and brings the citizenry into the constitutional order. It links them to the constitution that is "the supreme law of Canada."[8] It gives the citizens rights that are enforceable against governments. In some circumstances, as in official-language minority education rights, it requires positive action by governments. In the language of former Prime Minister Trudeau, the Charter puts the rights of people above the rights of governments, the precise antithesis of the philosophy of the amending formula.

The tension between bringing the citizenry into the constitutional order via the Charter and firmly placing that same citizenry on the sidelines when constitutional amendments are undertaken might lie dormant if formal constitutional change were only a rare event, a kind of Halley's comet in terms of its constitutional frequency. Formally, however, Meech Lake promises the reverse with its requirement of annual constitutional conferences and the concomitant assumption that constitutional fine-tuning is an ever-present requirement.

The tension might be reduced if amendments could be restricted to housekeeping matters of interest only to the governments of Canadian federalism but, as Meech Lake illustrates, the constitution is somewhat of a seamless web. No division of constitutional matters into those only of relevance to governments and those only of concern to citizens is possible. In any event, government domination of the amending formula is not restricted to the spending power, the institutions of federalism, the division of powers, and other federalism concerns.

There is, therefore, no escape from the conflict between these competing views on the constitution. Although governments may be mainly concerned with federalism, the Charter is not thereby extraneous to their interests. Indeed, in 1980-81 the desirability of the Charter was a major point at issue between the contending government alliances, and now the power of governments, expressed in the amending formula, encompasses the Charter. Equally, although citizens' groups may focus on the Charter – and often on particular clauses in it – as their major constitutional concern, they are not indifferent to the division of powers or the impact of changes in the latter on the waxing and waning of the national and provincial communities vis-à-vis each other. Indeed, one of the strongest reactions against Meech Lake comes from Canadians who feel that their national government and national community are being weakened.

In sum, the fact that some parts of the constitution are of more concern to governments and other parts of more concern to the citizenry does not invalidate the essential interdependence of the constitutional order. Governments and citizens view that interdependence through different lenses, but each is interested in the domains of greater concern to the other. The Charter contributes to a participant citizen ethic that applies to the whole written constitution, which, by courtesy of the amending formula, is nevertheless wholly under the control of the political executives of eleven governments. This unequal interdependence is more palatable to the governments in charge than to the citizen groups that Meech Lake defines as spectators.

To understand and to respond sensitively to the transformed role of the constitution brought about by the Charter requires a voyage of constitutional introspection on which Canadians have barely embarked. Students of federalism may not be the best guides for that journey. They may suffer from a disciplinary disability, what Veblen calls a trained incapacity, to appreciate a constitutional order in which federalism in relative terms has lost status as a constitutional organizing principle.

Meech Lake and the Frustrated Culture of Participation

. . . the atmosphere that has surrounded this whole accord [is] that it is a sort of "ark of the covenant"; that it is sacred; that it must not be touched; that even criticism is rather nasty of people – they should be prostrating themselves before this enormous achievement and not questioning anything in it.[9]

No reader of the proceedings of the Special Joint Committee on the Meech Lake Accord or of the Senate Committee of the Whole[10] can fail to be struck by the vehemence and bitterness with which the spokespersons for various groups challenged the legitimacy of a closed-door elite bargaining process restricted to governments. Their anger and the language they employed are constitutionally significant facts deserving examination. They reveal an attitude to the constitution completely at variance with the behaviour of those elites wielding government power who fashioned Meech Lake.

Those who speak for the various groups that have won a constitutional niche for themselves are deeply suspicious of processes of constitutional change from which they are excluded. They do not view executive federalism as simply an expeditious way of striking intergovernmental deals away from the probing television camera. Rather, it is a potential threat to whatever constitutional status they have won or, as for aboriginals and women in the 1980-81 constitutional discussions, were on the verge of winning. They are deeply hostile to the Meech Lake process in which private intergovernmental bargaining is followed by an *ex cathedra* announcement of a constitutional *fait accompli*, and in which ten of the eleven governments, all but Quebec, are almost sphinx-like in their subsequent unwillingness to describe the probable or even desired policy consequences expected to flow from particular clauses.

The composition of the bargaining elite and the governmental interests to which it gave pride of place were often cited by groups as reasons why their own constitutional concerns were ignored, misinterpreted, or overridden. George Erasmus, National Chief of the Assembly of First Nations, categorically rejected the statement of the Special Joint Committee Report that aboriginal First Nations were appropriately represented by first ministers that aboriginal voters helped to elect. "This bland assertion," he retorted, "that First Nations and their governments are represented by non-aboriginal politicians who have no interest, demonstrated or latent, in advocating our rights is bogus and is without foundation in fact or action."[11] The National Association of Women and the Law observed pointedly that the "agreement is only between eleven people, at this time all of them men."[12] Donna Greschner, a feminist legal scholar, asserted that the political battles of 1980-81 against "unsympathetic politicians" are "still too fresh in the memories of national women's organizations for them not to be suspicious of a deal struck in private by eleven men."[13]

These concerns about the biases in a system of closed-door bargaining by an elite of first ministers are not restricted to disgruntled interest groups but are shared by scholarly observers such as John Whyte and Wayne MacKay.[14] Indeed, the evidence of bias and concentration on the interests of governments in the Meech Lake process is so blatant that John Stuart Mill's observation seems as if penned for the occasion: "In the absence of its natural defenders, the interest of the excluded is always in danger of being overlooked; and, when looked at, is seen with very different eyes than those of the persons whom it directly concerns."[15]

Government leaders and citizens from Yukon and the Northwest Territories, which had further impediments placed in the way of their possible attainment of provincial status, could not conceal their incredulity over an outcome they had no reason to anticipate, and that subsequently received only a fragmentary explanation. Their evidence, diligently collected by a special Senate Task Force that held hearings in the northern territories, conveys an impassioned sense of outrage at the new barriers blocking their advance to provincehood and a conviction that paranoia is the appropriate response for northerners to adopt when their affairs are discussed in their absence.[16] In the strong but entirely representative remonstrance of Tony Penikett, government leader in the Yukon, "it is fundamentally unfair that our fate should be decided by others; by everybody else in the country except us, by 11 men in a locked room, most of whom could not find us on a map without assistance. . . . I have to tell you . . . the process in Meech Lake is Kafkaesque. Some 11 men in a locked room decided to condemn us to some sort of constitutional limbo. We never even got a hearing. What was the evidence? What was the charge? Where was our defence?"[17] The brief of the Northwest Territories displayed a similar mixture of stunned puzzlement and fury at the process and the outcome to which it led. "No one knows what is going to happen because there are essentially no rules to these games. I mean, 11 people sit in a room and decide. Then they come out and say they have agreed, so be it."[18]

These are not idiosyncratic observations. On the contrary, they verge on the commonplace. Northerners, stated a northern MP, suffered from "total exclusion from the process. . . . Everything was done behind our backs. We were unable to protect our rights that were bartered away at Meech Lake. We were treated as expendable pawns in the constitution game."[19] One aboriginal advocate referred to the "blackmailers among the provincial first ministers."[20] Alliance Quebec deplored "the abusive process . . . which has stifled democratic debate. . . . We must never again be faced with the kind of cynical constitutional *fait accompli* which confronts us today." [21] The Canadian Labour Congress criticized the anti-democratic process in which "public participation has been intentionally excluded in every meaningful way." [22] To the Human Rights Institute of Canada the Accord left the impression of being one in which "two groups of white males have agreed to increase their own powers at the expense of everyone else's." [23] To the organizing leader of the Canadian Coalition on the Constitution, "eleven men sat around a table trading legislative, judicial, and executive powers as if engaged in a gentlemanly game of poker, with little regard for the concerns of individual Canadians, who will ultimately feel the impact and bear the burdens of their moves." [24]

Similar statements from a remarkable variety of groups could be multiplied many times over. [25] The process is considered to be dishonourable, shameful, immoral, undignified, abusive, selfish, demeaning, and thus simply and categorically unacceptable. Academic voices can be readily added to these protestations. To Albert Breton the efforts "to muzzle the Canadian public [are] truly indecent." [26] For Wayne MacKay, anything less than Joint Committee hearings with a real possibility of change in the text and details of the Accord would be "something of an insult to the Canadian public." [27] Seldom have first ministers been subjected to such wholesale denunciation, the extent and tenor of which reveal a fundamental change in Canadian constitutional culture that can only be ignored at peril.

This deep distrust of the integrity of governments in the amending process is a serious concern when, should Meech Lake pass, Canadians will face a never-ending parade of annual conferences on the constitution. A Meech Lake-type procedure is almost perfectly designed to maximize the frustration of non-governmental groups who do not believe that eleven first ministers meeting in secret can be trusted to protect or serve interests that conflict with their own governmental ambitions. The extension of an invitation to some of the excluded groups, as on this occasion, to present ineffectual briefs before impotent committees threatens to delegitimize further the constitution that is the ultimate basis of the authority of governments.

The Emergence of a Shaky Citizens' Constitution

The linking of individual Canadians and various groups to the constitution is the end result of a lengthy period of adaptation as the Canadian constitution detaches itself from its British origins and adjusts to Canadian society without the benefit of external imperial supports. The declining significance of the British connection, formally signalled by various statutes – the 1931 Statute of Westminster, the 1949 ending of appeals to the Judicial Committee of the Privy Council, the partial domestication of the amending formula in the same year, and the elimination of a role in amendments for the British Parliament in 1982 – was more than a simple replacement of Britons by Canadians in working the constitution. It stimulated constitutional introspection and changed the grounds of constitutional legitimacy by weakening imperial and strengthening indigenous rationales for the various components of the Canadian constitutional order.

It is now evident that, for most of post-Confederation history, parliamentary supremacy and the British approach to the protection of rights without a Charter were, to a considerable extent, sustained by the imperial connection. Much of the support for parliamentary supremacy was derivative, the product of a constitutional tradition that, until World War Two, was based on Canadian links with the governing centre of a still powerful empire. Its capacity to differentiate Canadian from American constitutional practices enhanced its attractiveness.

The constitutional disentangling of Canada from the mother country in the last half-century was fostered not only by the diminished status of the United Kingdom in world affairs but also by the declining British proportion of the Canadian population. Concurrently, another stream of thought, driven by a reaction against the state-engineered brutalities of World War Two and the overthrow of imperial racial hierarchies in Africa and Asia, defined charters of rights as increasingly desirable attributes of modern statehood.

In the Canadian case, the domestic attractiveness of the charter idea was initially stimulated by the increasing ethnic and racial heterogeneity of the Canadian population, an early response to which was the weak 1960 Bill of Rights, a manifestation of Diefenbaker's one-Canada or pan-Canadianism. In socio-ethnic terms the Diefenbaker bill was an attempt to outflank the definition of Canadian society in terms of the two charter groups or founding nations. Put differently, it was an attempt to define Canadian society in a way that relatively downgraded the status of the descendants of those who met on the Plains of Abraham two centuries earlier. The constitution, by way of the Bill of Rights, was becoming an instrument of social recognition.

That constitutional role was dramatically enhanced by the 1982 Charter, which was simultaneously an instrument for the protection of traditional rights, a vehicle for the constitutional recognition of various groups defined by gender, ethnicity, and language, and a weapon to combat centrifugal pressures deriving from nationalism in Quebec and provincialism elsewhere, what Pepin-Robarts called dualism and regionalism.

The Charter redefined the citizenry as bearers of rights; it stressed the Canadian (not provincial) dimension of their identities; and it gave them a stake and a status in the constitutional order. The Charter developed roots in a remarkably short period of time. Indeed, it is almost certainly one of the best-known parts of the written constitution. The fact that the override clause, Section 33, appears to be on the defensive as a residual survivor of the previously potent theory of parliamentary supremacy testifies to the broadly based support for the Charter. That support is both general and diffuse. The former has an organizational expression in the various civil liberties groups that are scattered from coast to coast. The latter is spread across the numerous groups and organizations that see their interests reflected in and protected by specific Charter clauses that classify Canadians in terms of gender, race, ethnicity, and language.

Thus the citizen's new relation to the constitution in the 1982 Constitution Act is the product not only of traditional fundamental freedoms, democratic rights, and legal rights, but also of various particular recognitions for official-language minorities, for aboriginals, for multiculturalism, and for gender equality. Along with the equality rights in Section 15 (1) and (2), the latter of which gives constitutional sanction to affirmative action programs, these constitutional clauses selectively incorporate particular social categories of Canadians into the constitution. Women, aboriginals, and others are given specific constitutional recognition and constitutional identities they had previously lacked. Accordingly, they tend to see the written constitution not as an undifferentiated whole but through the lens of particular sections or clauses that speak directly to them in the same way as Section 92 is of special concern to provincial governments and Section 93 to denominational schools. For women it is Section 28; for ethnics concerned about multiculturalism it is Section 27; for official-language minorities it is Section 23; for aboriginals it is Section 25, along with Section 35 of the Constitution Act, and Section 91 (24) of the BNA Act for status Indians; for yet others it is the listed categories, including race, religion, and physical disability, in the Section 15 equality rights section of the Charter.

These varied constitutional recognitions, and the differences among them, have made the constitution a major instrument for the awarding and adjusting of the relative status of Canadians encompassed by them. The failure to include gays or lesbians or sexual orientation in the listed categories of Section 15 makes it clear that the Charter is an instrument of discrimination as well as an instrument for its prevention.[28]

The incorporation of various social categories into the Charter, alongside the more traditional rights in Sections 2 to 14, has changed the nature of the constitution and its relation to Canadian society. As the constitution reaches down selectively into Canadian society it has become a social document of great symbolic value, the supreme instrument of social recognition and its denial.

Thus, the 1982 Charter greatly expands the number of actors with explicit constitutional concerns. It supplements the still powerful government actors with various citizen groups who are directly linked to the post-Charter constitution. Many of these groups see their constitutional status as having been extracted or won in a bruising constitutional process in which their interests were in constant danger of being deliberately ignored, inadvertently overlooked, or casually encroached upon. Accordingly, they are suspicious and distrustful of governments. "Some women," stated Barbara McDougall, "still have fears that hard-earned gains can disappear with one stroke of the pen."[29] Other recent recipients of constitutional recognition feel the same way.

For women the Section 28 equal guarantee of the Charter's rights and freedoms to men and women "notwithstanding anything in this Charter" is a reminder of a protection won only after a dramatic political mobilization. It was largely due to the pressures of women's groups that Section 28 was included in the Charter and that it was exempted from the Section 33 override clause, which in turn was a response to the objections of several provincial governments to the Charter's erosion of parliamentary supremacy.[30]

That victory, graphically described in a book appropriately titled *The Taking of Twenty-Eight*,[31] plays a role in the mythology of the women's movement similar to that of victorious past battles for the inheritors of a military tradition. Consequently, "28 has a very strong symbolic significance to thousands of women who fought to get it there."[32] Feminist activists view Section 28 not as something granted to women, or as the automatic and logical application of a principle to women, but rather as something seized, in a way akin to a trophy. Thus the language of the women's movement tends to describe Section 28 as being possessed by women, or as a beachhead occupied by women in not altogether friendly land.

The relation of women to Section 28 is not dissimilar to that of provincial governments to Section 92. Like Ontario Premier Oliver Mowat of an earlier generation, women's groups see the courts as a potential ally and they have established legal funds to serve their litigation strategy. Feminist lawyers provide intellectual weaponry and legal insights for the political and constitutional controversies that involve women's concerns. For women, as is noted below, Meech Lake was seen as a setback.

For many of Canada's ethnic communities and the umbrella organizations that speak for them, Section 27 of the Charter is the focus of their constitutional identification. (It appears, however, that Section 27 is more significant to traditional "third-force" Canadians, primarily of European background, than to visible minorities whose numbers and political profile greatly increased in the seventies after the multiculturalism policy had been introduced. For the latter groups, Section 15 with its equality rights and affirmative action possibilities is more highly valued.) Section 27, with its directive that the Charter is to be interpreted in a manner "consistent with the preservation and enhancement of the multicultural heritage of Canadians," is only the most recent example of a hard-won recognition by third-force Canadians that ethnic backgrounds and cultures outside of the founding peoples have a place in the Canadian constitutional pantheon. They have engaged in recurrent struggles to remind constitutional reformers and policy-makers dealing with culture, language, and ethnicity that the descendants of Wolfe and Montcalm occupy a shrinking place in Canadian society. Like women's groups seeking recognition and equality in a "malestream" society, the various ethnic associations also look back on a succession of struggles, in their case to redefine Canada so that they are not engulfed in the primary French-English dualism of Canadian history.

The Royal Commission on Bilingualism and Biculturalism had been troubled by the distrust its dualist mandate elicited from mobilized third-force ethnics who lobbied for greater commission attention to their concerns and to their contributions to Canadian society. The emergence of the 1971 policy of multiculturalism testified to their modest success in gaining recognition. Officially the federal government divorced culture from language, summing up their coexistence in the phrase "multiculturalism within a bilingual framework." In illustration of the complexities of the ethno-linguistic domain, the federal government multiculturalism policy, designed to deflect criticism of its more central bilingualism policy, had the negative side effect of antagonizing Francophone Quebecers, who saw it as depreciating their own status as a founding people.

Multiculturalism was not mentioned in the first version of the Charter released by the federal government shortly after the breakdown of constitutional talks in the late summer of 1980. Section 27 was inserted in response to the pressures of umbrella ethnic organizations and the Ukrainian Canadian Committee.[33] It was a stronger statement than the government had hoped to make. According to a recent author, Section 27 "was a constitutional endorsement of the multiculturalism policy. It was regarded by the ethnic groups as a significant counterbalance between their interests, and the Charter provisions on the rights of the 'founding' and native peoples."[34]

On the other hand, the Meech Lake Accord, with its singling out of the existence of French-speaking and English-speaking Canadians as a "fundamental characteristic of Canada" and its "recognition that Quebec constitutes within Canada a distinct society," is considered a rebuff, as the latest indication that the multicultural components of Canadian society are not to enjoy equivalent constitutional status with founding peoples. These ethnic groups, like women's groups, perceive their constitutional recognition as precarious, and constantly threatened by the tendency of power-holders to forget their existence.

For aboriginals, a term that lacked popular currency until the 1970s and had no significance in the original BNA Act, the 1982 Constitution Act was a major advance, one not repeated in the Meech Lake Accord. An understanding of the former as a victory and the latter as a defeat requires a brief resort to history.

Indian leaders, as Sanders notes, reject the application of the term "ethnic" or "cultural minority" to their peoples, and hence are hostile to being considered as just another strand in the multicultural mosaic. There is also little contact or mutual support between aboriginal and ethnic organizations. As the original inhabitants, as "First Nations," and as aspirants to greatly enhanced powers of self-government, native groups find the cultural and symbolic recognitions held out by the multiculturalism policy to fall far short of aboriginal goals.[35]

Section 91 (24) of the BNA Act, which gave jurisdiction over "Indians, and Lands reserved for the Indians" to the federal government, accorded status Indians a unique constitutional position, although not necessarily to their advantage, in the first century of Canada's existence. That constitutional allocation of powers in the 1860s elicited a department of the federal government responsible for Indian affairs and an Indian Act. For Indians it led to a distinctive reserve culture, an antipathy to the provinces, and an ambivalent attitude to the federal government. For many Indians their separate identity is buttressed by treaties and is sustained by the existence of distinct political authorities at the band level. While the structure of band government is considered far from satisfactory it provides a focal point for political aspirations. It helps status Indians in the modern period to think of themselves as a political people and thus fosters their use of the language of states and nations. Indian special status, which strengthens both their identity and their political will, is summed up by Sanders as resting on five related elements: "federal status, the reserve system, the treaties (or aboriginal rights claim where treaties have not been signed), the Department of Indian Affairs and the *Indian Act*."[36]

The 1982 Constitution Act multiplied the aboriginal content of the constitution. Section 25 of the Charter guaranteed aboriginal, treaty, or other rights or freedoms of the aboriginal peoples against constructions of the Charter that would abrogate or derogate from them. Section 35 (1) of the Constitution Act recognized and affirmed the existing aboriginal and treaty rights of the aboriginal peoples, and Section 35 (2) defined aboriginal peoples as including Indian, Inuit, and Métis peoples of Canada. The inclusion of the Métis, their first overt constitutional recognition, increased the heterogeneity of the overall aboriginal population, produced a major uncertainty as to the actual number of aboriginal peoples, meant that aboriginal policy now had to encompass a more diversified ethnic base than hitherto, and clearly hindered the organizational and political unity of the redefined aboriginal peoples.[37] Section 37 of the 1982 Constitution Act required the holding of a conference on constitutional matters "that directly affect the aboriginal peoples of Canada, including the identification and definition of the rights of those peoples to be included in the Constitution of Canada." Overall, the 1982 Constitution Act, according to Louis "Smokey" Bruyère, president of the Native Council of Canada, treated aboriginal peoples as partners in Confederation and "provide[d] some countervail, some balance, to allow our people, otherwise weak and without influence, to effectively negotiate our place in Confederation."[38]

Recent aboriginal history has been a roller coaster of alternating recognitions and rebuffs.[39] In 1960 status Indians were given the franchise previously withheld on the ground that they were wards of the Crown. By the end of the 1960s they were threatened with assimilation by a federal government that thought their special status was the source of discrimination and contributed to their social and economic backwardness. Their original success, along with other aboriginals outside the status category, in gaining recognition of their rights in an early version of the Constitution Act in 1981 in Section 34, while it worked its way through the Joint Committee, Parliament, and the federal-provincial processes of executive federalism, was reversed in the fall of 1981 when a closed meeting of first ministers, at the behest of several western provinces, rolled back the recognition aboriginals thought they had won. Their successful counter-mobilization led to a modified reinstatement, in a renumbered Section 35, of rights that had been included and then removed. The holding of four constitutional conferences to identify and define their rights initially raised and subsequently dashed expectations as agreement could not be reached.

Meech Lake confirmed aboriginal weakness, in spite of Section 16 of the Accord, with its protection of the aboriginal constitutional status quo from the effect of the interpretation section (Section 2) of the Accord. They were not included as a fundamental characteristic of Canada, nor were they recognized as one or more distinct societies. The additional barriers put in the way of future provincehood for the northern territories had overtones of ethnic discrimination, given the high percentage of aboriginals, especially in the Northwest Territories. Further, in contrast to 1982, the aboriginal constitutional agenda was not part of the identified subject matter of future constitutional conferences. This last exclusion, stated George Erasmus, "just a little over a month after we had had a meeting with those same individuals . . . was a tremendous blow to us. We could not believe that they were doing that to us."[40]

Constitutional politics have been central to the concerns of aboriginal elites for over two decades. They have been encouraged to couch their demands in constitutional language. They have experienced a generally enhanced recognition of their status as constitutional actors. They have had some triumphs. In general, at least for status Indians, the debate between equality with its assimilationist assumptions and special Indian status has decisively tilted to the latter.[41] Thus status Indians specifically (and Inuit, who are also encompassed by Section 91 (24) of the BNA Act), and other aboriginals more tentatively, have attained a recognition that their distinctiveness deserves accommodative state measures, on the details of which, of course, significant disagreement remains. On the other hand, aboriginals have also learned that, compared to federal and provincial governments, they are marginal actors, and that when meetings take place in their absence their concerns may be disregarded or overridden.

The combination of having carved out several niches for themselves in the constitution, which nevertheless fall far short of their ambitions, and a suspicion of the motives of non-aboriginal leaders produces a recurrent abrasiveness and aggressiveness in aboriginal constitutional discourse. They speak the language of aggrieved minorities frustrated by the contrast between the limited constitutional recognition they have already achieved and their self-description as nations and first peoples. Their generally depressed status on virtually all socio-economic indicators, their dependence on governments for the funding of their own organizations, the lack of consensus that prevails in the overall aboriginal community, and their inability so far to achieve their goals add to their resentment. They bridge the gap between their aspirations and their attainments with a truculent, accusatory, and often confrontational style.

Official-language minorities, unlike the socio-ethnic categories discussed above, have been central to federal government constitutional strategy since the late sixties. Their protection, and in particular the provision of official minority-language education rights in provincial settings dominated by majority users of the other official language, have been at the core of federal government definitions of dualism for two decades. For Trudeau the nurturing of official-language minorities has been a primary objective since federal government interest in a strong Charter resurfaced in the late sixties. Both the Anglophone minority in Quebec and Francophone minorities elsewhere have thus been beneficiaries of government sponsorship, for national unity reasons, in ways that have been denied to other minorities.

On the other hand, both minority linguistic communities, while sustained by constitutional supports in the 1982 Constitution Act, know that they exist in the midst of provincial majorities that, if left to their own desires, would often treat the minorities less generously than the constitution requires. Further, the potency of their constitutional position is related to the governmental power that can be mobilized on their behalf. As Canada returns to a species of constitutional normality in response to a perceived decline in Québécois nationalism, official-language minorities justifiably fear that the succouring concern of the federal government may lapse, the political support behind their constitutional protections might diminish, and the approach to their rights might be niggardly rather than generous. They recognize, in a nutshell, that the respect accorded to their constitutional status – especially where it requires the expenditure of public funds, as in education – is contingent, and fluctuates for reasons largely beyond their control. The return of an effective working relationship between the Quebec and federal governments, along with the perceived decline of separatism in Quebec, weakens the political clout of Francophones outside Quebec and of Anglophones within Quebec.[42] Meech Lake confirms that in such circumstances their role as instruments of national purpose diminishes in importance.

Francophone minorities have too long a history of indifferent treatment and insensitive disregard for their concerns not to view the enhancement of their position leading up to and including the 1982 Charter as somewhat fragile. Their apprehensions are fed by galloping rates of linguistic assimilation far more likely to generate pessimism than optimism about their future. They note that the duality and distinct society provisions of the Accord appear to be more sympathetic to linguistic majorities – Francophone in Quebec and Anglophone elsewhere – than to official-language minorities within provinces. They observe that the premiers of English Canada and the federal Prime Minister were unwilling to have the role of their legislative bodies affirmed as including the promotion of linguistic duality, but only its preservation – in contrast to the role of the Quebec government and legislature "to preserve and promote the distinct identity of Quebec," which was affirmed.[43] From the perspectives of Francophones outside Quebec, the Accord, with its distinctions between promote and preserve, gives the most help where it is least needed – for the French-speaking majority in Quebec – and least help where it is most needed – for Francophone minorities confronting powerful assimilationist pressures outside of Quebec.

The Anglophone minority in Quebec does not share the long history of indifference and coercive majoritarianism experienced by Francophone minorities outside of Quebec. Nevertheless, Quebec Anglophones have lived through a recent period in which their former privileged status has been under attack, their numbers have been reduced by emigration, and the supply of new members to their ranks has been cut back by Bill 101's siphoning of allophones into the Francophone camp. The number of English students in the schools of the Quebec Association of Protestant School Boards has declined precipitously from approximately 120,000 in 1976 to 66,000 in 1985.[44] Education officials note that apparently no effort was made at the Meech Lake or Langevin meetings to persuade the Quebec government to bring Section 23 (1)(a), known as the mother tongue section of the Charter's language rights, into effect under Section 59 (1) and (2) of the 1982 Constitution Act – thus preserving a constitutionally based asymmetry in the treatment of linguistic minorities in Canada.

Only a few years ago the Parti Québécois leaders publicly speculated on the illegitimacy that might attach to a provincial referendum result in which a majority Francophone "yes" vote was overturned by the massive support of non-French speakers for the "no" side. The insecurities and apprehensions of the Anglophone community in Quebec are not fanciful. For Alliance Quebec the Meech Lake Accord underlines their weakness:

"our community is the group that has been consciously forgotten in this whole process ... our concerns have been systematically denied and denigrated by a number of powerful people in this country."[45] The Quebec Association of Protestant School Boards agreed that neither the federal nor the Quebec government, "and certainly not the other nine premiers," spoke for the English of Quebec in the Meech Lake meetings. "We are ignored ... we are obviously unimportant."[46] The fact that the English-speaking community of Quebec has a larger population than six of the ten provinces is no guarantee of influence in the government-dominated councils of executive federalism.

Thus members of both official-language minorities are watchful, nervous, and suspicious. Like aboriginals, women, and third-force ethnic groups, official-language minorities seek refuge and support in a constitution they fear may be subverted by governments more responsive to power and numbers than to rights. As the delicately nuanced language of the Commissioner of Official Languages suggests, the Meech Lake Accord displays more concern for provincial governments and majorities than for the sustenance of linguistic minorities.[47]

These specific constitutional clauses, along with the Charter as a whole, attract organizations, often government-funded, to their defence. They are the constitutional base for a counter-elite of group leaders who have been marginalized in the Meech Lake process. From their perspective and those of the groups they represent, the security that constitutional inclusion was to bring seems hollow. Meech Lake underlines the discrepancy between the constitutional gains they have made and their exclusion from processes that might erode these gains. This leads to a pervasive constitutional paranoia and a rhetoric of outsiders with noses pressed to the windows that separate them from the constitutional potlatch of governments to which they have not been invited.

Constitutional Competition for Status

This committee is hearing from many different groups which say: But we are not involved; we are left out and we feel the accord is something that has been created at our expense.[48]

The developing tendency to use the constitution as an instrument of community formation and of social management, which was a feature of the 1982 Constitution Act, was further elaborated in the Meech Lake Accord. Opposition to these aspects of Meech Lake sprang from two sources. The first, with former Prime Minister Trudeau as its champion, defended the national community against what was perceived as the crippling provincializing tendencies of Meech Lake; the second, with disparate membership, opposed the perceived relative decline in status of their group – women, aboriginals, and others – occasioned by Meech Lake.

Any constitutional change beyond the trivial modifies the relative status of the national and provincial communities that lie at the base of the federal system. The direction of change is perceived as pleasing or disturbing depending on its fit with citizens' preferences. While Meech Lake seems to have been perceived by Francophone Quebecers as a gratifying and appropriate, albeit modest, response to their demands of the past quarter of a century for a strengthened Quebec government, it was clearly viewed by many citizens and groups outside of Quebec, at least as judged by their public statements, as an undesired diminution of their sense of themselves as Canadians.

In normal constitutional times one might expect the national community to be vigorously defended in constitutional discussions by the federal government. The federal government's unwavering support for a Charter of Rights in the Trudeau years was premised on its anticipated contribution to nation-building. Remarkably, however, it is generally assumed that the central government did not strongly defend its own interests, nor those of the national community, in the Meech Lake round. Indeed, this is one of the major sources of disquiet at the elite process, the acceptability of which would have been enhanced if the excluded – in this case, believers in a strong national community and government – had been convinced that they were at the table in proxy.

In addition, therefore, to the grievances of particular groups that their constitutional ox had been gored, there was a larger malaise expressed by Don Johnston, by Deborah Coyne on behalf of the Canadian Coalition on the Constitution, by Al Johnson with his apprehension that the spending power and amending power provisions (with opting out with compensation) would deprive future central governments of valuable nation-building instruments, and by John Whyte, Roger Gibbins, and numerous others who saw the overall thrust of the Accord as provincializing.[49] In general, all of the groups who feared that the Accord, especially the distinct society provision, might weaken the Charter were prominent in defending the national community against an agreement that overwhelmingly reflected a provincialist, not just Quebec, view of Canada.

The most prominent advocate of this view was former Prime Minister Trudeau, whose defence of a strong federal government and a pan-Canadian community drawing much of its identity from the Charter found no echo among the eleven first ministers at Meech Lake or from the leadership of the three major parties in the House of Commons. For Trudeau, Meech Lake is a recipe for a "massive shift towards provincial patriotisms," with its weakening of instruments, such as the spending power, that develop "a sense of national belonging . . . a sense of belonging to one nation." [50]

The absence of support for the Trudeau version of Canada among first ministers and in the leadership of the three national parties was not based on an accurate reading of the sentiments of Canadians. Pan-Canadianism, support for the Charter, belief in a leading role for the central government, and a deep uneasiness at the provincializing thrust of the Accord were generously represented, indeed probably dominant, among the groups and individuals that appeared before the Joint Committee and in other forums outside of Quebec. It is scarcely disputable that in the Meech Lake round the processes of executive federalism and of debate in the House of Commons did not represent the spectrum of views in the electorate.

The Quebec dimension and the overall provincial dimension were well represented at Meech Lake. The national dimension was absent. There is no substantial evidence to gainsay Roger Gibbins's criticism that the Meech Lake Accord "appears to be a document drawn up by provincial governments for provincial governments, the result of a constitutional contest in which the federal government was a referee but not a player aggressively pursuing its own interests and vision." [51] Apparently, the return of Quebec to the constitutional family necessitated the provincializing of English Canada because the other provincial governments exacted a provincial price for their co-operation. If briefs are even minimally representative of how Canadians feel, significant numbers experience Meech Lake as an unwelcome shrinking of their capacities to act as Canadians and an undesired strengthening of the provincial dimension of their existence. [52]

In addition to strengthening the Quebec dimension specifically and the provincial dimension more generally as a by-product of the principle of equality of the provinces, Meech Lake readjusted the relative status of aboriginal, ethnic, and official-language communities of Canada. The possibility that the distinct society clause might weaken the Section 28 gender equality clause of the Charter added women's organizations to the long list of those who feared that the Accord would or might result in a relative weakening of their constitutional rights or status.

The distinct society clause was consistent with the concentration of Canada's French-speaking population in Quebec and its numerical dominance in the Quebec electorate. The definition of linguistic duality as a fundamental Canadian characteristic was consonant with the historical status of French and English as founding nations and charter peoples and, but much more tenuously, with the elevated status of bilingualism since the Official Languages Act of 1969. Nevertheless, the much more elaborate constitutional recognition of these historic and contemporary realities in the interpretive clause and the constitutional terminology employed were deeply upsetting to women, aboriginals, third-force ethnics, and official-language minorities. They understood that the constitutional recognition of any reality changed its nature and elevated it status relative to other realities not given similar treatment.

For official-language minorities the Accord appears to tilt the constitution's approach to language toward the interests and prejudices of provincial majorities and away from the needs of minorities for constitutional protection and support. For aboriginal Canadians the designation of others, but not themselves, as a distinct society is an insult and a distortion of history.[53] For those Canadians who can claim no founding status the stress on priority of arrival as the basis for constitutional ranking is unacceptable, based on "a rear-view mirror vision,"[54] and the "outdated and discredited concept of two founding nations."[55] Third-force Canadians and aboriginals are not placated by Section 16 of the Accord, which states that "Nothing in section 2 of the Constitution Act, 1867 affects section 25 or 27 of the Canadian Charter of Rights and Freedoms, section 35 of the Constitution Act, 1982 or class 24 of section 91 of the Constitution Act, 1867." Ethnic groups note that Section 27 only applies to the Charter, while the Accord requires "the Constitution of Canada" to be interpreted consistent with linguistic duality and Quebec as a distinct society.[56] The appropriate and necessary response to this unequal recognition, which appears to weaken multiculturalism relative to linguistic dualism, is to add multiculturalism as a fundamental characteristic.[57]

The anger of aboriginals is compounded by the fact that the ambiguities and imprecisions that had stood in the way of constitutional recognition of aboriginal self-government did not prevent acceptance of the equally elusive distinct society concept,[58] the ambiguities of which are touted as a virtue by Quebec Premier Robert Bourassa. They claim that their own constitutional recognition as one or more distinct societies is justified by both history and contemporary social and cultural facts. For aboriginals the Accord's vision of Canada is insufficiently historical; for ethnic groups, such as Ukrainians, it is insufficiently contemporary.

For women's groups the problems posed by the Accord are both specific and general. Specifically, they are concerned that the distinct society clause might weaken Sections 28 and 15 of the Charter. Their concern is stimulated by the fact that Section 16 of the Accord protects relevant constitutional clauses of concern to aboriginals and ethnics against the new Section 2 interpretive clause, but does not do the same for the Charter equality clauses of special concern to women. Women's groups, accordingly, seek the same protection for their constitutional interests in an amended Section 16 as has been granted to aboriginals and ethnic Canadians.[59]

In the previous round of constitutional bargaining in 1980-81 women's groups were successful in obtaining a strong Section 28 ("Notwithstanding anything in this Charter"), one clear purpose of which was to trump the Charter's Section 27 multiculturalism clause and ensure that the latter could not be used as justification for sex-based discrimination.[60] Their comparable efforts to trump the distinct society clause have so far (May, 1988) been unsuccessful, primarily because the distinct society clause, in contrast to the multiculturalism clause, has the backing of a government, indeed of the government whose reconciliation is the official justification for this round of constitutional bargaining.

For women's groups, however, the particular deficiencies of Meech Lake are less troubling than the larger symbolic message that women's equality rights are once again publicly identified as of secondary concern. "It is amazing," according to Dalhousie professor of constitutional law Wayne MacKay, "that Canada's constitution builders have, for a second time, ignored the position of women in Canada."[61] To women the deeply troubling message of Meech Lake is their powerlessness.[62] As Professor Beverly Baines pointed out, the response in the Joint Committee Report to the concerns of women was patronizing, unhearing, and sexist.[63]

The significance of these indigenous, ethnic, and women's objections to the sociological portrait of Canada offered by the Accord can be misunderstood if careful attention is not paid to the language in which grievances are expressed. It is not the traditional constitutional language of the division of powers but the language of national, ethnic, and sexual identity and of stigmatic exclusion versus honourable inclusion and recognition.

For aboriginals, women's groups, and members of the non-Charter communities Meech Lake is a rebuff. The logic of their perception is explained by George Erasmus, who observes that "You cannot deal with the rights of some Canadians without affecting the rights of others. If you upgrade the rights of the French and do not the same to the rights of everyone else, by definition, you have just lowered everyone else's."[64]

The Ukrainian Canadian Committee asserted that its past support for bilingualism and minority language rights had not been reciprocated by support from the government of Quebec and from Francophones outside of Quebec for recognition of the "multicultural reality of Canada in the Constitution." As a result the Committee "feels a great sense of betrayal"; Ukrainians "do not feel represented by the Constitution . . . we are being abandoned."[65] For Louis "Smokey" Bruyère of the Native Council of Canada, the Accord "totally misstates Canada as it is," and "provides a vision of the future in which aboriginal peoples cannot hope to share."[66] For Howard McCurdy, NDP MP from Windsor-Walkerville, the Accord tells one in three Canadians "that they are not really an inherent part of the country . . . second class citizens [who must] be welcomed into the Constitution."[67] Similar language was employed by Sergio Marchi, who spoke for those Canadians "who feel the isolation of being left out." "I do not feel, according to Section 1 [*sic*]," he continued, "that I am as constitutionally relevant as my French Canadian or English Canadian colleagues in this House of Commons."[68]

Citizens in the northern territories also experienced the Accord as a rebuff. With its requirement of unanimity for the creation of new provinces, and the possibility that existing provinces could extend their boundaries into the territories without the agreement of northern citizens or governments, the Accord aroused northern reactions similar to those of aboriginals – who, of course, are numerically influential in the territories – and of women and of ethnic minorities. According to Tony Penikett, government leader of the Yukon, northerners "were naturally flabbergasted or staggered" by the Meech Lake provisions.[69] Another northerner, "confused, hurt, and angered" by the process, was "outraged at the callous treatment. . . . Second-class citizens banished forever to colonial servitude, a voice unsought . . . this national shame."[70]

Although the intemperate language and passion, which run like threads through so many of the criticisms of Meech Lake, can also be found in earlier controversies, the present situation has certain unique attributes. First, the explosion of ethnic and feminist self-consciousness generates a much more pervasive and demanding assertiveness than was previously the case. Second, the ethnic and racial diversity of Canada has dramatically increased as a result of changed immigration policies that have reduced the numerical significance of the French and English charter groups. Third, the state role in the management of ethnic and linguistic tensions and in responding to gender-related issues has visibly grown in the last quarter of a century. Fourth, the written constitution has become a central policy instrument for the recognition, management, and transcendence of cleavages based on language, ethnicity, and gender. And fifth, the digesting of the major constitutional change of 1982 was not completed before a further bout of constitutional change upset the understandings that were emerging from the previous round. To some extent the constitution has become a source of instability and uncertainty rather than the reverse.

The constitution is now the central arena within which the groups of an increasingly plural society defined, *inter alia*, by gender, ethnicity, and language vie with each other for recognition and acceptance. That competition underlines the lack of consensus in Canada over the criteria to be employed, which in turn has the effect of making particular constitutional outcomes unstable. Canadians have stumbled into a constitutional game without having agreed on the rules to govern the competition or the norms that the results are to serve.

Aboriginal peoples and the French and English charter communities employ the language of historical priority, which ethnic supporters of multiculturalism reject. Feminist claims are based on their numbers, more than one-half of the population, and sometimes on the argument that there is a feminist culture, the nourishment of which would have positive social consequences. Past inequalities are selectively cited by all groups as justifying equal or even privileged future treatment. Those groups that made it into the constitution in 1982 view the constitutional status then achieved as a minimum, and as one that should not suffer a relative decline if others are to be advanced.

The contest by various groups to improve their ranking in the constitutional pecking order is not a discrete game. Indeed, it is played out in the shadow of the constitutional controversies of federalism, in which governments are the players and in which cleavages of particular relevance to governments receive priority. Thus Meech Lake responds to those diversities of language and territory that derive directly or indirectly from federalism, not to the more free-floating cleavages based on ethnicity and gender. Further, the attention paid to official-language minority communities was much greater in 1980-81 when the Quebec and federal governments were at loggerheads over the future of Canada than in the Meech Lake process, for which a rapprochement between the Quebec government and the other governments of the federal system was the guiding objective.

For the non-governmental interests involved the coexistence of two separate but overlapping constitutional games is deeply frustrating. The absence of agreed norms to govern the constitutional ranking of Canadians defined by such cross-cutting criteria as language, gender, race, ethnicity, and aboriginal status is compounded by the unpredictability of

131

which groups will be involved as allies of one or more governments, whose competition with each other is privileged by government domination of the amending formula. It is not even clear that the overarching Canadian community will be represented at the bargaining table.

Conclusion

I have heard too many statements, from too many quarters, high and low, suggesting that a constitutional agreement by a First Ministers' Conference is now, by convention, though not by law, the final word, as unchangeable as the law of the Medes and Persians.

Acceptance of such a convention would reduce Parliament and the provincial legislatures, in relation to constitutional amendments, to not much more than echoes. It would be subversive of parliamentary government. It would establish a new supreme, sovereign, omniscient, inerrant, infallible power, before which the function of Parliament and the Legislatures would be simply to say: "Roma locuta est. The First Ministers have spoken. Let all the earth keep silence before them."[71]

The bitterness and passion that inform the presentations of the numerous groups objecting to the Accord are not based on a narrow instrumental calculation of its effects on the future flow of material benefits. Their anger is not driven by the fear of tangible gains forgone but by a more complex battery of emotions. The representatives of women's groups, of aboriginals, of visible minorities, of supporters of multiculturalism, along with northerners and basic defenders of the Charter, employ the vocabulary of personal and group identity, of being included or excluded, of being treated with respect as a worthy participant or being cast into the audience as a spectator as one's fate is being decided by others. They employ the language of status – they are insulted, wounded, hurt, offended, bypassed, not invited, ignored, left out, and shunted aside. They evaluate their treatment through the lens of pride, dignity, honour, propriety, legitimacy, and recognition – or their reverse. Their discourse is a minority, outsider discourse. They clearly distrust established governing elites. They are in, but not of, the constitution. They are apprehensive parvenus.

Their most basic message is that governments do not own the constitution. The logic of their situation pulls them toward acceptance of the position that ultimate "sovereignty rests with the *people* of Canada, not with the governments or First Ministers."[72] Their anger is compounded by the symbolic importance of the amending formula, which indicates where power ultimately resides in a constitutional system, with its disturbing message that governments are in charge of the very constitution that gives citizens rights against governments. The advances they had made in 1980-82 were not repeated, and to some extent are repudiated by the Meech Lake process that relegates them to the sidelines, restricted to giving voice but not to being heard while their place in the constitution is being rearranged.

Their language and claims underline the recent changes in the relation of the constitution to Canadian society. The constitution that emerged from the battlefields of 1980-82, with the Charter's individual rights and various group recognitions, speaks past governments and directly to Canadians. From one perspective, the constitution is now an instrument of selective social recognition in an increasingly diversified society whose multiple groups have a high degree of self-consciousness. Its larger role is one of social management – of encompassing all Canadians within the official definition of Canadians as a people.

For many of the groups involved the language of federalism, of territorial particularisms, is largely irrelevant. They think of themselves in national terms, and accordingly they are somewhat distrustful of provincial governments. They know full well that the Charter, which for most of them is the major basis of their constitutional identity, was a national government instrument to which most provincial governments only gave reluctant agreement in exchange for constitutional concessions elsewhere. In a very explicit sense they are new Charter Canadians who take their place alongside the older meaning of Charter Canadians derived from our history, the French and English who, as "French-speaking" and "English-speaking Canadians," are singled out in Section 2 of the Accord as "a fundamental characteristic of Canada." Inevitably, the new Charter Canadians object to an Accord that appears to reassert the primacy of federalism over non-territorial characteristics and symbolically, and to an indeterminate sense legally, weakens the Charter relative to those federalism concerns encompassed in the distinct society and linguistic duality interpretation sections.

The constitution is now an arena in which these groups – defined by language, ethnicity, culture, race, and gender – vie with each other for status and recognition. The struggle is structured by the constitutional recognitions that already exist. Women, official-language minorities, aboriginals, and the ethnic supporters of multiculturalism already have niches in the constitution. They have constitutional identities and, especially in the case of aboriginals, they have unsatisfied constitutional ambitions.

All of the groups involved, especially their leaders, are keenly aware of their position in the constitutional pecking order, sensitive to the nuances of constitutional terminology, apprehensive that constitutional change might damage their relative constitutional status, and thus critically concerned with the processes of constitutional change that determine whose voices will be heard, and at what stages, as potential amendments move from conception to implementation. Constitution-watchers are no longer restricted to governments, constitutional lawyers, and a handful of social scientists. They have been joined by the elites from the various groups that have received specific constitutional recognition, along with a more diffuse category of Charter supporters and defenders. Tenured academics are involved. They specialize in the understanding of specific constitutional clauses and often identify with the interests of particular constitutional clienteles. They spin out refinements that work themselves into the understandings of more full-fledged participants.

As long as the constitutional issue is on the agenda – which the Meech Lake requirement of annual meetings on the constitution means will be forever – these groups are involved in the nerve-wracking sport of constitutional Kremlinology. Rather than scrutinizing the podium for the placement of individuals near to or far from the "leader" at the May Day parade, these constitutional spectators nervously watch threatened constitutional change to see if their clause is likely to receive more or less recognition as a result of a pending constitutional reshuffle.

The self-interest of the potentially affected groups generates demands for involvement in a process so consequential to their constitutional fate. In the making of the 1982 Constitution Act governments and citizens' groups, especially those with Charter concerns, were jointly involved. While governments made the final decisions, they did so in a context of high visibility and public pressure that had major effects on the outcome. By contrast, citizen groups have been effectively excluded from the Meech Lake process involving major amendments to a constitution no longer perceived as belonging to governments. The message of Meech Lake is that citizens are not to venture from the audience onto the playing field. They are cast in the old-fashioned role of spectators at the gladiatorial battles among governments that was their fate at the original Confederation debates in the 1860s and, with the crucial exceptions of the Quebec referendum and public participation in the 1980-82 constitutional process, has usually been their fate ever since.

In fact, even the status of spectator exaggerates the role of the public if Meech Lake is to be the prototype of the future. The essential characteristics of Meech Lake are the secrecy, the unwillingness of the leading actors to respond to criticisms, and the failure to produce position papers explaining the purpose of particular constitutional changes. (The recurring suggestion I have heard, that position papers are unnecessary as these issues have been discussed before by Lesage, the Canadian Bar Association, Pepin-Robarts, or whomever, is breathtakingly absurd. The mountain of past discussion papers, constitutional proposals, and the like is capable of justifying an incredibly diverse range of responses to Senate reform, to the spending power, and to other constitutional problem areas. Coherent constitutional dialogue requires the enacting governments to justify explicitly in reasoned language precisely what they are proposing now.)[73]

Without major changes in the process surrounding the formal requirements of the amending formula an annual Meech Lake exercise will be perceived as a constitutional affront by citizens who have been conditioned by the Charter to believe that they have legitimate niches in the constitution, that in some sense the constitution, at least in part, speaks to them and belongs to them. The insipid function offered to the public in the federal government's paper *Strengthening the Canadian Federation*, to "explore the implications of the *Constitution Amendment 1987* so it is well understood by everyone,"[74] and to help set the agenda for future constitutional conferences, will not satisfy the expectations the Charter has aroused.

Meech Lake reflects the historic assumption that the constitution, or at least the major part of it found in the Constitution Act, is about federalism, and that federalism in turn is primarily an affair of governments, the modification of which accordingly is properly a task for governing elites. Thus the Meech Lake process was dominated by governments who conducted their business in an almost clandestine manner, and then sprung on a surprised citizenry, especially in English Canada, the second most significant series of constitutional amendments since Confederation. The proposed changes were not presented as tentative proposals but as a firm agreement subject to change only if egregious errors – as defined by first ministers who had a concern for not seeing any – were to be discovered in the controlled and limited hearings process that could not be entirely avoided. Somewhat paradoxically, the Meech Lake process would have been more compatible with accepted constitutional assumptions leading up to 1980-82, when it was not employed, than in 1987, when it has been. With isolated exceptions at the margins, the Meech Lake process has looked more like a military manoeuvre by governments to keep the citizens at bay than one appropriate to the new constitutional culture that builds on the 1982 Constitution Act.

The hostility to the Meech Lake process is the expression of new constitutional realities that are the product of the 1982 Constitution Act. The political purposes of the Charter included the attachment of Canadians to the constitutional order by protecting their rights. In a surprisingly short time this has happened in English Canada; the Charter has taken root and generated a broad base of support. The various group recognitions and entitlements of the Charter have had their entirely anticipated consequence of inducing their possessors to believe that the written constitution is no longer an exclusive affair of governments. They could only believe otherwise if they assumed that the Charter was designedly fraudulent from the beginning, a Canadian version of the irrelevant paper charters that mock the reality of citizen-state relations in much of the world. Further, the possession of rights and recognitions logically generates a political culture increasingly sympathetic to constitutional participation by citizens, at least when their own status and rights are likely to be affected. This participant impulse is further stimulated by the general enhancement of the constitutional status of citizenship to which the Charter contributes, with its corollary of a diminished deference toward elites and governments.

It is not surprising that governments, especially provincial governments – most of which had little initial enthusiasm for the Charter – have been slow to understand the changed constitutional context in which they now have to operate. The master tradition in which they have been reared is one of executive supremacy, legislative weakness, and popular indifference and deference to their monopolistic possession of government power. That a freshly minted Charter still in its first decade should have generated a cluster of elites outside of government who see themselves as legitimate players in the constitutional game is a remarkable development in Canadian constitutional culture. The result of this changed relation of the constitution to Canadian society is that an amending procedure adequate to an era of government domination of the constitution becomes anachronistic and even insulting when Canadian society is honeycombed with interests whose elites have a vision of a citizens' constitution. Thus the amending procedure fashioned in 1980-81, particularly when employed in the manner of Meech Lake, contradicts the constitutional assumptions of citizen involvement that flow directly from the Charter, the other major component of the 1982 Constitution Act.

Further, as John Holtby noted in his impressive brief to the Special Joint Committee on the Accord, the parliamentarians' role in the amending process needs to be strengthened. No special procedures exist in either house of the federal Parliament or in most provincial assemblies for handling constitutional amendments. While "the amendment of the least significant statute requires three readings and committee study in both Houses . . . an amendment to the constitution is accompanied by the passage of a Resolution – the same process as is used for an extension of the luncheon recess." [75]

Unfortunately, not only is it self-evident that an annual repetition of the Meech Lake process can only damage the constitutional order, but it is equally clear that formal modification of the amendment procedure by an amendment will not be easy when unanimity gives each government a veto over the proposed change. Referenda, in particular, are exceedingly unlikely to attract the requisite degree of government support. No other aspect of the federal government constitutional package made public after the failure of the September, 1980, First Ministers' Conference attracted as much hostility and opposition from provincial governments as its referendum proposals. [76]

In the short run the best that may be hoped for is greater public involvement in committee hearings in all eleven jurisdictions both before and after governments meet, the release by governments of serious position papers revealing their constitutional purposes, and a greater degree of tentativeness in the constitutional agreements reached by governments until they digest the feedback from involved citizen groups, constitutional experts, and others.

None of these changes, which would modify the dynamics of the amending process and facilitate citizen input in advance of the release and hardening of government positions, requires resort to the amending procedure for implementation. They are simple acts of political will. While the viability of this halfway house between Meech Lake and referenda is unclear, it would unquestionably be a step in the right direction.

Significantly, the Report of the Special Joint Committee obliquely criticizes the Meech Lake process by suggesting that certain "special facts of the 'Quebec Round' " stood in the way of the "active and open consultative procedure across the country" that the Report recommends for the future. [77] However, the distinctly muted support for future "parliamentary and public consideration of the issues before governments reach agreement on amendment texts" [78] recently offered by Senator Lowell Murray, Minister of State for Federal-Provincial Relations, indicates a minimal understanding of what has happened to the constitutional culture of Canadians.

Thus, necessary changes are unlikely to come easily or to be granted graciously. Those who govern us may have to relearn the ancient democratic message that they are servants of the people, and learn the new message that the constitution under and by which we all now live does not belong to them. By agreeing, however reluctantly, to the 1982 Charter they also agreed, perhaps unknowingly, to a challenge to the Meech Lake process that they developed from the amending formula that was born with the Charter.

Chapter Five

Federalism and the Provinces

The specific nature of the Meech Lake process compounds the difficulties that always attend commentary on such a moving target as the Canadian constitution. The honourable and socially necessary role of constitutional critic requires the co-operation of governments for its effective performance. The minimum requirement for such co-operation is a reasoned exposition by the governments that dominate the process, of the ends they have in view and the relations of the chosen means to their attainment.

Elucidation of Ends Is Not Enough
The elucidation of ends requires more than homilies about reuniting the Canadian family, healing wounds left over by the Constitution Act of 1982, and producing a more harmonious federation. Desirable as these objectives are, their citation does not allow the outside commentator to engage in effective dialogue with those who, as our elected servants, have the major responsibility for keeping up-to-date a constitution that belongs to all Canadians.

In what way have the eleven governments violated their trust; or more precisely, ten of the eleven governments? The government of Quebec must be exempted from the bulk of my strictures. Both the Parti Québécois and the Quebec Liberal Party developed constitutional proposals, the meeting of which would produce the willing adhesion of the government of Quebec to the constitution. The election of the Quebec Liberal Party in December, 1985, was followed by the speech of Gil Rémillard, Minister for Canadian Intergovernmental Affairs, to a conference in Mont Gabriel in May, 1986, at which time he laid down the five requirements of the Quebec government. In ways that for the moment are irrelevant for our purposes, these proposals, modified by the process they have gone through and now clothed in legal language, have found their way into the constitution, or will do so if the Meech Lake amendments are passed by the legislatures of all eleven governments.

So, from a Quebec perspective the Meech Lake process has been open, the objectives of the government and the constitutional instruments to achieve them were laid out in advance, and the proposed Meech Lake amendments can be assessed as adequate or inadequate in the light of known means and ends. In such circumstances, the constitutional constituency of journalists, scholars, intellectuals, and engaged citizens in Quebec can have an intelligent debate on Meech Lake.

Such a possibility does not exist outside of Quebec. This exercise in constitutional change, the second most significant package of constitutional amendments in 120 years of our Canadian existence, is unaccompanied by serious position papers from Ottawa or from any of the other nine provincial governments. I speak with clinical accuracy when I state that the federal government has not gone beyond rhetoric and platitudes in explaining the consequences for all Canadians of the Meech Lake proposals.

It cannot be argued that since the proposed changes are ostensibly addressed to Quebec that no further explanation is required, that Canadian citizens from Bonavista to Vancouver Island can piggy-back an understanding relevant to the *Canadian condition* of proposals drafted by the Quebec government, which quite properly address Quebec concerns. It is not the responsibility of Premier Bourassa to speak for or to Canada. The major responsibility for that concern can only reside with the federal government. What Meech Lake will do to and for the government of all Canadians, its effect on the Charter, the kind of federal system envisaged by Meech Lake, the effect on such institutions as the Senate and the Supreme Court, and the effect of the immigration provisions on a policy area that virtually defines the central task of the modern democratic state – the ethnic and social composition of its future citizenry – surely these are constitutional concerns that require a careful analysis and response from the federal government. No such response is available.

Significant Change – An Example

To take one example only: under the guise of a transitional measure Canadians are embarking on probably the most significant explicit change in parliamentary government since Confederation, the change in the nomination and appointment procedures for Senators that will eventually produce a Senate whose membership is entirely derived from lists –

which may have only one name on them – prepared by provincial governments. To what kind of Senate are these changes directed? The Senate is not only a regional chamber, but also a house of review – of sober second thought – for legislation that often has no regional incidence. It is little short of incredible that the federal government has not publicly addressed the issue of the responsibilities of the reconstituted second chamber.

New Roles for the Provinces

The shortcomings of the Meech Lake process also apply to the behaviour of many, possibly all of the provincial governments outside of Quebec. Meech Lake unquestionably shifts the balance of power in the federal system toward the provinces. The government of British Columbia will have: (a) a new role in appointments to the Senate and the Supreme Court; (b) an enhanced role in the amending formula; (c) potentially enlarged responsibilities in immigration; (d) new tasks via annual conferences on the constitution and on the economy in running the federation as a partnership; (e) constitutionally protected capacities to opt out of future national spending programs with full compensation in specified circumstances; (f) greater responsibilities with respect to any future decision to transform the northern territories into provinces.

Further, the government of British Columbia, along with the other governments of the federal system, now governs a people who have been redefined by Meech Lake in terms of linguistic dualism.

The cumulative effect of these changes, which are not hypothetical or mere proposals but concrete changes well on the way to implementation, at least parallels in significance the constitutional package put forth by former (provincial) Premier Bill Bennett in 1978. That package was preceded by numerous public speeches by the Premier and was presented in nine constitutional booklets amounting to over 100 pages of reasoned analysis. There is nothing comparable from the government of his successor. To be specific, there is nothing at all.

How does the government of British Columbia view its new status in the federal system? Are the changes proposed consonant with those laid out by its predecessor? What has become of the drive of the previous government to achieve recognition as a fifth region? At the time of writing (January, 1988) we have no answers to these questions.

Thus, both as a resident of British Columbia and as a citizen of Canada, I have been deprived of the information necessary to make an informed judgement on Meech Lake. I have heard it suggested that explanations or position papers would be superfluous because, after all, our history of recent decades is littered with constitutional discussions and proposals of which this is simply a culmination. That is, if I wish to find the explanation for the Senate reform proposals, or the distinct society clause, I should rummage in my files for the proposals of other governments, task forces, and suchlike. But this is preposterous; the welter of proposals from the past does not speak with a clear voice and, in any event, many of the particulars of Meech Lake changes have idiosyncratic features not seen before. The citizen and constitutional commentator need to know why this particular government is in favour of these particular changes, and what their likely effects will be on a constitutional system that is the heritage of all Canadians, and of which our governments are only temporary custodians or trustees.

Constitutional Morality

It is easy to misunderstand my criticisms. It is not just an offended sense of *amour propre* that lies behind them, although I strongly feel that all citizens outside of Quebec should be offended by the manner of Meech Lake. Rather, my concern is with the larger issue of constitutional morality and with the damage done to the interdependent community of constitutional actors and constitutional commentators who together should play key roles in the evolution of the constitution. Thus, in the same way as judicial decisions are often described as the product of court and company – which includes the attorneys in court, the law professoriate, and so forth – I view the desirable manner of constitutional evolution as being the product of political decision-makers and the accompanying community of analysts and commentators. The capacity of the latter to contribute depends on the willingness of the former to provide relevant information about intentions, means, and goals. The functionally useful professional examination of judicial decisions could not survive a situation in which judges did not give reasons for their decisions.

Since the government has not been forthcoming, those who do not sit in the seats of power, but who nevertheless have a legitimate role in the development of a constitution, are incapable of effective performance. It is my considered opinion that this shortcoming of the Meech Lake process reduces the quality of the constitutional product that will emerge.

One reply to these criticisms would be that the bringing of Quebec back into the constitution was an act of such high statecraft, one so fraught with danger, and likely to produce such perilous consequences should it founder, that extraordinary stratagems were required to pull it off successfully. If that were publicly claimed to be the case several benefits would follow:

(1) We could have an open debate as to whether such an assessment of the situation was reasonable. Could the constitutional package have been crafted slightly differently and still have accommodated Quebec? Was there no alternative to extending the response to Quebec to the other provinces?

(2) The procedures, with their secrecy, absence of position papers, and stated intent to make changes to the constitutional package only if egregious errors were found – as defined and agreed to by all eleven first ministers – could be isolated as an abnormal response to an abnormal situation. They thus would be removed from the stream of precedents that will otherwise control future constitutional decision-makers.

This, however, is not the way that Meech Lake has been defined. Indeed, the impression conveyed is that Meech Lake is the appropriate way to generate constitutional change. For example, the aboriginals have been advised that, if they really wish to have their rights constitutionally defined, the Meech Lake process is the proper route to follow.

Accordingly, I view the Meech Lake process as a failure in constitutional morality. In a constitutional democracy, governments involved in major constitutional changes should provide either reasoned explanations for the particulars of the changes they propose or reasoned explanations that significant reasons of state require departures from otherwise appropriate behaviour. To do neither of these conflicts with a developing constitutional tradition, based on the Charter and a rights-bearing citizenry, which suggests at a minimum that the constitution does not belong to governments alone. The Charter, with its diverse recognitions of gender, ethnicity, aboriginal peoples, the disabled, and so on, has created constitutional niches for numerous social categories. The spokespersons for these groups are offended by constitutional changes that do – or may – affect their rights and status, but which they cannot influence. In the words of the government's paper *Strengthening the Canadian Federation* the task of public participation is to "explore the implications of the Constitutional amendment, 1987 so it is well understood by everyone," and to help set the agenda for future constitutional conferences. This is not a particularly robust role.

A Laudable Goal and Its Results

The entirely laudable goal of Meech Lake was to bring Quebec back into the Canadian constitutional family after the unwillingness of the Quebec government of Lévesque to accept the Constitution Act, 1982. The latter was considered an inadequate response to Quebec's demands and to the implied promises of the federal government in the Quebec referendum.

While former Prime Minister Trudeau is correct that the Constitution Act applied to Quebec, whether or not its government voluntarily assented to it, it is also true that the psychological sense of exclusion, of having been cheated, was a festering by-product of 1982, which, if unattended, could have become a significant political resource for a future independence-oriented government of Quebec. Further, the Parti Québécois government had signalled its constitutional alienation and defiance by systematically employing the "notwithstanding" clause (Section 33) of the Charter wherever possible, and by limiting its participation in the intergovernmental arena, including constitutional conferences.

To put it differently, the government of Quebec employed its disagreement with the Constitution Act as a resource to embarrass the other government partners in the federal system, to hamper the effective functioning of federalism, and to indicate clearly that the national unity/ integration purposes of the Constitution Act, especially the Charter, would be ill-served by the continuing official estrangement of the Quebec government.

The election of new governments in Quebec City and Ottawa produced a constitutional opening that both governments skilfully exploited. Quebec's official demands were almost universally viewed as modest when contrasted with the positions of previous Quebec governments. The other provincial governments were subsequently congratulated for altruistically shelving their own constitutional demands to some future round of constitutional discussions.

Hence, this was to be the Quebec round, the occasion for the return of Quebec to the constitutional family. However, the process of constitutional amendment required the agreement of the other provinces, either seven or ten (including Quebec), and the federal government, depending on the subject matter. Further, although not all the amendments individually required unanimity, the federal government decided to treat the whole package as subject to a unanimity requirement. Thus, each government had a veto.

The possession of ten provincial vetos meant that the self-sacrifice of the nine provincial governments outside of Quebec in shelving their constitutional demands did not go unrewarded. The payment for not exercising the veto was that the response to the constitutional package demanded by Quebec was, with the exception of the distinct society clause, generalized to all the provinces.

This outcome was rationalized in terms of the principle of the equality of the provinces. While this principle has an extensive history as part of the constitutional desire not to accord special status to Quebec, it was also an inescapable by-product of the equality of provincial power in the possession of a veto. Accordingly, it is surely misleading to characterize the Meech Lake-Langevin process and outcome as the Quebec round. It is more appropriately described as a provincial round, whose substance was primarily determined by Quebec. There are, of course, some exceptions. The place of "roles and responsibilities in relation to fisheries" as a permanent agenda item for future annual constitutional conferences was a side payoff to Premier Peckford of Newfoundland. The placating of Peckford has traumatized fisheries processors and fishermen's unions in the other Atlantic provinces, who are subjected to the unending constitutional uncertainty as to which government will have future jurisdiction over their affairs.

A One-Way Street

The fact that the Quebec round became the provincial round presupposes, of course, that unlike the 1982 Constitution Act, in which both orders of government enhanced their constitutional status in different ways, the 1987 Accord is much more of a one-way street. The one possible exception to this is the constitutionalized recognition of the federal spending power in areas of provincial jurisdiction. This has been seen by some as a gain for the federal government, in the sense that its former exercise of the spending power in provincial arenas was viewed as constitutionally ambiguous. However, the repeated justification the federal government employed for its spending power amendment was to "civilize the spending power," which unquestionably suggests imposing new constraints on its future use. Further, most of the social policy presentations to the Joint Committee, including that of Al Johnson, a former deputy minister in both Saskatchewan and Ottawa, assumed that the spending power would be a less available instrument in the future than it had been in the past. Its former use was, of course, central to the creation of the Canadian welfare state.

Another critique of the thesis that the Meech Lake Accord is characterized by provincial government gains and federal government losses is to deny the relevance of such zero-sum analysis, and to suggest instead that federalism is about interdependence, co-operation, and sharing, and that Meech Lake should be viewed as contributing to a more fruitful management of an intergovernmental entanglement that none can escape. The raw material for this thesis is found in the correct perception that Meech Lake increases the number of arenas in which governments are thrown together – annual conferences on the constitution and on the economy, the nomination and appointment processes for the

Supreme Court and the Senate, the accentuated juxtaposition of the two orders of government in the immigration field, the intergovernmental bargaining that the new spending power provisions will produce – and even in the enlargement of the scope of the unanimity requirements of the modified amending formula.

While these changes can all be seen through the lens of an increasing recognition of an inescapable interdependence, it is somewhat odd not to note that within this new interdependence the muscle of the provincial governments is much increased and that of the federal government is much reduced. To fail to make this distinction is to presuppose that all systems of intergovernmental interdependence and of constitutional requirements for co-operation are equal in the eyes of the gods who watch over federalism, which is surely an untenable position.

The detachment of the Conservative government from the standard political/bureaucratic desire to protect and expand turf is to be found in some combination of the following factors:

(1) A partisan desire to strengthen the election prospects of the party in Quebec is clearly central. Precisely the same partisan motivation has induced the federal New Democratic Party to support an Accord that is opposed by most of its natural constituents.

(2) The perceived urgency of bringing Quebec on board surely suggested that the precarious venture of getting the agreement of the other provincial governments would be jeopardized if they, and Quebec, were asked to cede power of whatever kind to the federal government. Thus the federal government role as a combined umpire/facilitator doubtless flowed in part from certain realities of power it could not ignore.

(3) New governments often desire to differentiate themselves from their predecessors in key policy areas, especially those possessed of high symbolism. Quebec/Ottawa relations specifically, and federal-provincial relations more generally, were obvious candidates given the centrality of constitutional matters to the Trudeau government and the confrontational style it brought to their resolution.

More generally, the adversarial relation between the opposition Conservatives and the governing Liberals in the Trudeau years had induced the former to define themselves antithetically to the centralist nationalism of Trudeau. Hence the Kingston communiqué, signed in 1977 between Conservative leader Joe Clark and four Conservative provincial premiers, which supported various provincial demands, Clark's subsequent definition of Canada as a community of communities, and the later Conservative defence of the "Gang of Eight" dissenting provinces in the stormy parliamentary battles of 1980-81, which led to the Constitution Act, 1982. The posture of the Conservative government was clearly a continuation of the constitutional philosophy the party had espoused in the decade before the 1984 Mulroney victory.

(4) In any event, there is little recent evidence of a well-developed Conservative position supportive of a strong central government, little evidence that the Mulroney government was keeping a well-developed preference for a strong Ottawa under wraps for the sake of a higher cause. Some time ago John Meisel argued that governing parties too long in office come to forget and ignore the federal nature of the society they govern. It may equally be true that new governing parties, which have enjoyed long spells on the opposition benches, may see the world through a provincial lens, and relatively forget and ignore the overall coast-to-coast Canadian community which, incidentally, the Charter has invigorated.

Charter Implications

No one who observed the parade of angry Canadians who appeared before the Joint Committee can doubt that the Charter is transforming the psyche of the Canadian people, that it has given women, aboriginals, ethnic communities, and others niches in the constitution they formerly did not have. That on the whole these groups, or at least their leaders, see themselves in Canadian, not provincial, terms is eloquently confirmed by their testimony. These new cleavages, which are constitutionally entrenched, clash with the federal-provincial cleavage that goes back to Confederation, which is the superior cleavage for the governing elites of the federal system and to which Meech Lake was a response.

To make sense of Meech Lake it is necessary to keep in mind the extent to which it was a response to Quebec filtered through a process in which governments were the dominant actors, and within which the other nine provincial governments could gain increased power and status on the coattails of Quebec. Meech Lake has enhanced the significance of the provincial dimension for all Canadians.

Chapter Six

Ottawa, the Provinces, and Meech Lake

The Many Difficulties of Criticizing Meech Lake

... when you have matters as significant as defining the nature and character of Canada being set behind closed doors and then simply run past the people after the fact, then I have some difficulty with that.[1]

Two statements from Lord Acton's inaugural lecture on "The Study of History" have not lost their cogency in the more than ninety years since they were delivered to a distinguished Cambridge audience in 1895: "The living do not give up their secrets with the candour of the dead,"[2] and:

There is a popular saying of Madame De Stael, that we forgive whatever we really understand. The paradox has been judiciously pruned by her descendant, the Duke de Broglie, in the words: 'Beware of too much explaining, lest we end by too much excusing.'[3]

The first statement reminds us that the student of unfolding events is not aided by being a contemporary of the politicians whose work he evaluates. The reverse is true, for the living continue to seek glory, ever striving to protect and enhance their reputation, and if politically active still struggling to change the goals of the state. They often prefer, accordingly, serviceable fictions to a potentially damaging candour. Hence their disclosures of motive and purpose are typically coloured by their ongoing pursuits.

In democracies, as elsewhere, politicians give themselves the benefit of the doubt when their policies appear questionable or even sullied to outside observers. The criticisms of the latter are, indeed, often discounted on the ground that those who make them are naively unaware of the pressures that buffet men of action. The world of decision-making, it is implied or asserted, is another country, an alleged fact that disqualifies those who have never travelled in it from judging the behaviour of its inhabitants.

A stratagem highly appropriate to this defence is to make policy in secret, deprive the public of information on what went into its making, and then rebuff critics for not understanding the necessities that attend statecraft. Of course, the practices of confidentiality and of cabinet solidarity are conventional attributes of responsible government. However, the dangers of elite conspiracy, to which that system if unchecked might lead, are normally countered by the system of adversarial politics, which accords high status to the official opposition. The parliamentary battle challenges the seductions of power with the searchlight of criticism. The public is thus provided with flows of information and many-sided commentary, which are essential tools of a thinking citizenry. For the Meech Lake Accord, the atypical fact that both the Liberals and the NDP officially supported the agreement in the House of Commons has greatly restricted the information and alternative analyses available to the public.

The situation was succinctly summarized by Pat Nowlan, a Conservative dissenter on Meech Lake:

> . . . there really has not been a debate in the House of Commons. When all three Leaders and Parties are together on principle and have a hearing during the summer there is not time for it to percolate out from coast to coast. It is very politically astute to get the measure through, but that is not the way to have a meaningful debate and a better Constitution.[4]

The compliance of the opposition parties mutes their normal inquisitive aggressiveness, to the disadvantage of public knowledge. Further, the agreement of all three national parties to the Accord adds to the psychological sense of isolation and impotence that often accompanies the role of critic.

When policies emerge from the intergovernmental arena, as in Meech Lake, a supplementary checking arrangement often, but not always, operates. The different vantage points and hence interests of the eleven major governments of the federal system, allied with the recurring temptation for particular leaders to "go public" to enhance their bargaining power, or to reassure their constituents, often increase public awareness of the nature of controversies among elites. Such elite division also stimulates public involvement as well as public understanding. That was emphatically the case for the major intergovernmental constitutional discussions from the late sixties to the 1982 Constitution Act. In the words of one participant in those earlier struggles, the 1982 Constitution Act amendments

> . . . were the product of years of public debate, countless federal-provincial conferences, hundreds of hours of debate in Parliament and legislatures, thousands of newspaper articles, many election campaigns and the Quebec referendum. The debates centered on fundamental concepts, and equally important, on wording of proposed texts.[5]

This has not been the case with Meech Lake, for the politics of reaching agreement were held to require lengthy backroom negotiations and soundings prior to the "official" negotiating sessions in order to minimize the possibility of failure. Further, the actual Meech Lake/Langevin discussions took place in the absence of advisers in the bargaining room, with only two note-takers present from the federal and provincial sides.

The secrecy and deliberately low profile of a process that was carefully designed to ward off unwelcome probes or queries from non-participants were graphically underlined by the statements of both Senator Lowell Murray and Prime Minister Mulroney two weeks before the Meech Lake meetings: that the purpose of the pending session was simply to see if a basis existed for serious discussion. Mulroney stated in the House of Commons that the meeting would not be "a constitutional conference, it will be a normal meeting." Murray, Minister of State for Federal-Provincial Relations, "stressed," according to a *Globe and Mail* report, "that the gathering will not be a formal negotiating meeting."[6] The day after what had been publicly defined as an exploratory meeting Canadians were informed that an agreement in principle had been reached, which was to be quickly transformed "into a constitutional text" to be transmitted to a constitutional conference "within weeks to approve a formal text."[7] A few weeks later at Langevin House the Accord was given legal clothing and the eleven first ministers "commit[ted] themselves and the governments they represent" to seek approval of their separate legislatures for a resolution to amend the constitution accordingly.[8] Thus, five weeks after a declared exploratory conference Canadians were confronted with a definitive constitutional text, described as inviolable, and to be opened up only if egregious errors, as defined and agreed to by eleven first ministers, were discovered. Thus the intergovernmental process, moving from secrecy to unanimity and protected by confidentiality, did little to enlighten the public beyond making available the actual words of successive intergovernmental agreements struck and refined in slightly over a month. Within another three weeks the Quebec National Assembly approved the Accord and Premier Bourassa asserted that Quebec would not consider proposals for change arising from hearings in other provinces.[9] The process was beginning to look more like a military manoeuvre by governments to keep the citizens at bay than an acceptable process of constitution-making in one of the world's oldest liberal democracies.

The remarkable mustering of elite support for the second most comprehensive package of constitutional change since 1867 by all three parties in the House of Commons and by the first ministers of eleven governments has drastically reduced the base of information and competing analyses available to the non-participants. The threatened breach of intergovernmental solidarity by the new Liberal government of Frank McKenna, which replaced the Hatfield Conservatives in New Brunswick, and the wavering of Premier Pawley of Manitoba have not yet effectively broken down the united front of governing elites and the undersupply of information to which it leads.

In spite of these constraints, the politics of a free society has partially lifted the veil. The servants of this task essential to our democratic health include a handful of politicians who have broken party ranks, and paid a price, a former Prime Minister who has defended the constitutional vision that informed much of the 1982 Constitution Act, various members of the Liberal-dominated Senate who have balked at being rubber stamps, a few academics who have performed their duty of disrobing emperors, various citizen activists who dislike the provincialist vision of Canada embodied in Meech Lake, and a number of interest groups whose shotgun criticisms reflect their fear that their ox has been gored. Nevertheless, a contemporary Lord Acton could only agree that those who wield power over us have not been forthcoming in explaining exactly what they have done to the constitution. The overwhelming justification offered for the Accord has been political, the necessity of getting the willing agreement of the government of Quebec to the constitution.

The consequences for the constitution of accommodating Quebec and placating the other nine provinces in the process have been treated as secondary phenomena. The phrase "equality of the provinces" has done yeoman service in justifying why Newfoundland, Manitoba, British Columbia, and the other provinces should have received so much constitutional largesse from what the federal government misleadingly called the Quebec round.

The "Quebec round" label underscores the tendency for the defenders of Meech Lake to dwell on its overriding political purpose, healing the wounds left by the 1982 Constitution Act, which the Quebec government opposed. Since the Meech Lake critics frequently focus on the negative consequences of particular clauses, rather than on the noble objectives they are alleged to support, the resultant debate has been unproductive. In general, critics resent being labelled anti-Quebec when they question the ambiguities, vagueness, and other weaknesses they feel mar the Accord.[10] On the other hand, the federal government resists defending and explaining the Accord on its merits, preferring the high ground and unassailable criterion of reuniting the Canadian family.

A related aspect of the process gravely hampers the successful performance of the honourable role of constitutional commentator. With the exception of the known position of the Liberal government of Quebec there is an absence of position papers explaining the rationale for particular changes as appropriate means for explicit constitutional ends. From the federal government, which must assume the primary responsibility for the overall health of the constitutional order, there has been a virtual total silence on the implications of particular changes involving, for example, the Senate, the Supreme Court, the spending power, and immigration. We have only a handful of descriptive documents, public relations releases, and reassuring speeches, which put down the critics as anti-Quebec or as negativist nay-sayers. The Meech Lake Accord process represents an oracular, ex-cathedra style of governing more appropriate to theocratic rulers dictating to the faithful than to elected political leaders explaining themselves to the citizens to whom they are accountable.[11]

For students of Meech Lake, Lord Acton's approving citation of the admonition of the Duke de Broglie, "Beware of too much explaining, lest we end by too much excusing," is also highly apposite. The defenders of Meech Lake, by defying its critics to come up with a "better" package that could obtain the requisite agreement of the other provinces and bring Quebec back into the constitutional family on honourable terms, suggest not only that this was a minimum package of concessions but that it was an inevitable package, the best that could be achieved in the circumstances. The argument that the agreement is a seamless web, so interdependent and so fragile that an amendment will shatter it, also suggests that Meech Lake is what it is because it could be no other.

The fact that our leaders provide negligible information on what went on at Meech Lake and Langevin House means that their claim can only be accepted on faith. We simply do not know what alternative package, reflecting different leadership and a different group chemistry, might have gained the requisite agreement. We know that the federal government bargaining strategy was to keep adding concessions until agreement was reached. Whether there was a stopping point beyond which Ottawa would not go is unknown. According to one journalist, the Prime Minister gave Lowell Murray "carte blanche to negotiate away whatever federal powers were necessary to get Quebec into the constitution."[12] If this assessment, which differs little from that of Jeffrey Simpson,[13] is even approximately true it is unreasonable to imply that if critics cannot come up with modifications that will get unanimous agreement that Meech Lake is better than any alternative. Any agreement that occupies the field and has the backing of eleven governments has a practical advantage over a contender lacking any official support. However, such a statement implies neither the superiority nor the inevitability of the Meech Lake Accord, only that it has all the advantages that go with incumbency. Had the federal government conceded twice as much to the provinces the resultant agreement would have been even more difficult to dislodge, although even less attractive to many of its critics. Accordingly, the outside analyst is wise not to accept the self-interested explanations of political leaders at face value.

The barriers suggested by the preceding paragraphs, which stand in the way of seeing clearly what happened and why, are supplemented by an additional impediment, the politicization of the academic community of commentators, many of whom have worked for governments, and most of whom have taken sides in the constitutional battles of recent decades. I exempt myself from neither of these categories. So the reader is to be warned that clinical detachment may be engaged in a losing struggle with partisan commitment and official connections in the minds of those who, in person or on paper, address audiences while wearing the protective garb of scholarship. Lord Acton's ideal, detached historian, whose "most sacred and disinterested convictions ought to take shape in the tranquil regions of the air, above the tumult and the tempest of active life,"[14] does not find a congenial environment at conferences that discuss divisive contemporary issues.

What Really Happened, or How the Quebec Round Became the Provincial Round

The first half-truth to be held up to the light is the reiterated assertion that this was the Quebec round, intended in the words of the Meech Lake communiqué "to allow Quebec to resume its place as a full participant in Canada's constitutional development."

The fact that the government of Quebec did not give its approval to the 1982 Constitution Act, and denied its legitimacy, raised political rather than legal problems, for the constitution clearly applied to Quebec. Nevertheless, it was obviously eminently desirable to have the Quebec government signal its formal allegiance to the Canadian constitutional order. After all, the catalyst for nearly two decades of constitutional introspection culminating in the 1982 Constitution Act had been the nationalist demands of the government and people of Quebec. While the willing allegiance of the citizens and Quebec government might have incrementally developed with the passage of time, and the grievances of 1980-82 might have become faded memories as new political generations emerged, it was probably a safer course of action for the other governments of Canadian federalism to work toward a constitutional rapprochement with the government of Quebec. To achieve such a reconciliation would presumably strengthen Canada by eliminating a grievance that would otherwise remain available for exploitation in the next wave of Québécois nationalist fervour.

In the great political compromise that produced the 1982 Constitution Act both the federal government and the governments of the other nine provinces had achieved some of their objectives. The Charter and other provisions of the Constitution Act also responded to women, aboriginals, visible minorities, and multicultural Canadians. The major actor whose claims were still unaddressed was the government of Quebec. Thus, both concern for the health of the Canadian constitutional order and an elementary sense of justice suggested that, when circumstances allowed, a judicious statesmanship should seek the reconciliation of the Quebec government. Hence, that there should be a Quebec round of constitutional discussions when the time was ripe seemed to be no more than common sense.

Quebec's ambivalent status was not a trivial matter for the other governments of Canadian federalism. The other provincial governments knew that without Quebec's participation in the constitutional process their own demands for constitutional change could only be met with difficulty. Immediately prior to the federal announcement of the Meech Lake meetings Premier Bourassa had announced that Quebec was boycotting the pending First Ministers' Conference on aboriginal rights as a sign of its dissatisfaction with the slow response to its own constitutional proposals. In effect the government of Quebec employed its disagreement with the 1982 Constitution Act as a resource to embarrass its government partners in the federal system and to hamper the system's effective functioning. It was evident that the national unity/integration purposes

154

of the Constitution Act, especially of the Charter, would be ill-served by the continuing official estrangement of the Quebec government.

The other nine provincial governments, however, were not passive spectators as the federal government orchestrated a response to the Quebec government's constitutional demands. The threat of their power to block gave them significant constitutional leverage, which they employed for their own interests.

In the Meech Lake Accord, the governments of the other nine provinces gained new powers and responsibilities for the nomination of Supreme Court judges and senators, a potentially enhanced role in immigration, an increased blocking power with respect to constitutional amendments, protection against the "abuse" of the federal spending power – including guaranteed compensation for non-participation in certain circumstances – and an enlarged role in the federal-provincial partnership through the constitutional requirements for two annual federal-provincial conferences, one on the constitution and one on the economy. Alberta was given the side payoff of having "Senate reform" identified as a mandatory agenda item for future annual constitutional conferences. Newfoundland received the supplementary constitutional gift of having "roles and responsibilities in relation to fisheries" placed on the agenda of the annual constitutional conferences in perpetuity, or until resolved.

Along with this overflowing cornucopia of constitutional blessings the premiers of the provinces outside Quebec have been lauded by the Prime Minister for their self-restraint, altruism, and discipline in suspending their own constitutional demands while those of Quebec received prior attention. This is a somewhat restrictive definition of self-restraint. Much of the Accord is a response to the ambitions of provincial elites outside of Quebec who enhanced the status of their governments on the coattails of Quebec. By inference, they were prepared to leave Quebec out of the Canadian constitutional family until they received significant payoffs. Their self-restraint was relative.

The Quebec government received essentially the same constitutional treatment as the governments of the nine other provinces, with the significant exception of a new interpretation clause tailored to its requirements, which stated, *inter alia*, that the constitution of Canada was to be interpreted in a manner consistent with "the recognition that Quebec constitutes within Canada a distinct society," (Section 2(b)), and "The role of the legislature and Government of Quebec to preserve and promote the distinct identity of Quebec . . . is affirmed" (Section 3).

Further, Quebec was to be the first province to have increased powers in immigration given constitutional protection. The negotiation of similar agreements was held out to the other provinces. With respect to the provincial governments' nominating role for Supreme Court judges, the Quebec government received the right to nominate three Supreme Court judges, while the rights to nominate the remaining six were not allocated to specific governments in the other nine provinces. The right of appointment, of course, remains with the federal government.

Overall the Meech Lake constitutional outcome is best characterized as a provincializing round. The role of the Quebec government was to set the terms for the enhancement of the powers of all the provinces. This outcome was rationalized in terms of the principle of the equality of the provinces. This principle, however, was elaborated and strengthened in the very process of bargaining that produced Meech Lake.

The requirements of the 1982 amending formula, as modified by the policy of the Mulroney government to treat the whole package of constitutional change as requiring unanimous provincial government agreement, gave an equality of veto power to each provincial government. Constitutional bargaining translated this into equal treatment of the other nine provinces as beneficiaries of whatever the federal government was willing to concede to Quebec. Thus the means employed to respond to Quebec transformed the Quebec round into a provincial round. The provincial governments of English Canada, which had profited from the 1982 Constitution Act compromise that left the government of Quebec on the sidelines, profited again from the reconciliation of Quebec.

The staggered two-stage process of constitutional change in 1980-82 and 1987, in conjunction with the amending formulas applicable to the separate stages, strengthened the provincializing tendencies in the composite package of 1982 and 1987. The 1981 Supreme Court decision, which allowed Quebec to be left out of the patriation package while requiring, by convention, a substantial measure of provincial consent, led to a 1982 Constitution Act that was a true compromise. Both the dissenting provinces and the federal government gained some of their objectives but had to concede in other areas. The Meech Lake response to the flaw of 1982, given a new amending formula that required unanimity to satisfy some of Quebec's demands, imparted an overall provincializing thrust to this second round that was not initially anticipated.

This provincializing outcome was facilitated by the Mulroney bargaining style, which appears to put a higher premium on getting agreement than on the substance of the agreement reached. Certainly in this constitutional round the federal government promoted no national vision, nor did it seek to strengthen a pan-Canadianism derived from the Charter. This absence may be partly attributed to a bargaining process that suggested that a federal government assertiveness requiring provincial government concessions would simply have made agreement impossible. Given the very strong desire of the federal government for an agreement, the provincial governments held most of the bargaining chips. On the other hand, there is little evidence of the existence of a Mulroney vision of a national community that was suppressed as a statesmanlike gesture in support of the higher objective of bringing Quebec into the constitutional family.

In sum, the general tenor of the Meech Lake Accord is unquestionably provincializing, although not always decentralizing. A number of commentators, seeking to find some confirmation that the flow of power was not entirely from Ottawa to the provinces, cite the recognition of the spending power in areas of "exclusive provincial jurisdiction" as a net gain for the federal government. This interpretation, however, rests on the premise either that there was a serious risk that the constitutionality of the federal spending power in provincial areas of jurisdiction might be successfully challenged in court, or that a more restrictive amendment than the Meech Lake proposal would otherwise emerge in the future. While neither of these can be discounted it is relevant that both Lowell Murray and Prime Minister Mulroney repeatedly described their objective and achievement as the civilizing of the federal spending power.[15] Whether or not this is desirable, it clearly suggests constraining and limiting its future use.

The provision for annual conferences on the constitution and on the economy enhances the provincial government role in executive federalism. The provincial government roles in the nomination of senators and Supreme Court judges are examples of intra-state reforms designed, in the language of the seventies, to federalize the centre.[16]

The extension of the unanimity principle for amendments to new areas, beyond those covered by the amendment provisions of the 1982 Constitution Act, reflects similar constitutional tendencies – provincial government input receives greater recognition and federal government discretion is correspondingly reduced from what it was prior to the Accord. With respect to the creation of new provinces the federal government has experienced successive encroachments on the discretionary power it formerly enjoyed. Prior to 1982 the creation of new provinces was a matter for the federal government alone. The 1982 Constitution Act subjected the creation of new provinces to the 7/50 amending formula, the agreement of at least two-thirds (seven out of ten) of the provinces with 50 per cent of the population, and that of the federal government. Meech Lake requires the unanimous consent of all eleven governments, and thus gives the smallest province a constitutional weight equivalent to that of Ottawa. It is symptomatic of the Meech Lake process that it has been left to the governments and citizens of Yukon and the Northwest Territories to resist this encroachment on federal government constitutional powers. The federal government itself has been mute; unwilling to direct attention to its own losses, it prefers to speak of gains for the federal system.

Other defenders of the Accord also resist the language of winners and losers and prefer to describe the Accord in terms of a more effective intergovernmental partnership. Interdependence, so the argument goes, requires a higher degree of intergovernmental co-operation and co-ordination if the single citizenry served by both governments is not to be damaged by counterproductive clashes between competing governments. While there is some validity to this perspective, it should be noted that the new stress on interdependence is purchased almost entirely at the cost of reducing the autonomy and the discretion of the federal government, and of strengthening the role of provincial governments in virtually every area touched by the Accord.

The Meech Lake vision is one of intensified executive federalism and intergovernmental contact within which the relative power of provincial governments is enhanced. This is true of the new procedures for Senate and Supreme Court appointments, for immigration, and for the annual conferences on the economy and the constitution. In sum, the Meech Lake vision of federalism postulates more provincialized central government institutions, an enhanced provincial government role in an enlarged intergovernmental arena, and a federal government that has voluntarily fettered much of the discretion it formerly enjoyed and wielded. This enhanced provincial role is not the product of a triumphant political theory that irresistibly champions this direction of change, nor of a sensitive judgement of the most appropriate structure of federalism to respond to the policy demands of the future. These possible rationales are conspicuously absent from the Meech Lake discussions. Meech Lake is a product of the internal dynamics of the intergovernmental arena responding to a problem within the constitutional system itself.

The Emerging Constitutional Culture and the Challenge to Government Domination of the Amending Process

The Meech Lake/Langevin Accord was an affair of governments. In Quebec the well-publicized constitutional policy of the Quebec Liberal Party became government policy after the provincial Liberals replaced the Parti Québécois as the government of Quebec. The proposals were subsequently refined at a carefully staged and well-reported conference in Mont Gabriel, Quebec. Elsewhere there was negligible public involvement leading up to Meech Lake. A brief flurry of lobbying between the Meech Lake and Langevin meetings resulted in some limited changes from the initial version to protect the interests of aboriginal Canadians and supporters of multiculturalism. The post-Meech Lake role of the public in Joint Committee hearings was defined by the federal government as "explor[ing] the implications of the Constitution Amendment, 1987 so it is well understood by everyone" and thus helping to set the agenda for future constitutional conferences.[17]

Government domination of the Meech Lake process meant that the outcome would reflect the interests of government. This domination, perhaps natural in earlier periods of Canadian history, turned out to be much less so in the Canada of the Charter. At this Calgary conference, as in some of the journalistic commentary that attended the interventions of former Prime Minister Trudeau, there has been a tendency to define Trudeau as a figure from yesterday, and his views and concerns as almost medieval, so drastically has the *Zeitgeist* allegedly been transformed. These assessments, however, rest on a profound misunderstanding of the significance and consequences of the 1982 Constitution Act, and particularly of the Charter, which is Trudeau's major legacy. The process leading up to the 1982 Constitution Act and much of its content – the symbolism as well as the substance of Section 28 dealing with gender equality, Section 27 with its provision that the "preservation and enhancement of the multicultural heritage of Canadians" is a criterion for Charter interpretation, Section 25 recognizing the rights of aboriginals, along with other clauses dealing with aboriginals, and Section 15 (1) and (2) with its identification of particular groups in the equality and affirmative action provisions – have transformed the Canadian constitutional culture in a manner that explains much of the hostility that Meech Lake has aroused.

These groups identify with particular clauses of the 1982 Constitution Act, primarily those found in the Charter. They no longer therefore see the constitution and its amendment as an affair of governments. Typically, although aboriginals resist easy categorization, these groups are sympathetic to the federal government; they, or at least their elites, think of themselves as Charter Canadians. They have acquired a constitutional recognition that gives them status and supports aspirations for an improvement in their socio-economic condition. Accordingly, they are disturbed when they see or fear that the recognitions they have so recently won are threatened by constitutional changes worked out in secret and reflecting government concerns.

In brief, they view government domination of the constitutional amending process as illegitimate. Their anger confirms that the Trudeau government's nation-building purposes for the Charter are already being realized, at least at the level of non-governmental elites. In that sense Trudeau is not a museum piece, for he speaks through the numerous groups that have attached themselves to the Charter, which he was so influential in fashioning.

Thus, although Meech Lake may be seen correctly as a Quebec round that became a provincial round, it should also be seen as highlighting a constitutional incoherence that will have to be worked out in the coming decades. The Charter and the groups it has brought into the constitution have weakened the status of federalism as a constitutional organizing principle. This has reduced the legitimacy of government domination of the amendment process, especially when it is employed by governments to serve their own interests as governments.

In this constitutional culture that is beginning to take shape as a result of the 1982 Constitution Act, especially of the Charter, government control of the amending process, once considered natural, now appears as an arrogant elitism. The rights and recognitions entrenched in the Charter have generated beliefs that their possessors are entitled to participate in constitutional change. The Charter fosters a participatory ethic, the frustration of which, as in Meech Lake, reveals a basic contradiction in the Canadian constitutional culture. At the present time the historic government domination of the formal procedures of constitutional change confronts a new set of actors who have acquired a presence in the constitution – women, aboriginals, linguistic minorities, multicultural groups, the disabled, and a more diffuse category of rights bearers who support the Charter as a progressive advance.

The reforms of 1982 have changed the relation of the Canadian constitution to Canadian society. The post-1982 written constitution is a much more comprehensive instrument than was the BNA Act. It incorporates and responds to various cleavages to which the BNA Act was indifferent. This enhanced constitutional sensitivity to Canadian social diversity diminishes the pride of place that governments based on territorial diversity formerly enjoyed in the constitutional order. The written constitution is now a major instrument for the regulation of the relative social status of different categories of Canadians. Failure to recognize that fact is the fundamental shortcoming of Meech Lake. That is why Meech Lake, both in its process and in its vision, is an anachronism, out of touch with what Canada has become.

Chapter Seven

Political Science, Ethnicity, and the Canadian Constitution

If the need to feel worthy is a fundamental human requirement, it is satisfied in considerable measure by belonging to groups that are in turn regarded as worthy. Like individual self-esteem, collective self-esteem is achieved largely by social recognition. Everywhere . . . collective social recognition is conferred by political affirmation. For this reason, struggles over relative group worth are readily transferred to the political system. . . . Political affirmation confers something else that ethnic groups seek . . . ethnic identification with the polity.[1]

Constitutional Change and Constitutional Commentary: The Declining Relevance of Political Science?

For the foreseeable future Canadians will be working out the changed internal structure of the constitution and its modified relation to Canadian society occasioned by the 1982 Charter. At a minimum these tasks include the following:

1. Refining the complex relationship of the Charter to both federalism and parliamentary government, each of which has lost relative status in the constitutional order.

2. Rethinking the role of the courts, especially the Supreme Court, given its new responsibilities for Charter adjudication that supplement its former role as umpire of federalism. This requires attending to the procedures and criteria for appointments to the bench, and the elaboration of an indigenous jurisprudence appropriate to the enhanced judicial role in making significant value choices for the Canadian people.

161

3. Developing a constitutional theory of citizenship applicable to the more explicit and prominent status citizenship now enjoys. Historically, citizenship has been a thin, almost non-existent category in Canadian constitutional analysis. This neglect is now glaringly unacceptable.
4. Modifying the language of political discourse by incorporating the language of rights that the Charter legitimizes.
5. Alleviating the tension that now exists between governments and various citizen groups over their respective roles in future processes of constitutional amendment. Governments' monopolization of the amending formula, in the manner of Meech Lake, is incompatible with the new culture of constitutional participation toward which the Charter leads.

In sum, the task is to respond to the emerging centrality, enhanced visibility, and increasing comprehensiveness of the constitution, as the supreme law of the land, in Canadian life.

These challenges are all well known, although the nature of the answers they will receive is unclear. The latter will depend on the skills with which tomorrow's constitutional players perform and on the nature of the ends they pursue within the leeway that the constitution provides.

The "living" constitution of the future, however, will emerge not only from the efforts of explicit constitutional actors but also from ongoing constitutional commentary that responds to and influences constitutional evolution. That commentary, marked as it will be by intellectual creativity, is itself unpredictable, as also is its symbiotic relationship with the actions of those who more directly work the constitution. Thus, how the relevant academic communities respond to their task of interpreting the changed constitutional order that the Charter has bequeathed to Canadians will influence future constitutional evolution. Clearly, the understanding and analysis required of the academic community cannot be confined to yesterday's world of parliamentary government and federalism. The rearrangement of our constitutional structure tinges previous research focuses and even the disciplinary division of labour with obsolescence. Much of our former scholarship reflects constitutional assumptions no longer valid. The impediments to relevant constitutional analysis, therefore, reside in inherited intellectual patterns sustained by the organizational structure and status system of academic life.

There are, however, some grounds for optimism that an intellectual reorientation is occurring. The new Canadian Law and Society Association, and the *Canadian Journal of Law and Society* it publishes, help to pull understandings out of traditional disciplinary grooves. New centres for constitutional studies and the study of law and policy at Calgary and York, respectively, testify both to interdisciplinarity and to an expanded conception of law and the constitution. In general, a developing interaction between law and the social sciences is evident on university campuses around the country, and in the footnoting practices of scholars. Indeed, the response of the academic community to the Charter and to the new constitutional arrangements of which it is a central component has been considerable, including changes in curricula, in research focus, and in the shedding of disciplinary parochialism.

Nevertheless, I believe that the academic/intellectual community is having some difficulty in responding to the new constitutional arrangements, and that the difficulty is especially pronounced in political science.[2] Political science students of the constitution have built up sophisticated expertise and extensive intellectual capital around the twin concerns of parliamentary government and federalism, the primary institutional components of the Canadian constitutional order since 1867. Both have attracted sympathetic scholarly attention from political scientists.[3]

The response of political scientists to the Charter and the courts, however, is much less developed, partly because of the recency of the 1982 Constitution Act. Also, historically, constitutional law has not enjoyed the prominence for political scientists in Canada that it has had for their American counterparts. Retooling, therefore, requires overcoming what Veblen called the trained incapacity of experts to respond to new challenges for which their expertise has diminished relevance. This is not just a matter of technical knowledge but also of basic values. The mainstream political scientists' version of the biographer's disease of identifying with their subjects is to become committed to the defence of the institutions they have long and lovingly studied. Accordingly, a successful response to the prominent role of the Charter in the post-1982 constitutional order will require a move away from past attitudes.

Impressionistically, at least, political scientists displayed limited interest in, or empathy for, the unremitting federal government support for a Charter from the late sixties to the Constitution Act of 1982. In general, political scientists saw the constitutional issues of the sixties and seventies in terms of a resurgent government-led provincialism that had to be given a more expansive constitutional recognition. Such assumptions clearly lay behind the pioneering introduction of the intrastate federalism thesis into Canadian constitutional discourse by Donald Smiley in his seminal 1971 article.[4] The necessity of a positive response to dualism and regionalism advocated by the Task Force on Canadian Unity in the late seventies was informed by similar assumptions.[5]

An alternative reform posture, that provincialism/regionalism should be contested and that institutional engineering should aim at drawing Canadians out of provincial frames of reference by giving them enforceable pan-Canadian rights, and thus, a national lens through which they could assess the performance of provincial political systems, had only limited support among political scientists. It was, however, central to federal government objectives, via the instrumentality of a Charter of Rights, through the entire Trudeau period. Thus, in general, political scientists and federal government practitioners of constitution-making did not share a common frame of reference in the Trudeau era. That disinclination to see the significance of a Charter, and the related propensity to see Canada in terms of its territorial particularisms also accounts, I suppose, for the tepid reception of the Constitution Act, 1982 by most political scientists, a response summed up in the volume appropriately titled *And No One Cheered*.[6]

While there may have been little cheering at the time, from the vantage point of 1988 it is evident that the Charter has not only elicited a broad basis of general support, but it has also attracted the specific support of particular groups – women's groups with Section 28, ethnic Canadians with Section 27, official-language minorities with Section 23, aboriginals with Section 25 (and Section 91 (24) of the BNA Act of 1867, plus Section 35 of the Constitution Act, 1982 and the now obsolete Section 37 with its requirement of constitutional conferences on aboriginal matters), and of those Canadians whose interests are encompassed in the various social categories listed in Section 15 (1) and (2) with their equality rights and affirmative action possibilities. Thus the 1982 Charter has positively linked many Canadians to the constitution and given them constitutional identities they formerly lacked. On the whole, however, these groups have received limited attention from political scientists who, possibly for that reason, appear to have underestimated the political significance of their constitutional recognition.

Also revealing of the political science perspective is the relatively positive political scientists' response to the Meech Lake Accord, which contrasts markedly with the responses of historians and law professors, both of whom have been much more critical of the Accord's ambiguities, its provincializing thrusts, its concern for governments, and its repudiation of the more open process of constitution-making of 1980-82.[7] Political scientists, by contrast, appear to support a highly federalist and governmental view of Canada that accords limited significance or credibility to the numerous groups that lack automatic government sponsorship – women, aboriginals, third-force Canadians, visible minorities, official-language minorities, and the numerous groups that cluster under the rubric of the various categories of Section 15 of the Charter. In these circumstances, the tendency of the federal government to strengthen the legitimacy of the Accord by citing supportive political scientists is not surprising. Eight of the twelve academics who signed a brief to the Special Joint Committee that was strongly supportive of Meech Lake were political scientists. They described themselves as a group "all of whom have devoted much of their professional careers to the study of Canadian federalism."[8] Another political scientist, Kenneth McRoberts, passionately defended the Accord on the ground that if it "accomplishes nothing else, at least it will establish once and for all that Canada is a federal country."[9]

Richard Simeon suggests that lawyers "anxious to cross every t and dot every i have generally been more critical of the Accord than have political scientists," because the latter "have more faith in political forces."[10] An alternative explanation would be that lawyers are less prone to collapse the constitution into its federalism component, and, partly because of a strong cadre of feminist women lawyers, treat both the Charter and the groups that support it with greater seriousness than do political scientists.

If this somewhat impressionistic assessment of the intellectual orientations of mainstream political science commentary over the past two decades is even approximately correct, there are good reasons to fear that political scientists will lose ground as constitutional analysts in the future. In the absence of a significant intellectual reorientation they will correctly come to be viewed as too wedded to institutional arrangements, such as federalism, of diminished constitutional importance.

This concern is strengthened when the qualitative changes in the relation of the post-1982 constitution to Canadian society are further explored. These changes go far beyond the stimulation on the one hand of a rights-bearing consciousness among the citizenry and a rearrangement of the relative powers of various institutions of government on the other. They draw constitutional discourse into new themes of ethnicity, culture, race, and identity, which, apart from the French-English cleavage, have historically attracted limited attention from political science students in Canada. The expansion of constitutional language to encompass new themes requires political scientists to modify their understanding of the constitution and its role in Canadian society. Much assistance is available in the pioneering work of the sociologist Raymond Breton on the state's management of ethnicity, partly by its manipulation of the symbolic order.[11]

The following section briefly notes the recent tension between competing views of the constitution, with particular reference to ethnicity.

From the Constitution Act, 1982 to Meech Lake: What Is the Constitution About?

The Constitution Act, 1982, mainly by the vehicle of the Charter, has made the constitution the supreme instrument of social recognition in a society whose multiplying cleavages are not so much transcended as differentially included in its clauses. The 1982 Act is honeycombed with particular recognitions – women, aboriginals, official-language minorities, third-force Canadians and visible minorities under multiculturalism, and the disabled and others in the equality rights section.

These varied recognitions differ in their nature, in their probable policy consequences, and in their psychological significance to the groups they encompass. Further, these constitutional categories, which have been explored elsewhere,[12] are still in flux. They are viewed as temporary constitutional stopping points rather than as settled equilibrium arrangements by the groups whose interests they reflect.

This instability is due partly to the recency of the Charter and partly to the constitutional developments that followed its introduction. Before these newly constitutionalized social categories had adjusted to their new status, and only two years after the coming into effect of the equality rights of Section 15 in 1985, the 1987 Meech Lake Accord aggravated the uncertainties derived from the previous bout of constitutional change.

The challenge that Meech Lake offered to the Constitution Act was not trivial but, as various authors have suggested,[13] was a powerful counter-attack to reinstate the dominance of governments, and to reassert the primacy of federalism, and to do so essentially from a provincial perspective. Meech Lake addressed Canadians largely in terms of their membership in national and provincial communities, especially the latter, rather than as aborigines, visible minorities, women, rights bearers, and related constitutional categories indifferent to federalism's spatial construction of communities. Further, by its processes Meech Lake clearly defined Canadians as subjects of an elite government-dominated constitutional order rather than as citizen participants in its unfolding.

Both the implicitly asserted primacy of federalism and the explicit domination by governments of the levers of constitutional change, along with the constitutional theory behind them, confront a counter-constitutional discourse that stresses non-federal cleavages and a citizen role in constitutional change. This counter-discourse, like the official discourse of governments, displays a crude intellectual symmetry within its own framework of assumptions. As long as constitutional change can be defined as a response to problems of federalism the primacy of governments as constitutional change agents plausibly follows. Conversely, if governments do control the working of the amending formula they will rework the issues pressing for constitutional attention to make them compatible with their concerns as governments of the federal system.

On the other hand, if the issues on the constitutional agenda pertain to women, aboriginals, ethnic Canadians, and the disabled, for example, the appropriateness of involving spokespersons from the affected groups in modifying the constitution has considerable plausibility. Again, if these groups are involved they will try to structure the constitutional debate in terms of their concerns that display remarkably less sensitivity to federalism and its governments than the latter automatically bring to the constitutional bargaining table. Thus how the constitution is defined, as an affair of governments, of citizens, or both, is relevant to the decision of who should be allowed to participate in changing it. The converse is also true. Whoever controls constitutional change will pull the working definition of the constitution in the direction of their natural preferences.

Although women, aboriginals, official-language minorities, and others have been defined as outsiders – as audience – by the processes of Meech Lake, they have explicit niches in the constitution. Their constitutional status, recognitions, and rights were typically achieved against the resistance or hostility of most governments,[14] and were sought because of their distrust of governments. Further, since it is not possible in major packages of constitutional change to sever the concerns of governments from those of other actors who enjoy a constitutional presence, it is scarcely surprising that Meech Lake has unleashed a challenge to official constitutional discourse, the examination of which tells us much about the constitutional disarray in which we find ourselves.

Among the various critical public reactions to Meech Lake in English Canada – from frustrated northern residents, from social policy activists, from women, from basic defenders of the Charter and supporters of the national community and its government – one of the most revealing comes from Canadians outside the privileged category of the two founding peoples. These ethnic critics of Meech Lake from traditional third-force groups such as Ukrainians, newly prominent visible minorities, and the various aboriginal communities contested definitions of Canada that gave privilege to French and English founding peoples and created community cleavages defined by federalism.

This ethnic/aboriginal discourse not only reveals pervasive disagreement with government definitions of community structured by federalism, but also underlines the extent to which the Canadian constitution is now embroiled in the tensions of an ethnically plural society. This discourse also confirms the enhanced role of the constitution, in the way so brilliantly described by Raymond Breton,[15] as an instrument of selective social recognition, engaged in fashioning and refashioning the Canadian symbolic order and differentially allocating official status to the multiplying ethnic diversities of a heterogeneous society. In general, it confirms that the constitution is now an arena within which competing ethnic and aboriginal Canadians battle for relative status vis-à-vis each other and with the two founding peoples privileged by past history and, even now, by the contemporary constitution.

This constitutional discourse grapples with issues of community and identity that are not reducible to federalist terminology. Nevertheless, it is now anchored in the constitution in the same way as constitutional controversies over preferred forms of federalism. As Canada becomes more multicultural and multiracial and the population of British and French descent continues to decline in relative strength, the impact of ethnicity on the theory and practice of the Canadian constitution can only increase.

The British background component of the Canadian population slipped below 50 per cent in about 1940 and soon may drop below 40 per cent. The French background component fell below 30 per cent in the early sixties and is now nearing the 25 per cent mark. By 1981 the "other" – non-British and non-French – had passed the French component and is now nearly one-third of the population. By the first half of the twenty-first century the "other" could be the largest single element of the population.[16] Thus the evolution of Canadian society confirms William H. McNeill's assertion that polyethnicity is the norm in contemporary societies.[17]

The constitutional theory of the future will have to seek an intellectual rapport with the sociology of race and ethnicity. Put differently, constitutional scholars have to try and understand the reciprocal relations between the constitution and ethnicity – how on the one hand, the Canadian constitution has responded to ethnic (and linguistic) pluralism, and how on the other ethnicity is itself shaped and given meaning by the constitution. For those political scientists who have stressed class and regionalism as the most relevant or exciting cleavages, and who have seldom strayed beyond the French-English dualism in their analysis of ethnicity, this reorientation will not come easily.[18] In general, social scientists are much more likely to find virtue in class conflict than in ethnic conflict, partly because, "especially in the West, ethnic affiliations have been in disrepute, for deep ideological reasons," with the consequence that the study of ethnic relations was for long a "backwater of the social sciences."[19] Similar deficiencies exist in "Western political thought," which, according to Kenneth McRae, "in general has shown little understanding or respect for the cultural diversity of mankind and has made scant allowance for it as a possible concern of government."[20] An additional impediment to the requisite intellectual reorientation is suggested by my UBC colleague Robert Jackson, who observes that the question "What have constitutions to do with ethnicity? . . . is not asked as often as one would expect in today's world of pervasive ethnic awareness." He finds the reasons for this unfortunate weakness in the division of labour between legal theorists and social scientists, with the former typically neglecting ethnicity and the latter devoting limited attention to jurisprudence concerns.[21]

A political scientist, perhaps especially one with an ethnically privileged WASP background, may fail to see the relevance of a constitutional discourse that does not focus on federalism, parliamentary government, or even rights, but seems more concerned with status, identity, recognition, dignity, etc. The constitutional language of ethnicity wielded by ethnic elites is emotional and passionate – a Mediterranean language – rather than calculating and instrumental. Its affinities are with such concepts as shame, envy, resentment, honour, and pride.

The overriding issue is how one's ethnic group is recognized and treated relative to other groups. It is a language haunted by comparison, driven by the ubiquitous fear that one has lost, or might lose, constitutional ground relative to some other group. In an odd way it is like a court language in which the processes of constitutional change are the contemporary equivalent of a dyspeptic monarch who might unpredictably cast a jaundiced royal eye on a formerly favoured courtier.

The next section of this paper will illustrate the constitutional language of ethnicity by sampling the responses of representatives of various ethnic groups and aboriginal Canadians who feared a relative loss of status occasioned by the distinct society and linguistic duality clauses of Meech Lake. If space allowed, similar examples could easily be taken from women's groups and official-language minorities who also saw Meech Lake as weakening their recently won constitutional status.

Meech Lake, Ethnicity, and the Constitution

The Accord's portrayal of Canada is unacceptable to ethnic and aboriginal Canadians.[22] To the Inuit the prominence given to French- and English-speaking Canadians, whose existence is a "fundamental characteristic of Canada," "continues to be an insult."[23] To the president of the Makivik Corporation the apparent move from multiculturalism to biculturalism is "offensive and insulting to the fact that we [Inuit] are not being recognized as being contributing members to this country." The failure to give "the Inuit and the aboriginal people . . . the same level of recognition we find to be stating a falsehood into the Constitution."[24]

Not surprisingly, aboriginal groups assert that historical priority, in which they ranked first, and which is the logic behind their self-descriptive label as "First Nations," should be the central factor in determining constitutional ranking. Indigenousness, as Horowitz notes, is "by far the most common claim to legitimacy."[25] Aboriginal advocates are particularly upset at the recognition of Quebec as a distinct society when they see that their own much greater distinctiveness, with deeper historical roots that, according to one Yukon Chief, go "back to before Christ and [are] synonymous with the great flood of the world,"[26] is not recognized. John Amagoalik, co-chairman of the Inuit Committee on National Issues, repudiated the status of French and English as founding nations on the grounds that "My ancestors occupied this land when the Mulroneys and the Bourassas and Vander Zalms of the world were still living in caves in Europe."[27]

Aboriginal frustrations are fostered by the fact that the conceptual fuzziness that was a barrier to the constitutional recognition of aboriginal self-government was not a barrier to constitutionalizing the vague distinct society concept,[28] whose lack of definition is defended as a virtue by Premier Robert Bourassa of Quebec. Some aboriginal leaders also suspect that the raising of the barriers to provincehood in the North is partly explained as an act of discrimination against the majority native population in the Northwest Territories.[29] Further, status Indians, with their special link with the federal government, are concerned that, whenever the federal government is weakened, their own influence diminishes.[30]

The aboriginal position is effectively summed up by George Erasmus of the Assembly of First Nations in his criticism that the distinct society "perpetuates the idea of a duality in Canada, and strengthens the myth that the French and the English peoples are the foundation of Canada. It neglects the original inhabitants and distorts history. It is as if the peoples of the First Nations never existed. . . . If anyone is more distinct, surely it is the peoples of the First Nations."[31]

For those Canadians who can claim no founding status the stress on priority of arrival as the base for contemporary ranking is unacceptable. They seek to deny the truth in the jest that "the definition of a Canadian is an immigrant with seniority."[32] To Liberal MPs Charles Caccia and Sergio Marchi the Accord is a voice from the past, "a rear-view mirror vision which may have been valid two generations ago,"[33] an "outdated [definition of Canada] ... primarily satisfied with only depicting our people's past and our country's history."[34] "Millions of Canadians are left out who do not identify with either French or English. They have no place in the Accord, and they are outside the Constitution."[35] In Marchi's words, "not all the people of this country have been dealt the same constitutional card, nor have they been equally credited with being a dignified and contributing part of this country ...."[36]

The Ukrainians cannot support a constitution "whose underlying rationale is the outdated and discredited concept of two founding nations."[37] The Canadian Institute of Minority Rights asserts the inappropriateness of giving constitutional recognition to "societal concepts dictated by 19th century realities" in the "increasingly pluralistic and multicultural society" of Canada.[38] The brief of the National Association of Canadians of Origins in India asserts that the use of the constitution to single out and rank Canadians is wrong in principle and divisive in practice. A preferred strategy would be for the constitution to "regard all persons, regardless of their cultural, linguistic, racial, or political background, as Canadians, and other definitions should be discarded."[39]

The protection of Section 27 of the Charter from the interpretation clause of the Accord by Section 16 of the latter[40] does not mollify third-force Canadians. They see an unacceptable distinction in the fact that Section 27 applies only to the Charter, in contrast to the Accord's requirements that "the Constitution of Canada" is to be interpreted consistent with linguistic duality and Quebec as a distinct society.[41] Accordingly, this invidious distinction that seems to weaken multiculturalism relative to linguistic dualism should be rectified by adding multiculturalism as a fundamental characteristic of Canada.[42]

For the ethnic and aboriginal minorities who feel left out by Meech Lake the latter's provisions are experienced as a sense of loss, of status deprivation, of non-recognition, of being rebuffed. For the Ukrainian Canadian Committee, "if there are groups within society that are alienated and do not feel represented by the Constitution, they will have less respect and affection for that Constitution. That is the way we feel, that we are being abandoned."[43] To the Ontario Black Coalition, the "overt recognition of English and French and the non-recognition of all the other groups, including large numbers of blacks, seems to be a denial of our existence on the part of Canada."[44]

For NDP MP Howard McCurdy, the Accord's message "to a third of the population – the blacks, the Ukrainians, the Poles, the Italians, ... and the variety of other people who compose my riding – [is] that they are not really an inherent part of the country. There is still the recognition inherent in all that has happened that there is some primacy to the two founding people. As long as that message is maintained, the country cannot be whole ... it implies that those of us who are neither English nor French are not really a part. ... It is unacceptable to me and all others ... that we should in any way be considered as second class citizens ... those of us who are neither French nor English [must] be welcomed into the Constitution."[45]

For Liberal MP Charles Caccia, "a constitution must include all members of society, rather than putting some in and leaving some out. ... Let us not drift with the divisive notion that some are members of a founding group and some are not."[46] For Sergio Marchi, what is the government "to say to those Canadians whose origins are neither English nor French, and who feel the isolation of being left out? I am one of those Canadians, and I do not feel, according to Section 1 [*sic*] that I am as constitutionally relevant as my French Canadian or English Canadian colleagues in this House of Commons, for instance. I do not accept that while they can be recognized in Section 1, I must accept to be in Section 16 at the very end of the Accord. ... "[47]

For Louis "Smokey" Bruyère, president of the Native Council of Canada, the Accord "promotes a view of reality that ignores the first founding people of Canada – the aboriginal peoples. It provides a vision of the future in which aboriginal peoples cannot hope to share ... it completely ignores aboriginal peoples and their place in the existing constitutional order. In that sense, it totally misstates Canada as it is. It takes us back to a myth of 120 years ago that the fundamental character of Canada is of the French and the English."[48] Spokespersons for the Nishnawbe-Aski Nation lamented that "we are the first nations of this country and we have been left out of Meech Lake. They do not want us. ... It is our land and resources that built your country."[49]

The purpose of this litany of emotional outbursts is to underscore the pervasive nature of ethnic and aboriginal constitutional grievances, and to indicate the existence of an admittedly inchoate but not formless style of constitutional discourse. The following section attempts to draw out some of the salient characteristics of ethnic and aboriginal constitutional discourse in Canada.

The Nature of Ethnic Constitutional Discourse

These ethnic grievances, which could be multiplied many times over and which, with suitable modifications, could be supplemented by similar protestations by women, official-language minorities, and northerners, as well as by basic Charter defenders, graphically reveal the many constituencies outside of governments that now see themselves in constitutional terms. They all accept the basic proposition that the constitution is now the crucial instrument for defining one's place in Canadian society.

This ethnic and aboriginal minority constitutional discourse has the following salient characteristics.

(1) It is predominantly a non-official discourse. Indeed, in the Meech Lake process it is explicitly an anti-official discourse that overtly challenges the legitimacy of an elite-dominated executive federalism as the instrument of constitutional change as well as the government-sensitive outcomes to which it leads. Ethnic and aboriginal groups do not trust the elected leaders of government to deal fairly with them when the constitution is on the agenda and they are not present.

(2) They are not, however, complete outsiders. They have constitutional identities. They occupy niches in the constitution and often think of particular clauses as specifically theirs, clauses whose presence and wording in the constitution is the result of past battles successfully fought. Thus they think of themselves as legitimate constitutional actors. Their situation is not the same as status Indians who were treated as wards before receiving the vote in 1960, or gays and lesbians excluded from explicit inclusion in Section 15 of the Charter. Although their discourse is non-official, it is grounded in the constitution.

(3) Their agenda is to protect or strengthen the constitutional recognition of their members. They clearly view the constitution as a vehicle for the enhancement (and loss) of status. Indeed, their distrust of majorities and their perception that only rarely do they have the ear of government make them especially dependent on the constitution as a lever.

(4) They do not view the constitution as fixed or stable, but as highly mutable. This belief is a product of the recency of the Constitution Act 1982, followed three years later in 1985 with the implementation of the Section 15 equality provisions of the Charter, in turn followed shortly after by the Meech Lake Accord. These developments coincided with a series of high-profile, but ultimately unsuccessful, aboriginal constitutional conferences. The previous history of tentative constitutional recognition and rebuffs of ethnic groups and aboriginals in the 1980-82 constitutional exercise, allied with their success in extracting the protections of Section 16 of the Accord by a frantic application of pressure,

undoubtedly leads them to view the process of constitutional development as whimsy moderated intermittently by *ad hoc* political pressure.

(5) Their language is often highly emotional. It is the language of shame, pride, dignity, insult, inclusion or exclusion, humiliation or recognition. Their concerns are not narrowly instrumental. Recognition of constitutional status seems to be sought for its own sake rather than for what tangible benefits might be expected to flow from it. Raymond Breton has described how the policy of multiculturalism evolved to quell the status anxieties of the non-British, non-French element that the language of charter groups, two nations, and biculturalism would lead to their marginalization.[50] Meech Lake generates similar tensions with the basic difference that the ethnic and aboriginal communities are now larger, more diversified, better organized, and can wield constitutional clauses in their self-defence.

(6) Ethnic and aboriginal constitutional discourse employs multiple criteria in the making of claims, unfailingly in the self-interest of the advocate, ranging from claims for special recognition based on historical priority of arrival to egalitarian denials of any form of special status as inimical to a common citizenship.

An alternative strategy to challenging the criteria employed by ethnic rivals is to make claims in terms of criteria that might initially be thought to be more applicable to other ethnicities. Thus the Ukrainian Community Development Committee (Prairie Region) has pleaded for "a concept of founding peoples that is more elastic," and capable of including the Ukrainians as a "founding settler people in the Prairie provinces" whose forefathers settled on lands that "had hardly felt the hand of man before . . . [and] . . . were open and sparsely populated by natives."[51] A functionally similar claim is made by the Ontario Black Coalition in the statement that "Black people have been a part of Canadian history since approximately 1600. Historians have downgraded or completely ignored the facts about blacks in Canada."[52]

(7) An emerging distinction that will grow more important in the light of anticipated demographic change is between visible minorities and the older, more traditional European groups outside of the French-English duality. Section 27, with its reference to the preservation and enhancement of the multicultural heritage of Canadians, is of more significance to the latter, while the former, especially those of lower status, see Canada through a multiracial rather than multicultural lens. For them, Section 15 is of more significance and their goals are less those of cultural protection than of equal treatment or positive discrimination. As their numbers grow to an anticipated 10 per cent of the Canadian population

by the turn of the century,[53] excluding aboriginals, the two groups will probably diverge in their constitutional demands. The older European groups will maintain their concern with the expressive dimension of ethnicity and cultural recognition, while the newer visible minorities will be motivated by more instrumental concerns of economic advancement and race relations issues. As Daiva Stasiulis observed, the 1981 establishment of a Race Relations Unit within the Multiculturalism Directorate was a response to "the increased proportion of non-white immigrants from Third World countries for whom the major substantive concerns – such as securing employment, and seeking protection from racial harassment, discrimination and inequality – diverge from the cultural and linguistic priorities of European groups whose political pressures were operative during the initial development of the Multicultural policy. In addition, these 'visible minority' groups began to voice their own status anxieties over the symbolism of a multicultural Canada which was not also conceived as multiracial." [54]

(8) An anomalous characteristic of the constitutional language of ethnicity is the relative absence of unofficial voices from the big battalions of the two linguistic majority communities of Francophones and Anglophones. As majority communities in Quebec and the rest of Canada respectively, their concerns are normally incorporated in the objectives of the governments they control. The unofficial Anglophone voice comes from the English minority in Quebec and the unofficial Francophone voice from French-speaking minorities outside of Quebec, neither of whom, with the possible exception of the Acadians in New Brunswick, see their provincial governments as allies.[55] This asymmetrical participation damages the quality of the debate.

(9) Organizational fluidity occasionally precipitates battles over which organization is the proper representative of a constituency with a constitutional identity. Organizational competition is especially evident for aboriginals, whose concerns are ill-served by the cacophony of dissimilar peoples grouped under the aboriginal rubric.[56] If Meech Lake is ratified and constitutional discussions take place on an annual basis, and there is meaningful public involvement, the state will acquire an interest in the representativeness of the various elites that claim to speak for particular communities/constituencies. Federal funding may facilitate the employment of selective inducements.

(10) The constitutional language of ethnicity is still in its infancy, somewhat rudimentary and dominated by the various ethnic claimants seeking to protect or improve their constitutional recognition. The ethnic and aboriginal population from which it derives only recently attained

the visibility, heterogeneity, numerical strength, organizational infra-structure, and self-confidence that now command constitutional atten-tion. The very labels under which the competing groups vie for status are often of recent vintage – Inuit, Dene, visible minorities, third-force, and First Nations. Their proliferation indicates the complexity of Canada outside of the charter peoples, and the search for status-giving identities.

In its early stages this language suffers from two fundamental weak-nesses. It is a centrifugal language more successful in capturing our separate ethnic selves than in addressing our common membership in a single polity by a contemporary theory of citizenship appropriate to our linguistic, multicultural, and multi-racial composition in the era of the Charter. No less demanding than the construction of the latter is the necessity of developing a composite constitutional discourse that simul-taneously captures the territorial dimensions of national and provincial communities fostered by federalism and the growing racial and ethnic diversities within them. At the moment, these two languages of commu-nity and identity, one sponsored by federalism and the other largely by the Charter, appear more as rivals than as complementary versions of the same phenomena viewed from alternative perspectives.

Conclusion

Constitutions and ethnicity are locked in an inescapable interdependence. The full meaning of each depends on an intimate understanding of the other. To Lord Durham constitutional engineering was to be directed to the assimilation of the backward French-Canadian population. To the subsequent generation of statesmen, escape from the French-English impasse under the Act of Union required a resort to federalism that would minimize ethnic conflict by its principle that fences make good neighbours. The other half of the Confederation agreement, however, parliamentary responsible government, confirmed the British political heritage of the colonists, captured in the preamble to the BNA Act in the phrase "a Constitution similar in Principle to that of the United King-dom." The British cast of the constitution was reflected in parliamentary supremacy and allegiance to the Crown, the "Mother" country, and the Empire.

The other explicit link between ethnicity and the constitution was Section 91 (24), which gave legislative authority over "Indians, and Lands reserved for the Indians" to the federal Parliament. That grant of authority and the policies based on it gave status Indians a uniquely intimate relationship with the federal government, a suspicion of the provinces, and a political identity that separated them from other peoples of aboriginal descent who lacked explicit constitutional recognition.

Various developments in the decades that followed World War Two upset the ethnic constitutional equilibrium that had functioned tolerably well for three-quarters of a century. A simple listing underlines the magnitude of the ethnic challenges even if it does little justice to their complexity: the emergence of an independence-seeking Quebec nationalism that challenged the survival of the Canadian state; the emergence of the aboriginal peoples as political actors with distinct political and constitutional demands; the emergence of the third force of white ethnics outside of the French and English founding peoples as a political constituency that resisted the second-class citizen status that it feared was a byproduct of the attempt to define Canada in terms of French-English dualism; and the numerical growth and enhanced political profile of visible minorities that emerged in response to more liberal immigration requirements.

These domestic developments in ethnic demography and political demands were stimulated by various international trends. The crumbling of the great European empires destroyed the legitimacy of ideas of racial hierarchies on which they had rested and stimulated ethnic consciousness and sub-state nationalism within Western states. The intellectual legacy of World War Two included a renewed search for mechanisms to protect citizen rights and, with the strong backing of the United Nations, not only stimulated a rights consciousness that swept across national borders but also fostered support for entrenched, judicially enforced charters as instruments for their protection. In Canada this climate of assumptions chipped away at the principle of parliamentary supremacy at a time when, for many additional reasons, the United Kingdom was receding in importance for Canadians. For Canada the retreat of imperial Britain was accompanied by the transformation of Empire into a multi-racial and multi-ethnic Commonwealth. The desire of successive Canadian governments to play a leading role in the Commonwealth, partly to give Canadians a prominence in an arena in which the United States could not participate, contributed to the more open immigration policy that changed the ethnic and racial composition of Canadian society.

For many students the central challenge to the constitutional order that emerged from World War Two has been the accommodation and containment of widespread centrifugal pressures, which were strongest in, but not confined to, Quebec. The response to dualism and regionalism, which sometimes took the form of a combative pan-Canadian nationalism, is undeniably the dominant theme of recent decades. Its centrality in our collective self-analysis reflects its status as the traditional fare of a century-old federalism and the dominance by governments of the constitutional agenda.

For political scientists who study governments the focus on federalism, dualism, regionalism, province-building, and similar subject matter appears natural, almost inevitable. Indeed, if such a disciplinary focus did not exist we would need to invent it, for it clearly reflects realities that require constant analysis and attention.

However, the Canadian people, their governments, and the constitution have simultaneously been responding to the ethnic and racial transformation of the Canadian population, which, as noted earlier in this paper, has markedly reduced the proportion of the population of French and British background and politicized those of other backgrounds. These demographic facts, in conjunction with the international phenomena identified above, are the social base and intellectual currents that lie behind a succession of state responses to accommodate and incorporate the galloping ethnic and racial diversities that have emerged in the past half-century. These responses include the post-war extension of the franchise to formerly excluded groups; the pan-Canadianism that lay behind the Diefenbaker Bill of Rights; the defeated assimilationist thrust of the 1969 policy paper on Indians; the changed immigration requirements of the sixties; the 1971 policy of multiculturalism; Quebec language policies to channel immigrants into the French-speaking community; the development of human rights commissions and codes at both federal and provincial levels; and the Constitution Act, 1982 with its clauses pertaining to aboriginals, to multiculturalism, and to "race, national or ethnic origins, [and] colour." These examples of a broad current of policy emanating from both orders of government are not issues of federalism as such, but rather of our response to who we are as a people.

Meech Lake, with its distinct society and distinct identity clauses, its statement "that the existence of French-speaking Canadians, centered in Quebec but also present elsewhere in Canada, and English-speaking Canadians, concentrated outside Quebec but also present in Quebec, constitutes a fundamental characteristic of Canada," its immigration provisions, and its Section 16 protection for aboriginal peoples and Canadians' multicultural heritage, is the most recent constitutional response to the changed composition of Canadian society. As shown earlier, third-force, visible minority, and aboriginal Canadians oppose what they see as a constitutional package that reasserts the primacy of governments, of majorities, and of founding peoples. They define Meech

Lake as speaking to the Canada of yesterday. They share the apprehensions of Dean John Whyte of Queen's University Law Faculty that

> constitutional changes in our present age that do not strive to express the worth of cultural diversity fail to perform one of the chief roles of a Constitution – the expression of a social vision, even a utopian social vision. In Meech Lake we have let this opportunity for visioning our future fall prey to the frantic process of recapturing our past.[57]

Constitutions are always in transition. The society that they shape and that shapes them is continuously transformed by socio-economic pressures emanating from the domestic and international environments. The necessary adaptation of the constitution to these new pressures is inevitably constrained by the bias of past arrangements and the historic values embedded in them. These constraints operate in intellectual communities as well as in the mentalities and behaviours of governing elites. To an earlier generation of English-Canadian political scientists, responsible parliamentary government was the revered centrepiece of the Canadian constitutional tradition. For Brady and Dawson the British heritage was central and positive, an orientation that, especially for the latter, distracted attention from the French fact in Canada and from the significance of federalism for its accommodation.

By contrast, federalism became the leading institutional focus for the next generation of political scientists. Further, as the popularity of the province-building rubric suggested, federalism lost many of the negative connotations it had acquired in the thirties depression as a barrier to central government leadership and as a constraint on the development of the national community. While this disciplinary orientation was an understandable response to the centrifugal pressures emanating from Quebec and elsewhere, and also to the trauma of constitutional introspection to which they led, it is the argument of this paper that students of the constitution should now recognize the diminished significance of federalism in the constitutional order and the emerging role of the constitution, especially the Charter, in responding to ethnicities other than French and English.

The Charter is not a minor addition to the Canadian constitutional system but a profound, wrenching transformation. It elevates the constitution as a whole to a level of symbolic and practical significance far surpassing its previous status as an instrument of governance. It brings new groups into the Canadian constitutional order and gives them constitutional identities. And from the perspective of this paper it generates a vigorous constitutional discourse responsive to aboriginal Canadians, visible minorities, and white ethnics who are not linked to the communities that did battle more than two centuries ago on the Plains of Abraham.

The constitution is not the only arena within which our ethnic, aboriginal, and other diversities jostle for recognition and power. Further, it is in part an historical accident – a by-product of the salience of the constitutional issue originally directed to concerns arising from dualism and federalism – that the constitution has become so intimately connected to those aspects of Canadians' ethnic composition that transcend French-English dualism. However, now that the constitutional connection has been made its repudiation is impossible.

"Ethnic conflict," as Donald Horowitz observes, "is, at bottom, a matter of comparison."[58] In the Canadian case the use of the constitution to allocate ethnic status greatly facilitates and stimulates comparison because its categories are so public and so heavily freighted with symbolic meaning. What was formerly implicit, and hence somewhat indeterminate and supportive of coexisting conflicting interpretations that did not confront each other, is now explicit. The constitution thus reinforces ethnic consciousness in a society whose ethnic and racial heterogeneity can only increase.

The desire for ethnic identification with and inclusion in the polity "derives ... from a quite general urge to be in harmony with one's surroundings, to belong in a territory, to be comfortable and at home."[59] In Canada the constitution has become a key instrument for the attainment of these objectives. Success, however, has been only relative. Elliot Tepper is correct in his prediction that a new definition of Canada will be required for the twenty-first century. "Canada tomorrow will be more than a country with no single majority. *It will be a country where no group is a dominant plurality.* ... The task of politics is to keep the definition of nationality related to the actual composition of the nation. It is time now to prepare for a more pluralistic future."[60]

Chapter Eight

Political Scientists and the Constitutional Crisis: The View from Outside Quebec

Introduction: Political Analysis and Constitutional Evolution

Constitutional evolution cannot be divorced from the constitutional commentary of academics, journalists, and the partisans of special interests. Since a functioning constitution is a product of the learned behaviour of the citizens and elites who work it, its development is continuously informed by the never-ending public seminar by which a political people constantly refreshes its constitutional understandings. This recognition lies behind the focused efforts of scholars and publicists to modify the interpretations that influence the behaviour of those who work the constitution more directly. Thus, as Canadians began to assimilate their new inheritance of British parliamentary government in the last half of the nineteenth century, Alpheus Todd, the Parliamentary Librarian, contributed two massive volumes to the task of educating a rude frontier society in the intricacies and nuances of their new constitutional arrangements. Todd responded to "the great and growing necessity for properly instructing the public mind upon a vital question of practical politics,"[1] by which he meant the threats a developing democratic spirit posed to executive stability in the modern state.

Another stream of commentary, to which the lawyer John S. Ewart made notable contributions,[2] sought to quicken the pace toward Canadian autonomy and thus to diminish the British role in such areas as judicial review of the constitution, Canada's external relations, procedures for amending the British North America Act, and in the role of and manner of appointing the Governor General. This colonial nationalism, which ultimately triumphed in area after area, most recently and belatedly in the 1982 Constitution Act ending the role of the British Parliament in constitutional amendments, had to struggle against a competing system of ideas that found solace, status, and security in the British connection.[3]

Another linkage between ideas and constitutional evolution is examined in a valuable recent work by Doug Owram. He analyses the efforts of Canadian scholars and constitutional commentators in the first half of the twentieth century to bring social science to the service of the enhanced role for the central government that they advocated in response to the various crises of their time.[4] They constituted, in an apt phrase, "The Government Generation," who believed that the governing of Canada would be more efficient and sensitive if its conduct was informed by intelligences such as theirs. And, as Owram tells the story, the demands of wartime administration and post-war reconstruction, both under central government leadership, led to the triumph of their views by the 1940s.

The way in which citizens and elites come to view the political world is immensely consequential for constitutional development. Neither governments nor the purveyors of analytical and normative frameworks are ignorant of the political significance of ideas, labels, and social science theories. Thus, the Rowell-Sirois Report was commissioned with a clear idea of the general direction its reform proposals were to take.[5] That royal commission, the first one to recruit academics to an extensive research role, employed legal and social science scholarship to provide the intellectual underpinnings for a revamped federalism under central government leadership. And, as Tom Courchene points out, it cast a long shadow, as the "equalization provision in the Constitution Act, 1982 is virtually identical to the wording used by the [Rowell Sirois] Commission in discussing the National Adjustment Grants."[6]

The Duplessis government's appointment of the Quebec Royal Commission of Inquiry on Constitutional Problems led to the Tremblay Report, which provided intellectual ammunition for Quebec's defence of provincial autonomy. More generally, the genesis and publication of the Tremblay Report revealed the Quebec government's recognition of the need for a supportive analytical and normative infrastructure to bolster its constitutional position. Otherwise, constitutional evolution might be excessively influenced by centralist theories propagated in Ottawa and circulating in English-Canadian intellectual communities.

Accordingly, a change in constitutional understanding – whatever its source – amounts to a *de facto* change in the working, living constitution. Sometimes the movement of ideas is slow and cumulative, and not easily attributable to a single source, person, or event. Such was the case in overcoming the constitutional impasse of the 1930s. It was resolved not by the dramatic sequence of formal constitutional change that critics of federalism so often advocated in the depression, but rather by governing elites learning to work the system by throwing the committee networks, which later came to be called executive federalism, across the relatively unchanged jurisdictional divisions of an historic federal system.

An analogous example of the slow but decisive development of a new intellectual consensus was the erosion of support for parliamentary supremacy and the steady growth of support for an entrenched Charter of Rights. This remarkable transformation in governing constitutional assumptions, in the context of the changing ethnic demography of Canadian society, reflected the vanguard role of the United Nations as international propagandist for entrenched rights and the concomitant declining allegiance to British constitutional values, such as parliamentary supremacy, as Canada and Great Britain drifted apart.

Given the link between ideas and constitutional change, it was entirely predictable that the constitutional turmoil of the past quarter of a century would channel much of the intellectual activity of relevant academic disciplines to the task of influencing the country's constitutional future. Members of the Quebec social science community defined themselves as "agents for social change and collective liberation,"[7] as the Quiet Revolution was followed by the accession to power of an independence-seeking Parti Québécois. More generally, Québécois social scientists played an intellectual leadership role in the necessary and basic introspection that accompanied the efforts of this newly politicized people to come to grips with modernity and to determine what kind of state structure – varying from an enhanced provincehood to independence – was appropriate to that task. While political scientists and other scholars outside of Quebec were involved in the somewhat less heady enterprise of seeking to preserve Canada through reform of its governing arrangements, they, too, were pulled away from their academic cloisters by both the sense of civic duty and the exciting prospect that they might influence the Prince.

The Multiple Roles of Political Scientists in the Constitutional Crisis

One manifestation of the symbiotic relationship between political science and public policy occurs in the constitutional field. The most serious constitutional crisis in Canadian history – the challenge to inherited constitutional arrangements initially posed by Québécois nationalism, which was subsequently reinforced by an aggressive provincialism in English Canada – directed scholarship to the analysis of constitutional ailments and the search for cures. The inducements for political scientists to participate were especially compelling because the pressures for reform focused on the institutions of government and the constitution, subject matters they thought fell peculiarly within their discipline's purview. Institutions were the levers whose manipulation might reduce the tensions that threatened to tear the country apart. Political science involvement was further stimulated by the massive expansion of the Canadian political science community in the sixties and seventies, including a proportionate increase in those studying Canadian politics.

A more ambitious paper than this would compare the analyses offered by all the major disciplines that tried to influence constitutional developments. It would also contrast the nature of involvement by Quebec academics with that of their counterparts elsewhere in Canada. Success in such an ambitious undertaking would have highlighted the impact of ethnicity and cultural context on academic/political behaviour, on the one hand, and of disciplinary differences, on the other. The former has recently been undertaken by Brooks and Gagnon for the social sciences in Quebec and English Canada. They contrast the evolution of the social sciences, drawn into the service of Québécois nationalism in the post-Duplessis years, with the more diffuse, less involved role of their counterparts outside of Quebec.[8] Disciplinary differences have recently been examined by Richard Simeon, with respect to the lawyers, political scientists, and economists employed as researchers on the Macdonald Royal Commission on the Economic Union and Development Prospects for Canada. He found that economists, by contrast with political scientists, were much less intellectually diverse, much more influenced by a prevailing paradigm, and much more confident in offering prescriptions to policy-makers.[9]

Although this essay will offer hints on some of these issues, its disciplinary focus is restricted to political scientists in English Canada. Inevitably, however, the discussion will be extended occasionally to the broader constitutional debate in which political scientists contributed only one of the many voices clamouring for attention.

The contributions of political scientists were scattered throughout the arenas in which the constitutional struggle was played out. They were employed as research directors on the Laurendeau-Dunton Royal Commission on Bilingualism and Biculturalism,[10] on the Task Force on Canadian Unity,[11] and on the Macdonald Commission.[12] The leading Canadian student of comparative federalism, Ronald Watts of Queen's University, was a key commissioner on the Task Force on Canadian Unity and was deeply involved in drafting and writing the final report.[13]

Political scientists participated on the constitutional advisory committees established by several provincial governments.[14] Through their leading role in the Canada West Foundation, they provided much of the intellectual basis for western Canadian criticism of existing federal arrangements.[15] A more direct involvement occurred in the 1980 summer constitutional discussions, when several of the government negotiating teams employed political scientists in an advisory capacity. Political scientists have held key positions in intergovernmental affairs units in Alberta, Ontario, and Ottawa.[16] Peter Meekison, one of the leading political science students of Canadian federalism, who at the time was deputy minister of federal and intergovernmental affairs for the province of Alberta, played a key role in fashioning the amending formula contained in the 1982 Constitution Act, particularly the opting-out provisions.

These examples, culled from personal knowledge and, thus, far from constituting an exhaustive listing, suggest that the "paucity of participation from its scholars" in political life and the separation of "the Canadian political system . . . from the world of the higher learning" that John Porter lamented two decades ago may now have diminished validity, at least as far as political scientists are concerned.[17]

More recent evidence of a visible, if more diffuse, role played by political scientists is provided by the Report of the Special Joint Committee of the Senate and the House of Commons on the 1987 Constitutional Accord. Among the academic commentators cited on page after page for their conflicting evaluations of the Meech Lake Accord, political scientists and law professors had a conspicuously higher profile than representatives of other disciplines.[18]

These indications of explicit involvement in various constitutional arenas were supplemented by an expansive outpouring of commentary, advocacy, and analysis in a stream of books, articles, and conference proceedings devoted to the constitutional introspection that flourished in the quarter of a century from the early sixties to the present. Political scientists enlarged the repertoire of constitutional vocabulary with such new terms as federal-provincial diplomacy,[19] executive federalism,[20] intrastate federalism,[21] and province-building.[22] In each case, these descriptive labels highlighted some constitutional features or processes at the expense of others. In one case, intrastate federalism, a battery of proposed reforms emerged to rectify the constitutional weakness identified by its underlying theory.[23] These and other contributions modified the way in which constitutional ailments were diagnosed by political and bureaucratic elites directly involved in the constitutional reform process.

As the constitutional debate proceeded, expertise built up around particular concerns. Electoral reform,[24] the possible contribution of the Charter to national unity,[25] the composition and role of the Supreme Court,[26] the role of second chambers,[27] and language policy[28] attracted small coteries of experts. They often advocated reform of the instrument on which they had lavished attention as one key to constitutional renewal.

Dominant Tendencies in Analysis and Prescription by Political Scientists

To sum up in a few pages the vast and disparate literature of constitutional analysis and prescription stretching over several decades, much of which did not go beyond mimeographed conference presentations, is to do an inevitable injustice to its richness and complexity. However, to descend to a forest of particulars and to concentrate on the minutiae of small differences is to risk losing sight of common intellectual tendencies that were part of the prevalent climate of opinion in the discipline outside Francophone Quebec. Thus, in the comments that immediately follow, I am interested in individuals and their specific contributions primarily for what they reveal about the role of political scientists and the governing intellectual paradigms they employed in the constitutional debate. There is a time and place for nuance and shadings, and a different time and place, of which this conference is one, for stark pictures and simplifications.

CONTEMPORARY FOCUS

The tendency of political scientists to concentrate on contemporary phenomena, or to see the past through the eyes of present concerns – a pervasive tendency among North American political scientists at the best of times – was strengthened by the emergence of a long-lasting constitutional crisis for which their expertise seemed especially relevant. The resultant present-mindedness also pulled political scientists in the direction of journalistic commentary. In my own case, for example, on looking back I am struck by the amount of effort and time I devoted to successive attempts to analyse the unfolding Canadian constitutional drama. Some future student of the sixties and seventies may reasonably conclude that the desire to be timely and relevant consumed an excessive share of intellectual resources, and that more theoretical concerns, which would have added to the intellectual capital of the discipline, were understudied.

THE TUG OF INVOLVEMENT

The political science response to the constitutional agenda mingled civic concerns and disciplinary understandings in an uneasy tension. The depression of the thirties had a similar effect in pulling the then fledgling Canadian social science community out of the academic cloister and into the political marketplace. This led to academic "hot gospellers" spouting insubstantial panaceas, according to Innis, or to what others saw favourably as an appropriate response to the call for intellectual service on behalf of the nation.[29]

While "rush[ing] into print before all the research is in" sometimes caused uneasiness to political scientists in recent decades, it was justified by a pace of change that required "all citizens . . . [to] make [their] voices heard before it is too late to do anything but write history."[30] The same point was made by David Easton in his 1969 presidential address to the American Political Science Association, in which he argued, in effect, that the noble long-run enterprise of building a science of politics had to be temporarily accorded a lower priority so that more resources could be devoted to the problems of an America ravaged by urban blight, race riots, and the Vietnam War.[31]

The Canadian participant thrust was justified, and reasonably so, by the belief that political science had something to offer to a polity verging on disintegration. However, it is also evident that the partial escape from more narrowly defined disciplinary issues that it offered was experienced by some political scientists as a relief, as an opportunity for involvement in the real world of pressing issues and urgent concerns. In this sense, the constitutional issue underlined the extent to which a purely reclusive, scholarly existence, at least in times of great troubles, is experienced as emotionally stultifying and personally unsatisfying. One can also occasionally detect a certain envy on the part of Anglophone scholars for their Quebec colleagues who were thought to be in the vanguard of a liberating change. By contrast, the conservative, defensive task of trying to save a threatened constitutional order produced distinctly smaller doses of exhilaration. One reviewer of the first edition of Donald Smiley's *Canada in Question* described it as "studded with the thorns of pessimism."[32] My own psychological state differed little from Smiley's. As the Quebec referendum approached, I wrote that "the future" for the believers in Canada would be "a long twilight struggle of coping, compromising, revising, and adapting. Success in the endeavour is likely to be fragile."[33]

ABSENCE OF SUPPORT FOR THE USE OF FORCE

In tune with the predominant dispositions of Anglophone elite opinion, political scientists did not advocate force to keep a reluctant Quebec in Confederation.[34] Earlier, Denis Smith had probably represented mainstream political science opinion in his indictment of the use of the War Measures Act at the time of the 1970 FLQ crisis.[35] Further, although it is not easy to document, political scientists showed scant sympathy for the federal government threat, in the absence of extensive provincial government support, to proceed unilaterally with a request to Westminster to amend the BNA Act. In general, political scientists seem to have preferred compromise or stalemate to a Gaullist unilateralism of action, and a fractured Canada to one held together by force.[36]

The roots of this pacific disposition, and this stress on procedural proprieties, doubtless lie, in part, in the weak military tradition in Canadian political culture, the accompanying lack of military intellectuals focusing on problems of internal order, and the related absence of a metaphysical view of the Canadian state as transcending the interests of a transient regional citizenry bent on its breakup. Highly relevant to the Anglophone response was the fact that after the 1970 FLQ crisis the Quebec nationalist forces were irrevocably committed to the democratic, non-violent means that culminated in the May, 1980, referendum. The stress on a democratic process within Quebec and the eschewing of a military response outside of Quebec obviously fed on each other. By contrast, any attempt to hijack the Quebec state by a narrowly based Québécois elite bent on a UDI (unilateral declaration of independence) strategy might have generated Anglophone support for the use of countervailing force, from which at least some political scientists would not have dissented.

LITTLE DESIRE/CAPACITY TO SPEAK FOR THE ANGLOPHONE SIDE OF DUALISM

In Quebec, many political and other social scientists served the cause of Québécois nationalism, either as supporters of an independent Quebec or of an enhanced Quebec role within Canadian federalism. They saw the Quebec state, according to Brooks and Gagnon, as the instrumentality by which Québécois would come to grips with modernity, and they gave little support to the federalist option espoused by Trudeau, Marchand, and Pelletier.[37] Their academic lens faced inward to Quebec, rather than outward to Canada.[38]

In marked contrast, political scientists outside Quebec displayed a remarkable unwillingness or inability to play the role of intellectual elite for the English-speaking side of a dualist Canada and gave virtually no overt commitment to an English-Canadian nation as the functional equivalent of the Québécois nation.[39] The sources of this hesitation, which had a major impact on the evolution of the constitutional debate, merit examination.

Anglophone Canada is not a cohesive community with a coherent sense of itself.[40] It is fractured by the physical separation of the Atlantic provinces from Ontario, by multiculturalism, and by the provincialism stimulated by powerful provincial governments. It is unable to "contemplate its own existence as a national collectivity."[41] Further, English-speaking Canada is headless. No one has the authority or official status to speak on its behalf. Provincial governments speak only for those within their borders, and they express the provincialism of their residents. The central government, by contrast, addresses the Canadian dimension of the citizenry, but this necessarily stresses the involvement of Anglophone Canada in the country-wide community it shares with Francophones. In other words, the federal system discourages Anglophone Canada from having a distinctive political sense of itself. It is either provincialized, loses its separate identity in a country it shares with others, or is relegated to minority status within Quebec. A prospective Canada without Quebec has no focal point within the federal system, no locus of power that would automatically be the centre of its future existence. Thus Canada-without-Quebec is a concept with a limited capacity to stimulate creative thinking about the constitutional arrangements in which its future citizenry would live. The absence of an organizational vehicle, or institutional container, for the Anglophone side of dualism deprived Anglophone academics of a bounded separate political identity around which they could organize a discussion of an autonomous Anglophone future. They participated in a constitutional debate structured by the dominant actors who would ultimately be involved in its resolution. These were governments, none of whom had a mandate or the desire to speak for English-speaking Canada. Thus, for an individual to do so was to risk being marginalized.

The nature of the Quebec challenge also inhibited positive thinking about the political future of the Anglophone side of dualism. Unlike the independence-oriented Quebec nationalists who hoped to break away from a constricting relationship with a dominant partner, Anglophones were asked to break up a political system of whose creation and century-long existence they were proud. To have seen in the Quebec challenge an opportunity to escape would have required a denial of the goodness of the country they had played a key role in making. Indeed, in recent decades the nation-building enterprise had required Anglophone Canada to dilute its Britishness by stressing its multicultural, and subsequently its multiracial, nature. At the same time as British Canada, defined by history, was accommodating itself to the more capacious, but thinner, concept of Anglophone Canada, defined by language, the latter had to relax its hold on the central government and accept the decline in its relative status that accompanied the elevation of the Francophone side of dualism. These developments, as Kenneth McNaught argued in the mid-sixties, contributed to a non-racial sense of nationality that gave little sustenance to the idea that Anglophone Canada was a potential nation requiring political autonomy to fulfil itself.[42]

Accordingly, both recent history and the powerful tendency of federalism to structure their identity into complementary provincial and country-wide frames of reference encouraged English-speaking Canadians to define themselves in terms of the country they were trying to save, rather than in terms of an autonomous English Canada they might have tried to create. As Latouche observes, the "frame of reference" for English Canadians is not English Canada but "an undifferentiated Canada."[43] And, as Resnick recently argued, the English-Canadian sense of nation "is in many ways rooted in the federal government. . . . To weaken or dismantle it is to strike a blow at our identity."[44]

Political scientists, influenced by the preceding factors, displayed an almost total absence of desire to foster an English-Canadian nationalism and to clothe it in the garments of its own state. To have done so would have required a rejection of the dualist concept of Canada they had imbibed much more wholeheartedly than their predecessors, and would have involved, accordingly, not just the repudiation of a political theory but the shedding of an identity. It would have required Anglophones to accept the equation of French-speaking Canada with Quebec, and thus implicitly to have sanctioned the sacrifice of Francophone and Anglophone minorities outside of their areas of majority strength.[45] This disinclination to act as intellectual servants for the Anglophone side of dualism received additional fostering from the networks of connections and involvements many political scientists had with governments outside of Quebec, none of whom spoke for English Canada.

Finally, the physical location of Quebec, sandwiched between Ontario and the Atlantic provinces, made it difficult to visualize Canada-without-out-Quebec, given the assumption that the ideal-type nation-state is characterized by a territorial oneness. Indeed, Rotstein argues that English-Canadian nationalism, largely devoid of other supports for its Canadian identity, focuses on territorial integrity, what he calls "mappism," as its *raison d'être*.[46] Symbolically, this orientation clearly heightens the assault on the psychic integrity of Anglophone Canadians that territorial dismemberment would produce. Practically, the location of Quebec meant that its independence would pose many serious problems for the divided Canada that would be left behind.

If Quebec and Newfoundland had changed places, Canada-without-Quebec would have had a geographical cohesion that would have greatly facilitated Anglophone Canada having a sense of itself, both before and after the exit of a Quebec existing at the hither edge of eastern Canada. In such circumstances, the dynamics on both sides would have strengthened the forces of disintegration.

For Francophone social scientists, the postulation of an independent Quebec built on the reality of an existing, expansive government, and thus was a relatively straightforward intellectual exercise. The intellectual construction of an independent Quebec was further stimulated by the nationalist elite's tendency to shed the inhibiting concept of a French Canada extending beyond Quebec that could not easily be given a political expression.

For social scientists outside of Quebec, by contrast, the postulation of an autonomous self-governing Anglophone Canada required a leap of the imagination, an intellectual disentanglement from the known, that did not come easily. They were encouraged by their environment to fight a rearguard action to save a threatened constitutional order and the pan-Canadian nation it served. Thus, even those university-based intellectuals in English Canada who sympathized with the *indépendantiste* option were in general opposed to its realization.[47] For Anglophone Canada, what existed posed a conceptual and practical barrier to an autonomous political future. For Québécois *indépendantistes*, this was not the case.

Somewhat paradoxically, the intellectual and political weakness of the Parti Québécois case was its governing assumption that the Québécois nation it sought to build had a functional counterpart in an English-Canadian partner. The latter, one of "two distinct nations" concealed "behind the fiction of ten provinces,"[48] according to René Lévesque, was considered potentially amenable to the political division of the northern half of North America. No such counterpart existed. Thus, the Quebec appeals to the English-Canadian nation in the Beige Paper of the Quebec Liberal Party and in the sovereignty-association proposals of the Parti Québécois fell on deaf ears. They were addressed to a non-existent entity. Anglophone Canada, rendered internally heterogeneous by its ethnic and racial cleavages, and politically fragmented by its provincialism, was given a larger political expression only in the country-wide setting where its sense of self was blended into a Canadianism to which it contributed, but which also reflected the other side of duality.

These aspects of Anglophone Canada frustrated the possibility of a positive reception to the idea of a division of Canada into Quebec and the rest. The presence of so many factors militating against a distinctive, autonomous political existence for Anglophone Canada generated the resistance to an independent Quebec that culminated in the referendum defeat.

NEGLIGIBLE ATTENTION TO CANADA-WITHOUT-QUEBEC
In 1977 Charles Pentland described the absence of thought by "any party" to the nature of a prospective economic association between the rest of Canada and an independent Quebec as "remarkable."[49] Equally remarkable was a lack of attention paid by political scientists to more explicitly political and constitutional concerns – the functioning and constitutional shape of the one or more residual Canadas that would survive the accession of Quebec to independence.[50]

In part, of course, this inattention reflected the previously noted lack of desire for such an outcome. There were also fears that open canvassing of such a future might give sustenance to the other side and thus contribute to its unsought arrival. This explains why governments outside of Quebec "could not be seen to undertake such thinking of the unthinkable."[51] Yet, the fact remains that a victory for the "yes" side in the referendum was very plausible, and that might have set in motion a process leading to the breakup of Canada. In addition to the direct evidence that some political scientists considered the breakup of the country to be a distinct possibility,[52] the urgency that drove scholars to intervene presupposed that Canada, the object of their affectionate concern, was threatened. Further, both the Bilingualism and Biculturalism Royal Commission in its 1965 Preliminary Report and the later Report of the Task Force on Canadian Unity categorically informed Canadians that they lived in a country whose survival was problematic.

Accordingly, the relative absence of attention to Canada-without-Quebec cannot be explained as an appropriate neglect of a highly improbable outcome. Part of the explanation emerges from the experience of one economist, Dan Usher, who published an article on the prudential need for "those of us in the rest of Canada to plan for the reconstruction of our country without Quebec."[53] The barrage of criticisms that he received clearly indicated that the area was a minefield in which it was better not to tread.

Occasionally, it was suggested that the constitutional impasse might become so grievous and incapable of resolution that an amicable if unenthusiastic parting of the ways might be mutually advantageous.[54] The political philosopher David Braybrooke suggested with impeccable logic that if Quebec had the right to secede, the other nine provinces had an equal right to secede from Quebec, thus removing Quebec from a Confederation that it might not wish to leave.[55] However, these observations were only that – asides, or *obiter dicta*, not agenda for action, and not the occasion to outline the contours of the new state of Canada-without-Quebec.

The most serious attempt to come to grips with the "unthinkable," and how the process of disentanglement might develop, was in *Must Canada Fail?* The book sets out to describe for English-speaking Canadians the nature of the federal crisis, possible strategies for its resolution, and the "possibility of a Canada without Quebec."[56] However, the promised "thinking of the unthinkable" only occurs interstitially, halfheartedly, and defensively. Although the volume represents the most serious collective effort by English-Canadian academics to see the political future of the peoples north of the United States in forms other than the existing or a modified federal arrangement, and although it also contains numerous valuable *aperçus*, it did not succeed in thinking creatively and tenaciously about the long-run future of the separate political system(s) of English Canada that would survive Quebec's departure.[57] The fact that this major effort can be described as a valiant attempt, and yet one that fell seriously short of adequacy as any kind of guide for the citizens and elites who would have to reconstruct what a departing Quebec had shed, reveals the state of unpreparedness with which Canada outside of Quebec would have confronted its future should the referendum vote have been positive and sovereignty-association negotiations begun.[58]

The sense of isolation and marginality visited on those who depart from the official line, the intellectual dominance of inherited thought patterns that presupposed Quebec within Canada, and the emotional impediments that powerful sentimental attachment to the loved and the known posed to incisive thinking about a novel and unsought future – these all contributed to the paucity of analysis of a grave future situation English-speaking Canadians had a very good chance of facing. While the relative avoidance of "Canada-without-Quebec" as a research and publication focus is psychologically understandable and strategically comprehensible – in the desire not to aggravate a delicate situation – the overall conclusion is irresistible. The allocation of intellectual resources between the objective of saving Canada by constitutional reform and preparing for the possible failure of that reform effort was overwhelmingly biased toward the former. Had Canada broken up, to be replaced by a sovereignty-association link with Quebec or a less harmonious coexistence of two or more independent states, the successor generation would have found little guidance in the pre-referendum literature directed, with few exceptions, to the reform of a country that had ceased to exist.[59]

ALTERNATIVE REFORM ORIENTATIONS
AND CULTURAL LAG

Prior to the 1982 Constitution Act, prescriptions to salvage an historic constitutional system fell roughly into two omnibus categories, which disagreed on the nature of the sickness and thus on the medicine designed to cure it.[60]

In the Anglophone political science community, the dominant reform thrust defined the problem as the insensitivity of the federal government to a combination of sub-state nationalism in Quebec and an aggressive provincialism elsewhere, both of which were simultaneously reflected in and reinforced by the province-building of provincial government elites. The reform task, from this perspective, had two possibilities – the devolution of additional jurisdiction to the provincial governments that expressed what Pepin-Robarts called dualism and regionalism, or a reconstruction of federal government institutions to incorporate the provincial dimension more fully and visibly into the institutional arrangements of the centre. While most provincial governments saw the opening up of the constitution as an opportunity to expand or protect their jurisdiction, Anglophone political scientists were more likely to search for ways to strengthen the central government and/or the Canadian community on which it rested. Their preferred way of achieving these goals was by attaching that government more effectively to the provincial realities of Canadian existence.

A crucial assumption behind the reform thrust for a more provincially sensitive central government was bluntly stated by one of its major supporters in the assertion that "territorialism," which meant provincialism, "is the dominant circumstance of our political life."[61] Thus the centre could only be saved if its majoritarianism and pan-Canadianism were diluted by the incorporation of a provincial dimension into its decision-making.[62] "Federalizing," "regionalizing," or "provincializing" the centre became a commonplace of reform proposals derived from this political science analysis. These proposals, especially those that enhanced provincial government input in areas and arenas otherwise under exclusive or predominant central government control, were most attractive to provincial governments, especially in the West, had some support in the Conservative opposition party, and were never adhered to – except sporadically for tactical reasons – by the Trudeau government.

Another, competitive reform thrust defined the Canadian problem as a basic weakness in the citizen base of the constitutional order, as a deficient Canadianism that could be alleviated by a Charter of Rights stressing individual citizen membership in a pan-Canadian community. This approach, supplemented by the constitutional protection of official-language minority education rights, was at the heart of the federal government's constitutional policy throughout the Trudeau years. The Trudeau analysis disagreed fundamentally with the tendency of most Anglophone political scientists to accord primacy to society, defined in regional terms, to which a revised constitution was to adapt. For Trudeau, by contrast, the constitution was an immense lever that could be employed to reinforce the national dimension of Canadians' civic existence and thus strengthen the ultimate resource base of the national government, an allegiant citizenry oriented to Ottawa.

From Trudeau's perspective, the citizen base of the constitutional order was far more national and sympathetic to the federal government than was apparent in the rhetoric of provincial governments that stressed, and claimed to speak for, the provincial dimension of the citizens' existence. He saw an institutional blockage in the practice of executive federalism, and the exaggerated ambitions of provincial governments to which it led, that prevented the Canadian dimension of citizen identity from flowering. With appropriate incentives, such as a Charter and, in the 1980 constitutional proposals, an amending formula that would give the citizenry, via referenda, a deadlock-breaking role when governments were in disagreement on proposed amendments, Trudeau sought to strengthen the identity of and multiply the instruments available to a coast-to-coast community of rights-bearing Canadians. Although there was some sympathy for the Trudeau interpretation among political scientists,[63] the latter were much more likely to adopt an accommodative than a Trudeauite confrontational approach to provincialism, whether of provincial communities or of the provincial governments that claimed to speak for them. They were also less likely to see citizens as an appropriate constitutional counterweight to (especially provincial) governments.

Thus, in the first round of constitution-making, culminating in the 1982 Constitution Act, the basic political science reform thrust lost out to the very different reform orientation of the Prime Minister.[64] Indeed, the influence of all external "advice," from that of individual academics to that of the state-sponsored Task Force on Canadian Unity, was largely determined by its compatibility with the deeply held views of the Prime Minister about federalism and appropriate constitutional change. As a result, there is a sense in which political scientists saw themselves as having lost in 1982, a fact that helps to explain their striking lack of enthusiasm for the Constitution Act of that year.

The tendency of political scientists to see the constitution as an affair of governments, and its chief organizing or structural principle as federalism, deflected their attention from the appearance of new actors in the constitutional game. Political science students of the written constitution were primarily specialists in federalism, around which they had built up considerable intellectual capital. Partly owing to the dominance of lawyers in the study of constitutional law, and partly because political scientists had, as a group, paid little attention to the Diefenbaker Bill of Rights, they were ill-prepared to sympathize with the political role that Trudeau assigned to the Charter. Indeed, several of the most negative critiques of the Charter project were authored by political scientists.[65] Political scientists were not in the vanguard as Charter advocates, nor were they prominent among the spokespersons for aboriginals, women, third-force Canadians, and visible minorities who broke into the constitutional order in 1982. Subsequently, they tended to downplay the gains in constitutional recognition these groups achieved in 1982, and as a further result expressed limited sympathy for their frustration with the closed executive federalism that produced Meech Lake. Thus, eight of the twelve academics who signed a brief to the Special Joint Committee on the 1987 Constitutional Accord supportive of Meech Lake were political scientists. They grounded the credibility of their support in the fact that they all had "devoted much of their professional careers to the study of Canadian federalism,"[66] a background that encompasses a diminishing proportion of the post-1982 constitutional order and provides an insufficiently comprehensive perspective to make a rounded appraisal of a constitutional package such as Meech Lake.

The core analysis of Canadian constitutional discontents by political scientists explains their lack of impact on a Trudeau-led central government; makes comprehensible their lukewarm or negative attitude to the 1982 Constitution Act, especially the Charter; contributes to their tendency to support Meech Lake; and lies behind their relative lack of empathy for the latter's heterogeneous opponents. Many opponents sport constitutionalized identities, derived from the Charter, that are the legacy of Trudeau's constitutional vision.

It may be suggested, therefore, that there is some tendency for Anglophone political scientists to suffer from a cultural lag; their contemporary attitudes to the constitution appear to be unduly influenced by pre-Charter assumptions, when federalism and parliamentary government were still the dominant features of a constitutional order with nineteenth-century roots.

Conclusion

Five major observations are readily drawn from this brief analysis of the recent involvement of Anglophone political scientists in the constitutional debates.

(1) The extensive and variegated involvement of political scientists underlines their relative lack of detachment from their Canadian subject matter. The eagerness with which they participated suggests that their citizen identities are not easily separated from their academic roles. Further, the evident excitement and passion they displayed indicate that, in times of turmoil, confinement to the study in the pursuit of purely disciplinary questions is viewed as a pallid substitute for advising and interacting with the Prince.

(2) Political scientists were overwhelmingly committed to the survival of a Canada in which Quebec was a full and voluntary partner. They showed almost no desire to speak for Canadians outside of Quebec as an incipient nation, and they devoted negligible resources to the study of how such a Canada-without-Quebec would function if, despite their best efforts, Quebec's departure could not be prevented.

(3) Anglophone political scientists brought to constitutional discussions the core assumptions that had come to permeate their discipline's study of Canadian constitutional politics. They attributed great potency to the provincial/regional dimension of Canadian life and tended to explain the weakness of the central government as due to its relative incapacity to reflect and incorporate that dimension in its own workings. In general, they were not prominent as supporters of the Charter of Rights reform thrust that obsessively informed Ottawa's constitutional thinking from the late sixties to the entrenchment of the Charter.

(4) It is not possible to single out the specific impact of their contributions on constitutional change and constitutional thought. With a few important exceptions, they wielded words rather than power, and their voice was only one of many vying for attention. It was, however, an important voice. Political scientists had an intellectual capital that could be and was brought to bear on the subject of the multiple relations between citizens and states that was central to their discipline. Had the

terminology and analysis they had partly inherited and partly developed, in conjunction with the global community of political scientists, not existed, it is undeniable that the Canadian bout of constitutional introspection would have been seriously impoverished. In area after area – proportional representation, second chambers, federalism, judicial review, and consociational democracy, for example – they and others could turn to their bookshelves and thus locate the Canadian debate in rich and elaborate literatures.

(5) Answers to the obverse question, of the impact of the constitutional crisis on political science, are almost equally elusive. In part, this is because Meech Lake remains on the Canadian agenda as I write, and its fate is unclear. We cannot, therefore, yet look back on a finished episode of constitutional transformation beginning in the sixties and assess its lessons for the study of political life. At a minimum, however, Anglophone political scientists have been made aware of the fragility of an old political system that they can no longer assume is part of the natural order. Perhaps some of the innocence and optimism that come from living in the new world of space, plenty, and long freedom from invasion has been chastened. Tragedy has knocked at our door, and if it was kept temporarily at bay we now know that it will probably knock again and again. As a result, the basic premises from which we begin thinking about our country have decisively shifted. Contingency has displaced stability as the starting point.

Chapter Nine

Ritual, Taboo, and Bias in Constitutional Controversies in Canada, or Constitutional Talk Canadian Style

David Crombie, defining "the essential way in which we go about Constitution making," stated: "It does not involve some kind of ideological purity. It is not some kind of academic event flowing only from legal classrooms. It has to do with the blood and guts of the country."[1] Meech Lake "is supported by a veritable Who's Who of Canadian constitutional scholars in this country."[2] (David Daubney, MP)

It is an honour for many reasons to deliver the Mabel F. Timlin Lecture at the University of Saskatchewan. Professor Timlin was a distinguished academic who was influential in introducing Keynesian ideas into Canada. For our generation, she is an obvious role model for female academics making their way in university departments where they still constitute a minority. Further, the university, now as always, exists in an environment that is somewhat uncomprehending of and sometimes hostile to academic values. So, on occasions such as this, when we celebrate the career of a noted predecessor, we simultaneously underline our commitment to the academic vocation. We employ ritual in the service of reason.

I am particularly pleased to give this lecture against the backdrop of Mabel Timlin's scholarship because she was acutely sensitive to the influence of context and personal background on our capacity to understand the world outside our windows. In 1968, she wrote: "As one who was born in the United States and had the greater part of her education there, the writer is well aware of the number of years it takes before the newcomer can become fully cognizant of the deep cleavages in ideology which may underlie the superficial resemblances between the two societies." She went on to note that the presence in Canada of first-class foreign scholars enriched the Canadian social sciences, while expressing her concern that in some Canadian departments there were few "native-born Canadians" or "long-term residents" to socialize them into Canadian folkways.[3]

This lecture addresses a different aspect of the impediments to analysis and public understanding. I plan to explore, tentatively and incompletely, some of the difficulties that attend our efforts at constitutional introspection and dialogue, especially at times when major constitutional changes are on our agenda. My analysis and illustrations are drawn from the last three decades during which our annual GNCT (Gross National Constitutional Talk) has been surpassed by few if any members of the United Nations. Clearly, we have talked much. Have we also talked well and wisely?

Introduction

In its largest sense, the constitution makes fundamental and authoritative statements about who Canadians are as a people. This has always been the case, of course, but that role has become more explicit with the addition of the Charter to the constitutional order at a time when the Canadian population was becoming ethnically and racially more diverse.

As our British past becomes decreasingly relevant to our identity, Canadians have undergone massive bouts of constitutional introspection, have implemented, in the 1982 Constitution Act, the most extensive single package of constitutional reform since 1867, and now in 1989 are embroiled in a wrenching debate over the Meech Lake Accord to "bring Quebec back into the constitutional family." For several decades Canadians have been involved in a comprehensive search for the constitutional conditions under which their togetherness could fruitfully continue, failing which Canada's termination as a noble but failed experiment might have to be considered.

In the real world of comparative constitutional politics – do other governments and peoples handle such potentially explosive issues better? – Canada would rank as a modest success story. In the seventies, we faced the possible breakup of the country with civility and tolerance. We have brought new actors – women, aboriginals, third-force and visible minority Canadians, and others – into the constitution. We have added the Charter as a third major pillar to a constitutional order hitherto dominated by parliamentary government and federalism.

It is nevertheless self-evident that our recent constitutional journey is not universally viewed as a success story in which all are winners. The Constitution Act generated anger and resentment from the intellectual and political elites of Quebec for its failure to respond to their definition

200

of Quebec's constitutional aspirations. The Meech Lake Accord, the attempt to overcome the constitutional isolation of the Quebec government, whether it passes or falls by the wayside, will confirm that the relative absence of cheering in 1982 was not idiosyncratic.[4] Dark cries of betrayal, accusations of bad faith, vitriolic language, and threats have been constant companions as Canadians have sought the constitutional Jerusalem, which ever beckons but tantalizingly fades as we approach it.

A vast descriptive and prescriptive literature has accompanied the ebb and flow of public introspection that stretches across three decades of constitutional reform efforts. A flood of official inquiries and government position papers, a veritable Niagara of briefs and presentations before legislative committees, and the profusion of scholarly and not-so-scholarly constitutional analyses that fill our bookshelves confirm our facility with words. Such a plethora of material might appear to suggest that there is little chance of saying anything new, and that this generation of constitutional commentators can only be parasitical on what has gone before.

Somewhat paradoxically, however, it is the very mountain of material we have produced that stimulates the nagging, insistent questions about its quality. What systematic shortcomings and biases might strike the attentive reader of the massive body of published materials directed to the constitution? How good are Canadians at constitutional talk? Is our constitutional conversation shot through with lacunae to the detriment of our constitutional understanding? Do we have too much bullying and too little reasoning as we do battle over rival constitutional futures? In general, what are some of the obvious impediments to a high-quality Canadian constitutional discourse?

The answers to such questions do not come easily. The material is too vast for comprehension by a lone scholar. Further, it would not be easy to get agreement on what an ideal constitutional debate would look like. Inevitably, therefore, the analysis in the following pages will be somewhat impressionistic and idiosyncratic. In fact, the reader may conclude that my difficulties in grappling with my elusive subject confirm my thesis that there are major impediments to lucid, high-quality constitutional analysis. Be that as it may, the effort is worth making.

My perspective is, in a broad sense, sociological. That is, I am concerned with the social and institutional constraints and incentives that are operative. My subject matter is the public debate among governments and private actors over alternative constitutional futures. In general, I have excluded case-oriented legal analysis directed to influencing judicial interpretations of the constitution. My purpose is not to pass judgement on individuals or on particular contributions, but to tease out some of the factors that shape constitutional discussion in Canada. I have concentrated on three major impediments to an open, high-quality constitutional discourse. (1) Procedural disputes about the manner of employing the formal amending process deflect attention from the substance of proposed amendments and thus lower the extent and quality of the discussion they receive. (2) Some constitutional subject matters – two of which are examined below – are so sensitive and delicate that there is a virtual taboo on discussing them openly and honestly. (3) Discussion of particular constitutional clauses is often dominated or monopolized by the clientele whose self-interest is served by their favourable constitutional interpretation. These "insiders" do not welcome "outsiders" into their constitutional territory, especially if the analysis of the latter is hostile to the claims of the former.

Disagreement Over the Amending Process

Constitutional discussion, as is true of all structured political behaviour, is subject to various constraints. One set of constraints is broadly institutional, the most important of which deserves to be singled out.

Up until 1982, the absence of a comprehensive agreed-on domestic amendment procedure constantly deflected attention from the substance of proposed amendments to the process that should be employed in implementing them. It is now evident, as the Meech Lake drama unfolds, that the adoption of the 1982 Constitution Act, giving Canadians for the first time a comprehensive set of amending formulae that could be domestically applied without resort to the British Parliament, did not end the procedural disputes over who should participate in formal processes of constitutional change, and in what ways and with what power. Indeed, to look back over the past three decades is to receive depressing confirmation of the striking extent to which our constitutional talk and behaviour have focused on the process of constitutional amendment. Controversy over the appropriate criteria has surfaced not only when proposals for a domestic amending formula were explicitly on the agenda, but also as a by-product of attempts to generate constitutional amendments using the available machinery of the time.[5]

Major controversies recently erupted over what their employers thought were legitimate and legal amendment processes in 1978 (Bill C-60), in 1980-81 (the patriation resolution), and in 1987-89 (Meech Lake). In each of these cases, the governments that played the leading role – the federal government (1978), the federal government and its two allies of Ontario and New Brunswick (1980-81), and the eleven original governments that agreed to the Meech Lake package – asserted the constitutional propriety of the manner in which they sought constitutional change. In the first two cases, the interpretations of the governments advocating change were successfully challenged. Although the Meech Lake outcome remains unclear (i.e., as of November 13, 1989), the process has been bitterly criticized by most of the opponents of this reform package.

Much of the discussion of the federal government's proposed Bill C-60 in the late seventies focused on the constitutionality of the federal claim that what it sought to do in phase one of a two-stage reform process was clearly within the federal government power of unilateral amendment contained in Section 91 (1), which had been added to the BNA Act in 1949. When the federal government, responding to political pressures and informed legal reservations about the constitutionality of the proposed course of action, submitted a reference to the Supreme Court on the power of Parliament to alter or abolish the Senate, the Court answered in the negative.[6]

In 1980-81, the debate over what became the Constitution Act was also deflected from the substantive issues in the proposed resolution to the legal question of whether the federal government was within its constitutional powers in requesting, with support from only two provinces, the Parliament at Westminster to pass a major package of constitutional change. Ultimately, three provincial courts of appeal, in Manitoba, Quebec, and Newfoundland, passed judgement on the constitutionality of the federal government initiative, as did the Supreme Court. The latter's decision supported the legality of Ottawa's proposed action, seven to two, but nevertheless held (six to three) that a constitutional convention existed that required "a substantial degree of provincial consent" where the federal request concerned matters affecting federal-provincial relationships or provincial powers.[7] The Supreme Court decision induced the eleven governments to return to the bargaining table from which the 1982 Constitution Act emerged, without the support of the Quebec government.

In this episode, the deflection of extensive political effort into the judicial arena was supplemented by the efforts of federal and provincial governments, and aboriginal peoples, to influence public and official opinion in the United Kingdom should the federal government proceed with a unilateral request. The opponents of unilateralism argued that the British Parliament had a trusteeship role on behalf of the provincial governments that gave it a discretion it should exercise by either rejecting or delaying its response to such a federal government request. When, following the Supreme Court decision in the 1981 patriation reference, the federal and nine provincial governments struck an agreement that the British Parliament duly enacted as an amendment to the BNA Act, the government of Quebec then challenged the constitutionality of the action in the Quebec Court of Appeal and in the Supreme Court, and lost in both judicial arenas.[8]

Meech Lake is the latest example of how discussion of the proposed substance of constitutional change gets entangled with the process by which it is to be achieved. The amendment formulae incorporated in the Constitution Act, 1982 require authorizing resolutions by Parliament and provincial legislative assemblies. The plausible inference that this was to allow a limited degree of public participation that was more than ritual was not initially apparent to the eleven first ministers who signed the Meech Lake agreement. Those outside the charmed circle of executive federalism were confronted with a *fait accompli*, defined as "outsiders," and informed that their criticisms would be without effect unless they uncovered "egregious" errors, as defined by the "insiders." The role offered to the public in the federal government's *Strengthening the Canadian Federation* was to "explore the implications of the *Constitution Amendment, 1987* so it is well understood by everyone."[9] To the federal government, the role of citizen was to be a public relations cheerleader, in effect to join the monarchy as part of the dignified components of the constitution. Further, as Eugene Forsey noted, the federal government systematically failed to respond to criticisms, no matter how cogent they appeared to be.[10] The federal government produced no substantive position papers linking the particular means it recommended in the Accord to explicit constitutional purposes.[11] This stratagem deprived opponents of the Accord of the leverage that comes from detecting inconsistencies in official processes of reasoning. Finally, in an unseemly display of constitutional McCarthyism, opponents of the Accord were tarred with the brush of being anti-Quebec.

The Meech Lake controversy over process is the meeting point for a conflict between a tradition of government dominance in the amending process and an emerging Charter-influenced constitutional culture. The leadership role of governments in formal constitutional change was evident at Confederation and throughout the next century. The debates that occurred in our first century swirled around the issue of which governments – British, federal, or provincial – should play what roles in constitutional change. The debate over the British role was clearly an affair of governments concerning the manner and pace of devolving the amending capacity from the British government to some combination of federal and provincial governments in Canada. Further, as long as the written constitution was conceived primarily as an instrument of federalism, which in turn could also be viewed as an affair of governments, the latter's dominance of the domestic component of the amending process appeared natural. Accordingly, given this background, it is not surprising that the elected office-holders of Canadian federalism came to view their leadership role in formal constitutional change as entirely natural and appropriate. It was seen as little more than a confirmation of the standard executive dominance in British systems of responsible government and the related dominance of governments in the executive federalism arena of intergovernmental policy-making. By the late eighties, however, the playing out of this tradition was no longer unchallenged.

The Charter, by giving rights to citizens and by handing out particular constitutional niches to particular categories of Canadians, such as women, aboriginals, and ethnic and visible minorities, implicitly suggests some citizen role in constitutional change, a suggestion given at least mild support by the new Constitution Act requirements that legislative ratification is necessary before intergovernmental agreements can become constitutional law. Where that requirement has led to legislative hearings – in Parliament, separately in the Senate, in Ontario, in New Brunswick, and in task force hearings in Manitoba – numerous citizen groups have vehemently challenged the Meech Lake process as incompatible with the kind of constitutional people Canadians are becoming under the influence of the Charter. To simplify only slightly, the Meech Lake controversy underlines a conflict between the "Governments' constitution," focusing on federalism and reflecting the formal monopoly of governments in the amending process, and a "Citizens' constitution" derived from the Charter and the new constitutional status and identities that it gives to Canadians in general, and to racial minorities, the disabled, official-language minorities, and others in explicit terms.[12] While the conflict ultimately focuses on the amending formula, its larger message is that Canadians and their governments profoundly disagree on what is central and what is secondary in their constitutional existence. As a result, constitutional discussion does not take place within a framework of shared assumptions but founders on the disharmonious coexistence of divergent first principles.

A crucial factor, accordingly, with a significant negative effect on the quality of constitutional discourse in Canada is the recurring disagreement over the criteria that should govern formal constitutional change, both in determining who the legitimate participants should be and in defining what the relationships of power and influence among them should be. In an evolutionary sequence, these controversies have included the relative roles of the United Kingdom government and governments in Canada, the relative roles of the federal and provincial governments, and, most recently, and somewhat implicitly, the relative roles of citizens and governments. As Robert Vipond has cogently argued, at base these are debates about the locus of sovereignty in Canada.[13] The emergence of the Charter and the bitter Meech Lake controversy suggest that in the near future the sovereignty issue, too long avoided, will be discussed on its own terms rather than as an appendage to substantive constitutional proposals.

Historically, disagreement over procedures has unquestionably seriously damaged the quality of substantive constitutional debate. Thus, some provincial government opponents of the Charter found it easier to criticize the unilateral process by which it was to be achieved than to debate its merits. Further, attacks on the narrow legality or the broader constitutionality of a particular amending process affix a taint of illegitimacy to the outcome it produces. One strategic purpose thus served is to strengthen the claim for compensatory treatment in the next constitutional round. This was clearly evident in the successful effort of successive Quebec governments to define the 1980-82 process and outcome as illegitimate, and for the Bourassa government to employ that definition as a potent bargaining chip for what became the Meech Lake round. Similar calculations unquestionably underlie the vehement objections of many of the Meech Lake opponents.

Criticism of the fairness of a decision-making process is a standard tactic of losers in all policy areas. In the constitution-making process in Canada, however, especially in recent decades, such criticisms are simultaneously remarkably pervasive, unusually acerbic, and profoundly damaging to the quality of constitutional discourse. Debates over the substance of amendments get sidetracked into debates over the legitimacy of the process being employed. While the latter debate deals with a major constitutional issue, it, too, is often poorly conducted because it emerges as a by-product of efforts to delegitimate one or another constitutional package or, as in Meech Lake, as a diffuse sense of outrage unaccompanied by suggestions for reform of the amendment process. The quality of Canadian constitutional discourse will continue to suffer as long as the formal and informal processes of constitutional amendment are viewed as illegitimate by one or more of the major public or private interests possessed of a significant stake in the constitution.

Taboo Subjects

The Canadian debate over alternative constitutional futures was remarkably open. Indeed, especially from the 1976 Parti Québécois victory to the 1980 referendum, the political behaviour of Canadians deserves high praise for the civility with which the possible breakup of the country was discussed. It is nevertheless true that the overall constitutional debate was subject to implicit constraints that tended to rule certain subjects or orientations out of bounds. Two of these taboo subjects, Canada-without-Quebec and the viability and potential of aboriginal self-government as an effective response to the myriad problems of aboriginal peoples, deserve a brief examination.

In each case, definitions of what should not be publicly said or written appear to have been widely shared. Further, although governing elites no less than outside academic commentators were party to these taboos, the former did not overtly dictate their observance to the latter. Rather, both those wielding official state power and subject to electoral pressures and the professoriate wielding tenure appear to have viewed the world from the same vantage point. We may assume, therefore, the existence of political/cultural norms that limited the oral and written contributions of both groups. The inevitable result of such constraints is to impoverish our understanding of the subject matters that are relatively cocooned from public examination.

CANADA-WITHOUT-QUEBEC

In the period leading up to the Quebec referendum, no serious, focused discussion took place of the constitutional structure, institutional arrangements, etc., of the one or more Canadas that would have survived Quebec's departure.[14] Clearly, this inattention was not based on the belief that an independent Quebec was such a slim possibility that it would be irrational to allocate intellectual resources to the examination of its consequences for other Canadians, nor did the inattention come from a belief that a separated Quebec would cause no more than a mild spasm of indigestion should it happen. On the contrary, the possible breakup of the country was widely considered to be a serious and threatening possibility. It logically follows, therefore, that a different referendum outcome and the different dynamism of events to which that might have led would have left Anglophone Canadians ill-prepared for a future they had tried to avoid. The explanations for the absence of analysis and prescription directed to Canada-without-Quebec, accordingly, are to be found neither in the thesis that its future existence was inconceivable nor in the position that its parturition would be a form of natural childbirth requiring no advanced political/constitutional technology.

An important part of the explanation was that Canada-without-Quebec, or Anglophone Canada, has no sense of itself. It is headless. No political elites have the roles and authority to speak on its behalf. The governing structure of federalism either provincializes English-speaking Canada into nine distinct communities, each of whose governments can only speak for a territorially delimited segment of the Anglophone population, or links it to a federal government for which English-speaking Canada is only one of the two official-language communities whose interests the federal government must express. The Anglophone Quebec community is particularly voiceless as the ideology of Quebec as a French state extends its sway. Further, the galloping ethnic heterogeneity of English-speaking Canada, especially in recent decades, erodes the unity that yesterday's British Canada derived from its historic links with the mother country.

All of these factors limit the capacity of Anglophone Canadians to see themselves as the functional counterpart of a Québécois nation tied to an aggressive provincial government that can articulate the constitutional concerns of the 80 per cent of Francophone Canadians who live in the province. As Latouche observes, the "frame of reference" for English Canadians is not English Canada but "an undifferentiated Canada."[15] Thus academic and other commentators outside Quebec did not see themselves as spokespersons for an English-Canadian nation seeking or needing the garments of statehood for its fulfilment. Also, no government, federal or provincial, saw itself as a servant of that ambition. Outside Quebec, the efforts of governments and constitutional commentators in the pre-referendum period were devoted to healing a wounded polity, not to separating the partners in a soured marriage.

Given the opposition of governments and most commentators outside Quebec to the breakup of Canada, obvious strategic considerations additionally channelled the debate in Anglophone Canada. The adversarial structuring of the debate pitted a Quebec elite seeking to take its province and people out of Canada against a pan-Canadian elite that sought to keep Quebec in. The political requirements of the debate on the Canadian side, accordingly, were to portray the disadvantages or unattainability of sovereignty-association or independence to Quebec, and conversely the advantages of staying within a suitably reformed Canadian constitutional framework. Neither of these goals would be served by examining how a Canada-without-Quebec might function, and even less by any indication that such a Canada might, on some grounds, be preferred. Indeed, the public examination of Canada-without-Quebec might appear to legitimate an outcome that English-speaking Canadians did not seek. While this constraint was most evident in the behaviour of incumbent politicians in Ottawa and the provinces other than Quebec, it also, to only a slightly lesser extent, constrained the constitutional analysis and prescriptions of the Anglophone academic community.

The considerations that led governments and academics in English Canada to focus the overwhelming bulk of their efforts on preventing the breakup of Canada rather than coolly preparing for such a possibility were not, of course, narrowly instrumental. The civic identity and patriotism of English-speaking Canadians were bound up in the Canada that was threatened by Quebec's possible departure. For those outside of Quebec to question Canada's continuity was to break a taboo. The historic Canadian nation-state was part of the given for Anglophone Canadians. It was not a disposable container but a crucial component of their self-definition and of a sense of belonging.

For its believers there are always elements of the sacred attached to a nation-state. And the sacred is not to be approached casually or in a purely calculating fashion. Thus, when one economist suggested that simple prudence required "those of us in the rest of Canada to plan for the reconstruction of our country without Quebec,"[16] he was reproved by a senior British Columbia civil servant who argued that the possibility of Canada breaking up was remote, and would be even more so "if governments and scholars would concentrate their energies on positive changes to the current federal system."[17] This was, to say the least, a somewhat bizarre criticism given the fact that in this period needles in haystacks are easier to find than are either official or scholarly explorations of the future of what Quebec might leave behind.

While a few authors gingerly and tentatively broached the possibility of Canada-without-Quebec, they were distinctly in the minority, and often they were overtly uncomfortable about what they were doing.[18] They did not succeed in hard, creative thinking about the constitutional structure of the one or more countries that might emerge from the nine provinces, shattered central government, and two territories left behind by a departing Quebec.

Thus, to conclude this discussion: a potentially traumatic and not improbable outcome for Anglophone Canada received scant attention from governments or scholarly analysts. A degree of attention appropriate to the probability and seriousness of such an outcome would have violated a taboo and encroached on the sacred,[19] as well as possibly increasing the likelihood of its happening.

ABORIGINAL SELF-GOVERNMENT

A second constitutional policy area affected by a taboo was aboriginal self-government.[20] The minefields that threaten to blow up or derail the unwary traveller in this policy area are too numerous for comfort.[21] The issue acquired prominence because Section 37 of the Constitution Act, 1982 (as amended) required the holding of a series of constitutional conferences, with the participation of aboriginal representatives, to discuss "constitutional matters that directly affect the aboriginal peoples of Canada, including the identification and definition of the rights of those people to be included in the Constitution of Canada." As the conferences proceeded, attention was concentrated on the self-government issue. In total, four constitutional conferences were held, three of which focused on the issue of self-government. In addition, a small body of political and academic literature emerged to explore aboriginal self-government. The difficulties and inhibitions that attend the making of effective aboriginal constitutional policy are clearly revealed in the literature and in the constitutional discussions between aboriginal leaders and the political leaders of the governments of Canadian federalism.[22]

Much of the difficulty in discussing self-government at such an abstract level was due to the inherent complexity of the subject matter, especially its application to the large and growing aboriginal population that lacked a land base. These difficulties, however, were compounded by what can only be described as a taboo that constrained many non-aboriginal participants from honestly communicating some of their concerns to aboriginal leaders. For example, Douglas Sanders, one of the country's leading legal students of Indian affairs, recently referred to the "reality, which none of the politicians has been frank enough to admit ... that self government has no content for non-status Indians and most Métis. It can only be given content if special lands are set aside for those populations," the prospects of which are less than minimal.[23] The most exhaustive analysis of the Section 37 constitutional process, produced by a participant, described the level of discussion as uninspiring, claimed that at the "preparatory stages" there was "an almost total failure to engage in serious discussions of the legal and policy details associated with self-government,"[24] and attributed a lack of candour to non-aboriginal politicians. One researcher noted explicitly a problem inherent in the taboo: "Some of those who do have ideas are guarded about sharing them with the public. No politician wants to appear reactionary: sincere and sometimes reasonable concerns about enhancing the various rights of aboriginal peoples tend to be left unvoiced."[25] Another researcher observed that the central question of the financing of aboriginal self-government had been "studiously avoided, for the most part," by the participants in the constitutional negotiations.[26]

Similar inhibitions are present in academic commentary. In several cases, non-aboriginal scholars displayed considerable discomfort when their analysis appeared to be leading them to conclusions that did not seem supportive of aboriginal claims or constitutional demands. Negative assessments were resisted on the grounds that it was not for "outsiders" but only for aboriginals to draw such conclusions. In an article pointing out some of the pitfalls that may attend self-government, two authors asserted that "we are not taking a position on the desirability of Indian government. We are merely pointing out problems of which the architects of Indian government will have to be cognizant. It is for the Indian people, not non-Indian academics like ourselves, to weigh the advantages and problems of Indian government and decide on its acceptability."[27] Non-aboriginal authors seek not to be misunderstood politically, for they fear inclusion in a "reactionary" camp.[28]

Given these restraints and hesitations that impede scholarly inquiry, it is perhaps not surprising that much of the literature on aboriginal self-government is a lament for the absence of rigorous analysis. A leading anthropological student of Indian policy, Sally Weaver, recently observed: "I think the notion of Indian government at the moment remains essentially at the level of a 'value-notion.' It is as yet an unarticulated, vaguely conceptualized ideology or philosophy."[29] Two other students described the aboriginal self-government literature as "rich in eloquent rhetoric and philosophy but largely lacking in rigorous analysis and specific, concrete proposals."[30] A volume on *Public Administration Questions Relating to Aboriginal Self-Government*, published in 1987 when the constitutional process was winding down, commenced with the prefatory statement that little had been written "to date" on such issues, which were crucial to the viability of self-government.[31]

These illustrations of the apparently very weak quality of the political discussions on constitutionalizing aboriginal self-government and of the major gaps in the published literature suggest the existence of cues, incentives, and disincentives coming from the larger political, cultural, and intellectual environments that threaten the integrity of political discourse and intellectual exchanges between aboriginals and non-aboriginals, especially when they focus on large constitutional principles. Particularly at this level, "Politicians cannot oppose aboriginal issues publicly in Canada."[32] For academics, according to a recent analysis of the politics of aboriginal studies, high costs may follow any "deviation from the generally sympathetic orientation towards native rights."[33]

Self-evidently, such constraints are not conducive to honest discussion of aboriginal constitutional policy, whether contributed by academics in treatises or by politicians before inquisitive television cameras. These constraints are informed by the varied domestic and international currents shaping the climate of opinion that attaches to the contemporary discussion of aboriginal and racial issues.

Now, as in the past, domestic discussion of aboriginal policies is powerfully influenced by the international environment. The post-World War Two replacement of an international system in which European empires controlled much of the globe and of mankind by a successor multiracial international system in which most of the independent states in the United Nations are former colonies of European powers has transformed the internal Canadian debate. The former international climate was consonant with and supportive of a military-style Indian Affairs Branch administering wards being eternally prepared for civilization, and thus was hostile to ideas of self-government. The successor era redefines the situation, especially of status Indians, as one of internal colonialism, for which the external analogy elicits the obvious response of some form of independence or self-government.[34] The natural tendency of aboriginal political elites to assert the latter as a right is hostile to practical concerns about viability.

The replacement of the wardship concept by ideas of rights, equality, and self-government is a major political advance, with its positive evaluation of aboriginal peoples. For aboriginal elites, observing the explosion of Third World non-Western peoples onto the global stage and reconstructing their own peoples' pre-contact past, the rhetoric of sovereignty, the language of nationhood, and the self-descriptive label of "First Nations" are emotionally satisfying and status-raising. For peoples who see their recent past as one of degradation and poverty, such language is profoundly dignifying.

However, the translation of this language into functional institutional arrangements is not easy. Indeed, the language does not facilitate down-to-earth analysis and may even impede its translation into workable structures. The language of nationalism does not make easy contact with the reality that most of the political units for which self-government is possible have the population of small villages. The status Indian population is scattered in 578 bands across the country. In terms of 1981 figures, about 22 per cent of the population are in bands of less than 500 members, more than half of the population in bands with less than 1,000 population, and there are only eight bands with more than 3,000 population. In terms of bands, 370 of 578 had less than 500 population and

486 had less than 1,000 population. These figures must be further reduced by the extensive off-reserve migration, which constitutes slightly under one-third of the total population. On the other hand, demographic growth will increase the average band size in coming decades.[35]

Thus, the First Nation governments described by the Penner Report,[36] which are to have the potential of wielding jurisdiction over a variable range of matters now the responsibility of federal and provincial governments, will in fact be the governments of small struggling villages. In most cases, they have limited economic bases, high unemployment levels, negligible revenue-raising capacity combined with an historic antipathy to self-taxation, and a relative absence of the professional personnel that local government administration will require. Further, even this limited potential self-government has almost no applicability to most of the aboriginal population, especially Métis and non-status Indians, who live off reserves and thus have no land base.[37]

The hesitations and inabilities of politicians to say what they think when aboriginal issues enter the constitutional arena, and the tendency of academics to conceal their private doubts because of a desire to be on the "right" side of the self-government issue, when it is viewed as a matter of principle, have historical roots. The unimpressive history of Indian administration and the failure of recent efforts to repudiate that legacy have left contemporary politicians and students with little firm ground on which to stand. In its "Statement of the Government of Canada on Indian Policy," tabled in the House of Commons in 1969, the federal government recommended, in effect, the termination of Indian status with the unavoidable exception of residual treaty rights, the rapid phasing out of specialized Indian administration, the repeal of the Indian Act, and the assimilation of status Indians as individuals into Canadian society, where they were to receive the same services as other Canadians from the same government agencies. A few short years later, the federal proposal had been shelved, defeated by the organized objections of Indians. Since that time it is only a slight exaggeration to describe Indian policy as a stalemate. Gibbins and Ponting portray the seventies as "a period of *turmoil and floundering*."[38] This stalemate weakens the capacity and will of non-aboriginals to play a leadership role in determining the means and ends of policy for status Indians, or more generally for the aboriginal population, and thus makes them more receptive to proposals emanating from the aboriginal people themselves.

Past efforts are perceived to have failed. The depressing litany of social indicators of profound malaise in aboriginal communities – from suicides to excessively high unemployment rates – constitutes a standing reproach to past and still surviving policies. This fact gives the advocates of change a decisive edge over the defenders of the status quo, a category virtually devoid of members.[39] It also accounts for a tendency for academics to replace objectivity by zealotry when studying aboriginal issues. According to Schwartz, "an academic may be so sincerely outraged by the injustice that has been done to aboriginal groups that he or she loses the ability to rationally and fairly assess the merits of differing evaluations of the past or proposals for the future."[40]

The failure of past policies, the colonial analogy, and the extraordinary sensitivity that attends policy areas where race is involved combine to lower the quality of policy discussion and discourage egalitarian discourse when aboriginal issues are discussed from constitutional perspectives. For scholars there is a "subtle, though not imperceptible, pressure to come down on the 'right' side of [aboriginal] issue[s] – to be 'politically correct.' "[41] Under the guise of deference or sensitivity, perhaps motivated by a sense of guilt, such constraints lead to the concealment of negative information, sustain a form of paternalism that resists treating aboriginal leaders as equals, and reduce the likelihood that aboriginal constitutional policies will be efficacious.

In these circumstances, the attempt to entrench a right to self-government in the constitution for aboriginal peoples may have been misconceived. The diverse conditions and peoples to which such a right might apply virtually deprived the concept of any clear operational meaning. The focus on rights fostered a discussion that raised all the big issues and fundamental principles at a level of abstraction, hence encouraging rhetoric on one side and obfuscation on the other. The suggestion by Cassidy and Bish that a bottom-up approach at the local level, concentrating on practical details of Indian government, might be a more profitable route deserves serious consideration.[42] Logically, it is far more likely to generate realistic and honest discussions and serious bargaining than thus far has occurred at the constitutional level, where principles dominate.

Insiders and Outsiders

Inadequate attention has been paid to the unequal distribution of the "right" to speak or write on particular constitutional matters. From a sociological or political perspective, it is evident that the constitution is not viewed as an undifferentiated whole, all of whose parts are equally available to any would-be constitutional discussant for public analysis or commentary. Rather, especially with respect to the Charter, different constitutional themes and clauses are deemed to be of special concern to particular groups who, usually from an advocacy perspective, play a leading role when constitutional discussion turns to them.

This is, no doubt, perfectly understandable when constitutional lobbying takes place, when the advocates of feminist, aboriginal, official-language minority, multicultural, visible minority, and other particularistic perspectives appear before legislative committees to nudge constitutional change in preferred directions. These groups, in competition with each other and with governments, struggle to have their interpretations prevail in times of constitutional uncertainty. Given the constitutional politics of self-interested behaviour, the absence of such a pattern of representational activity would be abnormal. It extends, however, into volumes of academic constitutional commentary – ostensibly more dispassionate – that also display a marked tendency to give to authors who identify with a particular constitutional interest, or who share the characteristics of its clientele, the chapters dealing with that clientele's constitutional concerns. Again, this is scarcely surprising, as the constitutional involvement of particular groups generates in their elites and academic sympathizers an intimate and empathic understanding of their constitutional concerns that others are unlikely to possess. Particular patterns of the distribution of constitutional scholarship across the cleavage lines of Canadian society are thus partly to be explained as by-products of prior political involvements and the competence thus built up. They may also, of course, simply represent a "natural" distribution of interests that, for example, attracts women to Section 28 studies and third-force Canadians to Section 27 of the Charter.

The pattern, in any event, is clear. Academic constitutional analysis is highly sensitive to representational considerations, especially for issues pertaining to gender, race, ethnicity, and language. In collections of essays devoted to a range of constitutional concerns, the chapters on the women's movement, on Section 28 of the Charter, or on the sex equality guarantees in Section 15 will almost invariably be written by women, a gender correlation between authors and subjects that is generally true of feminist scholarship.[43] In the subsection on "Women" in a recent "Equality Rights" bibliography almost four-fifths of the eighty-four publications written by named individuals were by women.[44] While the authors of the literature focusing on the aspirations, triumphs, and constitutional defeats of aboriginals have a more eclectic background, the explanation partly resides in the limited representation of aboriginals in university departments. The pattern, nevertheless, is clearly present in volumes touching on aboriginal constitutional claims. About half of the more than forty articles in *Pathways to Self-Determination* and *The Quest for Justice: Aboriginal Peoples and Aboriginal Rights*, appear to have been written by aboriginals.[45] An analogous practice is to accord chapters on Quebec to Francophone Quebecers.[46]

These distributional characteristics of authors generate the concept of the "intruder," someone who has either blundered into constitutional realms viewed as the property of others, or who has been insufficiently diffident or hesitant, or who has not been cleared by those whose legitimacy is unquestioned.

These political, academic tendencies are manifestations of the recurrent academic debate, brilliantly analysed by Robert K. Merton, of whether "insiders" or "outsiders" should be considered privileged bearers of insight and truth.[47] Insiders are members of the group that is being examined or that is making claims; outsiders, by contrast, are not part of the culture of emotional ties, affinities, and understandings that come from introspection and lived experience. The standard insider argument, that one has to "be one to understand one" and that no third party can acquire the intimate knowledge only insider status brings, is countered by the outsider claim – the claim of the stranger to see more clearly precisely because he or she is not affected by the passions of the moment, by the bias that comes from belonging, or by "the corrupting influence of group loyalties upon the human understanding."[48]

The opening up of the constitution, via the Charter, brings new social movements into the constitutional arena, distributes constitutional identities to numerous categories of Canadians, and stimulates insider claims. These movements, organized around such solidarities as race, ethnicity, gender, language, nationhood claims, and sexual orientation, seek to enhance the group consciousness and self-confidence of their members. As Katherine Swinton notes, at least in the short run, the Charter "reinforce[s] concepts of community based on shared characteristics such as race, sex or handicap, that transcend provincial boundaries."[49]

As the constitution, by means of the Charter (and, prospectively, under the Meech Lake interpretation clause), makes official statements about the relative status and public recognition of the groups it differentially mentions, these groups have gotten involved in constitutional change to protect or enhance their place in the constitution. There is now, for example, an explicit ethnic constitutional discourse within which French and English founding peoples, the older third-force European communities, aboriginal peoples, and visible minorities do battle with each other in the constitutional arena to protect or advance their ranking on the ethnic constitutional ladder.[50] A specialized sub-discourse focuses on the claims of aboriginals as a distinctive category seeking to enhance their status vis-à-vis other Canadians, and is also the vehicle by which the more disadvantaged aboriginals, such as the Métis, strive for some of the recognitions and perquisites that attach to their status aboriginal brethren. For the Métis, the use of the constitution as a resource was greatly enhanced by their inclusion in Section 35 of the Constitution Act, 1982 as one of the "aboriginal peoples of Canada." Finally, a sophisticated feminist constitutional discourse is articulated by various feminist groups that monitor, *inter alia*, constitutional developments in judicial arenas and in proposed packages of constitutional amendments.[51] The nature of these groups, most of them organized around ascribed status and thus closed to outsiders, along with the political pressures requiring leaders to be representative of the group's defining characteristics, weaken the perceived legitimacy of outsider commentary, especially of a critical nature.[52]

The general thesis is that knowledge and understanding not derived from existential membership in the group concerned are unreliable because of their source. The attempted denial of the participation rights of outsiders or their downgrading is not a trivial matter that only operates at the margin of constitutional discussions. In the period of the most intense nationalism leading up to the referendum in Quebec, the assumption took hold that it was for Québécois to decide their future, and that outside commentary seeming to verge on advice was somehow impertinent. Hence, those provincial premiers who spoke in Quebec in the referendum debate did so somewhat apologetically, as if it was not also their country whose future might be determined by the unfolding debate in which they hesitatingly participated, and as if they were not talking to fellow Canadians. The clear implication was that the people of Quebec were being consulted in their capacity as Québécois, not in their civic capacity as Canadians.

An even more remarkable example of insider pressure was the attempt by Premier Lévesque to denigrate Prime Minister Trudeau's credentials in the referendum debate on the grounds that his mother was Scottish.[53] Precisely the same insider assumption lay behind the recurrent suggestion that a referendum defeat occasioned by the votes of the 20 per cent non-Francophone minorities in Quebec would lack credibility if the "true Quebecers," defined by blood and history and with roots going back to the Conquest, had by a majority voted "yes."

The insider phenomenon, therefore, is pervasive, comes in many guises, and will not disappear.[54] It has significant constitutional consequences.

The original BNA Act, with its focus on federalism, generated competing visions of the appropriate roles of federal and provincial governments and backed these visions by the organizational clout of governments and the intellectual resources they could muster. Analogously, particular Charter clauses are backed by organizations that muster professional expertise in their defence. The elites of these organizations have a proprietary attitude toward the clauses of particular concern to them. Their clauses were "won" by their predecessors in battles only a few short years ago, battles that have become part of the folk memory of the groups concerned, a memory nourished and wielded as a resource in the next round of battles.[55]

These groups tend to view themselves as minorities, marginalized and victimized. "Women's lives," for example, according to a recent feminist analysis, "are characterized by a lack of control over all the conditions of their lives, over their bodies, their sexuality, their homes, and their workplaces. They are devalued as human beings and exploited as workers, and they lack power in the institutions that govern them."[56] From this perspective, Canadian society is viewed as "a very well designed, finely tuned affirmative action program for white, temporarily able-bodied men."[57] Given such a pattern of belief, the constitution is viewed as a weapon or a resource, and the scholarship of interest groups is purpose-driven and laced with advocacy.

While analogies, especially highly imperfect ones, are among the weakest forms of analysis, it nevertheless helps our understanding to assert that the relationship of the feminist movement to Section 28, and to sex equality rights in Section 15, and of multicultural groups to Section 27, and so on, bear striking resemblances to the relationships of provincial governments to Section 92 of the BNA Act, "Exclusive Powers of Provincial Legislatures." In each case, intellect and organization are mobilized for the defence and enhancement of constitutional positions. In the same way as provincial governments argued the compact theory to provide historical legitimacy to their subsequent constitutional demands, women's groups wield the historical background to Section 28 to support their claim that it was intended to overcome the historical disadvantages of women, not merely, as its language suggests, to support the formal equality of "male and female persons" vis-à-vis each other.[58] And, in the same way that Premier Oliver Mowat of Ontario advanced the cause of provincialism before the Judicial Committee of the Privy Council in the nineteenth century, "increased proactive strategic litigation by women" is recommended in a recent study "if women are to make positive gains. Women's voices need to be heard more often in more courtrooms."[59]

The difference between where we are now and pre-Charter days, accordingly, is not in the existence of constitutional competition between organized power groups, nor in the stratagems they employ, but in the greater pluralism of the interests that are now organized for constitutional pursuits. Further, the new interests are private, although often government-funded, and unlike governments they relate to the constitution not through federalism but through the Charter.[60]

Constitutional evolution, accordingly, is partly driven by an organized pluralism of public (government) and private interests. While there are tremendous variations in the resources they have at their disposal, they all tend to see the constitution through the lens of self-interest and concentrate on the constitutional clauses of particular concern to them. They generate most of the messages about the constitution that are transmitted to the citizenry.

The more overt processes of constitutional politics do not leave the academic community untouched. There is an extensive intermingling of the academic and political spheres. There was, for example, considerable coming and going between government and the academy in the period of constitutional introspection from the sixties to the eighties. The involvement, peripheral or central, that political scientists and lawyers have often enjoyed as leading actors in intergovernmental affairs units or as more intermittent members of the various advisory groups that flourished had the virtue of informing many scholars of how the real world of constitutional politics departed from their textbook understandings. This clear gain, however, comes at the potential cost of role ambiguity. Academic analysis may be knowingly or unconsciously influenced by a prior, ongoing, or prospective linkage with one or more of the government actors involved. An analogous problem exists for the many academic constitutional experts involved in consultative relationships with the proliferating constitutional pressure groups stimulated by the wide-open constitutional agenda of recent decades. Both scholars and readers of their work need to be more aware of the cross-pressures to which these overlapping roles can lead, and of the extent to which a diminished objectivity among scholars may have to be set against the gain in understanding acquired from participation.

To condemn the public involvement of scholars in constitutional matters on the ground that it may consciously or unconsciously damage their objectivity is akin to bewailing the law of gravity, a childish attempt to deny the inevitable. Further, like the law of gravity, scholarly involvement brings important benefits in its wake, both to the quality of constitutional policy-making and to the enhanced understanding that constitutional participation brings to scholarship. Further, the various private groups involved in constitutional affairs lack the in-house resources that governments routinely enjoy, and thus they could not compete effectively with the big battalions of government if they were deprived of enriching contact with the academic community. Such academic involvement with private groups weakens the domination that governments would otherwise enjoy in constitutional politics.

Nevertheless, if I may identify one more taboo, or at least inhibition, it is that of discussing the costs to objectivity and the role ambiguity that political involvement may bring to scholarship, and this needs to be breached. The assessment by Bryan Schwartz of the factors that distort scholarly criticism of the aboriginal reform process is of general application. He identified "One factor . . . [as] . . . the existence or prospect of a professional association with one of the political organizations involved in the reform process. Many academics acquire their knowledge of the process from first-hand participation in aboriginal matters as paid consultants to aboriginal organizations or governments. When writing or speaking in the academic mode, we do not always succeed in detaching ourselves from the self-persuasion or political sympathy that arises from an advocacy role. The desire to remain popular with current or potential clients may also colour attempts at independent and forthright criticism." [61] The validity of Schwartz's concern cannot be gainsaid by any constitutional scholar who has observed both his own behaviour and that of his colleagues.

The tendency to "insiderism" also needs to be resisted in scholarly literature. Tocqueville suggested, with some justification, that "there are certain truths which Americans can only learn from strangers." [62] Also, it should not be forgotten that Gunnar Myrdal was deliberately selected as an outsider to do the research that led to the classic *An American Dilemma*.[63] Without suggesting that we have a large untapped supply of Tocquevilles and Myrdals, it remains true that we need more outsiders involved in research and publication on many of the emerging constitutional focuses generated by the Charter and by the politicization of the aboriginal peoples of Canada. Otherwise we risk relative monopolies of constitutional interpretation that suppress the creative dialectic of opposing views on which our constitutional understanding feeds. Further, the tendency for insiders to concentrate on particular constitutional clauses also needs to be counterbalanced by a scholarship that is concerned for the whole, an orientation that outsiders are more likely to provide. The constitution must be analysed and understood as more than a political market within which rival armies clash.

Both insiders and outsiders, as Merton notes, have their special strengths as agents of inquiry and understanding.[64] The tensions between them are creative. They educate each other. The policy objective is to prevent one orientation from defeating the other. We need, in other words, intellectual checks and balances in constitutional scholarship. Since a shortage of insiders is not to be anticipated, it is the outsider role that requires strengthening. Some of the functionally necessary system of checks and balances must be provided by scholars who either shun or drastically limit their public involvement. Amidst the cacophony of constitutional voices, we must find a place for the scholar who, in the simple but elegant language of Julien Benda, is "the man of study, . . . the man who, silently seated . . . , reads, instructs himself, writes, takes notes."[65]

Conclusion

This lecture is far from exhausting the subject matter with which it deals; indeed, it barely scratches the surface. Had time, my energy, and the patience of the listeners allowed, much more could have been said. However, it makes more sense to conclude with an acronym I often employ in the closing minutes of a lecture, FRIN – Further Research Is Needed – a message entirely appropriate for this talk.

The particular examples running through this analysis are of little importance compared to the larger message they are intended to illustrate. That larger message is simply that our constitutional talk is structured by the very constitution it addresses. The written constitution structures its own debate among governments by the jurisdictions it gives them, and also among the citizenry whose links to specific Charter sections are given an organizational expression by such associations as the Canadian Ethnocultural Council, the Federation of Francophones outside of Quebec, and the National Action Committee on the Status of Women. The debates among these constitutional actors are further structured by the formal amending process, the manner of its employment by those with most power within it, and the extent to which the process and its employment are considered legitimate. A perception of illegitimacy, seldom entirely absent in Canada, weakens the quality of debate on the substance of constitutional change by deflecting attention to unacceptable elements in the process by which it is to be achieved.

Finally, we need to know more about the links between the academic community of constitutional commentators and the governments and private constitutional lobby groups that monitor constitutional evolution and try to influence its direction when an opening presents itself. The links and their consequences need to be traced so that we can at least crudely estimate at what point the benefits of extensive academic involvement carry too high a price in a diminished objectivity that exacerbates a constitutional partisanship requiring no academic contributions to flourish. The pole of disinterested constitutional scholarship is in much greater need of strengthening than the rival pole of special interest advocacy sustained by the driving ambitions of governments and by private interests with stakes in the constitution.

To study the sociology of constitutional discussion in this way requires organizing rubrics that capture major characteristics of how we talk to each other. The concept of taboos points to the subjects we approach with trepidation and avoid if possible, where we bite our tongue for fear we will offend the spirit of the times. The additional concept of insiders and outsiders helps to determine the varying degree to which, across the whole range of constitutional concerns, particular subject matters are relatively open to all intellectual comers or are relatively closed to those who do not have "the right stuff." If this mapping were done, we would have a much better idea of the extent to which the constitution is a common possession and where it has been colonized, and by whom. These, however, are unquestionably large topics for which further research is needed. This lecture may not qualify as much of a beginning, but sometimes even a hint has its utility.

Chapter Ten

Passing Judgement on Meech Lake

Introduction

A few days before the June 23, 1990, Meech Lake deadline, *The Globe and Mail* gloomily editorialized:

> The standard schoolbook portrait of our Fathers of Confederation depicts 33 men of apparent sound judgement, soberly reflecting on their accomplishment. And how might we depict the most recent inheritors of their fragile legacy? A portrait of Canada's contemporary nation-builders would depict a group of men and women arranged in a circle, each person eager to point the finger of blame at another, and each with his or her back turned on the ill-served public. It is an extraordinarily depressing image . . . at this perilous moment, with economic stability and constitutional gridlock in the offing, the search for blame – and the effort to avoid it themselves – wholly preoccupies every party to the looming fiasco. . . .
>
> Regardless of Meech's fate in the days ahead, incalculable damage has been done to the cause of national unity in Canada. No words ring more hollow in the land today than "honor and enthusiasm."[1]

As I write these lines only a few weeks after the June 23 deadline and the passing of Meech Lake into history, the "blame" industry decried by *The Globe and Mail* is in full swing. Premier Filmon of Manitoba spoke simple truth in stating that there is enough blame available for everybody.[2] Some, however, prefer to pass their share on to others who might be portrayed as more deserving. Those who fear the judgement of history on their Meech Lake role now struggle to plant evidence favourable to themselves, hoping it will become friendly "raw" material for future historians. For the political actors directly involved, and whose political ambitions remain alive, blaming someone else for the collapse of Meech Lake, or for the too-frequent sordid episodes that dogged its three years of existence, is a way of saving one's political skin and damaging an opponent's reputation. Further, those who feel their past behaviour has been misjudged re-enter the political-intellectual fray to set the record straight. Thus, according to former Prime Minister Trudeau, he and his fellow contributors decided to write *Towards a Just Society* to get their views on record, because "today's men and women were deforming the record of yesterday's men and those who shared those values."[3]

Blaming is an essential part of the larger, never-ending political game of treating the recent past as an exploitable resource for partisan purposes. For the studious Meech Lake watcher of the deceptions, prevarications, obfuscations, and manipulations that accompanied this failed effort at constitutional change it is perhaps time to step back, eschew participation in the contest of competitive vituperation, and try to clear away some of the underbrush. Such a pursuit of dispassion and objectivity doubtless will fall short of scholarly success, so commingled have become our civic, sometimes partisan, and academic roles. Nevertheless, with the condition of Canada now in much worse shape than before the Meech Lake cure commenced, a retreat from partisanship if not from civic concern is worth attempting, even if success will only be partial.

The demise of Meech Lake is not the demise of our constitutional troubles, but rather the occasion for a renewed bout of even more fundamental constitutional bargaining, the preparations for which are already under way. If we can find in the Meech Lake fiasco some lessons to improve the way we amend the constitution, Meech Lake may, like the losing battles at the onset of wars, inform the discretion of the political generals of the future with more wisdom. The concluding half of this paper explores the rudiments of a constitutional theory applicable to future attempts at formal constitutional change.

The simple fact of failure does not of itself make Meech Lake an object lesson in its substance and process of what should be avoided. If it did, no high-risk enterprise would ever be attempted, and human stagnation would be fostered. However, if the failure of a high-risk venture has predictably grave consequences, those who undertake it should proceed with a shrewdly informed intelligence and extreme sensitivity to the factors that might frustrate their efforts. That Meech Lake was high risk was clearly known to its architects, who proceeded with great care in the preliminary stages, leaving open the possibility of retreat should success appear unlikely, in which case the limited early efforts could be publicly defined as only exploratory. It was necessary, according to Gil Rémillard, to avoid another setback to Quebec "at all costs."[4] The Quebec City correspondent of *Le Devoir* stated that the leading actors had to walk on eggs, without breaking them.[5]

Given these understandings of the treacherous terrain of constitutional change, the Quebec and federal governments, particularly Rémillard and Lowell Murray, collaborated with each other and carefully sounded out the possibility of getting the agreement of the other provinces to Quebec's minimum demands. This unusual process, featuring a series of bilateral meetings, was "the result of an abundance of caution."[6] These meetings succeeded, with some slippage, in persuading the other provinces to put their own separate constitutional demands on hold until the pending "Quebec round" was over. Without such an agreement it was feared the agenda would become excessively cluttered, the primary equity requirement of responding to Quebec would be jeopardized, and a failure would aggravate the Quebec government's alienation from the constitutional order. According to one close observer: "The constitution is a genie in a corked bottle. Before uncorking it, one must be sure the genie will not grow to unpredictable proportions, or become unmanageable. One dare not expand Mr. Rémillard's list of five items." Other governments, therefore, must hold back.[7]

This agreement of the other provinces was accompanied by an implicit understanding that Meech Lake would be followed by yet another provincializing constitutional round, the reward to the other nine provinces for their statesmanlike restraint in allowing the Quebec round to proceed. Little attention was paid to this eventuality in the three years of Meech Lake discussions from 1987 through 1990, nor did the eleven governments openly address and defend the fact, discussed above in Chapter Six, that Meech Lake itself was a provincializing round as the other provinces received everything that Quebec did, with the exception of the "distinct society" clause.

These costs, or payoffs for Meech Lake, almost inevitably followed from the operational premises of the leading Meech Lake actors, the federal and Quebec governments. They assumed that the support of the other governments was both a necessary and sufficient requirement for implementing a package of constitutional amendments to bring Quebec back into the constitutional family, defined implicitly as a family of governments. This remarkable sensitivity to the concerns of (especially provincial) governments was coupled with an equally remarkable insensitivity to the symbolism of the Charter and the constitutional interests of a host of emergent new constitutional actors – women, ethnic groups, and others who were linked to the constitution by the Charter, and aboriginals. As Campbell stated: "The [preliminary] process was tightly controlled and engineered for the purpose of increasing the likelihood of success. Only the 11 governments were involved."[8] At the Mont Gabriel conference in May, 1986, which I attended, and at which Quebec presented its five conditions to a gathering mainly composed of government representatives and academics, several discussants voiced a clear preference for a deal done in the dark while Canadians slept.

As Meech Lake proceeded beyond its tentative intergovernmental beginnings and retreat was no longer an option, the constitutional blindness that assumed feminist groups, aboriginal organizations, and other non-governmental actors could be safely ignored generated a succession of misjudgements, bungling, and offensive behaviour that followed fast on each other's heels. The end result was a humiliating defeat for the federal government, a massive and outraged rejection of the process on all sides, an unsought boost to the alienation of Québécois, and enhanced support for the Quebec *indépendantistes* whose goal Meech Lake had been intended to stymie.

From genesis to post-mortems Meech Lake has been shrouded in symbolism. Its purpose, its substance, and its process have tapped deep and passionate emotions on both sides of the Quebec/rest-of-Canada divide. The process has been central to reactions to Meech Lake, partly because the substance, apart from the symbolism of the "distinct society," could only be understood by experts. Further, the process turned out to be based on a profound misconception of the kind of constitutional people Canadians are becoming. Finally, the substance of Meech Lake was directly linked to the intergovernmental process from which it emerged. Where the process was opened up to extensive public hearings after the Meech Lake and Langevin meetings, opponents of the Accord vastly outnumbered supporters.

Interpretations of Meech Lake

BACKGROUND: WAS QUEBEC BETRAYED IN 1980-82?

The immediate origins of Meech Lake lie in the major shortcoming of the 1982 Constitution Act, the unwillingness of the Quebec government to agree to its terms. This historical fact has given rise to a bitter, indeed vitriolic, controversy over whether Quebec was betrayed in 1980-82. The specific accusation is that the federal government, and Prime Minister Trudeau in particular, made commitments to Quebec in the referendum campaign that were not subsequently carried out. The most common argument of the supporters of the betrayal thesis is that in the context of the referendum, the vague Trudeau commitment to renew federalism could only be interpreted as a commitment to enhance the powers of the Quebec government and the status of Quebec in Confederation.

The passionate, polemical language in which the debate is conducted, particularly by the nationalists, reveals the treacherous emotional terrain of its subject matter and the wisdom of the traditional Oxford belief that academic objectivity is imperilled as we become part of the history we are seeking to understand. The debate is especially intense within Quebec. Why this is so is poignantly explained by Professor Guy Lafor-est, who writes, "In the world of Quebec intellectuals, the flux of the seasons has in a sense stopped with the spring of 1980. Intellectuals and politicians alike perpetually relive the [referendum] debate, they carry it in their luggage whenever they travel."[9] The rise and fall of the Meech Lake Accord gave new life to the debate as the Accord's protagonists and opponents both sought support in their interpretation of what really happened in 1980-82.

The subsequent failure of the Meech Lake Accord will inevitably enter into the next round of historical controversies over the genesis and consti-tutional morality of the 1982 Constitution Act. From one perspective, the failure of Meech Lake and the negative constitutional consequences likely to follow will further discredit the 1982 outcome by underlining the continuing constitutional disarray to which it has led. On the other hand, if the Meech Lake episode is viewed discretely the moral revulsion its process aroused in both its participants and the Canadian citizen as voyeur provides a comparison that defenders of the 1980-82 process and outcome will welcome and exploit.

The more limited purpose of the next few pages is not to predict the contours of the historical reappraisals of the future, or to judge who betrayed whom a decade ago, but to illustrate the nature of the latter debate, highlight its emotionalism, and indicate the debate's interde-pendence with the constitutional politics of Meech Lake.

The emotion that drives the debate derives from its roots in the elemental notions of honour, dignity, truth, shame, and deceit. Passion is further aroused by their linkages with such emotion-laden categories as citizen, nation, and self-determination. The fact that the central actor around whom controversy rages is Pierre Trudeau adds a further inflam-matory element.

The language employed by Premier Lévesque and his cabinet col-leagues in criticizing the November 5, 1981, constitutional agreement in the National Assembly debates includes the following: Quebec as "shamelessly betrayed"; the "night of treachery" in which the agreement that excluded Quebec was hatched; "the thieves of our rights"; "the farce and trickery from which we have just come out"; "this stab with a dagger"; and a description of Quebec as "isolated, betrayed – there is no other word – and despoiled at the same time."[10] More recently, Claude Morin wrote of the "poisoned heritage" left by Trudeau,[11] while Gil Rémillard informed reporters that the 1982 constitution was a "poisoned fruit that everyone had tasted and because of it we are all sick. This country is sick."[12]

The language of betrayal leads to the assertion that the guilty must show contrition and repentance. Thus in his resignation letter to Prime Minister Mulroney, Lucien Bouchard referred to the "villainy of 1982" and the requirement for "the whole country [to] make an act of atonement to Quebec, which had been ostracised by Pierre Elliott Trudeau's strong-arm coup."[13] Similar language was employed by the journalist Marcel Adam, who described Meech Lake as "reparation" to Quebec for the Trudeau reforms that were contemptuous in manner and fraudulent in content.[14] To a Francophone academic, one purpose of Meech Lake was to "blot out the original sin" committed by the other governments in 1980-82.[15]

The betrayal and iniquity of the 1982 outcome were central to the Prime Minister's rationale for the Meech Lake Accord. At various times, he spoke of the need to remember how in 1982 "Quebec was left alone, isolated and humiliated . . . the worst injustice ever inflicted on Quebecers . . . the broken promises made to Quebecers for a constitutional renewal founded on cultural and linguistic survival."[16] To Mulroney, Canada was "a country paralyzed by an incomplete Constitution brutally imposed on Quebec by the federal government. . . . There was change, just as Mr. Trudeau had promised. The following year Quebec was excluded from the Constitution."[17] It is of some historical and moral interest that at the time, as noted in the Introduction to this volume, Mulroney was a supporter of patriation over the objections of the Quebec government, as he considered Trudeau had no alternative.

Accusations of betrayal were not restricted to Quebec nationalists and Conservative partisans supporting the Accord. Donald Smiley, perhaps the leading English-Canadian student of federalism,[18] Gordon Robertson, a retired and highly regarded public service mandarin with extensive constitutional experience,[19] and two elder statesmen, Jack Pickersgill and Robert Stanfield, all explicitly employed the language of betrayal.[20]

The thesis that promises had been made and broken, that Meech Lake was the righting of an historical wrong, the belated payment of a debt that had been cavalierly put aside, gave a remarkable moral flavour of accusation, guilt, confession, and repentance to the constitutional debate. It contributed a sense of rectitude to the Quebec position and deflected attention in Quebec away from the constitutional concerns of Canadians elsewhere. Those who seek a justified repayment for past wrongs customarily are indifferent to the difficulties they may be visiting on the guilty parties. This high moral ground tended to justify Bourassa's rigidity because those who have been wronged do not have to bargain. From Quebec's perspective, it made the demands of citizen groups in English Canada appear illegitimate, for they had not been isolated and ostracized in 1980-82. Also, it meant that for opponents to assess the merits or demerits of the Accord in a calculating fashion seemed vaguely offensive, rather like bartering in a cathedral. This moral background also raised the stakes should Meech Lake not carry, for such a failure would not be seen as merely the failure of a project, but as the non-performance of a moral obligation to a wronged people.

Was Quebec betrayed? Some of the key factors relevant to an informed judgement are discussed in the remaining pages of this section.[21]

The 1982 Constitution Act, the focus of the betrayal debate, was a compromise between the demands of the two competing groups, the Gang of Eight (including Quebec) and the Gang of Three (the federal government, Ontario, and New Brunswick). The former dictated the amending formula that became part of the constitution, and the latter, with the federal government in the leading role, provided the requisite support for the Charter. The provinces also won a new natural resources clause (Section 92A) advantageous to their province-building objectives. The have-not provinces benefited from the constitutionalization of the commitment of the Parliament and government of Canada to "the principle of making equalization payments" in Section 36 (2).

The goal of patriating the constitution from Great Britain was a high-priority federal government objective. While the federal government was the catalyst for ending the vestigial relic of colonialism involved in the British Parliament role in amending the Canadian constitution, the gains accrued to all Canadians in the form of a more complete political independence. Within Canada, which order of government, federal or provincial, gained from patriation would be determined by the amending formula that was to replace the Westminster route. From this perspective, patriation was unquestionably a provincial triumph. The federal government would have gained had its own preferred amending formula been adopted, but that was dropped because of provincial government opposition. In fact, the federal government was better off under the Westminster process it was leaving behind than it would be under the provincialist amending formula that replaced it and became part of the constitution.[22]

The Charter, while conceived of as a potent instrument to shape the constitutional culture of Canadians and strengthen the pan-Canadian community, did not directly strengthen the federal government as such. Logically, it was just as likely to lead to the striking down of federal as of provincial legislation. Although all governments had the notwithstanding clause to bypass portions of the Charter in selected circumstances, its addition to the Charter was undeniably a response to pressure from provincial governments in western Canada. Nevertheless, overall the Charter was a federal government victory. If the Charter strengthened pan-Canadian and weakened provincial identities over the long run, the federal government would be strengthened in the competitive struggle for the allegiance of the citizenry. From the provincial perspective, the encouragement it offered provincial residents to think of themselves as Canadians was precisely why most provincial governments opposed it. On balance, however, the argument occasionally heard that the 1982 Constitution Act was a federal government victory, which then required a countervailing provincial round, as in Meech Lake, to restore an appropriate constitutional equilibrium, appears to be strained.[23] The 1982 Constitution Act was clearly a compromise. Between the federal and provincial governments, considering the latter as a single category, there was no unequivocal victor.

The basic elements of the 1982 Constitution Act, including the changes sought by provincial governments, applied to Quebec. In that elementary sense, Quebec was not left out; it received the "goods" of the Constitution Act, as well as the "bads." Two last-minute concessions failed to budge the Parti Québécois government from its opposition. A modification to the amending formula providing "reasonable compensation" to a province that opted out of an amendment transferring "provincial legislative powers relating to education or other cultural matters from provincial legislatures to Parliament" was explicitly designed and seen as a concession to Quebec. Since education and cultural matters were presumably central to Quebec's identity, this concession was significant, although it fell short of Quebec's original demands.[24]

The second concession applied only to Quebec. Section 23 (1)(a), according minority-language educational rights to the children of Canadian citizens whose first language was that of the English or French linguistic minority population of their province of residence, would not come into force in Quebec until so authorized by the Quebec government or legislative assembly (Section 59). Functionally, this was the equivalent of a supplementary notwithstanding clause available only to Quebec and applicable to a key aspect of the Charter's educational language rights.

From this somewhat limited perspective, therefore, it can be asserted that in 1982 Quebec gained slightly more than any other province. It is, however, also true that in spite of Section 59 Quebec jurisdiction was more seriously challenged by the Charter's minority-language educational rights clauses than any other province. Such rights were more likely to constrain Quebec's sensitive educational policies than those of other provinces and, in so doing, to disturb an extremely volatile Quebec policy area.

The Parti Québécois government attacked the Charter for reducing the National Assembly's powers in general, and specifically for its encroachment on Quebec's legislative powers over the language of education. Second, it opposed the Charter's mobility rights, even as qualified by Section 6 (4),[25] and even though the opposition Liberal members reiterated that such a "basic freedom of movement [was] . . . elementary in a federation."[26] The third major Quebec government objection was the failure of the amending formula to provide full fiscal compensation when a province opted out of an amendment transferring provincial legislative powers to the federal government. This was logically seen as impairing the government's jurisdictional autonomy by forcing it to pay a price for refusing to cede constitutional powers it legitimately possessed to the federal government, when enough other provinces were willing to do so. Even those who doubted the good bargaining faith of the Quebec government admit that this was a "point of dissent with a claim to be taken seriously."[27] While the probability of such future amendments was no doubt low, the symbolic message was clear – in certain crucial circumstances the province where one of the two founding European peoples was concentrated would either pay a price for continuing to exercise its rights, or it would give them up because the decision-making rule was biased in favour of the federal government, in which both Quebecers and French Canadians were a minority.[28]

The Parti Québécois objections to the 1981 agreement should not be generalized to the whole Quebec political class without qualification. Although the provincial Liberals also regarded the 1981 agreement as inadequate, their opposition was at least somewhat ambivalent. The Liberal leader, Claude Ryan, thought that the agreement had "enough positive elements" that the Quebec government had the duty to work to improve it and thus render it acceptable.[29] Further, a number of opposition members thought that the minimum conditions established by the Quebec government for its agreement to the constitutional package were designed either to subvert the agreement or to force Ottawa to bypass Quebec and thus stimulate a nationalist reaction.[30] Accordingly, thirty-eight Liberals voted against the resolution establishing the minimum conditions.[31]

The ambivalence of the Liberals toward the constitutional package sprang not only from the natural adversarial incentives for opposition members to differentiate themselves from the government, but also from their own constitutional preferences. The 1980 Beige Paper of the Quebec Liberal Party, *A New Canadian Federation*, had advocated a strong, entrenched Charter with fewer concessions to the provinces – no notwithstanding clause, for example – than were in the actual Charter. Further, the Quebec provincial Liberals' proposals on mobility rights and minority-language education rights did not contain the qualifications and exceptions of the 1982 Charter, and thus were also further removed from the Parti Québécois position than was the 1982 Charter.[32] On several key rights issues, then, the Quebec Liberals were constitutionally closer to the federal Liberals than to the provincial Parti Québécois.

For both the Parti Québécois and the provincial Liberals the deficiencies of the 1982 Constitution Act lay as much in what it failed to do as in the weakness of its actual contents. According to Gil Rémillard, the 1982 Constitution Act did not respond to the needs and profound aspirations of Quebec society, and in some respects was in opposition to its most legitimate interests.[33] In the sympathetic and cryptic words of two Ontario government briefing papers, "the 1982 amendments did not address adequately Quebec's place in the Federation, which was the driving force behind the current phase of constitutional discussions which began in the 1960s,"[34] and the "constitutional settlement of 1982 addressed none of Quebec's historic concerns."[35]

This failure was particularly infuriating to the nationalists because they believed that, given Quebec's recent political history and the contemporary intellectual climate, Trudeau's promise of renewed federalism could only have been understood by the voting majority to have meant more power for the Quebec government and a sympathetic redefinition of Quebec's role in Canada.[36] This Quebec-centred interpretation was no doubt encouraged by the fact that the Liberal leader, Claude Ryan, was the official leader of the "non" forces in the 1980 referendum campaign. The Ryan Liberals looked like a government in waiting while the Parti Québécois appeared headed for imminent electoral defeat after the referendum. The Quebec-oriented constitutional proposals of Ryan and the Quebec Liberals clearly would have achieved what the critics faulted Trudeau for not doing.

The 1982 Constitution Act made no serious overtures in the direction of enhancing the powers of the Quebec government, and thus of Quebecers as a political collectivity, or of recognizing Quebec as a distinct society or as the homeland of the French-speaking people of Canada. The public image of the 1982 Constitution Act, dominated as it was by the Charter, reflected Trudeau's pan-Canadian vision of a country of individual rights and of two linguistic communities with a country-wide existence. Symbolically, the Constitution Act via the Charter was a repudiation of the *indépendantiste* vision of Quebec as an incipient French-speaking nation with the right and duty to take appropriate measures of self-preservation in the threatening English-speaking environment of North America. In substantive terms, this entrenchment of Trudeau's rival vision in the constitution was the trigger for the betrayal allegation, when his pre-referendum promise, at least to those who lacked the skill to decode his words, could be read as more power for Quebec. The vigour and comprehensiveness of the Parti Québécois reaction to the Charter are closely linked, therefore, to the context of its introduction.[37]

While the bitterness of the nationalists' reaction is understandable, the question of betrayal cannot be definitively answered. Former Prime Minister Trudeau has vigorously defended both his role in the referendum and the federal government's contribution to the 1982 constitutional package as being consistent with his public statements since he entered politics. He adds that shortly before the referendum René Lévesque clearly understood and publicly referred to what Trudeau meant by the renewal of federalism. Further, since the Parti Québécois lost the referendum campaign, it was only to be expected, Trudeau argues, that the victors would have more influence on the direction of constitutional change than the losers. "There was no point in winning the referendum," he somewhat exaggeratedly put it, "if we were going to give to those who had lost it everything they were trying to get by winning it."[38] Trudeau and those who argue this way unfailingly add that the support of the 1982 Constitution Act by the federal cabinet and the Liberal Party in Parliament, both of which had strong Quebec representation, cannot be discounted as irrelevant to Quebec's desires and interests simply because a separatist Quebec government, angry and demoralized from its recent referendum defeat, did not support the Constitution Act with its signature.[39] Finally, although the evidence from the polls is somewhat ambiguous, at least some polls at the time of the proclamation of the Constitution Act in 1982 indicated that "most Quebecers who had an opinion wanted the province to sign the agreement."[40]

The passions of the betrayal debate cannot be adequately understood without paying close attention to the conditioning contexts out of which that debate emerged. It was driven by the two major historically rooted competing visions of how a minority French-speaking population could survive in a North American English-speaking sea. Trudeau and Lévesque personified the two dominant competing answers to this dilemma: Trudeau's vision of a bilingual Canada where linguistic minorities could survive away from their areas of majority concentration, and the Lévesque view of an independent Quebec state as the leading servant of a Francophone majority no longer torn by the divided identity fostered by federalism. The structural context of both the referendum debate and the constitutional reform process that followed pitted the protagonists of these competing views directly against each other. Their encounter confronted both of them with agonizing dilemmas that need to be understood by the armchair critics.

On one side of the debate, the incumbent Quebec government was ostensibly engaged in the renovation of Canadian federalism, its clear responsibility as a government following the referendum result. However, it was "viscerally incapable" of truly contributing to such an objective, the equivalent of committing "hara-kiri" by losing the party's "raison d'être." [41] This is the assessment of a Trudeau opponent and an advocate of the betrayal thesis.

According to various sources, the Parti Québécois resolved the dilemma by not bargaining seriously for renewed federalism. This is the opinion of academic supporters of the Meech Lake Accord, [42] authors of scholarly accounts, [43] and Liberal defenders of the 1982 Constitution Act. [44] Claude Morin, the Parti Québécois minister who handled the constitutional portfolio throughout the period from the referendum to the Constitution Act, could scarcely be more explicit in his agreement. Quebec, he asserted, could make no further concessions beyond the Gang of Eight provincial accord of April, 1981. It could go no further on the amending formula, and it could not tolerate any reduction of its powers by means of the Charter of Rights, especially in linguistic matters. "Nothing would make us change our minds." [45]

Since that accord of April 16, 1981, was only a provincialist amending formula, and it was made public after the Charter had been introduced and strengthened in a gruelling hearings process, it was inconceivable that the totality of post-referendum constitutional reform could be restricted to that amending formula alone. Clearly, the Parti Québécois position invited either deadlock or proceeding without Quebec. [46]

The Parti Québécois dilemma was paralleled in reverse for the governing federal Liberals. Either the delivery of the federalism renewal promise was to be controlled by the Parti Québécois that had lost the referendum, with the kind of minimalist results just indicated, or renewal had to proceed without the agreement of the Quebec government. The former would have deprived the referendum outcome of the conventional meaning that is attached to victory and loss in such contests, while the latter inevitably would give the nationalists the propaganda resource of betrayal to wield in future constitutional controversies.

A third possibility for the federal government would have been to accept a stalemate, implicitly to agree that Quebec had a *de facto* veto even if the Supreme Court decision[47] had found that unanimity was not a constitutional requirement. However, the admission that this time, following the most intense period of constitutional politics in Canadian history, like all the other times – Fulton-Favreau, the Victoria Charter, and Bill C-60 – Canada was once more incapable of constitutional decisiveness, would have been received as a humiliating defeat by the federal government and by many Canadians. It would also have provided precisely the ammunition sought by the supporters of Quebec independence to prove that federalism was incapable of renewal. Stalemate would also have meant that the many Canadians who participated in the constitution-making enterprise, especially with respect to the Charter – women's groups, visible minorities, French and English linguistic minorities, the disabled, civil rights activists, aboriginals who gained a more secure place in the constitution and promises of constitutional discussions to identify and define their rights, and the Métis who gained constitutional recognition as an aboriginal people for the first time – should all have been rebuffed in order to avoid constitutional change unacceptable to a Quebec government whose commitment to federalism was at best half-hearted. Stalemate would have come with a heavy price tag.

Given these extraordinarily ambiguous situations in which both the Quebec and federal governments found themselves, with both of whom, given their perspectives, it is easy to sympathize, both governments' behaviour made sense from their separate perspectives. For the Quebec government its non-agreement, which either blocked the enterprise or gave it the resources to delegitimate a negative outcome from the position of a victim, was preferable to agreement on the only terms it could get. For the federal government, proceeding without Quebec was preferable to letting the Parti Québécois dictate the terms of an acceptable agreement or create a stalemate.

Occasionally, it is suggested or implied that after the referendum the federal Liberal government should have delayed constitutional reform until the return of a federalist government in Quebec. This apparently was broached by Claude Ryan, the Quebec Liberal leader, and rejected by Trudeau.[48] A Quebec journalist recently suggested that Trudeau could have indicated that he could not proceed with his reform commitment until the Quebec population had an election opportunity to determine who should negotiate for Quebec.[49]

Politically, however, acceptance of this advice by the federal government would have carried risks equal to or greater than the various alternatives it was intended to displace. It would have meant sacrificing the momentum of the referendum outcome, banking on a federalist provincial election victory in the next year and a half, which was far from certain, or confronting a newly elected and reinvigorated Parti Québécois government. Success in such an endeavour would also have required managing the puzzled and probably angry public reaction to months of silence following the referendum and what had been defined as the gravest crisis in Canadian history. In addition, when the provincial election came, the federal government would certainly have been chastised for so overtly favouring the federalist side in a provincial election with promises of constitutional gifts, conditional on a particular election outcome. Finally, this theoretical possibility foundered on the divergence between the Trudeau and Ryan versions of constitutional renewal. The only circumstance in which it would have come to pass would have been the calling of an election by Lévesque immediately after the referendum defeat, resulting in the election of Ryan's federalist Liberal Party. Had such an election been quickly announced the federal government would have had to delay the constitutional reform process until after the election results. Further, it would not have subsequently been politically possible to bypass the objections of a freshly elected federalist government in Quebec City by proceeding without its support.

While Trudeau might have preferred to bypass a Parti Québécois government than to have to get an agreement from a federalist Quebec government with a vision of Canada considerably different from his own, the immediate post-referendum emergence of the latter depended on the willingness of the Parti Québécois to call an early election they were almost certain to lose. They didn't. Of course, had the referendum been held closer to the final date before an election had to be held, then the Lévesque government would have had no choice, and the constitutional history of Canada in the last decade would have turned out differently.

The more extreme version of the betrayal thesis, that Trudeau explicitly lied to the Quebec people in the referendum campaign, has negligible support because it cannot be documented.[50] The softer version, espoused by some scholars, journalists, and political opponents, concludes that Trudeau was deliberately and carefully ambiguous "at a crucial moment, possibly the most important time in the history of the people of Quebec."[51] Even this milder version, however, is hotly disputed by Trudeau.[52]

Given that the truth of the betrayal thesis even in its softer version is indeterminate, its political salience has been dictated by the political capacity and will of the contending political forces to have their interpretation of the events and outcome of 1980-82 prevail. In this political context, the betrayal forces had the advantage. The Trudeau government was old and tired as well as preparing for a new leader in the few remaining years left to it in office after 1982. The Liberals were defeated in 1984 and replaced by a Conservative government with a Quebec leader who had close links with Quebec nationalists. The new Conservative governing party had achieved a significant but fragile breakthrough in Quebec. Its consolidation would be well served by discrediting the federal Liberals in Quebec. The mutual interest of both major parties in Quebec provincial politics and of the governing federal Conservative Party in popularizing the betrayal thesis or, at a minimum, a negative view of the 1982 Constitution Act, has put opponents of the betrayal line and defenders of the 1982 Constitution Act in Quebec at a serious disadvantage. Numerically, most federal and provincial representatives from Quebec from 1984 to the present have found it politically advantageous to be critical of the treatment received by Quebec in 1982. This imbalance was compounded by Trudeau's retirement and the dilution of his vision implicit in the official support offered to the Meech Lake package by the Liberals under his successor, John Turner, in 1987.

Justification of a major constitutional enterprise such as Meech Lake required the delegitimation of the status quo from which escape is sought. In such a task, truth is helpful but not essential, and not always available. Plausibility and repetition will suffice for short-run political purposes, as they have in this instance. The more dispassionate scholarship of the future may produce more convincing if more nuanced answers to the betrayal question than this generation can provide. Even then, a tantalizing question mark will probably remain.

SUBSTANCE: WAS MEECH LAKE A LIMITED PACKAGE?

Some of the simplest questions about Meech Lake – such as 'Was Meech Lake a limited package?' – defy straightforward answers and thus underline the political factors that pervade scholarly attempts to come to grips with Meech Lake.

In two addresses to the Quebec National Assembly Premier Bourassa underlined the magnitude of Quebec's Meech Lake gains, including "the potential to obtain new powers," and asserted that "Quebec has realized one of the most important political victories of its history, a victory recognized by most objective observers as one of its greatest in two hundred years." He reminded the critics who pointed to unsettled areas that "there will be another round of negotiations."[53] Significantly, Bourassa never made such claims outside of Quebec, where these and similar statements were repeated by opponents of the Accord.[54]

Outside of Quebec, Meech Lake supporters, including Bourassa, Rémillard, the federal government, and academics, defended the Accord, in the phrase of the Attorney General of Ontario, for the "limited, focused and modest character" of its answer to the question, what does Quebec want?[55] Even within Quebec, occasional political statements to the contrary, the Accord tended to be viewed as a vital, indispensable minimum.[56] The changes proposed by the Accord were further minimized by the claim that they had been debated and examined for decades.[57] To another group of supporters, the Accord did not represent "a radical departure from Canadian constitutional practice."[58] Such supporters also invariably added that the Accord was the absolute minimum the Bourassa government or any succeeding Quebec government could accept. This claim was often accompanied by the suggestion, prediction, or threat that Quebec's five Meech Lake demands would appear trivial when contrasted with those that would build on the nationalist passion that would follow from a Meech Lake failure. These interpretations of the Accord were indirectly supported by the Parti Québécois, which described the minimal contents of the Accord in scathing terms, although René Lévesque's assessment had been hesitant and wavering.[59]

The assertion that neither Bourassa nor a successor Quebec government would ever accept less after the Meech Lake package had been publicly agreed to by all first ministers is almost certainly true, at least in the short and middle run. This, however, is to be explained at least as much by the politicized inflexibility of Quebec bargaining in constitutional politics as it is by the scope of the Quebec demands.

The argument that a Meech Lake failure would lead to greater demands, possibly including independence, was also plausible, but the implicit inference that all increases in demands would increase the indigestion of English Canada was problematic. Constitutional indigestion is partly a product of whether Quebec is thought of as part of Canada, as a province (almost) like the others, as subject to the Charter, and as sharing in a single Canadian citizenship. From these perspectives, at some point a larger Quebec package of demands is less challenging to Canadianism than is a smaller package. That an independent Quebec would not be subject to the Charter is tautological and innocuous, whereas the same statement about the province of Quebec is threatening. Thus, in certain circumstances less can be more, and more can be less.

This paradox does not exhaust the difficulty of assessing the "size" of Meech Lake. The seemingly simple statement that the Meech Lake package was limited and modest is simultaneously true, false, and indeterminate, depending on the context in which it is judged. Compared to sovereignty-association, to the 1980 Quebec Liberal Party Beige Paper proposals, and to the post-referendum position of the Parti Québécois in the mid-eighties, Bourassa's demands were clearly restrained. Thus Prime Minister Mulroney contrasted the "five reasonable conditions [of the Quebec Liberal Party] for healing the breech [*sic*] and returning to the fold" with the twenty-two conditions that had been proposed by the Parti Québécois, which "would have, among other things, removed Quebec from the application of virtually every provision of the Charter."[60] From a slightly different perspective, Senator Lowell Murray, Minister of State for Federal-Provincial Relations, positively contrasted the focused, "limited and manageable agenda" of Meech Lake with the overloaded agenda of 1980-82 and the "paralyzing linkages" among a diffuse range of constitutional issues to which that led.[61]

For Premier Bourassa, the reiterated claim that Meech Lake was a small package made his inflexibility appear reasonable outside Quebec and mandatory inside the province. It also explained his odd use of "compromise" to describe the Quebec position, by which he meant that he had made all of his compromises in establishing Quebec's non-negotiable initial minimum conditions. According to Bourassa, Quebec's demands had been tailored "in such a way that they would be acceptable to all,"[62] and were "mild" compared to Lévesque's previous demands.[63] Unfortunately, this approach, designed to protect the government from the nationalist criticisms that would inevitably attend any Quebec concessions, undermined the normal meaning of compromise that applies to the mutual adjustment of opposing parties at the bargaining table.[64]

Thus, attaching the adjective "modest" to Quebec's demands or to the Meech Lake response (not precisely the same thing) was widespread, was defensible from a number of perspectives, and was functional for many of the players. For example, when Lucien Bouchard referred in his resignation letter to the Prime Minister to the "five paltry little conditions

[Quebec] timidly set for its constitutional return,"[65] his purpose was to underline the unreasonable intransigence of English Canada and the appropriateness of a powerful nationalist response to the pending humiliation of Quebec should Meech Lake not pass.

Yet, modesty and limitation were clearly in the eye of the beholder. To assert the smallness of the Quebec demands or of the Meech Lake package on the ground that they were not as extensive as the 1980-82 agenda or the 1982 outcome or as the Parti Québécois pre- or post-referendum demands is analogous to describing a 6-foot-4-inch Harlem Globetrotter as a midget by comparing him only to his other teammates. The Meech Lake package of amendments would unquestionably have been the second largest package of formal constitutional change since 1867, surpassed only by the 1982 Constitution Act. Even what might appear to be a small change from some detached, Olympian perspective, such as the extension of the unanimity principle to the creation of new provinces, was viewed as a gratuitous humiliation by the citizens of the Yukon and the Northwest Territories and as a major roadblock to their constitutional aspirations. What might appear as an even smaller change, the transitional changes to the Senate giving provincial governments the power to nominate the candidates from which Ottawa would then make appointments, was potentially the single most important change to the operation of the Senate since 1867.

The portrayal of Meech Lake as a small, limited package was facilitated by describing it as the Quebec round, a labelling that deflected attention from the fact that everything Quebec requested was given to all provinces in response to the principle of equality of the provinces, with the exception of the "distinct society." Once the Quebec round was correctly seen as a provincial round, the perceived magnitude of its impact on the federal system was much greater.

From these perspectives, the Meech Lake Accord was far from being a limited, modest package. It was, as John Whyte, Dean of Law, Queen's University, put it, "no mean document. This is big-time constitutional stuff."[66] It strengthened the provinces, encroached on the Charter, repudiated in its process the participant citizen role in constitution-making that had briefly surfaced in 1980-81, and espoused a French and English founding peoples image of Canada at a time when the country's changing ethnic demography was leading to a more multicultural, multiracial, and aboriginal definition of Canada. Thus little imagination was required to support the claim of many of the Accord's opponents that Meech Lake represented serious, fundamental, extensive constitutional change.

From yet another perspective, the scale of the Meech Lake package was indeterminate in the sense that much of its language, especially the "distinct society," was ambiguous and thus could be interpreted or distorted in line with the political purposes of the speaker. For Ramsay Cook, the distinct society clause was a Lewis Carroll Alice in Meechland phrasing that had no clearly understood meaning.[67] The words employed in the Meech Lake spending power restrictions were, according to Dean John Whyte, "constructively ambiguous . . . . chosen for their lack of clarity," a result to which he was unwilling to apply the label "statesmanship."[68] This characteristic of the Accord was summed up by one bemused and frustrated critic who refused to describe Meech Lake as an agreement, since there was no agreement on what had been allegedly agreed on.[69] This indeterminacy, of course, allowed those who disagreed whether Meech Lake was a big or small package both to have their way and to put off to the future the determination of who was right.

Thus, depending on perspective and context Meech Lake might be seen as a small package (bigger ones had been put forward in the recent past) or as a big package (if implemented it would have been surpassed only by the 1982 Constitution Act) or as a package of indeterminate size, as its terms had more than the normal imprecision of constitutional language.

Finally, those opponents of Meech Lake who characterized it as a large package partly did so because they perceived it as unbalanced, as a package of one-sided concessions to the provinces.[70] For such critics it is probable that additions to the package that gave more gains to the federal government and the Canadian community would have made the resulting even larger package appear smaller. To such critics, assessments of size derived as much from the one-sided direction as from the extent of change. Somewhat paradoxically, Quebec supporters of Meech Lake would also have seen a more balanced larger package as smaller, for it would have reduced Quebec's gains, at least in a relative sense.

RETROSPECTIVE: DOES THE MEECH LAKE FAILURE MEAN ENGLISH CANADA HAS REJECTED QUEBEC?

The political/constitutional fallout of the Meech Lake failure will depend on whether it is interpreted as a rejection of Quebec by English Canada. Such an interpretation, already widespread in Quebec, will not die for lack of support. That support will feed one of the most disturbing and damaging aspects of the Meech Lake debate, most dangerously personified by the Prime Minister, that is, the tendency of the Accord's supporters to label its opponents as anti-Quebec and to engage in the self-fulfilling prophecy that its rejection would be, or at least would be perceived as, English Canada rejecting Quebec.[71]

Such an interpretation of the Accord's failure is at best questionable. When the Accord was initially drafted and refined in two sessions at Meech Lake and Langevin Block all eleven governments were on side, as well as both opposition parties in the House of Commons. When Meech Lake died all but two provincial governments were still on side, as well as all three party leaders in Manitoba, albeit unenthusiastically, and probably somewhat less than half of the Newfoundland legislators. An impressive array of prestigious Anglophone elites volubly in support of Meech Lake, and active in various groups to encourage its ratification, achieved a high visibility as the deadline approached. The Toronto *Globe and Mail*, the leading newspaper of English Canada, gave consistent and passionate editorial support to Meech Lake from its birth to its burial. Premier Clyde Wells of Newfoundland insisted that he was not opposed to Quebec, but only to the ways in which Quebec's demands were to be met. Any attempt, therefore, to portray the Meech Lake outcome as analogous to the 1980-82 results in which the government of Quebec was isolated while the other governments struck a mutually self-interested compromise agreement would clearly be an exaggeration.

Some of the support for Meech Lake in the closing months was no doubt based on fear of the consequences should the Accord fail. For provincial elites this fear mingled with the recognition that their own provincial governments would also gain power if Meech Lake were to be accepted. It is also evident that some of the support in the three federal parties was based on partisan hopes of future electoral success in Quebec that might be dashed for the party that opposed Meech Lake. However, these qualifications do no more than underscore the reality that in political life motives are often mixed.

At the grassroots level, there was clear, if limited, evidence of anti-French sentiment in parts of the country. When the British Columbia Social Credit Party voted overwhelmingly in convention to rescind support for Meech Lake, this was coupled with a motion proclaiming English as the official language of British Columbia.[72] Journalistic accounts suggest that opposition to the Accord from rural Manitoba municipalities was coloured by anti-French sentiment.[73] Premier Devine of Saskatchewan admitted that passage of the Meech Lake Accord was hampered by "[a]nti-French sentiment ... prevalent in Western Canada."[74] In his own province, the Saskatchewan Association of Rural Municipalities, resentful at special support for the French language, unanimously supported a resolution backing the idea of a "one-culture province."[75]

An Angus Reid-Southam News poll, taken in February, 1990, indicated that a majority of respondents in Saskatchewan and Manitoba would support English-only municipalities.[76] In Ontario, the passage of English-only resolutions in Sault Ste. Marie, Thunder Bay, and several dozen more municipalities was deeply embarrassing to the Ontario government and to Meech Lake supporters.[77] In a poll taken after the failure of Meech Lake, 44 per cent of home-language English speakers approved such resolutions, while 52 per cent disapproved.[78]

It is almost certainly the case, as well, that much of the opposition to the distinct society clause in the three prairie provinces reflected their own heterogeneity and the smallness of the local Francophone populations. The idea of singling out in the constitution French-speaking Canadians and English-speaking Canadians as "a fundamental characteristic of Canada," and of identifying Quebec as a "distinct society" in Canada, was alien to the cultural perspectives and ethnic demography of the Prairies. The Manitoba Task Force on Meech Lake validly reflected the position of those who appeared before it when it recommended a Canada clause that would add aboriginal peoples and Canada's multicultural heritage as fundamental characteristics of Canada.[79]

An initial assessment, therefore, of whether English Canada rejected Quebec would conclude that there was simultaneously strong Meech Lake support from various private elites and from the federal and provincial governments, often in defiance of their own electorates, and scattered but not insignificant evidence of specific anti-French/anti-Quebec opposition to the Accord from local politicians and grassroots activists.

This, however, does not take us very far, mainly because most of the opposition to Meech Lake outside of Quebec was not driven by anti-Quebec or anti-French sentiments but by a mix of particularistic concerns and general conceptions of Canada that clashed with the competing vision and contents of Meech Lake. The Charter, as is discussed in more detail below, has taken hold outside of Quebec to a degree that even its strongest early supporters would not have predicted. There is thus considerable truth in the claim that the Accord foundered on the English-Canadian view of the Charter as "a central part . . . of what constitutes Canadian federalism"[80] or, perhaps more accurately, the Canadian constitution. In less than a decade it has become almost an icon to its more passionate supporters, who referred angrily to "the assault on the Charter contained in the Meech Lake proposals."[81]

A recent scholarly comparison of the differences between the Meech Lake debates in English Canada and Francophone Quebec underlines their contrasting attitudes to the Charter. In English Canada the Charter has become a sacred symbol that is profaned by Meech Lake. In Quebec, by contrast, the Charter is seen to go beyond the simple task of rights protection and is viewed as a straitjacket whose dynamism leads to centralization and uniformity. In Quebec, accordingly, the debate is not driven by a fear that the Charter might be weakened but by a doubt whether the distinct society clause will be an adequate defence against the Charter's insensitivity to the particular needs of Quebec.[82]

From this perspective, the central Meech Lake conflict was between the Quebec government that wished to limit the Charter's impact, by means of the distinct society provision, and the positive orientation to the Charter, which translated into opposition to that objective in the rest of Canada.[83] This conflict was exacerbated by the fact that the distinct society concept was, in Gil Rémillard's language, the generating principle and common denominator of all of Quebec's original conditions and hoped-for gains.[84]

From a different perspective, the opposition to Meech Lake that was played out before various legislative committees was highly fragmented and particularistic, not driven by rival conceptions of what Canada was all about but rather by the fears of feminist groups, aboriginals, visible minorities, social policy activists, and the disabled that Meech Lake threatened their existing status or future goals. To assume, however, that such groups were speaking or acting for English Canada as such is either to trivialize their goals and often distinctive identities or to postulate a brilliantly orchestrated conspiracy that is inconceivable.

The reality is that the Charter and various constitutional clauses referring to aboriginals have introduced a minoritarian counter-culture into the constitution, which comprises a variety of interests and social categories and is endowed with organizations and elites, each of which sees the constitution as a vehicle to advance or protect particularistic concerns. In the various Meech Lake arenas in which they were allowed to participate, that is precisely what was done by the National Action Committee on the Status of Women, the Canadian Ethnocultural Council, the Assembly of First Nations, and others. Essentially, they were for themselves, and they opposed whatever got in the way of their objectives. Their self-interested behaviour paralleled that of provincial governments, with the exception that they could not exact concessions by withholding the employment of a veto.

While the various groups that opposed the Accord from outside of Quebec may be accused of constitutional selfishness, the assertion that they spoke for English Canada or that their particularistic concerns were driven by anti-French or anti-Quebec motivations is implausible. In functional terms, their actions paralleled the responses of the Federation of Francophones outside Quebec and the various organizations speaking for the Acadian population of New Brunswick, who obviously did not speak for English Canada and who could not be accused of anti-French or anti-Quebec motivations. They initially opposed the Accord out of fear that its content would weaken their own French-language position, and they belatedly came to its support out of the greater fear that its defeat, by stimulating support for independence in Quebec, would leave them even less protected than they would be under Meech Lake. These Francophone and Acadian early opponents and subsequent supporters of the Accord, like the other non-governmental actors outside of Quebec, pursued their own constitutional self-interest because they did not trust governments to do so.

The preceding observations underline what is too often ignored or misunderstood. English Canada is headless and voiceless. It has no corporate existence. Given the existing structure of power in the federal system, it is incapable of accepting or rejecting anyone or anything. (See the Introduction and Chapter Eight.) No authority figure can speak for English Canada as such and advise its members on the advantages and disadvantages of alternative English-Canadian constitutional futures. Thus, to the question "Did English Canada reject Quebec?" the nuanced answer must be the Scottish verdict "not proven."

To some extent the Charter contributed to competing conceptions of constitutional virtue between Francophone Quebecers and English Canadians, whose reconciliation was difficult. The Charter and various aboriginal constitutional clauses also fostered diverse self-interested minoritarian tendencies that became barriers to the Accord's acceptance. While these developments fostered resistance to the Accord, some of the blame, if that is the right word, for their strength must reside with the governments that tried to treat the Accord as a private affair for office-holders and assumed no responsibility for educating their citizens in the Accord's virtues. It was not an opponent of the Accord, but a group of its passionate supporters despairing of the crudities of its official defenders, who wrote: "Unfortunately, the principal defenders of Meech Lake have chosen to sell the Accord as nothing more than a deal required to get Quebec to 'return to the constitutional family'. It is presented as simply a saw-off, extracted by nationalist blackmail. Among constitutional options, it is the visionless alternative."[85]

What Went Wrong? A Failure of Constitutional Theory

The Meech Lake episode, now handed over to the historians as an instructive example of a major constitutional initiative that failed, graphically underlines the need for more sophisticated constitutional theorizing. Meech Lake is not simply a brilliant manoeuvre that narrowly failed because of a technical miscalculation about the applicability of the three years' rule, or because of bad luck, such as the unpredicted antagonistic chemistry between several of the key players in its later stages. Rather, it failed because it was based on an inadequate, outdated constitutional theory.

Canadians have not yet digested the 1982 Constitution Act. The governments of Canada tried to implement the second most extensive constitutional changes since Confederation as quickly as possible, and with as little public discussion as possible, by a collective act of intergovernmental unilateralism. They were either insensitive, indifferent, or oblivious to the impact of the 1982 Constitution Act on the citizenry. Accordingly, they were unaware that their leading role as agents of constitutional change was subject to new requirements of legitimacy that they failed to meet.

Governments mastered the technical aspects of the new amending formula with relative success, although even here they failed to appreciate the implications of the three-year time limit for certain classes of amendments (Section 39 (2)) and of the necessity for legislative ratification by each agreeing government. These errors, however, were trivial compared to their larger failure to appreciate that memories of the public role in the constitutional process in 1980-81, the 1982 Charter, the various aboriginal constitutional clauses, and the bitterness of aboriginals about the failure of the four aboriginal constitutional conferences had decisively changed the relationship of many Canadians to what they had come to think of as their constitution.

There was remarkable and appropriate sensitivity by governments to the formal exclusion of Quebec from the 1982 constitutional agreement, and an appreciation of the volatile situation to which that could lead. However, in preparing for Meech Lake there was almost no recognition that the constitutional culture outside of Quebec was no longer acquiescent and deferential.

INSENSITIVITY TO THE NEW SOCIAL, SYMBOLIC ROLE OF THE CONSTITUTION

This new civic orientation to the constitution derived from the new role of the constitution in the era of the Charter and from frustrated aboriginal demands for constitutional advances. The agreeing governments at Meech Lake, however, failed to realize that major constitutional change in the Charter era modifies the relative status and identities of an increasingly heterogeneous and constitutionally self-conscious citizenry. Meech Lake would have modified the relative importance of the federal and provincial governments to the advantage of the latter and thus would have reduced the scope of action of citizens and interests with a country-wide identification. Meech Lake would have reshuffled relationships of power and influence among the institutions of government, and by so doing simultaneously readjusted the relative influence of the various groups and interests in society that are differentially linked to those institutions. For example, to make executive federalism a more prominent vehicle for constitutional change, as Meech Lake both was in itself and purported to do for the future, threatened to erode the already limited role of citizens and legislators in constitutional change. To modify the procedures for nominating and appointing Supreme Court judges in the interest of provincial governments was to increase the insecurities of those who look to the Court for advancement but do not view provincial governments as allies.

Further, now that citizens have been brought directly into the constitutional order by the Charter, constitutional change is invested with high symbolic content. It may deliberately or inadvertently modify the official identities and public status of those who have been singled out for special constitutional attention. The social, normative, and symbolic significance of the contemporary constitution was a key reason for identifying French- and English-speaking Canadians as "a fundamental characteristic of Canada" and for stating that Quebec constituted "within Canada a distinct society," and this newly enhanced significance was a key factor as well in generating the opposition to Meech Lake triggered by these clauses. The "distinct society" and "distinct identity" of Quebec clashed with the civic identity other Canadians derived from the Charter. The constitutional defining of the two historic French- and English-language groups as "a fundamental characteristic of Canada" grievously offended the *amour propre* of the aboriginal people. For "multicultural Canadians," both clauses were perceived as chilling constitutional confirmations of their second-class status because they were later, and hence less worthy arrivals on Canada's shores. By such selective inclusions, exclusions, definitions, and redefinitions, constitutional change manipulates the symbolic order of society and redefines the people it serves. The governments that met at Meech Lake, in spite of the symbolic adjustments in their own Accord, do not appear to have understood the greatly enhanced psychological role of the constitution that followed in the wake of 1982, especially of the Charter. They forgot that the contemporary constitution speaks not only to governments but also, and directly, to Canadians.

As a result, they blundered casually and unknowingly into an emotional minefield, with consequences that frequently flow from such wandering.

THE LEADERSHIP FAILURE OF GOVERNMENTS

The lamentable quality of the Meech Lake debate, especially the contributions of its official government supporters, merits examination and explanation.

Those provincial governments that did not even bother to hold hearings and had only perfunctory legislative debates before passing the Accord, of which British Columbia was a prime example, both exploited and contributed to civic ignorance about a potentially major alteration in Canadian federalism and in the underlying philosophy of Canadianism. Provincial governments outside of Quebec further reduced the quality of the debate by their almost total unwillingness to defend the Accord in terms of the equality-of-the-provinces principle that made the Quebec round a provincial round. Presumably, for the provinces other than Quebec, strategy considerations dictated deflecting attention from their gains because that useful blindness would allow a subsequent constitutional round to be a "real" provincial round, a self-interested objective that a correct description of Meech Lake would not have served. As a result, the debate suffered from the pervasive bias of its label as the Quebec round, rather than dealing with the Accord as a provincializing round with Quebec playing the leading role for all the provincial government beneficiaries.

From the government of Quebec, all criticisms, questions, and suggestions for possible changes were almost invariably met with the categorical statement that Quebec's demands were minimal, non-negotiable, and hence non-discussable. The Quebec government position – that all of Quebec's compromises had been made by the time the agreement became public after the second round of meetings at Langevin Block – had a devastatingly deadening effect on subsequent debate.

After the Langevin meeting, the Quebec government moved quickly to ratify the Accord. Bourassa held no hearings at this time, not wishing to give a forum to the nationalist critics of the Accord, who had challenged its adequacy as a response to the traditional demands of Quebec in earlier National Assembly hearings held between the Meech Lake and Langevin meetings.[86]

Bourassa's strategy of having only limited hearings on the preliminary version of the Accord, no hearings after the Accord was finalized in legal language, and then proceeding to a quick debate in the National Assembly was widely criticized in Quebec as anti-democratic, elitist, and inappropriate for such an exalted activity as formal constitutional change.[87] These criticisms were remarkably similar to those that dogged the public debate outside of Quebec.

Bourassa's quick ratification, which took the opposition Parti Québécois by surprise, had several major consequences, all of them hostile to meaningful and informed public debate. It stifled the possible mobilization of Quebec opinion against the Accord. It gave an anti-Quebec colouring to opposition elsewhere in Canada, including that of any other government that, influenced by public opinion or its own reassessment, might wish to amend the Accord. It made any compromise or retreat very difficult for Quebec by requiring a return to the National Assembly for an amendment that would surely be attacked by the nationalists as a sell-out. It reduced the role of elaborate reasoned justifications by the Quebec government for particulars of the Accord, because reason invites responses, encourages debate, and generates uncertainty about proposed courses of action – far better, so the Bourassa government reasoned, to justify the package by its limited size and by defining it as the rectification of an historic injustice. While the overall Quebec strategy led to a deliberate and welcome rigidity for Bourassa, it gave an appearance of irrelevance and futility to subsequent debate about the Accord outside of Quebec.

The federal government defaulted on its responsibility to provide intellectual leadership for a major constitutional reordering of Canada, a point that was candidly admitted by some of the academic defenders of the Accord.[88] The initial federal government silence partly derived from an erroneous interpretation of the constitutional process and of how the Meech Lake dynamics would develop. According to Lowell Murray, the key federal minister, the federal government saw no need for "a large campaign . . . [or] a great sales pitch" because with all governments "on board" it was expected the agreement would be ratified in a year.[89] Accordingly, the only individuals who had to be convinced were the premiers, and that had already been done in two closed meetings, as Mulroney indicated. When told that some premiers might be having second thoughts, he commented: "I take it as given that all premiers signed the deal and will have it endorsed by their legislatures. . . . It's settled – it's done. . . . They gave their word – that's as good as gold for me."[90]

The federal government scheduled its hearings for the summer, leaving little time for the preparation of briefs by academics or interest groups. The hearings were clearly intended to be a formality, as the Accord was described as an untouchable seamless web that would only be altered if an egregious error, as defined by governments, was found. The total absence of major position papers elucidating the proposed changes further hampered would-be critics by depriving them of official rationales whose weaknesses they could try to penetrate. For major critics, such as Trudeau, the federal government carefully staged competing media events in order to minimize the visibility of several of his interventions.

In English Canada, the public was provided with homilies about bringing Quebec back into the constitutional family and an avoidance of specificity. Mulroney's personal difficulty in rigorously explaining and justifying the Accord may have been linked to his apparent belief that it emerged as a result of an almost ineffable "human dynamic" among those in the bargaining room, which could only be communicated with great difficulty, if at all, to non-participants.[91] This view of the Accord as an inexplicable product of the chemistry of private social interaction reduced the role of reason and increased the need for trust, which was in short supply, in getting support for the Accord.

The quality of the debate was further dampened by the unusual fact that all three parties in the House of Commons supported the Accord and suppressed internal caucus criticism by party discipline. This drastically reduced the flow of information and analysis to the public that is normally a by-product of adversarial relationships in the House of Commons. Thus, the federal government was not pressed to provide reasoned explanations of the purposes to be served by or the consequences expected to flow from particular changes, such as those dealing with immigration, the transitional arrangements for Senate reform, and the spending power.[92] Instead of providing particular justifications for particular amendments in the Accord, the federal government preferred to justify the entire Accord as the "product of nineteen years of comprehensive constitutional review and of extensive commentary in learned journals and the press."[93] Since the previous nineteen years had produced a chaos of competing proposals, this statement by the Prime Minister did not encourage focused debate.

This choking off of information was compounded by the fact that, initially, the intergovernmental agreement was unanimous. As a result, no dissenting provincial government provided an alternative view of the Accord until changes of government in Manitoba, New Brunswick, and Newfoundland broke the intergovernmental consensus and made major contributions to opening up the debate.

The deficiencies of Meech Lake as an exercise in constitutional education for a people asked to redefine itself and reassess its future have, therefore, several sources. Structural factors were crucial – such as the unanimity requirement that initially biased the flow of information in favour of the Accord, the practice of party discipline that bottled up minority dissent within party caucuses, and responsible government that allowed governing majority parties in some provinces to pass the Accord with little democratic fuss. Many "deficiencies," however, were chosen as strategies to thwart public discussion and public understanding.

These latter, "chosen" deficiencies in constitutional leadership are not just abstract ethical shortcomings devoid of practical significance, private vices, so to speak, relevant only for the confessional. On the contrary, they represent grievous shortcomings in constitutional morality that reflect an impoverished and anachronistic constitutional theory.

Constitutional education is a two-way street. Dialogue improves the understanding of governors as well as the governed. A more public, open, tentative process with opportunities for feedback would surely have been preferable to the shadow-boxing encounter between a rigidly brittle Accord and the resentful clashing views of other legitimate constitutional actors who felt unjustly ignored. There is now a public base to the constitutional order, whose implications need to be worked out. The democratic assumption that authority springs from below is extended to the constitution itself by the Charter. Consequently, constitutional change by executive coup is now illegitimate, as well as being counterproductive, as Meech Lake shows. It follows that the new constitutional actors need to be educated in their responsibilities, particularly those groups that have niches in the constitution, such as women, aboriginals, and others. In the long run, it is not helpful to see these new constitutional players as only awkward impediments to be bypassed, overcome, or outsmarted. They have memories; they observe and learn from their "betters"; they are in the constitution; they will not go away.

DISTRUST OF GOVERNMENTS AND OF EXECUTIVE FEDERALISM

Remarkably, the arsenal of arguments available to legitimate executive federalism and government dominance of the Meech Lake process was singularly unconvincing to the army of the suspicious. The representatives of women, aboriginals, multicultural Canadians, and various "equality-seekers," as they came to be called, simply did not believe that their voices would be heard and their interests served if one of their own was not at the table.[94]

On all occasions on which hearings were held, the subsequent committee reports, influenced by the indignation of the groups they heard, and even when controlled by government majorities, could offer only halfhearted justification for the process.[95] When reports based on hearings were prepared in provinces whose governments were not committed to the Accord,[96] or in the Senate with its Liberal majority,[97] their criticisms of the shortcomings of the process were scathing. The criticism of Newfoundland, although not based on hearings, was passionately expressed.[98] The report of the Manitoba Task Force is representative. It stated that the majority of those who appeared before it were gravely disappointed with the process. The Accord was seen as " 'a pressure cooker' deal agreed to in the wee hours of the morning by eleven First Ministers who were too tired to do otherwise." The Task Force members "were struck by the impression that the presenters felt a sense of being cheated, misled, and betrayed. . . . [and] realized the extent to which the process . . . undercut the legitimacy of the Accord." [99]

Distrust was aggravated by the perceived failure of the federal government to defend its own interests, to speak for a more than provincial vision of Canada, and to strike a compromise in which both sides of the federal bargain, the federal government as well as Quebec and the other provincial governments, would gain as well as give. Outside of Quebec, the federal government was thought to have abdicated its role as guardian of the federal interest, a view that is confirmed by insider accounts. According to one premier, Mulroney "kept asking if we had a deal. . . . It was as if he didn't have any idea what the deal was or he didn't care that much as long as he got one." [100] Remarkably, there is pervasive and convincing evidence in various hearings that the Accord was opposed even in provincial settings in English Canada because it weakened the federal government and threatened Charter-influenced conceptions of Canadian citizenship. The pro-Meech Lake governments in English Canada were either unable or unwilling to defend convincingly a province-serving constitutional package before their own provincial residents. Equally remarkably, the dissenting provinces of Manitoba, New Brunswick, and Newfoundland criticized the Accord for its provincializing thrust. Overall, distrust for the executive federalism process in English Canada was fed by its perceived failure to give appropriate weight to a strong central government and to the Canadian community as being more than an aggregation of provincialisms.

Unwillingness to trust or put one's constitutional fate in the hands of governments has especially strong roots among particular groups, such as women and aboriginals. They filtered the Meech Lake attempt to exclude them from meaningful participation through the memories of previous constitutional experiences that had instilled in them a distrust for political office-holders. Both women and aboriginals remembered that in 1981 a closed first ministers' meeting had weakened or removed rights they thought they had secured. They were only reinstated after a massive application of political pressure. Aboriginals could not help but contrast their failure to have their rights detailed and entrenched after four constitutional conferences with the much more extensive constitutional changes that were made for Quebec only a few weeks after the failed fourth aboriginal conference. They concluded that "in the final analysis [they are] ... an expendable group whose interests will be sacrificed to meet the dictates of larger and more powerful political constituencies."[101] After the (false) impression that a Meech Lake deal had been concluded, the leader of the Assembly of Manitoba Chiefs bitterly observed: "We're left on the outside, looking in. It's unfair and it's the perpetuation of a double standard. Quebec has been here for 350 years, but we've been here for thousands of years."[102]

Women's groups were aware that the application of pressure by aboriginals and multicultural groups between the Meech Lake and Langevin meetings had won both groups protection against the interpretive provisions of the Meech Lake Accord that women had not equally won.[103] Thus, from the perspective of one feminist scholar, Professor Beverly Baines, the Quebec round was also a "men's round" in which "these men simply forgot about us, just as their predecessors did in November, 1981, when they were negotiating the Charter's override provision."[104] Women's groups who appeared before the Manitoba Task Force were bitterly critical of the process and thought that women had been ignored, denied the dignity of reasoned answers, and symbolically treated as second class. They "[r]epeatedly referred to the eleven 'men' who drafted the Accord."[105] Multicultural groups had their own historical reasons for believing that the natural propensity of politicians engaged in constitutional discussions was to overlook them.[106]

Public reactions to the Meech Lake process initially challenged and ultimately repudiated the justifying assumptions of executive federalism in constitutional matters, namely that governments can be relied on as reliable proxies for the constitutional views of their electorate. In constitutional settings, the claimed responsiveness of responsible government is no longer believed. Indeed, by the end of the process even first ministers were unable to repress any longer their distaste for and frustration with elitist deal-making in private.[107]

In its largest sense, the Meech Lake process was a failed attempt to ignore or roll back the pressures for a more open democratic process of constitutional change. Those pressures derive from changes in cultural values, especially among elites, and from the message of the Charter and various aboriginal clauses that the constitution no longer belongs to governments. To ignore such pressures after the experience of Meech Lake would be inexcusable constitutional folly. This point is elaborated in the concluding sections of this chapter.

WHY DID GOVERNMENTS BLUNDER SO BADLY?

No definitive explanation can be offered of why the governments that tried to engineer Meech Lake were so little cognizant of the extent that the Charter and the aboriginal constitutional clauses had changed the constitutional order. Some of the likely contributing factors, however, can be readily identified.

The most obvious explanation, not to be discounted, is self-interest. To preserve a monopoly for governments over the process of constitutional change required no complex justification for those who thought they already possessed it. In addition, to keep constitutional change in the hands of governments was a great simplifier to the eleven actors who could meet and plan the future of the country. To have to think of women, visible minorities, aboriginals, and who knew how many others as constitutional participants seemed like a recipe for stalemate and a constitutional tower of Babel. These root and branch reasons, however, can be supplemented by several supplementary supporting considerations.

First, although both the Charter and a comprehensive amending formula appeared simultaneously in the 1982 Constitution Act, they did not have a common origin, and thus their potential interrelations were unexplored. The amending formula was fashioned by provincial governments in the private arena of the Gang of Eight provinces that opposed the threatened Trudeau unilateral patriation. Further, the provincial governments that created the amending formula were opposed to the federal government's proposed Charter, an opposition they preserved from challenge by keeping the public that overwhelmingly supported a Charter out of the private proceedings in which their constitutional package was crafted.[108] Thus, those who drafted the amending formula failed to consider its future constitutional coexistence with a Charter.

On the other hand, the Charter, the major constitutional policy objective of the Trudeau federal government, was modified by a vigorous public hearings process that gave the public, especially the groups that won concessions, a proprietary attitude to its contents. They developed no similar attitude to the amending formula. Accordingly, it was natural for governments, especially provincial ones, to see the amending formula as their responsibility and achievement, and the Charter, which originated elsewhere, as constitutionally irrelevant to its operation.

Second, the Quebec and federal governments, which played the leading role in generating the Meech Lake outcome, were not among the Charter's strongest advocates. In Quebec, the 1982 Charter was originally viewed by the governing Parti Québécois as the instrument of the federal government and *les anglais* to reduce Quebec powers. Although Quebec Liberals had historically been more sympathetic to the Charter idea, and under Bourassa put forth Meech Lake as a partial rapprochement with the Charter, the distinct society clause was clearly an attempt to soften its impact. The fact that both leading parties in Quebec have been willing to resort to the notwithstanding clause and have offered principled defences of its constitutional utility further underlines the relative weakness of the Canadian Charter in Quebec political culture. Thus the Quebec Liberal government was the least likely government in the country to understand the impact of the Charter on the constitutional culture of English Canada, although its sensitivities probably surpassed those of the Parti Québécois opposition.

The governing Conservative Party in Ottawa, Quebec's partner in orchestrating Meech Lake, had successfully delayed the patriation package in 1980-81 and had tended to see the Charter as Trudeau's Charter. Thus, Meech Lake was the joint product of the provincial government and the federal party least predisposed to sympathy with the Charter.[109]

A third more general reason why the constituencies that cluster around the Charter have so little salience when governments consider constitutional change is that the Federal-Provincial Relations Office and the various provincial intergovernmental affairs advisory units see the world in federalist rather than Charter terms. Their task is to manage federalism, not citizen-state relations. They are encouraged in this view in constitutional matters by the lead role given to governments by the formal structure of the amending formula. In the intergovernmental arena in which constitutional deals are struck, the support sought is that of other governments, not of the feminist defenders of Section 28 or of the Ukrainian Canadians concerned with the possible weakening of Section 27. The federalism assumptions that drive the amending formula, with their inherent stress on territory and jurisdiction, tend to generate a blindness to the social cleavages of sex and ethnicity that are not territorially based, even if they are now of constitutional import.

MEECH LAKE AS THE SETTING FOR A CONFRONTATION BETWEEN OLDER AND NEWER VIEWS OF THE CONSTITUTION

The implicit constitutional theory behind Meech Lake assumed that the bringing of Quebec back into the constitutional family was a federalism issue; that executive federalism backed by governments that controlled their legislatures by applying party discipline to one-party majorities was the vehicle for its achievement; and that the Quebec issue, with appropriate payoffs to the other veto-possessing provincial governments, could be discretely handled without seriously upsetting the new constitutional groups that clustered around the Charter or the politically awakened aboriginal peoples. This theory was wrong on every count.

Meech Lake was the setting for a confrontation between the federal and provincial governments, whose authority derived from federalism and responsible parliamentary government, and a cluster of ethnic, feminist, indigenous, social policy, minority official-language, and rights concerns that derived mainly from the Charter and from other clauses applying to the aboriginal peoples of Canada. Phrased differently, the confrontation was between older and newer conceptions of the constitution. To Trudeau, the constitutional struggle of the previous twenty years had been a contest between the rights of the people and the rights of governments, with the Charter as the instrument – admittedly imperfect because of the notwithstanding clause, and incomplete because of the absence of a referendum provision in the amending formula – "to establish the sovereignty of the people over all levels of government."[110] For Trudeau, and for other opponents of the Accord,[111] Meech Lake was an attempt to repudiate the new forces, to establish decisively the primacy of governments in the amending process, and to counter the nationalizing thrust of the Charter by enhancing the role of the provinces in the overall functioning of the federal system.

These purposes were especially important for the Quebec government. As William Thorsell succinctly put it: "What is Meech Lake but an effort by Quebec to regain more breathing room under the Charter of Rights, which bound it more closely than at any time in our history to a pan-Canadian ideal?"[112] Premier Bourassa's principled support of the notwithstanding clause is driven by the same purpose of carving out a sphere of governmental autonomy to respond to the specificity of Quebec.[113] In Francophone Quebec, the Meech Lake debate was driven by a political dynamic that was "unanimously decentralist and autonomist" and thus saw the Charter as a threatening constitutional instrument, against which defences were required.[114]

In English Canada, by contrast, the Charter fosters a view of citizenship based on equal rights that is hostile to the *de facto* differences in citizen treatment that were perfectly normal in Canadian federalism when rights derived from precedent and tradition rather than from a Charter. The fear that the Charter might be weakened was central to the reservations of Manitoba, New Brunswick, and Newfoundland about the Accord. Why was it impossible to view the Quebec government's use of the notwithstanding clause to apply its legislation on language of signs as simply a Quebec issue to be handled in terms of federalism's respect for provincial diversity? The answer is the Charter. It elevated Quebec's response to an issue of high constitutional principle and Canada-wide concern and provided Premier Filmon of Manitoba with a rationale to withdraw the Accord from debate in the provincial legislature. This attack on the Charter's symbolism by the Quebec government was probably the single most important factor in the erosion of support for Meech Lake outside of Quebec.

In the Manitoba and New Brunswick public hearings, defence of the Charter against the possible encroachments of the Accord, especially the distinct society clause, was probably the most recurring plea of various non-aboriginal citizen groups. In Manitoba, over half of those who spoke at the Task Force hearings were concerned about the Accord's impact on "Charter rights, particularly sex equality rights."[115] In New Brunswick, a major issue of those who appeared before the Select Committee was the necessity of defining the "Charter's supremacy in the Constitution."[116] The New Brunswick Select Committee declared that "of all the Constitutional Acts, the Charter is undoubtedly the most important for individual Canadians."[117]

Where public hearings were held, the non-aboriginal citizen groups that opposed the Accord were overwhelmingly drawn from the social categories singled out by the Charter for recognition – feminist groups, multicultural groups, official-language minorities, and the various groups listed in the Section 15 equality rights clause. Normally these groups fought to enhance or protect the constitutional clauses of particular concern to their clientele, as well as defending the overall prominence of the Charter in the constitution. Clearly, the Charter's capacity to slice through federalism's categories of territorial community membership was warmly received in English Canada by citizens whose identities and multiple senses of belonging derived from sex, ethnicity, language, the status of being disabled, and other geographically diffuse social categories.[118]

The confrontation between older and newer conceptions of the constitution waxed and waned as the locus of discussion or attention shifted. It was most evident when public hearings were under way, least evident when the media focus was on First Ministers' Conferences or on the pilgrimages of federal emissaries shuttling back and forth from Ottawa to provincial capitals seeking to patch up a faltering Accord. The two constitutional worlds of governments and citizens, of federalism and the

Charter, of the French and English founding peoples versus the others separately waxed and waned as the agenda shifted from the closed meetings of executive federalism to the cacophonous citizens' world of various interests driven by social and ethnic cleavages. Some merger of these worlds occurred as new governments were elected in Manitoba, New Brunswick, and Newfoundland that were not committed to the Accord and were sensitive to their provincial public opinion. Inevitably, this increased the rancour of subsequent first ministers' meetings.

As the ramifications of the Accord were clarified, it could no longer be seen as simply a pragmatic response to a federalism concern. It implicated all Canadians whose interests or identities or conceptions of Canada had come to be attached to the Charter.[119] Feminist groups in English Canada saw the Accord as a rebuff to their 1982 gains in the Charter. Ethnic communities, who initially sought to defend Section 27 of the Charter and who subsequently tried to have multiculturalism included as one of Canada's fundamental characteristics, saw the Accord as devaluing Canadians whose background was neither French nor English. The aboriginal peoples responded with even more passion in defence of their distinctive status as the real founding people of Canada. Here, the Accord clearly entered the social territory of competing claims for status and recognition of the traditional European founding peoples, the indigenous peoples whose ancestors long preceded them in North America, and the other contributors to the multicultural, multiracial dimension of Canada that could not make claims as founding peoples or First Nations. Not only did these interpretations of the Accord's subject matter deny that it was simply a response to a federalism problem, but as a corollary they challenged the domination by governments of the amending process. To the extent the Accord was seen as manipulating the social pluralism of a heterogeneous society rather than simply readjusting the relative status and powers of the territorial communities of federalism and their governments, the propriety of the governments' leadership role was weakened. The truculent aggressiveness of so many of the Accord's critics from outside Quebec derived from their belief that government monopolization of the amending process was illegitimate. Deference was conspicuously absent as the Accord's opponents challenged the legitimacy of governments to tamper with their Charter or their constitutional aboriginal status.

The defenders of government dominance of the amending process were not without arguments. They pointed to the historic virtues of democratic representative and responsible government fostered by competitive politics in a situation in which the electorate had the last say.

The more recently established practice of executive federalism, capped by First Ministers' Conferences, was itself almost a tradition, legitimated by its capacity to inject flexibility into a nineteenth-century division of powers. When these rationales did not assuage the critics, some of the Accord's supporters defended the process as clearly meeting the requirement of the Constitution Act, and thus as beyond reproach. Strong process defenders added that the Meech Lake process, with its requirement of legislative approval, "has in fact met a higher test of democracy than the 1982 constitutional changes did."[120] Other defenders suggested that the process problem was inherited from the 1982 Constitution Act, for which those who employed it in the late eighties bear no responsibility. This appears to be the rationale for the Prime Minister's assertion that the three-year waiting period is the Achilles' heel of the 1982 amending formula.[121]

However, these formalistic defences of the process or of the behaviours of the governments that employed it are unconvincing. They pay inadequate attention to the distinction between the technical requirements of the amending formula and the expanding or contracting, flexible or rigid, open or closed political process within which the technical requirements are met. While the technical requirements for amendment may have been more stringent in Meech Lake than in 1980-82, the political process surrounding the latter was much more open and sensitive. The public hearings process strengthened the Charter, with several basic features such as "protection of the rights of the disabled or the constitutional recognition of the concept of affirmative action for disadvantaged groups in society, . . . [emerging from] public hearings and public representations which changed the minds of governments." Indeed, even after the apparently final intergovernmental settlement in late 1981, there were further modifications that strengthened protections for women and aboriginals.[122] Thus, the federal package in 1980 was conceived very differently from the original seamless web of the Meech Lake Accord.

Nothing in the 1982 amending formula prohibited a flexible, open process of public consultation before first ministers meet; nothing prohibited first ministers from viewing their agreement as somewhat tentative and subject to modification as a result of informed public input; the 1982 formula did not require the abusive bullying visited on opponents of the Accord in its early days; the legacy of 1982 did not preclude treating Canadians who identified with the Charter as honourable participants in the exalted activity of constitutional politics. The processes that enveloped the 1987-90 Meech Lake effort were chosen by leaders, not dictated by formal constitutional requirements.

The confrontation between older and newer views of the constitution is a consequence of the 1982 incorporation of the Charter into the Canadian constitution. The Charter links Canadians directly to the constitution, while the amending formula, when applied in the Meech Lake fashion, presupposes an older constitutional view in which governments are in charge and the management of federalism is the task. This older view, however, is rejected by those whose link to the constitution is through the Charter or derives from the constitution's aboriginal clauses. Almost a decade after the Charter's arrival on the Canadian scene, original Charter supporters such as Jean Chrétien and early opponents such as former Premier Allan Blakeney agree that the Charter has permanently and drastically changed constitutional politics in Canada. For Chrétien the Charter makes "individual Canadians parties to the constitution with a legitimate claim of ownership to it."[123] For Blakeney, the Charter gives to women, ethnic groups, and aboriginal peoples what he variously called "a possessor interest . . . [or] a sense of proprietary rights" in the constitution that had not existed prior to the 1982 Constitution Act.[124]

These emerging realities necessitate a basic rethinking of the various roles and functions of the constitution, of the relationship of the constitution to a people that is more than federal, of the role of citizens as constitutional actors, and of the process of formal constitutional change.

Where Do We Go From Here?

The theory and practice of constitutional change appropriate for the Canadian future must recognize the new social role of the constitution in the era of the Charter. Federalism and parliamentary government remain as fundamental constitutional ordering principles, but they coexist with a Charter that incorporates the citizenry directly into the constitutional order.

The society over which the constitution presides can no longer sustain the ethnic constitutional hegemony of the French and English as founding peoples. They must retreat, move over, and give more constitutional space to the galloping ethnic and racial heterogeneity of contemporary Canada, including a growing and increasingly alienated aboriginal population.

The constitution by means of the Charter now speaks directly to Canadians. The elites of the groups with Charter recognition have stakes in the constitution. They have left the audience and are now on the playing field, as are the aboriginal peoples for whom the constitution is a potential lever to a less marginalized future.

The constitution has thus become a public affair and rests on a citizen base. Patient, honest explanation of the means and ends of constitutional change by leaders prepared to listen to citizens is the only viable alternative to the havoc-creating seamless web of future Meech Lake Accords. Since citizens can no longer be excluded, as the failed attempt to do so in Meech Lake confirms, they must be educated in their new constitutional responsibilities. Thus far, their bruising encounters with governing elites have been more likely to engender cynicism, distrust, and an aggressive self-interest rather than the reverse.

Outside of Quebec, these new constitutional players – women, aboriginals, ethnics, basic Charter supporters, and others – contributed to the demise of Meech Lake by challenging the constitutional philosophy on which it was based and by delegitimating the process by which it was to be achieved. To blame them for the collapse of Meech Lake is unfairly to forget how new they are to constitutional politics and how limited, indeed perverse, has been their education in the handling of constitutional responsibilities that attend their new status. If they had been taught anything by their previous constitutional interaction with and observations of governments, it was surely that to trust governments is a high-risk enterprise and that an obstinate self-centredness is the way to play constitutional politics. Constitutional selfishness turned out to be contagious. Quebec's demands were driven by self-interest; the acquiescence of the other provincial governments was purchased by side payoffs; and Newfoundland and Alberta ensured that their constitutional concerns pertaining to fisheries and the Senate were granted priority at future constitutional conferences. By inference, the message from the other provincial governments was that in the absence of such concessions they were prepared to block Quebec's return to the constitutional family. Thus, when Elijah Harper and the Manitoba Chiefs indicated their desire to kill the Meech Lake Accord because it did "an injustice" to native peoples by leaving them as "second-class citizens,"[125] they revealed the depth of their alienation, the particularistic aboriginal vision that guided them, and how well they had learned the hardball game of constitutional politics by assiduous observation of the elected leaders of governments.

One key reason for the failure of Meech Lake, therefore, was the too restrictive constitutional morality on which it was based. The basic Meech Lake process was designed to keep the citizenry at bay. Not surprisingly, when they climbed over the barricades, their mood was often truculent rather than co-operative. No one had bothered to educate the citizen leaders who acted as intermediaries for a range of societal interests in how they should handle responsibilities they had not been expected to bear. What is required is a more comprehensive version of what J.A. Corry pleaded for in 1978, a new constitutional morality.

In pre-Charter days, Corry's new morality required English Canadians and the federal government to cultivate and act on a nuanced empathy for and understanding of the sensitivities of Québécois and their government. More generally, he saw the need for a "constitutional morality," an intergovernmental comity that would reduce the abrasion in a system of big governments.[126] Corry's prescriptions remain apposite, yet they can no longer be restricted to relations among governments but must be extended to the new constitutional players linked to the Charter and to the aboriginal constitutional clauses. This multiplication of constitutional players and the correspondingly more demanding requirements of constitutional morality for civility, trust, and mutual respect among a diversity of public and private constitutional players do not ease the management of our constitutional business. However, in our era, these requirements, like the law of gravity, cannot be ignored. A deliberate constitutional blindness to the social changes that lie behind them has nothing to recommend it. We cannot return to simpler times.

There is no feasible alternative to making citizens worthy participants in the ongoing revision of the constitution of their country. The goal of a citizens' constitution and the participant imperatives it engenders can be justified as one more stage in the evolution of Canadian democracy. Or, it can be justified on the strictly pragmatic grounds that the Charter makes a move in that direction unavoidable. In the same way that the 1960 Bill of Rights paved the way for the 1982 Charter, the latter has paved the way for, indeed made inevitable, a more democratized amending process. Such a move flows from the logic of where we are now in constitutional terms. At this stage, the details of that democratized process – referenda, constituent assemblies, an open give-and-take process of legislative committees – are less important than the recognition that we have no choice but to move in that direction.

While warnings abound that to travel on this route may be a recipe for deadlock and stalemate,[127] we know that the existing process is devastatingly counter-productive. The premise behind the fear of change is that Canadian citizens are more divided from each other than are their governments. This is not self-evident, in part because citizen choice is less affected by the rigidities of vested self-interest that governments bring to the bargaining table. Also, citizens have less face to lose.

The old logic of executive federalism has left Canadians with the debris and humiliation of a badly bungled attempt to amend the constitution in the service of our togetherness, an attempt that has further divided us. It is both unsurprising and encouraging that a recent poll indicates that two out of three Quebec residents, and an even higher ratio outside of Quebec, believe that "Changes to the constitution should only be decided by the people voting directly in a referendum."[128]

Meech Lake has provided at least a preliminary answer to a question its formulators had not intended to ask. Can governments retain the leading role in formal constitutional change that they attempted to exercise in Meech Lake? The negative answer suggests that the further answer to the basic question Meech Lake did not resolve – what separate or shared constitutional futures are appropriate for the one or more peoples living north of the United States? – will emerge from a more open, pluralistic process than the discredited Meech Lake model.

Notes

Editor's Preface

1. Alan C. Cairns, "The Living Canadian Constitution," in Douglas E. Williams, ed., *Constitution, Government, and Society in Canada: Selected Essays by Alan C. Cairns* (Toronto, 1988), p. 12.
2. Alan C. Cairns, "Constitutional Minoritarianism in Canada," The J.A. Corry Lecture, Queen's University, March 6, 1990 (mimeo), p. 3.
3. See, for example, Alan C. Cairns, "Alternative Styles in the Study of Canadian Politics," *Canadian Journal of Political Science*, VII (1974), pp. 101-28; Cairns, "National Influences on the Study of Politics," *Queen's Quarterly*, 81 (1974), pp. 333-47; Cairns, "Political Science and the Americanization Issue," *Canadian Journal of Political Science*, VII (1975), pp. 192-234; Cairns, "Political Science in Canada: Some Observations and Speculations," *Transaction of the Royal Society of Canada*, Fourth Series, XVIII (1980), pp. 263-71; and A.C. Cairns and D.E. Williams, "Writings in Political Science," in W.N. New, ed., *The Literary History of Canada*, Second Edition (Toronto, 1989), Vol. 4, pp. 263-92.
4. Alan C. Cairns, "Author's Introduction," in Williams, ed., *Constitution, Government, and Society in Canada*, p. 13.

Author's Introduction

1. Denis Robert, "La signification de l'Accord du lac Meech au Canada anglais et au Québec francophone: un tour d'horizon du débat public," in Peter M. Leslie and Ronald L. Watts, eds., *Canada: The State of the Federation 1987-88* (Kingston, 1988), pp. 118, 156. The two solitudes are revealed with clarity in Philip Resnick, *Letters to a Québécois Friend, with a reply by Daniel Latouche* (Montreal, 1990).
2. Lynn Smith, "Could the Meech Lake Accord Affect the Protection of Equality Rights for Women and Minorities in Canada?" *Constitutional Forum*, 1 (Winter, 1990), p. 17.
3. Patrick Alexander McCartney, "An Examination of Federal and Provincial Government Sponsorship of Voluntary Associations in Canada" (M.A. thesis, Queen's University, 1990), pp. 17, 39.
4. Section 35 (1) of the Constitution Act, 1982, stated that "existing aboriginal and

treaty rights . . . are hereby recognized and affirmed." Section 35 (2) defined the "aboriginal peoples of Canada" to include "the Indian, Inuit and Métis peoples of Canada." Section 37 required the calling of a constitutional conference to identify and define aboriginal rights. Section 25 of the Charter protected certain aboriginal, treaty, and other rights from abrogation or derogation by the Charter. The original federal government jurisdiction over "Indians, and Lands reserved for the Indians" derives from Section 91 (24) of the BNA Act, 1867.

5. I have elaborated on a number of the preceding points in "Constitutional Minoritarianism in Canada," the J.A. Corry Lecture delivered at Queen's University, March 6, 1990.

6. Robert M. Campbell, "Eleven Men and a Constitution: The Meech Lake Accord," in Robert M. Campbell and Leslie A. Pal, *The Real Worlds of Canadian Politics: Cases in Process and Policy* (Peterborough, Ont., 1989), p. 238.

7. *Ibid.*, p. 239.

8. "Address by Mr. Gil Rémillard," in Peter M. Leslie, *Rebuilding the Relationship: Quebec and its Confederation Partners; Report of a Conference, Mont Gabriel, Quebec 9-11 May, 1986* (Kingston, 1987), p. 41.

9. The Constitutional Committee of the Quebec Liberal Party, *A New Canadian Federation* (Montreal, 1980), p. 32.

10. Cited in Paul C. Weiler, "Rights and Judges in a Democracy: A New Canadian Version," *University of Michigan Journal of Law Reform*, 18 (Fall, 1984), p. 88.

11. *Ibid.*, p. 90.

12. Cited in Calvin R. Massey, "The Locus of Sovereignty: Judicial Review, Legislative Supremacy, and Federalism in the Constitutional Traditions of Canada and the United States," mimeo (1990), p. 41.

13. Weiler, "Rights and Judges," p. 90.

14. "Draft Agreement on the Constitution: Proposals by the Government of Quebec (Released May 1985)," in Peter M. Leslie, ed., *Canada: The State of the Federation 1985* (Kingston, n.d.), pp. 64-68. See also the earlier 1981 proposals of the Parti Québécois government for giving Quebec's consent to the patriation package in Stephen A. Scott, "The Canadian Constitutional Amendment Process: Mechanisms and Prospects," in Clare F. Beckton and A. Wayne MacKay, eds., *Recurring Issues in Canadian Federalism*, Volume 57 of the Research Studies of the Royal Commission on the Economic Union and Development Prospects for Canada (Toronto, 1986), p. 103.

15. F.L. Morton, Peter. H. Russell, and Michael J. Withey, "The Supreme Court's First 100 Charter of Rights Decisions: A Quantitative Analysis," prepared for presentation at the annual meeting of the Canadian Political Science Association, May 27-29, 1990, Victoria, British Columbia, pp. 14-15.

16. Andrée Lajoie *et al.*, "Political Ideas in Quebec and the Evolution of Canadian Constitutional Law, 1945 to 1985," in Ivan Bernier and Andrée Lajoie, eds., *The Supreme Court of Canada as an Instrument of Political Change*, Volume 47 of the Research Studies of the Royal Commission on the Economic Union and Development Prospects for Canada (Toronto, 1986), p. 64.

17. One of the tantalizing historical might-have-beens is whether the Charter would have acquired the same degree and kind of popular support among Québécois that it acquired elsewhere if the provincial Liberals had controlled the Quebec government after the 1982 Constitution Act. If it had, the Quebec/rest-of-Canada tensions over the Charter that hounded Meech Lake to its grave might have been absent or much less salient.

18. The five Quebec conditions were:
    1. Explicit recognition of Quebec as a distinct society;
    2. Guarantee of increased powers in matters of immigration;
    3. Limitation of the federal spending power;
    4. Recognition of a right of veto;
    5. Quebec's participation in appointing judges to the Supreme Court of Canada.
"Address by Rémillard," in Leslie, *Rebuilding the Relationship*, p. 42.
19. Andrew Cohen, "That Bastard Trudeau," *Saturday Night*, June, 1990, pp. 38-46. According to William Thorsell, "Mr. Mulroney seems almost obsessed with his place in history relative to Mr. Trudeau. He fights him in the mirrors, he fights him in the smoke, he fights him in the fading memories of millions ready to scalp a scapegoat." "Mulroney playing a dangerous game in attacking the constitution," *Globe and Mail*, January 20, 1990.
20. This assessment of the events of 1980-82 by the Prime Minister necessitated a certain blurring of his own past, as his contemporaneous support for the Trudeau constitutional initiative has been noted by several commentators. See in particular Jeffrey Simpson, "His feelings then, his remarks now," *Globe and Mail*, January 4, 1990; Simpson, "With Liberals in pursuit," *ibid.*, April 14, 1989. See also Susan Delacourt, "Constitution attack surprises Chretien," *ibid.*, April 10, 1989; William Thorsell, "Mulroney playing a dangerous game in attacking the constitution," *ibid.*, January 20, 1990. Mulroney's support for proceeding without Quebec is also asserted in Ron Graham, *One-Eyed Kings: Promise and Illusion in Canadian Politics* (Toronto, 1987), pp. 160-61.
   For Mulroney's denials that he would have proceeded without Quebec, see Graham Fraser, "PM says 1982 flaws removed 'flexibility' in Meech Lake talks," *Globe and Mail*, June 13, 1988; Hugh Winsor, "Constitutional Accord not so high on cabinet's agenda, PM hints," *ibid.*, September 14, 1989.
21. "Mulroney's Magic Moment," *Maclean's*, June 15, 1987, p. 17.
22. Cited in Simon Schama, *Citizens: A Chronicle of the French Revolution* (Toronto, 1990), p. xiii.
23. "The Globe and Mail-CBC News Poll," and Hugh Winsor, "Nation sharply split over failure of Meech Accord," *Globe and Mail*, July 9, 1990; Hugh Winsor, "Wells was lightning rod for anti-French feeling, poll shows," *ibid.*, July 10, 1990.
24. Geoffrey York, "Native MLA blocks debate on Meech," *ibid.*, June 13, 1990.
25. Geoffrey York and Alan Freeman, "Native MLA advises PM to call chiefs with offer," *ibid.*, June 16, 1990.
26. For a generally critical appraisal of the English-Canadian academic response to the Quebec question, see Serge Denis, "L'Analyse Politique Critique au Canada Anglais et la Question du Québec, 1970-1990," communication presentée dans le cadre du colloque annuel de la Société Québécoise de Science Politique, Congrès de l'ACFAS, Université Laval, Mai 1990 (mimeo).
27. Adrienne Rich, *On Lies, Secrets, and Silence: Selected Prose 1966-1978* (New York, 1979), p. 18.
28. Donald Johnston, ed., *With a Bang, Not a Whimper: Pierre Trudeau Speaks Out* (Toronto, 1988), p. 105.
29. Robert Bothwell, Ian Drummond, and John English, *Canada since 1945: Power, Politics and Provincialism* (Toronto, 1981), p. 4.

Recent Federalist Constitutional Proposals

1. Pierre Elliott Trudeau, *A Time for Action: Toward the Renewal of the Canadian Federation* (Ottawa, 1978), p. 20.

2. Task Force on Canadian Unity, *A Future Together: Observations and Recommendations* (Ottawa, 1979); *Coming to Terms: The Words of the Debate* (Ottawa, 1979); *A Time to Speak: The Views of the Public* (Ottawa, 1979).

3. For another comprehensive appraisal of Pepin-Robarts and of the constitutional proposals of the Liberals, Conservatives, and NDP, see Réjean Landry, "Les projets de réformes constitutionnelles des grands partis politiques fédéraux et de la Commission Pepin-Robarts: essai d'évaluation," *Canadian Public Policy*, V, 2 (Spring, 1979), pp. 263-73. For the Communist Party, see Sava D. Bosnitch, "The Current Communist Party Line on the 'National Question' in Canada," paper presented to the annual meeting of the Canadian Political Science Association, Saskatoon, 1979.

4. Sterling Lyon, "Speaking Notes for the Honourable Sterling Lyon," document 800-8/034 (Ottawa, Federal-Provincial Conference of First Ministers, October 30-November 1, 1978, mimeo), pp. 4-7, 16; Ed Broadbent, *House of Commons Debates*, June 27, 1978 (photocopy). On the federal government's willingness to live with the existing division of powers, see Pierre Elliott Trudeau, "Prime Minister's Introductory Statement: Verbatim Transcript," document 800-8/048 (Ottawa, Federal-Provincial Conference of First Ministers, October 30-November 1, 1978, mimeo), p. 6.

5. For an exception, see Committee on the Constitution, The Canadian Bar Association, *Towards a New Canada* (Ottawa, 1978), pp. 33-36.

6. Province of British Columbia, *British Columbia's Constitutional Proposals Presented to the First Ministers' Conference on the Constitution* (October, 1978), p. 29.

7. For an exception, see Gordon Gibson, "Submission to the Special Joint Committee of the Senate and the House of Commons on the Constitution of Canada," September 5, 1978 (mimeo), pp. 14-15.

8. Trudeau, *A Time for Action: Toward the Renewal of the Canadian Federation*, pp. 20-21.

9. Government of Alberta, *Harmony in Diversity: A New Federalism for Canada* (1978).

10. Flora MacDonald, "Notes for Remarks to the Seminar on Canada-U.S. Relations," Harvard University, December 7, 1977 (mimeo), p. 25; Progressive Conservative Party, "Discussion Paper No. 3: The Constitution and National Unity" (n.d., mimeo), p. 4.

11. Progressive Conservative Party, "Discussion Paper No. 3," pp. 1-3, 6.

12. Joe Clark *et al.*, "The Kingston Communiqué: A Joint Statement by . . . Joe Clark and . . . Premiers Moores, Hatfield, Davis and Lougheed," Kingston, September 16, 1977 (mimeo), p. 5.

13. Progressive Conservative Party, "Discussion Paper No. 3," p. 8.

14. Broadbent, *House of Commons Debates*, June 27, 1978.

15. Ed Broadbent, "National Unity Illusions Outlined, Speech to the Men's Canadian Club of Vancouver," October 4, 1977 (mimeo), p. 2.

16. *Ibid.*, p. 3.

17. *Ibid.*, p. 2.

18. Ed Broadbent, "Opening Statement to the Joint Senate-House of Commons Committee on the Constitution," August 15, 1978 (mimeo), pp. 3-4.

19. Broadbent, *House of Commons Debates*, June 27, 1978.

20. Broadbent, "Opening Statement," p. 5.

21. Broadbent, *House of Commons Debates*, June 27, 1978.

22. Broadbent, "Opening Statement," p. 8.
23. *Ibid.*
24. NDP Federal Convention (1977), p. 36.
25. Trudeau, *A Time for Action: Toward the Renewal of the Canadian Federation*, p. 22.
26. *Ibid.*, p. 12.
27. Pierre Elliott Trudeau, *A Time for Action: Highlights of the Federal Government's Proposals for the Renewal of the Canadian Federation* (Ottawa, 1978), p. 1.
28. Trudeau, *A Time for Action: Toward the Renewal of the Canadian Federation*, pp. 12, 21.
29. *Ibid.*, pp. 8, 22.
30. Government of Canada, *Constitutional Reform: Canadian Charter of Rights and Freedoms* (Ottawa, 1978), p. 2.
31. Government of Canada, *The Constitutional Amendment Bill: Text and Explanatory Notes* (1978), Part I:4:i.
32. Trudeau, *A Time for Action: Toward the Renewal of the Canadian Federation*, p. 20.
33. *Ibid.*, p. 9.
34. Government of Canada, *The Constitutional Amendment Bill*, Part I:4:iii.
35. Government of Canada, *Constitutional Reform: House of the Federation* (Ottawa, 1978), p. 15. See also Peter McCormick, "The House of Federation – A Critical Review" (1978, mimeo).
36. Claude Morin, *Quebec versus Ottawa: The Struggle for Self-Government 1960-72* (Toronto, 1976), p. 130.
37. *Globe and Mail*, February 19, 1979.
38. Government of Canada, *Constitutional Reform: House of the Federation*, pp. 19, 12, 11.
39. *Ibid.*, p. 14. See also pp. 8-9 for criticism of the Bundesrat solution for Canada.
40. Richard Simeon, "Opening Statement to the Special Committee on the Constitution," discussion paper no. 4 (Kingston, 1978), p. 6.
41. Alan C. Cairns, "From Interstate to Intrastate Federalism in Canada," discussion paper no. 5 (Kingston, 1979).
42. Government of Canada, *The Canadian Constitution and Constitutional Amendment* (Ottawa, 1978), pp. 20-21.
43. Landry, "Les projets," p. 271.
44. For a very positive assessment, which provides a good summary of its political reception in Quebec, see Léon Dion, "Il est douteux que le rapport Pepin-Robarts serve de base à une révision de la constitution," *Le Devoir*, February 9, 1978. See also Mel Watkins, "Coming Apart Together: The Report of the Task Force on Canadian Unity," *This Magazine*, 13, 2 (May/June 1979), for a provocative assessment.
45. Task Force on Canadian Unity, *A Future Together*, p. 21.
46. *Ibid.*, p. 24.
47. *Ibid.*, pp. 46, 47, 51.
48. Province of British Columbia, *British Columbia's Constitutional Proposals*, Paper No. 7. As Castonguay notes, the Trudeau government deliberately turned a blind eye to data that disconfirmed the realism of its approach. Charles Castonguay, "Why Hide the Facts? The Federalist Approach to the Language Crisis in Canada," *Canadian Public Policy*, v, 1 (Winter, 1979), pp. 6-7.
49. Task Force on Canadian Unity, *A Future Together*, pp. 48, 53. In fact, the report's discussion of the desirability of entrenching minority language rights is not entirely clear. Contrast pp. 53 and 109.

50. *Ibid.*, pp. 26-27.
51. *Ibid.*, p. 118.
52. *Ibid.*, p. 36.
53. *Ibid.*, pp. 6, 32.
54. *Ibid.*, p. 6.
55. *Ibid.*, pp. 39, 17. See also the Task Force volume *A Time to Speak*, which implicitly and explicitly stresses the fragmentation, limited identities, and particularisms of the country.
56. Maurice Pinard, "Ethnic Segmentation, Loyalties, Incentives and Constitutional Options in Quebec," paper presented at twinned workshop organized by the Canadian Political Science Association and the Israeli Political Science Association, Israel, December 11-16, 1978 (mimeo). For the case of Nova Scotia, see G. Perlin and G. Rawlyk, "Atlantic Regionalism: The Nova Scotia Elite and Some of the Problems of Confederation," paper presented to the Workshop on the Political Economy of Confederation, Kingston, November 8-10, 1978 (mimeo).
57. Task Force on Canadian Unity, *A Future Together*, pp. 81, 85.
58. *Ibid.*, p. 88.
59. *Ibid.*, pp. 89-90.
60. *Ibid.*, pp. 83, 85, 118.
61. *Ibid.*, p. 85.
62. *Ibid.*, p. 87.
63. *Ibid.*
64. *Globe and Mail*, February 5, 1979.
65. Task Force on Canadian Unity, *A Future Together*, pp. 35, 91, 125.
66. *Ibid.*, pp. 106-09.
67. *Ibid.*, pp. 104-06.
68. *Ibid.*, p. 68.
69. *Ibid.*, p. 70.
70. *Ibid.*, pp. 70-71, 74.
71. *Ibid.*, p. 76.
72. *Ibid.*, p. 69.
73. *Ibid.*, p. 85.

An Overview of the Trudeau Constitutional Proposals

1. Donald V. Smiley, "The Structural Problem of Canadian Federalism," *Canadian Public Administration*, 14 (1971), p. 326.
2. Worded as follows: "The *Canadian Charter of Rights and Freedoms* guarantees the rights and freedoms set out in it subject only to such reasonable limits as are generally accepted in a free and democratic society with a parliamentary system of government."
3. Richard Simeon, "An Overview of the Trudeau Constitutional Proposals," *Alberta Law Review*, XIX, 3 (1981).
4. *Ibid.*

The Politics of Constitutional Renewal in Canada

I would like to thank the Hon. Eugene Forsey for catching several errors in an earlier version of this paper, and Keith Banting for his major editorial contribution.

1. See Denis Smith, *Bleeding Hearts . . . Bleeding Country: Canada and The Quebec Crisis* (Edmonton, 1971), for a discussion.

2. See Richard Simeon, *Federal-Provincial Diplomacy: The Making of Recent Policy in Canada* (Toronto, 1971), pp. 115-22, for the details.

3. Institute of Intergovernmental Relations, *The Response to Quebec: The Other Provinces and the Constitutional Debate*, Documents of the Debate no. 2 (Kingston, 1980).

4. Although Ottawa asserted that provincial consent was unnecessary for the enactment of Bill C-60 as a constitutional amendment, much of the bill would have been of only limited value, practically and symbolically, without provincial consent. For example, while the Charter of Rights and Freedoms, including language rights, would immediately apply to the federal government, it would not become applicable to the jurisdiction of a province until adopted by the province, and would become entrenched only when endorsed by a formal amending process. While the provisions relating to the Supreme Court would be part of the constitution upon enactment of the bill, they would only become entrenched after appropriate constitutional amendment processes involving the provinces had been undertaken. Even the proposed preamble and the statement of aims would only become entrenched after provincial approval, although they would become part of the constitution and applicable to Ottawa on passage of the bill. Thus the attempt to bypass the provinces in the enactment stage, while hoping for their subsequent opting in, seriously reduced the potential significance of Bill C-60, however unavoidable the federal strategy might have been.

5. See Allan Smith, "Quiet Revolution in the West," *Canadian Forum*, LVIII, 681 (June-July, 1978), for an incisive discussion of the transformation of western Canada.

6. David E. Smith, "Political Culture in the West," in David Jay Bercuson and Phillip A. Buckner, eds., *Eastern and Western Perspectives* (Toronto, 1981).

7. Province of British Columbia, *British Columbia's Constitutional Proposals, Paper No. 7, Language Rights and the Constitution of Canada* (Victoria, 1978), pp. 11, 13, 15.

8. Denis Smith, "Between Two Solitudes," *Canadian Forum*, LIX, 688 (April, 1979), p. 4.

9. Additional exceptions to Parliament's amending power were "rights or privileges . . . granted or secured . . . to any class of persons with respect to schools or as regards the use of the English or the French language or as regards the requirements that there shall be a session of the Parliament of Canada at least once each year, and that no House of Commons shall continue for more than five years . . ."

10. It would, of course, have been possible to achieve patriation with a provisional amending formula requiring unanimity while a permanent formula was worked out in Canada. This, however, raised the possibility that the temporary formula might confirm the French saying that nothing is so permanent as the provisional.

11. With the exception of Canadian Indians, who mounted extensive lobbying efforts in the United Kingdom, non-governmental participation in Britain was mainly restricted to massive letter-writing campaigns opposing patriation. Edward McWhinney, *Canada and the Constitution, 1979-1982* (Toronto, 1981), pp. 72-73.

12. See the assessment of Jeffrey Simpson, "Divided Canada puts UK in a hot spot," *Globe and Mail*, April 15, 1982. See also Ronald J. Zukowsky, *Struggle over the Constitution: From the Quebec Referendum to the Supreme Court, Intergovernmental Relations in Canada, The Year in Review*, 1980, vol. II (Kingston, 1981), p. 5.

13. Governor General Schreyer subsequently claimed his remarks were taken out of context, and Trudeau issued a statement, with the Governor General's concurrence, denying that the Governor General had "sought to exert pressure of some kind on me or

my ministry." *Vancouver Sun*, January 22 and 26, 1982. See McWhinney, *Canada and the Constitution*, pp. 129-31, for a discussion of the incident.

14. *Vancouver Sun*, May 26, 1981.

15. Other indications of that conservatism had already been vividly manifested in the defeat of several concerted efforts to get significant constitutional change in the previous two decades:

(i) The Fulton-Favreau amending formula of the mid-1960s, a formula almost excessively respectful of provincial prerogatives, was dropped and faded away because of the withdrawal of support by the Lesage government of Quebec.

(ii) The Victoria Charter package of 1971, which included an amendment formula, a limited Charter of Rights, and Supreme Court reform, was not proceeded with when the Quebec government made its support conditional on constitutional changes in the social policy area that were not forthcoming.

(iii) The federal government effort in Bill C-60 to institute a measure of change in areas that Ottawa insisted were within its own amending jurisdiction failed to get broad support from Parliament. The constitutionality of parts of the bill was challenged by several provinces and a fading Trudeau government nearing the end of its term could not keep it alive in the face of so much opposition. A belated Supreme Court ruling in the closing weeks of the subsequent Conservative government found that the proposed changes to the Senate were *ultra vires* the federal amending power under 91 (1) of the BNA Act.

(iv) The federal government attempt in Bill C-9, The Canada Referendum Bill, was a portent of later unilateralist attempts by Ottawa, and also of its recurrent strategy to bring in the people to bypass provincial governments in constitutional change. The bill would have allowed Ottawa to consult "the entire population . . . on future proposals for constitutional change," including reforms of any of the "customs, conventions and enactments that comprise the Constitution of Canada." The Conservative opposition fought the bill in Parliament, and it died with the 1979 election. Douglas Brown, *Intergovernmental Relations in Canada: The Year in Review, 1979* (Kingston, 1980), p. 32.

16. Peter H. Russell, "The Effect of a Charter of Rights on the Policy-making Role of Canadian Courts," *Canadian Public Administration*, 25, 1 (Spring, 1982), p. 26.

17. The poll is discussed in Sheilagh M. Dunn, *The Year in Review 1981: Intergovernmental Relations in Canada* (Kingston, 1981), pp. 5-7. See *Globe and Mail*, August 22, 1981, for the negative reaction of pollsters and academics.

18. Zukowsky, *Struggle over the Constitution*, p. 107.

19. Quebec Liberal Party, *Choose Quebec and Canada* (Montreal, 1979); The Constitutional Committee of the Quebec Liberal Party, *A New Canadian Federation* (Montreal, 1980).

20. For the Conservatives in office, see Brown, *Intergovernmental Relations in Canada . . . 1979*, pp. 9-10, and McWhinney, *Canada and the Constitution*, pp. 12-15. For their response to the Liberal government resolution of October, 1980, see Zukowsky, *Struggle over the Constitution*, pp. 83-85. For major statements of Conservative positions in the winter and spring of 1981, see Research Office of the Official Opposition, "Minority Report presented to the Canadian People," mimeo, February 16, 1981, and "Statement of . . . Joe Clark on Progressive Conservative Amendments to the Constitutional Resolution," Ottawa, April 21, 1981. The Clark statement is discussed in *Globe and Mail*, April 22, 1981.

21. Bob Rae, "Building Traditions," *Canadian Forum*, LIX, 692 (September, 1979), p. 11.

22. Thus the basic confidential federal strategy paper, the "Kirby document," stated: "Given the Government's lack of western representation, it would probably be more difficult to defend unilateral federal action on such a regionally sensitive issue as resources than it would be to withstand a ferocious attack by the Government of Quebec over the entrenchment of minority language education rights, given the federal government's strong representation from Quebec." "Report to Cabinet on Constitutional Discussions, Summer 1980, and the Outlook for the First Ministers Conference and Beyond," Ministers' Eyes Only, August 30, 1980, p. 41. Hence the political desirability of getting one western government on side, preferably Saskatchewan, and the need to court the NDP with its western base of support in Parliament.

23. See McWhinney, *Canada and the Constitution*, p. 57, for an assessment of the NDP contribution. See Zukowsky, *Struggle over the Constitution*, p. 91, for Joe Clark's summary of the Conservative contribution.

24. When the federal NDP indicated its support for official bilingualism in Ontario, the Ontario NDP provincial leader, Mike Cassidy, applied pressure on the federal party to drop the proposal. Cassidy, facing a provincial election, feared his party's chances would be hurt in a province where the Conservative government and popular opinion were against such a constitutional imposition. The federal party capitulated to the electoral necessities of its provincial counterpart. *Maclean's*, February 23, 1981, p. 24.

25. *Globe and Mail*, October 7, 1980.

26. Zukowsky, *Struggle over the Constitution*, p. 89. Four NDP Saskatchewan MPs broke with the national party as a result of these pressures. See also *Globe and Mail*, February 26, 1981, for a report by Blakeney of a secret meeting on January 18, 1981, between Broadbent and the NDP provincial leaders in Alberta and Manitoba, Notley and Pawley, which was unsuccessful in producing a common position on the constitution.

27. See Dunn, *The Year in Review 1981: Intergovernmental Relations in Canada*, p. 19, and William Johnson, "Quebec Liberals adrift in a sea of indecision," *Globe and Mail*, October 1, 1981, for the tensions and divisions in the Quebec provincial legislative party caucus over their response to a PQ motion condemning federal government unilateralism. Nine Liberals, mainly from Anglophone ridings, broke with the party leadership and voted against the motion.

28. Although these undoubtedly played a part. See McWhinney, *Canada and the Constitution*, pp. 57, 120.

29. See Zukowsky, *Struggle over the Constitution*, p. 8, on the actual strains in the Liberal Party in the winter of 1981, mainly from Quebec Liberals.

30. When one Alberta Conservative MLA, Thomas Sindlinger, disagreed with Premier Lougheed's opposition to Trudeau's patriation plans, he was immediately expelled from the party. *Globe and Mail*, October 17, 1980.

31. Four opposition parties appeared before the Joint Committee: the NDP and Social Credit parties from Alberta, the Saskatchewan Conservatives, and the Union Nationale from Quebec. Zukowsky, *Struggle over the Constitution*, p. 78.

32. However, some reports suggest that the breakaway of three NDP rebels in Manitoba, who formed a new Progressive Party in March, 1981, was partly due to their opposition to the constitutional position of the provincial party. *Globe and Mail*, March 3 and March 28, 1981.

33. On occasion, the working out of this tendency produced complex intra-party hostili-

ties. The British Columbia NDP strongly opposed the constitutional position of the British Columbia Social Credit government, which was aligned with NDP Premier Blakeney of Saskatchewan in opposition to the Trudeau package. NDP leader Barrett was reportedly so furious at the Saskatchewan government's "proselytising the rebel constitution position in B.C." that he threatened to retaliate by sending B.C. NDP opponents of nuclear power on a speaking tour of Saskatchewan where uranium mining and nuclear energy are strongly supported by the provincial government. *Vancouver Province*, July 6, 1981. Barrett was responding to the political proposition that the friend of my enemy is my enemy.

34. See Dunn, *The Year in Review 1981: Intergovernmental Relations in Canada*, pp. 37-39, for details.

35. "PM accepts Ryan's plan for Quebec agreement," *Vancouver Sun*, November 16, 1981; Charlotte Montgomery, "PQ Reign can be Outwaited: Trudeau," *Globe and Mail*, November 16, 1981. Trudeau was obviously trying to prevent a common PQ-Liberal front against the agreement, and he knew that a very high percentage of provincial Liberal voters felt that Lévesque should have signed (82 per cent according to one survey, *Vancouver Sun*, November 14, 1981), thus making it difficult for Ryan to side with Lévesque's seeming intransigence. Trudeau was successful to the extent that on a straight party vote the provincial Liberals voted against a PQ motion laying down Quebec's minimum demands, which passed 70-38. *Vancouver Sun*, December 1, 1981.

36. Seven of the eight dissenting provinces, all but Manitoba, passed resolutions in their legislatures hostile to federal unilateralism. Only in Alberta and Saskatchewan did the official opposition support the resolutions. Zukowsky, *Struggle over the Constitution*, p. 107.

37. See Zukowsky, *Struggle over the Constitution*, pp. 71-85, 91, for an analysis of the Joint Committee. For a criticism of the unrepresentative nature of the groups and lobbies appearing before the Joint Committee, reflecting "too much the golden triangle of Canadian political life – Toronto, Ottawa, and English Montreal," see McWhinney, *Canada and the Constitution*, pp. 50-51, 115-16.

38. Zukowsky, *Struggle over the Constitution*, pp. 110-12.

39. As originally proposed in the parliamentary resolution in the autumn of 1980, the amending formula was derived from the Victoria Charter amending formula of 1971. Amendments could be passed with the agreement of the federal government, the governments of Ontario and Quebec, and the governments of two provinces with more than half of the regional population in both the Atlantic and western regions. The proposal also, however, gave Ottawa the power to employ a referendum as an alternative to obtaining agreement of the requisite provincial governments. Such a referendum would pass if it obtained a national majority and a majority in those provinces, the support of whose governments would have constituted provincial approval of the proposed amendment. Subsequently, the federal government modified the proposal for the Atlantic and western regions so that the agreement of any two provincial governments in these regions, or the support of popular referendum majorities in any two western and any two Atlantic provinces would be sufficient for the passage of the proposed amendment. The federal strategy, portrayed as a deadlock-breaking procedure, was clearly designed to enhance the role of the people and employ them as instruments to bypass recalcitrant provincial governments that stood in the way of centralizing amendments.

40. See Dunn, *The Year in Review 1981: Intergovernmental Relations in Canada*, pp. 20-32, for a discussion of the final conference.

41. The three following paragraphs are taken, with minor changes, from the author's "Constitution-Making, Government Self-Interest, and the Problem of Legitimacy in Canada," to be published in a book tentatively titled *Political Support in Canada: The Crisis Years*, edited by Allan Kornberg and Harold Clarke. For additional analysis, see McWhinney, *Canada and the Constitution*, chapter 11; Dunn, *The Year in Review 1981: Intergovernmental Relations in Canada*, pp. 30-34; Robert Sheppard, "Lobby groups taste blood, and Ottawa quaking," *Globe and Mail*, November 26, 1981.

42. For the decisive impact of the Joint Committee process on the Charter, see the testimony of the Minister of Justice, Jean Chrétien, *Minutes of Proceedings and Evidence of the Special Joint Committee of the Senate and of the House of Commons on the Constitution of Canada*, no. 36, January 12, 1981; Robert Sheppard, "PMS Proposed Charter of Rights Could Have Far-Reaching Effects," *Globe and Mail*, February 14, 1981.

43. Zukowsky, *Struggle over the Constitution*, pp. 127-29.

44. See Donald Smiley, *The Canadian Charter of Rights and Freedoms, 1981*, Discussion Paper Series, Ontario Economic Council (Toronto, 1981), for a sophisticated discussion.

45. The Resolution was sent to the Supreme Court with all amendments having been considered and voted on, but without the Resolution itself having been passed. This strategy was to allow the Supreme Court to examine a "finished document" and then to allow the House of Commons an additional debate of two days if the Supreme Court upheld the Resolution. Zukowsky, *Struggle over the Constitution*, p. 90.

46. "The effect of the legislative override in diminishing judicial power should not be over-estimated. Legislators who contemplate recourse to the notwithstanding clause will face some powerful political disincentives. . . . Access to the crowded agenda of modern legislatures is never easy and may be especially difficult when influential groups have a vested interest in a position adopted by the judiciary. In proposing a legislative override, government will be committing itself to a policy position which is almost bound to be labelled by the media as 'subverting civil liberties'. This is bad politics, even for a government with a clear legislative majority." Russell, "The Effect of a Charter of Rights," p. 19.

47. See Smiley, *The Canadian Charter of Rights and Freedoms*, chapter 4, for a helpful discussion.

48. *The Constitution Act*, Section 23 (3) (a) (b).

49. See the critical comments of Max Yalden, Commissioner of Official Languages, *Globe and Mail*, March 17, 1982.

50. See Richard J. Joy, *Canada's Official Language Minorities* (Montreal, 1978); Réjean Lachapelle and Jacques Henripin, *The Demolinguistic Situation in Canada: Past Trends and Future Prospects* (Montreal, 1982).

51. The basic amending formula required resolutions of the Senate and the House of Commons, and resolutions of the legislative assemblies of at least two-thirds of the provinces with at least 50 per cent of the population of all the provinces, with an opting-out capacity for up to three provinces. Section 9 dealt with several matters for which unanimity was required, and Section 10 with several matters covered by the two-thirds plus 50 per cent requirement, but with no opting-out provisions. These included matters pertaining to the Senate, the Supreme Court, the establishment of new provinces, the extension of existing provinces into the Territories, and amendments to the delegation provisions of the Accord. Any amendment to the amending formula itself was subject to the requirement of unanimity. See *Amending Formula for the Constitution of Canada* –

Text and Explanatory Notes – Constitutional Accord: Canadian Patriation Plan, Canadian Intergovernmental Conference Secretariat, Document No. 850-19/004, Ottawa, April 16, 1981.

52. The agreement between nine provinces and the federal government on November 5, 1981, removed the clause of the provincial Constitutional Accord requiring the government of Canada to pay "reasonable compensation" to a provincial government opting out of an amendment transferring legislative jurisdiction to the federal government. Subsequently, in response to suggestions and pressures from Claude Ryan and the federal Quebec Liberal caucus, the agreement was amended so that "reasonable compensation" would be paid by the federal government to a province opting out of a constitutional amendment "that transfers provincial legislative powers relating to education or other cultural matters . . . to Parliament" (s. 40).

53. See *Globe and Mail*, November 4, 1981, "What Trudeau Has Said Before on Formula," for Trudeau's very strong criticisms of the formula on various occasions in 1980 and 1981.

54. Trudeau's phrase. Dunn, *The Year in Review 1981: Intergovernmental Relations in Canada*, p. 29.

55. Zukowsky, *Struggle over the Constitution*, p. 5.

56. Richard Gwyn, "The Big Constitutional Dice Roll," *Vancouver Sun*, April 22, 1981.

57. See John Gray, "A Magnificent Obsession," *Globe and Mail*, November 7, 1981.

58. This chronology was constructed with the assistance of chronologies in *Globe and Mail*, April 18, 1981; *Vancouver Province*, April 26, 1981; "The Magazine," *Vancouver Province*, April 18, 1981; David Milne, *The New Canadian Constitution* (Toronto, 1982), pp. 9-11; R.D. Olling and M.W. Westmacott, *The Confederation Debate: The Constitution in Crisis* (Toronto, 1980), pp. xiii-xviii.

Citizens (Outsiders) and Governments (Insiders) in Constitution-Making

1. Technically, the phrase "citizens' constitution" is something of a misnomer, as in addition to those Charter clauses referring to citizens, others refer to "everyone," "any person," and "every individual." Nevertheless, the latter categories all include citizens, and the impact of the Charter on the conceptions and practice of citizenship is what concerns me. Hence, I prefer the phrase even if, in terms of some Charter rights, it is under-inclusive.

2. See Deborah Coyne, "Brief to the Special Joint Committee on the 1987 Constitutional Accord," July 20, 1987 (mimeo).

3. Royal Orr, President of Alliance Quebec, *Senate Debates*, December 2, 1987, p. 2252.

4. Marsha A. Chandler, "Constitutional Change and Public Policy: The Impact of the Resource Amendment (Section 92A)," *Canadian Journal of Political Science*, 19 (1986), pp. 103-26.

5. (Gang of Eight), "Amending Formula for the Constitution of Canada: Text and Explanatory Notes," Ottawa, April 16, 1981 (mimeo), p. 3.

6. *Ibid.*, pp. 4, 6.

7. Constitution Act, 1982, Section 40.

8. *Ibid.*, Section 52 (1).

9. Eugene Forsey, *Senate Debates*, November 4, 1987, p. 2133.

10. In addition to hearing evidence in Committee of the Whole, the Senate established a

Senate Task Force on the Accord and the Yukon and Northwest Territories, which published a *Report* in February, 1988. The Senate also held and published supplementary hearings before a subcommittee: *Proceedings of the Senate Submissions Group on the Meech Lake Constitutional Accord*.

11. *Senate Debates*, November 18, 1987, p. 2201. See also Erasmus, *Minutes of Proceedings and Evidence of the Special Joint Committee of the Senate and the House of Commons on the 1987 Constitutional Accord*, (hereafter, Special Joint Committee, *Minutes*), No. 9, August 19, 1987, p. 61; M. Louis "Smokey" Bruyère, President, Native Council of Canada, *ibid*., No. 12, August 25, 1987, p. 101.

12. Special Joint Committee, *Minutes*, August 4, 1987, p. 2A:63. See also Margaret Mitchell, *House of Commons Debates*, October 8, 1987, p. 9839.

13. Donna Greschner, "A Constitution with 'Instructions Included': Some Questions about Interpretation after Meech Lake," presented to the symposium on the Meech Lake Accord, University of Toronto, October 30, 1987 (mimeo), p. 1. See also Sylvia Gold, President, Canadian Advisory Council on the Status of Women, Special Joint Committee, *Minutes*, No. 10, August 20, 1987, p. 87; Susan Riley, "The Meech Boys: Are Women up the Lake without a Paddle?" *This Magazine*, 21, 7 (1987-88), pp. 31-35.

14. John D. Whyte, "The 1987 Constitutional Accord and Ethnic Accommodation," presented to the symposium on the Meech Lake Accord, University of Toronto, October 30, 1987 (mimeo), p. 3; Wayne MacKay, Special Joint Committee, *Minutes*, No. 3, August 5, 1987, p. 43.

15. Cited in Fred Schindeler, "One Man One Vote: One Vote One Value," *Journal of Canadian Studies*, 3 (1968), p. 16.

16. See note 10 for material on northern attitudes.

17. Senate Task Force, *Proceedings of the Senate Task Force on the Meech Lake Constitutional Accord and on the Yukon and Northwest Territories*, No. 1, September 3, October 24 and 25, 1987, pp. 16, 30. See also Penikett's presentation to the Special Joint Committee: *Minutes*, No. 15, August 31, 1987, as well as the bitter denunciations of the treatment of the northern territories by two northern MPs, Audrey McLaughlin (*House of Commons Debates*, September 30, 1987, pp. 9505-07) and Dave Nickerson (*House of Commons Debates*, October 6, 1987, pp. 9704-07). Chapter 9 of the Senate Task Force *Report* (February, 1988) contains a selection of comments by northerners objecting to the Accord.

18. Michael Ballantyne, Northwest Territories Minister of Justice, Special Joint Committee, *Minutes*, No. 8, August 18, 1987, p. 74.

19. Nickerson, *House of Commons Debates*, October 6, 1987, p. 9705.

20. Tony Hall, Special Joint Committee, *Minutes*, No. 14, August 27, 1987, p. 14A:5.

21. Special Joint Committee, *Minutes*, No. 8, August 18, 1987, pp. 8A:4-5. See also *Senate Debates*, December 2, 1987, p. 2247.

22. Special Joint Committee, *Minutes*, No. 10, August 20, 1987, p. 5.

23. *Ibid*., No. 11, August 21, 1987, p. 24.

24. Deborah Coyne, *ibid*., No. 14, August 27, 1987, p. 8.

25. See in particular the very detailed critique by Sergio Marchi, *House of Commons Debates*, October 6, 1987, p. 9742.

26. *Senate Debates*, February 10, 1988, p. 2731.

27. Special Joint Committee, *Minutes*, No. 3, August 5, 1987, p. 43.

28. In addition, nine of the ten provinces "have chosen to leave out sexual orientation" as an expressly prohibited ground of discrimination from their human rights codes. The

exception is Quebec. Arnold Bruner, "Sexual Orientation and Equality Rights," in Anne F. Bayefsky and Mary Eberts, eds., *Equality Rights and the Canadian Charter of Rights and Freedoms* (Toronto, 1985), pp. 457-58.

29. *House of Commons Debates*, September 30, 1987, p. 9502. See also Pauline Jewett, *ibid.*, September 29, 1987, p. 9434; Lynn McDonald, *ibid.*, October 1, 1987, pp. 9532-33.

30. Mary Eberts, "Sex-based Discrimination and the Charter," in Bayefsky and Eberts, eds., *Equality Rights*, pp. 199-204.

31. Penny Kome, *The Taking of Twenty-Eight: Women Challenge the Constitution* (Toronto, 1983).

32. Louise Dulude, President of the National Action Committee on the Status of Women, Special Joint Committee, *Minutes*, No. 13, August 26, 1987, p. 38.

33. T.C. Christopher, "The 1982 Canadian Charter of Rights and Freedoms and Multi-culturalism," *Canadian Review of Studies in Nationalism*, 14 (1987), p. 337. See also Michael R. Hudson, "Multiculturalism, Government Policy and Constitutional En-shrinement – A Comparative Study," in Canadian Human Rights Foundation, *Multicul-turalism and the Charter: A Legal Perspective* (Toronto, 1987), pp. 72-79, for a brief background to Section 27.

34. Hudson, "Multiculturalism," pp. 121-22.

35. Douglas Sanders, "Article 27 and the Aboriginal Peoples of Canada," in Canadian Human Rights Foundation, *Multiculturalism*, pp. 156-58.

36. Douglas Sanders, "The Renewal of Indian Special Status," in Bayefsky and Eberts, eds., *Equality Rights*, p. 532.

37. Thus Sanders notes that a "persistent problem [at first ministers' constitutional conferences on aboriginal self-government] has been the grouping of Indians, non-status Indians, Métis and Inuit in one forum." Douglas Sanders, "An Uncertain Path: The Aboriginal Constitutional Conferences," in Joseph M. Weiler and Robin M. Elliot, eds., *Litigating the Values of a Nation: The Canadian Charter of Rights and Freedoms* (Toronto, 1986), p. 74.

38. Special Joint Committee, *Minutes*, No. 12, August 25, 1987, p. 97.

39. Sanders, "The Renewal of Indian Special Status."

40. *Senate Debates*, November 18, 1987, p. 2200.

41. Sanders, "The Renewal of Indian Special Status," pp. 530, 560.

42. It should be noted that this essay was written in early Meech Lake days, when Québécois nationalism and Quebec separatism were generally perceived to be in decline. Indeed, both Mulroney and Bourassa were encouraged to proceed with Meech Lake because they believed Quebec nationalism and separatism were at a low ebb, and thus would cause them little trouble.

43. Yvon Fontaine, President, Federation of Francophones outside of Quebec, Special Joint Committee, *Minutes*, No. 3, August 5, 1987; Canadian Parents for French, *ibid.*, No. 4, August 6, 1987; Lucille Blanchette, President, Société Franco-manitobaine, *ibid.*, No. 11, August 21, 1987.

44. Quebec Association of Protestant School Boards, "Brief . . . for Presentation to the Committee of the Whole of the Senate of Canada on the Constitutional Accord of 1987," December, 1987 (mimeo), p. 2.

45. *Senate Debates*, December 2, 1987, p. 2254.

46. *Ibid.*, February 3, 1988, p. 2616.

47. Commissioner of Official Languages, *Annual Report 1987* (Ottawa, 1988), p. 7. See

also the very powerful evidence in the same vein of John D. Whyte, Special Joint Committee, *Minutes*, No. 10, August 20, 1987, p. 70.

48. Human Rights Institute of Canada, Special Joint Committee, *Minutes*, No. 11, August 21, 1987, p. 18.

49. Donald J. Johnston, "Submission of the Honourable Donald J. Johnston to the Special Joint Committee on the 1987 Constitutional Accord, July 22, 1987" (mimeo); Coyne, Special Joint Committee, *Minutes*, No. 14, August 27, 1987, pp. 6-25; Johnston, *ibid.*, No. 11, August 21, 1987, pp. 32-49; Whyte, *ibid.*, No. 10, August 20, 1987, pp. 58-82; Roger Gibbins, "A Sense of Unease: The Meech Lake Accord and Constitution-Making in Canada," paper presented to Second Thoughts on Meech Lake: A Conference on Political Process, University of Calgary, November 19-20, 1987 (mimeo).

50. Special Joint Committee, *Minutes*, No. 14, August 27, 1987, pp. 121, 119-20. Trudeau's earlier intervention, between the Meech Lake and Langevin meetings, was published in the *Globe and Mail*, May 28, 1987.

51. Gibbins, "A Sense of Unease," p. 15.

52. For a sampling of these reactions, in addition to the references cited in previous paragraphs, see National Union of Provincial Government Employees, Special Joint Committee, *Minutes*, No. 3, August 5, 1987, pp. 90-110; National Anti-Poverty Organization, *ibid.*, No. 5, August 11, 1987, pp. 5-24; Timothy Danson, *ibid.*, No. 6, August 12, 1987, pp. 25-46; Canadian Nurses' Association, *ibid.*, No. 8, August 18, 1987, pp. 25-42; Canadian Labour Congress, National Farmers Union, and United Electrical, Radio and Machine Workers of Canada, *ibid.*, No. 10, August 20, 1987, pp. 5-22, 23-40, 106-21.

53. Zebedee Nungak, Co-Chairman, Inuit Committee on National Issues, *ibid.*, No. 3, August 5, 1987, p. 28; George Erasmus, National Chief, Assembly of First Nations, *ibid.*, No. 9, August 19, 1987, p. 50.

54. Charles L. Caccia, *House of Commons Debates*, September 30, 1987, p. 9508.

55. Thor Broda, Vice-President, National Executive, Ukrainian Canadian Committee, Special Joint Committee, *Minutes*, No. 7, August 13, 1987, p. 100.

56. Andrew Cardozo, Executive Director, Canadian Ethnocultural Council, *ibid.*, p. 52; Dieter Kiesewalter, German Canadian Congress, *ibid.*, p. 72.

57. George Corn, President, Canadian Ethnocultural Council, *ibid.*, p. 42; Dr. Lilian Ma, Immediate Past President, Chinese Canadian National Council, *ibid.*, p. 62; Kiesewalter, *ibid.*, pp. 70-72; Michael K.B. Hahn, Co-Chairman, Canadian Federation of Ethno-Businesses and Professionals, *ibid.*, No. 11, August 21, 1987, p. 9; George Corn, *Senate Debates*, January 27, 1988, p. 2563.

58. Nungak, Special Joint Committee, *Minutes*, No. 3, August 5, 1987, p. 30; Ernie Daniels, Interim President, Prairie Treaty Nations Alliance, *Senate Debates*, December 16, 1987, p. 2458.

59. Beverly Baines, National Association of Women and the Law, Special Joint Committee, *Minutes*, No. 2, August 4, 1987, pp. 85-86, and Brief, *ibid.*, pp. 2A:52-54; Beth Symes, Women's Legal Education and Action Fund, *ibid.*, No. 3, August 5, 1987, p. 118; Gold, *ibid.*, No. 10, August 20, 1987, p. 85; Dulude, *ibid.*, No. 13, August 26, 1987, pp. 24-27; Beverly Baines, "Women's Equality Rights and the Meech Lake Accord," for the Canadian Advisory Council on the Status of Women, August 25, 1987 (mimeo); Baines, "Accord Jeopardizes Women's Equality," *Financial Post*, September 7, 1987.

60. Eberts, "Sex-based Discrimination," p. 202.

61. A. Wayne MacKay, "Linguistic Duality in Canada and the Distinct Society in Que-

bec," presented to the symposium on the Meech Lake Accord, University of Toronto, October 30, 1987 (mimeo), p. 18.

62. Lynn Smith, "The Effect of the 'Distinct Society' Clause on Charter Equality Rights for Women in Canada," *ibid.*, pp. 24-26.

63. Beverly Baines, "Gender and the Meech Lake Committee," *Queen's Quarterly*, 94 (1987), pp. 807-16.

64. *Senate Debates*, November 18, 1987, p. 2202.

65. Broda, Special Joint Committee, *Minutes*, No. 7, August 13, 1987, pp. 101, 103.

66. Bruyère, *ibid.*, No. 12, August 25, 1987, p. 96.

67. *House of Commons Debates*, October 2, 1987, p. 9619.

68. *Ibid.*, October 6, 1987, p. 9743. See also Charles Caccia, *Senate Debates*, November 4, 1987, pp. 2138-46.

69. *Proceedings of the Senate Task Force*, No. 1, September 3 to October 25, 1987, p. 18.

70. David Philpott, Tourism Industry Association of the Yukon, *ibid.*, pp. 66, 68.

71. Eugene Forsey, Special Joint Committee, *Minutes*, No. 2, August 4, 1987, pp. 2A:94-95.

72. Coyne, "Brief to the Special Joint Committee," p. 3.

73. "One of the most astonishing, and frightening, things about the Proceedings before the Joint Committee of the Senate and the House of Commons has been that the defenders of the Accord seem to have made not the faintest attempt to analyze, and answer, the very specific, detailed adverse criticisms of one section after another, by people eminently qualified to speak." Eugene Forsey, "Submission on the Meech Lake Accord, to the NDP Public Hearings on that Subject," Calgary, September 22, 1987 (mimeo), p. 5.

74. Government of Canada, *Strengthening the Canadian Federation: The Constitution Amendment* (Ottawa, 1987), p. 9.

75. Special Joint Committee, *Minutes*, No. 4, August 6, 1987, p. 4A:13. See Holtby's brief in the appendix to this day's proceedings for his views on the role of legislative committees prior to first ministers' meetings, and on changes in the rules of legislatures so that amendments will require the same scrutiny in terms of debate and committee examination that now applies to the most insignificant bill. See also the remarks of Roland de Corneille (*House of Commons Debates*, October 8, 1987, p. 9834) contrasting the elaborate procedures applied to bills and the cursory treatment accorded to resolutions for constitutional amendment.

76. Stephen A. Scott, "The Canadian Constitutional Amendment Process: Mechanisms and Prospects," in Clare F. Beckton and A. Wayne MacKay, eds., *Recurring Issues in Canadian Federalism*, Vol. 57, Research Studies of the Royal Commission on the Economic Union and Development Prospects for Canada (Toronto, 1986), p. 88.

77. Special Joint Committee, *The 1987 Constitutional Accord, The Report of the Special Joint Committee of the Senate and the House of Commons* (Ottawa, 1987), p. 143.

78. Lowell Murray, "The Process of Constitutional Change in Canada: The Lessons of Meech Lake," *Choices* (Institute for Research on Public Policy), February, 1988.

Ottawa, the Provinces, and Meech Lake

1. A. Wayne MacKay, *Minutes of Proceedings and Evidence of the Special Joint Committee of the Senate and of the House of Commons on the 1987 Constitutional Accord*, No. 3, August 5, 1987, p. 64.

2. John Emerich Edward Dalberg-Acton, First Baron Acton, *Selected Writings of Lord Acton, Vol. II, Essays in the Study and Writing of History*, ed. J. Rufus Fears (Indianapolis, 1985), p. 505.

3. *Ibid.*, p. 550.

4. *House of Commons Debates*, October 5, 1987, p. 9684.

5. Edward S. Goldenberg, "Debate needed to make sure accord is right," *Globe and Mail*, July 14, 1987.

6. "PM invites 10 premiers to discuss Quebec constitutional proposals," *Globe and Mail*, March 18, 1987.

7. Meech Lake Communiqué, April 30, 1987, in Bryan Schwartz, *Fathoming Meech Lake* (Winnipeg, 1987), p. 232.

8. *Ibid.*, p. 238.

9. "Vote to ratify accord hailed as great victory for Quebec," *Globe and Mail*, June 24, 1987.

10. See "PM's comment on motive angers women's groups," *Globe and Mail*, August 20, 1987; Sergio Marchi, *House of Commons Debates*, October 6, 1987, p. 9742.

11. The comments of Sergio Marchi in the House of Commons, although lengthy, merit extensive citation. *House of Commons Debates*, October 6, 1987, p. 9742:

The absence of any true public input in the development of this resolution is a national tragedy. The package was not only assembled and hastily ratified in secret by the First Ministers, it was accomplished by marathon talks which continued into the early hours of the morning – two characteristics which are certainly not conducive to drafting the most essential piece of legislation governing Canada which is expected to meet the aspirations of all Canadians and the tests of time and circumstance.

To further aggravate the situation, the public hearings before the joint parliamentary committee were held during the summer months, the worst possible time of the year for any Government to encourage the participation, involvement and attention of Canadians. In addition, before the first witness had a chance to appear before the committee, government spokespersons made it painfully clear that the government-dominated committee would not be in any mood to accept any changes or consider any amendments. For once, unfortunately, the Government kept its word.

We saw the spectacle of individual Canadians and an impressive spectrum of organizations representing various constituencies travelling to the nation's capital to provide Members of Parliament and Senators with very moving and passionate presentations of their vision of Canada and of their dreams. All of these counted for absolutely nothing.

Canadians did not have a meaningful opportunity to share their dreams and their wishes for their country. This is a staggering and remarkable shortcoming because this stage in our constitutional evolution as a nation excluded the very people whom our Constitution is to serve and protect. There was no partnership. There was no give and take. The process was secret and dictatorial. It was a take-it-or-leave-it proposition from start to finish.

This approach, unfortunately, also gripped the elected Chamber. It was regrettable that many Members of Parliament of all stripes responded to those seeking changes and improvements by alleging that they were anti-Quebec or by promoting the concept that the inclusion of a new clause or the amendment of a current clause would scuttle the entire deal. The language and strategy used assumed that if the Accord could not convince Members on its own merit there was a need to intimidate individuals into accepting the Accord's version of Canada. This tack was not only unfortunate and misleading, it also depicted an air of desperation and insecurity as well as an attitude which was prepared to tolerate glaring and recognizable shortcomings in the Accord.

12. Charlotte Gray, "Clever Lowell Murray," *Saturday Night*, November, 1987, p. 14.

13. Jeffrey Simpson, "Anatomy of a Deal," *Globe and Mail*, June 2, 1987.

14. Acton, *Selected Writings*, p. 550.

15. See, for example, "Notes for an Address by Prime Minister Brian Mulroney on the Meech Lake Agreement," House of Commons, Ottawa, May 11, 1987 (mimeo), p. 7; Lowell Murray, Special Joint Committee, *Minutes*, No. 2, August 4, 1987, p. 23.

16. For a discussion of intrastate federalism, see Donald V. Smiley and Ronald L. Watts, *Intrastate Federalism in Canada*, Vol. 39, Research Studies of the Royal Commission on the Economic Union and Development Prospects for Canada (Toronto, 1985).

17. Government of Canada, *Strengthening the Canadian Federation: The Constitution Amendment* (Ottawa, 1987), p. 9.

Political Science, Ethnicity, and the Canadian Constitution

1. Donald L. Horowitz, *Ethnic Groups in Conflict* (Berkeley, 1985), p. 185.

2. Throughout this paper my references to political science are restricted to political science in English Canada. Their applicability to political science in the Francophone Quebec community is an open question.

3. In the depression of the thirties, of course, many English-Canadian scholars were highly critical of the constraints federalism placed on the central government, while more recently Quebec scholars have been critical of the constraints it put on Quebec nationalism.

4. Donald Smiley, "The Structural Problem of Canadian Federalism," *Canadian Public Administration*, 14 (Fall, 1971).

5. Task Force on Canadian Unity, *A Future Together: Observations and Recommendations* (Ottawa, 1979).

6. Keith Banting and Richard Simeon, eds., *And No One Cheered: Federalism, Democracy and the Constitution Act* (Toronto, 1983).

7. See, for example, Ramsay Cook, "Alice in Meechland or the Concept of Quebec as 'A Distinct Society,'" and John D. Whyte, "Submission to the Special Joint Committee of the Senate and the House of Commons on the 1987 Constitutional Accord," both in *Queen's Quarterly*, 94 (Winter, 1987); Bryan Schwartz, *Fathoming Meech Lake* (Winnipeg, 1987).

8. Ron Watts *et al.*, to the Special Joint Committee on the 1987 Constitutional Accord, July 22, 1987.

9. Kenneth McRoberts, "The Case for Meech Lake," *Canadian Forum* (December, 1987), p. 13. In marked contrast, the masthead of the Canadian Coalition on the Constitution, the organized focus of opposition to the Accord, which lists sixty-eight names, about one-third of whom are academics, has only three that I recognize as political scientists. Other political scientists who have serious reservations about the Accord are Roger Gibbins, Al Johnson, Orest Kruhlak, and the author of this article.

10. Richard Simeon, "Meech Lake and Shifting Conceptions of Canadian Federalism," *Canadian Public Policy*, 14, Supplement (1988), p. S-24.

11. Raymond Breton, "The Production and Allocation of Symbolic Resources: An Analysis of the Linguistic and Ethnocultural Fields in Canada," *Canadian Review of Sociology and Anthropology*, 21, 2 (1984).

12. Alan C. Cairns, "Citizens (Outsiders) and Governments (Insiders) in Constitution-Making: The Case of Meech Lake," *Canadian Public Policy*, 14, Supplement (1988).

13. See in particular Katherine Swinton, "Competing Visions of Constitutionalism: Of Federalism and Rights," and John D. Whyte, "The 1987 Constitutional Accord and Ethnic Accommodation," both in Katherine E. Swinton and Carol J. Rogerson, eds., *Competing Constitutional Visions: The Meech Lake Accord* (Toronto, 1988).

14. The protection of minority language education rights, of course, was the centrepiece of the federal government's constitutional goals.

15. Breton, "Production and Allocation of Symbolic Resources."

16. Elliot L. Tepper, "Demographic Change and Pluralism," paper presented to the Conference of Canada 2000: Race Relations and Public Policy, October 30-November 1, 1987, Carleton University, Ottawa (mimeo), p. 6.

17. Wm. H. McNeill, *Polyethnicity and National Unity in World History* (Toronto, 1986).

18. "Thus far the study of multiculturalism has been pursued mainly by sociologists, anthropologists, and historians. Other social scientists such as political scientists have largely ignored the area." Gilbert Scott, Director General, Multiculturalism, Department of Secretary of State, "Race Relations and Public Policy – Uncharted Course," June 8, 1987 (mimeo), p. 3. Howard Palmer also asserts that "Political historians and political scientists in Canada have shown very little interest in ethnic relations, other than their concern with the all-pervasive question of conflict and accommodation between English and French." "Canadian Immigration and Ethnic History in the 1970s and 1980s," *Journal of Canadian Studies*, 17 (Spring, 1982), p. 45. There are some exceptions – the work of Freda Hawkins and Gerry Dirks on immigration and refugee policy respectively, and John Wood and Elliot Tepper on East Indians and Southeast Asians in Canada. See also the impressive early work by University of British Columbia political scientist J.A. Laponce, *The Protection of Minorities* (Berkeley, 1960). John Solomos, "Trends in the Political Analysis of Racism," *Political Studies*, 34 (June, 1986), pp. 313-24, discusses the limited contributions of British political scientists to the analysis of racism, compared to the contributions of sociologists and anthropologists.

19. Horowitz, *Ethnic Groups in Conflict*, p. 13.

20. Kenneth D. McRae, "The Plural Society and the Western Political Tradition," *Canadian Journal of Political Science*, 12 (December, 1979), p. 685.

21. Robert H. Jackson, "Jurisprudence and Multi-Ethnic States," delivered at the International Congress of Anthropological and Ethnographic Sciences, Zagreb, Yugoslavia, July, 24-31, 1988 (mimeo), pp. 2-3.

22. Several of the quotations used in this section are also cited and discussed in Cairns, "Citizens (Outsiders) and Governments (Insiders) in Constitution-Making."

23. Zebedee Nungak, Co-Chairman, Inuit Committee on National Issues, Special Joint Committee, *Minutes of Proceedings and Evidence of the Special Joint Committee of the Senate and of the House of Commons on the 1987 Constitutional Accord*, No. 3, August 5, 1987, p. 28 (cited hereafter as Special Joint Committee, *Minutes*).

24. Special Joint Committee, *Minutes*, No. 14, August 27, 1987, p. 26.

25. Horowitz, *Ethnic Groups in Conflict*, p. 202.

26. Chief Hammond Dick, *Proceedings of the Senate Task Force on the Meech Lake Constitutional Accord and on the Yukon and the Northwest Territories*, No. 1, September 3, October 24, October 25, 1987, p. 96 (cited hereafter as *Senate Task Force*); Chief Charles K. Shawkenee of the Chippewa informed the Ontario Select Committee that "we

have been here at the very minimum of 10,000 years, and in the Ohio valley, at least 20,000 years." *(Ontario) Select Committee on Constitutional Reform 1987 Constitutional Accord,* February 25, 1988, afternoon sitting, draft transcript, p. C-71 (cited hereafter as *Ontario Select Committee).*

27. *Senate Task Force,* No. 3, November 2, 1987, p. 32.

28. Zebedee Nungak, Special Joint Committee, *Minutes,* No. 3, August 5, 1987, p. 30; Ernie Daniels, Interim President, Prairie Treaty Nations' Alliance, *Senate Debates,* December 16, 1987, p. 2458.

29. Hon. Stephen Kakfwi, *Ontario Select Committee,* February 16, 1988, morning sitting, p. C-19.

30. Gregg Smith, President, Indian Association of Alberta, *Proceedings of the Senate Submissions Group on the Meech Lake Constitutional Accord,* No. 4, March 15, 16, 1988, p. 26 (cited hereafter as *Senate Submissions Group);* Bill Cachagee, Chairperson Wabun Tribal Councils, *Ontario Select Committee,* March 7, 1988, p. C-12; Chief Gordon Peters, *Ontario Select Committee,* February 17, 1988, afternoon sitting, p. C-65; Harry Doxtator, President, Association of Iroquois and Allied Indians, *Ontario Select Committee,* February 18, 1988, morning sitting, p. C-7; Chief R.K. Miskokomon, Union of Ontario Indians, *Ontario Select Committee,* February 18, 1988, afternoon sitting, p. C-23.

31. Special Joint Committee, *Minutes,* No. 9, August 19, 1987, p. 50. See also Louis "Smokey" Bruyère, President, Native Council of Canada, *Senate Debates,* December 2, 1987, p. 2258. See the *Report of the Task Force to the Committee of the Whole, Senate of Canada,* February, 1988, ch. 6, for the recommendation that the Meech Lake Accord should also recognize "that the aboriginal peoples of Canada constitute distinct societies." However, not all aboriginals seek recognition as distinct societies. The legal counsel for the Four Nations of Hobbema argued that to put the distinct society label on the Indian people would be doing an injustice, for "a distinct society connotes something domestic, something within Canadian Confederation. This does not describe adequately what we as Indian people are. We, the Four Nations of Hobbema, are nations, a people in the international usage of the word. . . . We have our own unique culture, language, government, and political affiliations, and our own land. We are more than a distinct society, and to classify us as a distinct society would be to derogate and/or abrogate our right to self-determination." *Senate Submissions Group,* No. 5, March 18, 1988, p. 63. See also Chief Gordon Peters, Chiefs of Ontario, *Ontario Select Committee,* February 17, 1988, afternoon sitting, p. C-72.

32. Dr. Louis Melosky, National Director, Canadian Multiculturalism Council, *House of Commons, Minutes of Proceedings and Evidence of the Standing Committee on Multiculturalism,* No. 4, February 4, February 26, March 4, 1986, p. 13.

33. Charles Caccia, *House of Commons Debates,* September 30, 1987, p. 9508.

34. Sergio Marchi, *ibid.,* October 6, 1987, p. 9743.

35. Caccia, *ibid.,* September 30, 1987, p. 9508.

36. Marchi, *ibid.,* October 6, 1987, p. 9743.

37. Thor Broda, Vice-President, National Executive, Ukrainian Canadian Committee, Special Joint Committee, *Minutes,* No. 7, August 13, 1987, p. 100.

38. Arthur Heiss, Co-President, Canadian Institute on Minority Rights, *ibid.,* No. 12, August 25, 1987, p. 22. See also the briefs of the Canadian Ethnocultural Council, *ibid.,* No. 7, August 13, 1987, pp. 41-61, the German Canadian Congress, *ibid.,* No. 7,

August 13, 1987, pp. 70-80, and Council of Christian Reformed Churches in Canada, *ibid.*, No. 8, August 18, 1987, p. 105.

39. Tej Pal S. Thind, National Secretary, National Association of Canadians of Origins in India, *ibid.*, No. 7, August 13, 1987, p. 82.

40. Nothing in Section 2 of the Constitution Act, 1867 affects Section 25 or 27 of the Canadian Charter of Rights and Freedoms, Section 35 of the Constitution Act, 1982, or class 24 of Section 91 of the Constitution Act, 1867.

41. Andrew Cardozo, Executive Director, Canadian Ethnocultural Council, Special Joint Committee, *Minutes*, No. 7, August 13, 1987, p. 52; Dieter Kiesewalter, Executive Member, German-Canadian Congress, Special Joint Committee, *Minutes*, No. 7, August 13, 1987, p. 72.

42. National Congress of Italian Canadians, *Ontario Select Committee*, February 17, 1988, morning sitting, p. C-22; Canadian Ethnocultural Council, Special Joint Committee, *Minutes*, No. 7, August 13, 1987, p. 42. Spokespersons for virtually all ethnic groups made this demand in all the arenas available to them.

43. Broda, *ibid.*, No. 7, August 13, 1987, p. 103.

44. Roy Williams, President, Ontario Black Coalition for Employment Equity, *Senate Submissions Group*, No. 3, March 4, 1988, p. 108.

45. Howard McCurdy, *House of Commons Debates*, October 2, 1987, p. 9619.

46. Charles Caccia, *Senate Debates*, November 4, 1987, p. 2139.

47. Marchi, *House of Commons Debates*, October 6, 1987, p. 9743. See also the presentations of the Canadian Multilingual Press Federation in *Ontario Select Committee*, February 22, 1988, pp. C-15–C-30, and in the *Minutes of Proceedings and Evidence of the Standing Committee on Multiculturalism*, No. 11, December 7-8, 1987, pp. 26-41.

48. Bruyère, Special Joint Committee, *Minutes*, No. 12, August 25, 1987, pp. 95-96.

49. Deputy Grand Chief Lindbergh Louttit, Nishnawbe-Aski Nation, *Ontario Select Committee*, March 7, 1988, p. C-14.

50. Breton, "Production and Allocation of Symbolic Resources," p. 134.

51. Ukrainian Community Development Committee, *Building the Future: Ukrainian Canadians in the 21st Century* (Edmonton, 1986), pp. 5, 24.

52. Roy Williams, President, Ontario Black Coalition for Employment Equity, *Senate Submissions Group*, No. 3, March 4, 1988, p. 108.

53. T. John Samuel, "Immigration, Visible Minorities and the Labour Force in Canada: Vision 2000," paper presented at the Conference on Canada 2000: Race Relations and Public Policy, October 30-November 1, 1987, Carleton University, Ottawa (mimeo), p. 7.

54. Daiva K. Stasiulis, "The Antinomies of Federal Multiculturalism Policy and Official Practices," paper presented at the International Symposium on Cultural Pluralism, Montreal, October 19-20, 1985 (mimeo), p. 13. As Jean Burnet wrote in 1983, many new Canadians of non-European background "joined the Native peoples, now urbanizing, and earlier Asian and Black arrivals to constitute visible minorities far larger than Canada has been accustomed to. For them, the problems of learning English or French or maintaining ancestral languages and cultures is far outweighed by the problem of winning the right to be treated like everyone else by judges, policemen, teachers, employers, landlords, neighbours, and fellow passengers in buses and subways." Secretary of State of Canada, *Multiculturalism ... Being Canadian* (Ottawa, 1987), p. 14. See also Dr.

Harish C. Jain, *Minutes of Proceedings and Evidence of the Standing Committee on Multiculturalism*, No. 6, May 26, 1987, p. 18; the evidence of Jean Gammage, Vice-President, Urban Alliance on Race Relations, *Minutes of Proceedings and Evidence of the Standing Committee on Multiculturalism*, No. 10, December 7, 1987, pp. 41-56; John Cordice, Chairman, Research and Education Committee, Ontario Black Coalition for Employment Equity, *Minutes of Proceedings and Evidence of the Standing Committee on Multiculturalism*, No. 12, December 15, 1987, p. 20.

55. Both official-language minority communities, of course, had the strong support of the federal government during Mr. Trudeau's prime ministership.

56. Thus Doug Sanders notes that a "persistent problem [at first ministers' constitutional conferences on aboriginal self-government] has been the grouping of Indians, non-status Indians, Métis and Inuit in one forum." "An Uncertain Path: the Aboriginal Constitutional Conferences," in Joseph M. Weiler and Robin M. Elliot, eds., *Litigating the Values of a Nation: The Canadian Charter of Rights and Freedoms* (Toronto, 1986), p. 74. Note also the controversy over which organization speaks for Japanese Canadians seeking redress. See the statement of Otto Jelinek, Minister of State for Multiculturalism, *Minutes of Proceedings and Evidence of the Standing Committee on Multiculturalism*, No. 7, May 13, 1986, pp. 11-12, and the evidence of Arthur Miki, President, National Association of Japanese Canadians. No. 9, May 27, 1986, pp. 17-20.

57. John D. Whyte, "The 1987 Constitutional Accord and Ethnic Accommodation," in Swinton and Rogerson, eds., *Competing Constitutional Visions*, pp. 268-69.

58. Horowitz, *Ethnic Groups in Conflict*, p. 197.

59. *Ibid.*, p. 186.

60. Tepper, "Demographic Change and Pluralism," p. 24 (italics in original).

Political Scientists and the Constitutional Crisis

1. Alpheus Todd, *Parliamentary Government in the British Colonies* (Boston, 1880), p. x. See also his *Parliamentary Government in England*, 2 vols., 2nd ed. (London, 1887-89).

2. John S. Ewart, *The Independence Papers*, 2 vols. (Ottawa, 1925-32); and Ewart, *The Kingdom Papers*, 2 vols. (Ottawa, 1912-17).

3. See Carl Berger, *The Sense of Power: Studies in the Ideas of Canadian Imperialism 1867-1914* (Toronto, 1970).

4. Doug Owram, *The Government Generation: Canadian Intellectuals and the State 1900-1945* (Toronto, 1986).

5. *Ibid.*, ch. 9.

6. Thomas J. Courchene, *Equalization Payments: Past, Present and Future* (Toronto, 1984), p. 26.

7. Stephen Brooks and Alain G. Gagnon, "Social Scientists and Politics in Canada," in Alain G. Gagnon, ed., *Intellectuals in Liberal Democracies: Political Influence and Social Involvement* (New York, 1987), p. 24.

8. Stephen Brooks and Alain G. Gagnon, *Social Scientists and Politics in Canada: Between Clerisy and Vanguard* (Montreal, 1988); Brooks and Gagnon, "Social Scientists and Politics in Canada." See also Alain G. Gagnon, "The Role of Intellectuals in Modern Quebec: The Drive for Social Hegemony," in Stephen Brooks, ed., *Political Thought in Canada: Contemporary Perspectives* (Toronto, 1984).

9. Richard Simeon, "Inside the Macdonald Commission," *Studies in Political Economy*,

22 (Spring, 1987). See also R.A. Young, "Political Scientists, Economists, and the Canada-U.S. Free Trade Agreement," *Canadian Public Policy*, 15 (March, 1989), for disciplinary differences in assessing the free trade agreement.

10. Michael Oliver (Carleton) as Director and Léon Dion (Laval) as Special Consultant on Research.

11. David Cameron (Trent), who had earlier written on *Nationalism, Self-Determination and the Quebec Question* (Toronto, 1974), was the Research Director.

12. Alan Cairns (UBC), responsible for research on institutions, was one of three research directors. The other two were David Smith (Queen's), for economics research, and Ivan Bernier (Laval), responsible for legal research.

13. Further, two of the chief advisers the Task Force employed were political scientists, John Meisel and Léon Dion, while the third, Edward McWhinney, is a constitutional lawyer who teaches in the political science department at Simon Fraser University.

14. Four of the original eighteen members of the Ontario government's Advisory Committee on Confederation were political scientists – Alexander Brady, Eugene Forsey, Paul Fox, and John Meisel – as were two of the smaller seven-person advisory group established in British Columbia, Alan Cairns and Neil Swainson, with a third, constitutional lawyer Ron Cheffins, having taught previously in a political science department.

15. See, for example, David Elton, F.C. Englemann, and Peter McCormick, *Alternatives: towards the development of an effective federal system for Canada* (Calgary, 1978).

16. Peter Meekison was deputy minister of Federal and Intergovernmental Affairs for Alberta from 1978 to 1984. David Cameron, the former deputy minister of Intergovernmental Affairs in Ontario, previously held senior government responsibilities dealing with federalism and constitutional issues in the Federal-Provincial Relations Office and the Secretary of State's department. Norman Spector has moved from the position of senior constitutional adviser in British Columbia to his present position as secretary to the (federal) cabinet for federal-provincial relations. He has recently been joined by Peter Leslie, a leading student of federalism and former director of the Institute of Intergovernmental Relations at Queen's University, who is assistant secretary to the cabinet (policy development). A third political scientist, Jim Hurley, is a senior member of the FPRO. All of the preceding have been academic political scientists at one time or other.

17. John Porter, *The Vertical Mosaic* (Toronto, 1965), pp. 503-04.

18. *Report of the Special Joint Committee of the Senate and the House of Commons on the 1987 Constitutional Accord* (Ottawa, 1987).

19. Richard Simeon, *Federal-Provincial Diplomacy: The making of recent policy in Canada* (Toronto, 1972).

20. Donald Smiley, *Canada in Question: Federalism in the Seventies*, 2nd ed. (Toronto, 1976), ch. 3.

21. Donald Smiley, "The Structural Problem of Canadian Federalism," *Canadian Public Administration*, 14 (Fall, 1971).

22. Edwin R. Black and Alan Cairns, "A Different Perspective on Canadian Federalism," *Canadian Public Administration*, 9 (March, 1966).

23. See the discussion and analysis in Donald V. Smiley and Ronald L. Watts, *Intra-state Federalism in Canada*, Vol. 39, Research Studies of the Royal Commission on the Economic Union and Development Prospects for Canada (Toronto, 1985); Roger Gibbins, *Regionalism: Territorial Politics in Canada and the United States* (Toronto, 1982).

24. See William P. Irvine, *Does Canada Need a New Electoral System?* (Kingston, 1979), for a positive answer, and John C. Courtney, "Reflections on Reforming the Canadian

Electoral System," *Canadian Public Administration*, 23 (Autumn, 1980), for some reservations.

25. Rainer Knopff and F.L. Morton, "Nation-Building and the Canadian Charter of Rights and Freedoms," in Alan Cairns and Cynthia Williams, eds., *Constitutionalism, Citizenship and Society in Canada*, Vol. 33, Research Studies of the Royal Commission on the Economic Union and Development Prospects for Canada (Toronto, 1985). See also Peter H. Russell, "The Political Purposes of the Canadian Charter of Rights and Freedoms," *Canadian Bar Review*, 61 (March, 1983).

26. Peter H. Russell, "Constitutional Reform of the Judicial Branch: Symbolic vs. Operational Considerations," *Canadian Journal of Political Science*, 17 (June, 1984).

27. Roger Gibbins, *Senate Reform: Moving Towards the Slippery Slope* (Kingston, 1983); Donald Smiley, *An Elected Senate for Canada? Clues from the Australian Experience* (Kingston, 1985).

28. Jean A. Laponce, "Conseil au Prince qui voudrait assurer la survie du français en Amérique du Nord," *Cahiers québécois de démographie*, 17 (printemps, 1988); Laponce, *Languages and Their Territories* (Toronto, 1987).

29. See Owram, *The Government Generation*, chs. 6-10.

30. Richard Simeon, "Preface," in Richard Simeon, ed., *Must Canada Fail?* (Montreal, 1977), p. viii.

31. "The New Revolution in Political Science," Presidential Address to the American Political Science Association, 1969, reprinted in David Easton, *The Political System*, 2nd ed., (New York, 1971).

32. Smiley, *Canada in Question*, 2nd ed., p. viii.

33. Douglas E. Williams, ed., *Constitution, Government, and Society in Canada: Selected Essays by Alan C. Cairns* (Toronto, 1988), p. 190.

34. Arguments against the use of force can be found in Cameron, *Nationalism, Self-Determination and the Quebec Question*, p. 158; Simeon, "Introduction," in Simeon, ed., *Must Canada Fail?*, p. 4; Task Force on Canadian Unity, *A Future Together: Observations and Recommendations* (Ottawa, 1979), pp. 113-14. Frederick J. Fletcher, "Public Attitudes and Alternative Futures," in Simeon, ed., *Must Canada Fail?*, pp. 32-34, briefly discusses the majority antipathy of Anglophone Canada, based on poll data, to the use of force.

35. Denis Smith, *Bleeding Hearts . . . Bleeding Country: Canada and the Quebec Crisis* (Edmonton, 1971).

36. Two 1979 articles, by Reginald Whitaker and Donald Smiley, do not directly contradict this statement, but they both suggest that the breakup of Canada might not be a neat surgical separation. Whitaker eschews the language of a right to national self-determination for Québécois and asserts that the outcome will be determined by the relative bargaining power of Quebec and "English Canada"; and the latter "should take as tough a position as possible." Smiley, like Whitaker, does not advocate force, but he asserts that "liberal democracy is compatible only with piecemeal and incremental change," which would exclude such a "revolutionary act" as "the destruction of Canada." Hence, to Smiley, the idea of a peaceful Quebec route to independence is either naive or calculated deception by political leaders. Reginald Whitaker, "Competition for Power: Hobbes and the Quebec Question," *Canadian Forum*, 58 (January/February, 1979); D.V. Smiley, "Quebec Independence and the Democratic Dilemma," *Canadian Forum*, 58 (January/February, 1979).

These articles, however, were mild compared to the angry polemic of historian Donald

Creighton, whose message is summed up in its title, "No more concessions. If Quebec does go, let it not be with impunity," *Maclean's*, June 27, 1977.

37. Brooks and Gagnon, *Social Scientists and Politics in Canada*, p. 61.

38. An extreme illustration of this tendency was provided by Michael Brunet. In a lengthy review of Maurice Lamontagne's *Le Fédéralisme canadien* (Québec, 1954), Brunet asserted that "Le plus grave reproche qu'un critique canadien-français puisse adresser à M. Lamontagne c'est d'avoir systématiquement oublié qu'il est un Canadian français du Québec." *Canadians et Canadiens* (Montréal, 1954), p. 162.

39. Gad Horowitz was an articulate and prominent early exception. See his "Mosaics and Identity," originally from *Canadian Dimension*, December, 1965, and January, 1966, reprinted in Canadian Dimension, *Kit No. 4, Canadian Political Culture* (no date, no place). Horowitz wished to stimulate a class politics that was hindered in Canada by the unity-discord dialogue between French and English and by the provincial fragmentation of English Canada. A looser link with Quebec, he argued, would weaken the derivative provincialism of English Canada and stimulate a class politics focused on the national government of English Canada in Ottawa. Horowitz, however, was an exception in seeing benefits from a divided Canada. Further, his piece was written in the mid-sixties, almost before the constitutional debate was well under way.

In the seventies, Philip Resnick analysed and supported an "*English Canadian* sense of nationhood" that he argued was emerging to parallel the Quebec drive to independence, and which would result in two separate nations north of the United States. *The Land of Cain: Class and Nationalism in English Canada 1945-1975* (Vancouver, 1977), pp. 201 *passim*.

40. In a 1978 article, Abraham Rotstein argued that "English Canada's chief liability" in negotiating a new constitutional arrangement with Quebec "is its thin and underdeveloped sense of itself." "Is There an English-Canadian Nationalism?" *Journal of Canadian Studies*, 13 (Summer, 1978), p. 117. See also Kenneth McRoberts, *Quebec: Social Change and Political Crisis*, 3rd ed. (Toronto, 1988), pp. 310-21.

41. Daniel Latouche, *Canada and Quebec, Past and Future: An Essay*, Vol. 70, Research Studies of the Royal Commission on the Economic Union and Development Prospects for Canada (Toronto, 1986), p. 74.

42. Kenneth McNaught, "The National Outlook of English-speaking Canadians," in Peter Russell, ed., *Nationalism in Canada* (Toronto, 1966).

43. Latouche, *Canada and Quebec, Past and Future*, p. 77; see also p. 79.

44. Philip Resnick, "Letters to a Québécois Friend," unpublished ms., p. 14. Resnick's essay, with a reply by Daniel Latouche, has been published: *Letters to a Québécois Friend* (Montreal, 1990).

45. I am grateful to Cynthia Williams for drawing this point to my attention.

46. Rotstein, "Is There an English-Canadian Nationalism?" p. 114.

47. Latouche, *Canada and Quebec, Past and Future*, p. 92.

48. "An Address Given by Mr. René Lévesque, Prime Minister of Quebec, before the Members of the Assemblée Nationale, 'We are Quebeckers,' " (Paris, November 2, 1977), p. 13. An inability to appreciate the tenacity of provincialism in English Canada runs through Parti Québécois thinking. In 1968, Lévesque asserted: "by and large there are no serious reasons why nine provinces out of ten would not within the present constitutional framework accept readily, even eagerly, and in some cases with relief, strong central leadership with decentralization being limited to administrative procedures. . . ." René Lévesque, *An Option for Quebec* (Toronto, 1968), p. 78.

49. Charles Pentland, "Association after Sovereignty?" in Simeon, ed., *Must Canada Fail?*, p. 223.

50. There were, of course, occasional speculations. See, for example, Donald Smiley, "Central Institutions," in Stanley M. Beck and Ivan Bernier, eds., *Canada and the New Constitution: The Unfinished Agenda* (Montreal, 1983), vol. 1, pp. 76-83, for a brief analysis of the sovereignty-association option – described as "a design for deadlock" (p. 82) and concluding (pp. 82-83) that "sovereignty-neat" was probably more workable. Smiley's position was originally elaborated in *The Association Dimension of Sovereignty-Association: A Response to the Quebec White Paper* (Kingston, 1980). See also Peter Leslie, *Equal to Equal: Economic Association and the Canadian Common Market* (Kingston, 1979).

51. Retired Premier Leslie Frost of Ontario, as reported by Simeon, ed., *Must Canada Fail?*, p. vii.

Hugh Thorburn commented in 1977 that for the federal government "Even to permit subordinate officials to plan scenarios for separatism is to admit to a less than total commitment to the integrity of the country. The peremptory rejection of this suggestion in the past by the Trudeau government is ample testimony to the prevalence of this attitude." Simeon, ed., *Must Canada Fail?*, p. 206. See also Cameron, *Nationalism, Self-Determination and the Quebec Question*, pp. 128-29.

Earlier, Thorburn had given qualified support for a reconstituted Canada composed of a weakened central government and two national governments – Quebec would be the government of French Canada, with "the other to consist of the English-speaking provinces" who would come together in a new national government of English Canada. "Needed: A New Look at the Two Nations Theory," *Queen's Quarterly*, 80 (Summer, 1973), p. 271. The article was subsequently serialized in *La Presse*, Montreal, August 18, 20, 21, 1973. I am grateful to Hugh Thorburn for drawing this article to my attention.

52. Smiley, *Canada in Question*, 2nd ed., p. viii, referring to an earlier statement; Simeon, ed., *Must Canada Fail?*, pp. vii-viii, 1; R.M. Burns, ed., *One Country or Two?* (Montreal, 1971), pp. 2, 72, 73, 121, by various contributors.

53. Dan Usher, "The English Response to the Prospect of the Separation of Quebec," *Canadian Public Policy*, 4 (Winter, 1978), p. 58, and the replies by David L. Emerson and Daniel Latouche.

54. In *Canada in Question: Federalism in the Eighties*, 3rd ed. (Toronto, 1980), p. 261, Smiley wrote: "It may be that when Canadians in both Quebec and outside that province come to look at the alternatives cool-headedly they will decide that the creation of two or more jurisdictions possessing sovereignty in the fullest legal sense would be less than calamitous."

55. David Braybrooke, "Would the Crisis in Confederation be Resolved More Easily with Less Talk about Rights?" in Stanley G. French, ed., *Philosophers Look at Canadian Confederation* (Montreal, 1979), p. 313.

56. Simeon, ed., *Must Canada Fail?*, p. vii.

57. The same observation applies to an earlier volume with many of the same contributors: Burns, ed., *One Country or Two?*

58. An analogous point was made by David Cameron in a discussion of how English Canada had "sublimated" the question of Quebec's national independence. It is "not an issue which has received sustained and thorough consideration in English Canada. This is unfortunate and may prove to be a costly omission if, as is quite possible, Canada at some time in the future is faced with an independence movement which has come to power in

Quebec by the operation of the normal processes of representative democracy. Its cost may be high in any case if it can be shown that an unwillingness to think the problem through to the end has meant the closing down of options without serious assessment of them." *Nationalism, Self-Determination and the Quebec Question*, p. 127.

59. As David Cameron wrote: "There is no escape from responsibility; a public figure is as responsible for his silence as for his speech. It must in principle be admitted, I think, that there is a point beyond which the refusal to open consideration of such a painful and intractable issue may fairly be regarded as an avoidance of the duties of public office rather than as an exercise in restraint and statesmanlike caution. Acceptance of the idea that the initiation of discussion of a matter of public importance may in certain circumstances be irresponsible because it may help to bring on the very thing which is to be avoided includes as a necessary corollary the notion that the continuation of silence in other circumstances may be a serious abdication of responsibility." *Ibid.*, p. 129. The same logic surely applies to academics who seek to influence constitutional policy.

60. Ronald Watts appropriately reminded me in discussion that many reform proposals were a mixture of what, from a purist perspective, might look like rival prescriptions based on competing theories. I continue to think, however, that they can be usefully grouped according to their dominant reform orientations.

61. Donald V. Smiley, "Territorialism and Canadian Political Institutions," *Canadian Public Policy*, 3 (Autumn, 1977), p. 456.

62. Smiley and Watts, *Intrastate Federalism in Canada*, provide the best overview of this reform thrust.

63. See the various writings of the time by Garth Stevenson, Reg Whitaker, and Alan Cairns. Perhaps not surprisingly, lawyers were strong supporters of an entrenched Charter. See R.A. MacDonald, "Postscript and Prelude – the Jurisprudence of the Charter: Eight Theses," 4 *Supreme Court Law Review* (1982), pp. 340-41. Also, according to Janet Hiebert, law professor Walter Tarnopolsky, then president of the Canadian Civil Liberties Association, was especially influential in reining in the limitation clause. "The Evolution of 'Reasonable Limits' in the Charter," paper presented at the annual meeting of the Canadian Political Science Association, Windsor, June, 1988, pp. 17-18.

64. While the Constitution Act, 1982, contained an amending formula, an equalization commitment, and a resource section, as well as the Charter, the former were not central to the basic political science constitutional reform agenda.

65. See, for example, Donald V. Smiley, "The Case against the Canadian Charter of Human Rights," *Canadian Journal of Political Science*, 2 (September, 1969); Smiley, *The Canadian Charter of Rights and Freedoms, 1981* (Toronto, 1981); Peter Russell, "A Democratic Approach to Civil Liberties," in Frederick Vaughan, Patrick Kyba, and O.P. Dwivedi, *Contemporary Issues in Canadian Politics* (Scarborough, 1970). As Marc Gold observed, "some of the most articulate arguments against the Charter were offered by political scientists and not lawyers." "The Rhetoric of Rights: The Supreme Court and the Charter," *Osgoode Hall Law Journal*, 25 (Summer, 1987), p. 380 n13.

66. Ronald Watts *et al.*, letter to the Joint Clerks, July 22, 1987, and accompanying brief.

Ritual, Taboo, and Bias in Constitutional Controversies

1. *House of Commons Debates*, October 5, 1987, p. 9648.

2. Special Joint Committee, *Minutes of Proceedings and Evidence of the Special Joint*

Committee of the Senate and of the House of Commons on the 1987 Constitutional Accord, No. 7, August 13, 1987, p. 33.

3. "The Social Sciences in Canada: Retrospect and Potential," in Mabel F. Timlin and Albert Faucher, *The Social Sciences in Canada: Two Studies* (Ottawa, 1968), pp. 41-42.

4. On the 1982 Constitution Act, see Keith Banting and Richard Simeon, eds., *And No One Cheered: Federalism, Democracy and the Constitution Act* (Toronto, 1983).

5. See the remarks of Senator Jack Austin on the history of "bitter conflict" over the amending formula: *Senate Debates*, April 20, 1988, p. 3173.

6. *Reference Re Legislative Authority of Parliament to Alter or Replace the Senate* (1980), 1 S.C.R. 54.

7. *Attorney General of Manitoba et al. v. Attorney General of Canada et al.* In the Supreme Court of Canada, September 28, 1981.

8. *Re: Objection to a Resolution to amend the Constitution (Quebec Veto Reference) in the Supreme Court of Canada* (1982) 2 S.C.R. 793.

9. *Strengthening the Canadian Federation: The Constitution Amendment, 1987* (Ottawa, 1987), p. 9.

10. Eugene Forsey, "Submission on the Meech Lake Accord, to the NDP Public Hearings on that Subject," Calgary, September 22, 1987 (mimeo), p. 5.

11. The observations of Orest M. Kruhlak concerning the immigration provisions are to the point: "Without any discussion, the Government of Canada has decided to increase the role provinces other than Quebec can play in the selection of immigrants and apportioning of the number of immigrants between provinces. . . . where are the position papers that discuss the changes? Where is the Government of Canada's explanation of why it believes that Quebec and the other provinces should have an enhanced role in immigration policy?" "Constitutional Reform and Immigration," in Roger Gibbins, ed., *Meech Lake and Canada: Perspectives from the West* (Edmonton, 1988), p. 203.

12. For a more detailed analysis, see Alan C. Cairns, "Citizens (Outsiders) and Governments (Insiders) in Constitution-Making: The Case of Meech Lake," *Canadian Public Policy*, 14, Supplement (September, 1988); reprinted above as Chapter 4.

13. Robert C. Vipond, "Whatever Became of the Compact Theory? Meech Lake and the New Politics of Constitutional Amendment in Canada," *Queen's Quarterly*, 964, 4 (1989).

14. The analysis in this section is made at greater length in Alan C. Cairns, "Political Scientists and the Constitutional Crisis: The View from Outside Quebec," paper presented at the Inaugural Conference of the School of Policy Studies, Queen's University, "Policy Agendas for the 1990s," April 13-14, 1989; reprinted above as Chapter 8.

15. Daniel Latouche, *Canada and Quebec, Past and Future: An Essay*, Vol. 70, Research Studies of the Royal Commission on the Economic Union and Development Prospects for Canada (Toronto, 1986), p. 77.

16. Dan Usher, "The English Response to the Prospect of the Separation of Quebec," *Canadian Public Policy*, 4 (Winter, 1978), p. 58.

17. David L. Emerson, "Comments," *Canadian Public Policy*, 4 (Winter, 1978), p. 76.

18. Insight into the range of and limits to Anglophone academic analysis can be found in two volumes, R.M. Burns, ed., *One Country or Two?* (Montreal, 1971); Richard Simeon, ed., *Must Canada Fail?* (Montreal, 1977).

19. On the other hand, no prominent Canadian commentator employed nationalist rhetoric with the flourish of Lord Hailsham's reaction to the possible breakup of the United Kingdom: "if devolution is seen as a step towards complete separation, I wholly

reject it. Separation I regard as the destruction of my country, treason to the whole, treason to the separate parts, and worse still, treason to the Christian West of which we are all part and which now stands on the defensive against hostile forces determined to destroy everything that it stands for and all that it has contributed to human welfare." Lord Hailsham, *Elective Dictatorship* (London, 1976), p. 11.

20. Some of the material in this section is taken from an unpublished lecture: Alan C. Cairns, "Aboriginal Self-Government and Citizenship," presented to the Legal Theory Workshop, University of Toronto, April 24, 1987 (mimeo).

The probability that my observations in this section will be misunderstood is, regrettably, rather high. I do not deny that a body of literature tries to overcome some of the weaknesses in the discussion of aboriginal self-government. (See in particular the long list of publications from the research project on "Aboriginal Peoples and Constitutional Reform" organized by the Institute of Intergovernmental Relations, Queen's University.) However, much of this literature explicitly identifies many of the weaknesses I address. In any event, my concern is primarily with the explicit indications by various authors that candid discussion of many aboriginal issues is subject to pronounced and admitted psychological and cultural constraints.

21. Roger Gibbins and Radha Jhappan recently described "aboriginal politics as a field of study [that] abounds with polemics of various hues," and claimed it was "difficult to conduct dispassionate analysis of issues which essentially arise from Canada's ignoble historical treatment of aboriginal populations," a situation that makes most writers "in this field ... generally sympathetic towards aboriginal causes, and many feel compelled to take on an advocacy role." "The State of the Art in Native Studies in Political Science," paper presented at the Tenth Biennial Canadian Ethnic Studies Association Conference, Calgary, October 18-21, 1989 (mimeo), pp. 22-23.

22. See David C. Hawkes, *Aboriginal Peoples and Constitutional Reform: What Have We Learned?* (Kingston, 1989), for an assessment of the aboriginal constitutional process.

23. Douglas Sanders, "An Uncertain Path: The Aboriginal Constitutional Conferences," in Joseph M. Weiler and Robin M. Elliot, eds., *Litigating the Values of a Nation: The Canadian Charter of Rights and Freedoms* (Toronto, 1986), pp. 72-73.

24. Bryan Schwartz, *First Principles, Second Thoughts: Aboriginal Peoples, Constitutional Reform and Canadian Statecraft* (Montreal, 1986), p. 324.

25. *Ibid.*, p. 325. See also Sanders, "An Uncertain Path," p. 71, for a similar observation.

26. David C. Hawkes, "Preface," in Marc Malone, *Financing Aboriginal Self-Government in Canada* (Kingston, 1986), p. xi.

27. J. Rick Ponting and Roger Gibbins, "Thorns in the Bed of Roses: A Socio-political View of the Problems of Indian Government," in Leroy Little Bear, Menno Boldt, and J. Anthony Long, eds., *Pathways to Self-Determination: Canadian Indians and the Canadian State* (Toronto, 1984), p. 122.

28. For example, at the conclusion of a paper that addressed some of the problems that might attend the implementation of self-government, Roger Gibbins recently asserted that "I am left in the rather uncomfortable position of appearing to agree with opposition to aboriginal self-government expressed by some of the western premiers during the April, 1985, First Ministers' Conference. I hesitate to endorse their opposition, for by doing so I might appear to sanction the motivations that lay behind their opposition." "Citizenship, Political, and Intergovernmental Problems with Indian Self-Government," in J. Rick Ponting, ed., *Arduous Journey: Canadian Indians and Decolonization* (Toronto, 1986), p. 376.

29. Sally M. Weaver, "Indian Government: A Concept in Need of a Definition," in Little Bear, Boldt, and Long, eds., *Pathways to Self-Determination*, p. 65.

30. Roger Gibbins and J. Rick Ponting, "An Assessment of the Probable Impact of Aboriginal Self-Government in Canada," in Alan Cairns and Cynthia Williams, eds., *The Politics of Gender, Ethnicity and Language in Canada*, Vol. 34, Research Studies of the Royal Commission on the Economic Union and Development Prospects for Canada (Toronto, 1986), p. 174.

31. David C. Hawkes, "Preface," in C.E.S. Franks, *Public Administration Questions Relating to Aboriginal Self-Government* (Kingston, 1987), p. vi.

In a recent analysis, Frank Cassidy and Robert L. Bish, *Indian Government: Its Meaning in Practice* (Halifax, 1989), p. xx, the authors preface their volume as follows: "Nowhere in the literature . . . has a concerted effort been made to treat the practical issues of Indian government in a comprehensive and broad ranging manner – in a way that connects very specific subjects such as fire protection and child welfare services to such fundamental questions as: 'Who governs?' or 'How are Indian people governed and how do they govern themselves?'

"The major issues that have been treated systematically in debates and analyses of Indian government have, for the most part, focused on sovereignty, aboriginal rights, land claims, and constitutional entrenchment of self-government authority. While all of these issues are central, issue resolution has not proceeded very far because of the gap that appears to exist between these relatively general issues and the diversity of Indian government in Canada."

32. Sanders, "An Uncertain Path," p. 66.

33. Gibbins and Jhappan, "The State of the Art in Native Studies in Political Science," p. 24. They note that the "few scholars who have dared to express doubts about the appropriateness, and indeed authenticity, of aboriginal claims have been attacked and even ridiculed, regardless of the substance of their concerns."

34. See Ponting, ed., *Arduous Journey*, for frequent use of the colonialism analogy.

35. The data in this paragraph are from Andrew J. Siggner, "The Socio-Demographic Conditions of Registered Indians," in Ponting, ed., *Arduous Journey*; J. Perreault, L. Paquette, and M.V. George, *Population Projections of Registered Indians, 1982 to 1996* (Ottawa, 1985), pp. 53-55.

36. House of Commons, Special Committee on Indian Self-Government, *Report* (Ottawa, 1983).

37. "Most commentators," according to William J. Reeves, "would agree that the number of Métis and non-status Indians is greater than the number of status Indians and Inuit with a land base. For instance, recent estimates place the number of non-status Indians, including Métis, at 280,000 to 750,000, while about 30 per cent (100,000) of the approximately 350,000 status Indians live off-reserve, typically in the cities." "Native 'Societies': The Professions as a Model of Self-Determination for Urban Natives," in Ponting, ed., *Arduous Journey*, p. 344. An even larger figure is provided by Martin Dunn, who asserts that "a very rough (and very conservative) rule of thumb is that there are three [Métis and non-status Indians] for every registered Indian," which would produce a total figure of "at least 800,000 persons." *Access to Survival: A Perspective on Aboriginal Self-Government for the Constituency of the Native Council of Canada* (Kingston, 1986), p. 63 n1.

38. "Historical Overview and Background," in Ponting, ed., *Arduous Journey*, p. 35.

39. According to Douglas Sanders, Trudeau's reluctant conversion to support for self-

government was "on the basis that other approaches to aboriginal populations in Canada had failed." "An Uncertain Path," p. 71.

40. Schwartz, *First Principles, Second Thoughts*, p. 327.

41. Gibbins and Jhappan, "The State of the Art in Native Studies in Political Science," pp. 23-24.

42. Cassidy and Bish, *Indian Government: Its Meaning in Practice*.

43. For example, all five "women's" chapters in the following collections are by women: Banting and Simeon, eds., *And No One Cheered*; Gibbins, ed., *Meech Lake and Canada: Perspectives from the West*; K.E. Swinton and C.J. Rogerson, eds., *Competing Constitutional Visions: The Meech Lake Accord* (Toronto, 1988).

44. Gwen Brodsky and Shelagh Day, *Canadian Charter Equality Rights for Women: One Step Forward or Two Steps Back?* (Ottawa, 1989), pp. 303-09.

45. Little Bear, Boldt, and Long, eds., *Pathways to Self-Determination*; Menno Boldt and J. Anthony Long, eds., *The Quest for Justice: Aboriginal Peoples and Aboriginal Rights* (Toronto, 1985).

46. The four Quebec chapters in Banting and Simeon, eds., *And No One Cheered*, are written by Francophone Quebecers; the three chapters on Meech Lake and Quebec in Gibbins, ed., *Meech Lake and Canada*, are written by Quebecers, including former Prime Minister Trudeau and an Anglophone.

47. Robert K. Merton, "Insiders and Outsiders: A Chapter in the Sociology of Knowledge," *American Journal of Sociology*, 78 (July, 1972).

48. *Ibid.*, p. 30. This debate has an historic lineage in Canadian constitutional discussions. The controversy over continuing or ending appeals to the Judicial Committee of the Privy Council could be reconceptualized around the antithesis of "insider" versus "outsider," with the latter status attributed to the Judicial Committee by its defenders who found its virtue as a final appeal court in the fact that it was a distant, aloof arbiter that, in the language of the times, was "without local prepossessions." The Judicial Committee's opponents, the Canadian nationalists, the insiders, by contrast, argued the need for local knowledge, the intimate sympathies and understandings that could only come from long experience of living in the country whose future the decisions affected. See Alan C. Cairns, "The Judicial Committee and its Critics," *Canadian Journal of Political Science*, 4 (September, 1971), for a discussion employing different terminology.

49. Katherine Swinton, "Competing Visions of Constitutionalism: of Federalism and Rights," in Swinton and Rogerson, eds., *Competing Constitutional Visions*, p. 283.

50. See Evelyn Kallen, "The Meech Lake Accord: Entrenching a Pecking Order of Minority Rights," *Canadian Public Policy*, 14, Supplement (September, 1988).

51. For a recent example, see Brodsky and Day, *Canadian Charter Equality Rights for Women*.

52. "Insider" commentary that departs from the appropriate ideological stance arouses particularly virulent reactions. Thus Marie Smallface Marule, a member of the Blood tribe, lecturer in Native American studies, and a prominent administrator in aboriginal organizations, stated recently: "we must beware of the traitors in our midst – those of our people who have already accepted elitism, materialism, and individualism, who are trying to convince us that the Canadian way is the only way. Yes, it may be inevitable that our greatest enemies are within our own ranks." "Traditional Indian Government: Of the People, by the People, for the People," in Little Bear, Boldt, and Long, eds., *Pathways to Self-Determination*, p. 45.

53. Trudeau replied in a speech in Montreal. "Transcription de l'allocution du Tres

Honourable Pierre Elliott Trudeau du centre Paul Sauvé," Montréal, 14 mai 1980 (mimeo).

54. The issue of whether and in what ways members of majority groups can/should speak as or for minority group members is a controversial subject in literary studies. See Margery Fee, "Why C.K. Stead didn't like Keri Hulme's *the bone people*: Who can write as Other?" *Australian and New Zealand Studies in Canada*, 1 (1989), and the references there cited.

55. For good examples of this genre of rhetoric, see Brodsky and Day, *Canadian Charter Equality Rights for Women*, p. 17, for the women's movement, and the following, all from the *(Ontario) Select Committee on Constitutional Reform 1987 Constitutional Accord*: the evidence of Chief Gordon Peters, February 17, 1988, afternoon sitting, draft transcript, pp. C-67-68, for status Indians; Cathy McPherson, Co-ordinator, Persons United for Self-Help in Ontario, February 23, 1988, morning sitting, draft transcript, pp. C-10-11, for the disabled; and George Corn, President, Canadian Ethnocultural Council, March 10, 1988, afternoon sitting, draft transcript, p. 2, for multicultural Canadians.

56. Brodsky and Day, *Canadian Charter Equality Rights for Women*, p. 11.

57. *Ibid.*, p. 149.

58. *Ibid.*, p. 37.

59. *Ibid.*, p. 93.

60. The aboriginal peoples are an important exception in this regard.

61. Schwartz, *First Principles, Second Thoughts*, p. 327.

62. Cited in Merton, "Insiders and Outsiders," p. 33.

63. See *ibid.*, p. 35, for a discussion.

64. *Ibid.*

65. Ray Nichols, *Treason, Tradition, and the Intellectual: Julien Benda and Political Discourse* (Lawrence, Kansas, 1978), p. 22. Bryan Schwartz, after noting the tendency for academics to take the aboriginal "side," asserted: "There are enough skilled politicians, technical employees, and consultants available that academics are not needed to act as servants and mouthpieces for the competing interests. Their function ought to be to supply independent criticism and creative suggestions." *First Principles, Second Thoughts*, p. 326.

Passing Judgement on Meech Lake

1. Editorial, "Will Meech end not with a whimper but a whine?" *Globe and Mail*, June 21, 1990.

2. TV news program, June 25, 1990.

3. Hugh Winsor, "Trudeau message has great beat – but can you dance to it?" *Globe and Mail*, March 26, 1990.

4. Gil Rémillard, "L'Accord constitutionnel de 1987 et le rapatriement du Québec au sein du fédéralisme canadien," in Réal-A. Forest, dir., *L'adhésion du Quebec à l'Accord du Lac Meech*, (Montréal, 1988), p. 205 (translation).

5. Gilles Lesage, "Introduction," in Un Dossier du *Devoir*, Le Québec et le Lac Meech (Montréal, 1987), p. 20.

6. J. Peter Meekison, "The Meech Lake Accord: The End of the Beginning – or the Beginning of the End?" *Constitutional Forum*, 1 (Winter, 1990), p. 14.

7. Peter M. Leslie, *Rebuilding the Relationship: Quebec and its Confederation Partners; Report of a Conference at Mont Gabriel, Quebec 9-11 May, 1986* (Kingston, 1987), p. 33.

8. Robert M. Campbell,"Eleven Men and a Constitution: The Meech Lake Accord," in Robert M. Campbell and Leslie A. Pal, *The Real Worlds of Canadian Politics: Cases in Process and Policy* (Peterborough, 1989), p. 239.

9. Guy Laforest, "Ten Years Later: Trudeau and the Referendum," communication presentée au Congrès de l'Association canadienne de science politique, tenu a l'Université de Victoria, 27-29 mai 1990 (mimeo), p. 1.

10. Stephen A. Scott, "The Canadian Constitutional Amendment Process: Mechanisms and Prospects," in Clare F. Beckton and A. Wayne MacKay, eds., *Recurring Issues in Canadian Federalism*, Volume 57 of the Research Studies of the Royal Commission on the Economic Union and Development Prospects for Canada (Toronto, 1986), p. 105.

11. Claude Morin, "Trudeau nous a légué un héritage empoisonné," in Donald Johnston, ed., *Lac Meech: Trudeau parle ... Textes réunis et présentés par Donald Johnston* (Montréal, 1989), p. 134.

12. Graham Fraser, "Quebec will one day sign Constitution, PM says," *Globe and Mail*, June 25, 1990.

13. Canadian Press translation of Lucien Bouchard resignation letter to Prime Minister Mulroney, *Globe and Mail*, May 23, 1990.

14. Marcel Adam, "Laisser le Canada anglais faire de l'accord Meech son problème," in Johnston, ed., *Trudeau parle*, pp. 121, 123.

15. Robert Décary in Un Dossier du *Devoir, Le Québec et le Lac Meech*, p. 67 (translation).

16. "Notes for an address by the Right Honourable Brian Mulroney, Prime Minister of Canada, Meech Lake Accord Second Anniversary Speech," June 2, 1989 (mimeo), pp. 3, 10.

17. Editorial, "Cool the threats on Meech Lake," *Financial Post*, December 7, 1989, citing Mulroney.

18. Donald Smiley, "A Dangerous Deed: The Constitution Act, 1982," in Keith Banting and Richard Simeon, eds., *And No One Cheered: Federalism, Democracy and the Constitution Act* (Toronto, 1983), pp. 76, 78, 93.

19. Gordon Robertson, letter to the editor, *Globe and Mail*, March 25, 1989.

20. R.L. Stanfield and J.W. Pickersgill to Clyde Wells, February 21, 1990 (mimeo), p. 2; Stanfield, "Time for amends to Quebec," *Globe and Mail*, November 17, 1989.

21. The best discussion of the complex issues in this debate is Laforest, "Ten Years Later." The basic positions are vigorously expressed in Appendice A of Johnston, ed., *Trudeau parle*, with contributions by Marcel Adam, Trudeau, and Claude Morin.

22. Each provincial government received a veto over the Section 41 subjects covered by the unanimity requirement, including changes to the amending procedure itself. In Section 38 (2) a province was empowered to opt out of an amendment that derogated from the "legislative powers, the proprietary rights or any other rights or privileges of the legislature or government of a province." This opting-out principle was described by one of the amending formula's creators as "the cornerstone of the new amending formula," with the protection it gave "to each and every province" against constitutional amendments, falling in the above categories, that it opposed. J. Peter Meekison, "The Amending Formula," in R.D. Olling and M.W. Westmacott, eds., *Perspectives on Canadian Federalism* (Scarborough, 1988), p. 67. If opting out occurred on an amendment transferring

"provincial legislative powers relating to education or other cultural matters from provincial legislatures to Parliament," Canada was obligated to provide "reasonable compensation" to a non-participating province (Section 40).

23. This is an implicit assumption of many of the English-Canadian Meech Lake supporters, and it presupposes that the pan-Canadianism and potentially centralizing effects of the Charter greatly outweigh the provincial gains. A contrary view is expressed by Stephen Scott: "if assessed as the outcome of a negotiation, the November 5, 1981, agreement must, surely, be regarded as an overwhelming success for the provinces party to the April Accord. Their amending formula was adopted in almost every essential respect, and most of the guarantees of the Charter were subjected to the 'legislative override.' " "The Canadian Constitutional Amendment Process," p. 95.

24. Quebec had been the leading provincial proponent of full fiscal compensation in all cases conferring legislative jurisdiction on Parliament, a provision inserted in the Gang of Eight's April, 1981, Constitutional Accord, "and agreed to with varying degrees of enthusiasm by the other provinces." Meekison, "The Amending Formula," p. 65. The logic behind the demand for full fiscal compensation was explained in the accompanying text of the provincial accord: "This provision is designed to prevent a taxpayer, resident in a province to which the amendment does not apply, from paying twice: first, in his or her federal tax bill and second, to the province which continues to exercise the jurisdiction." [Gang of Eight], "Amending Formula for the Constitution of Canada: Text and Explanatory Notes," Ottawa, April 16, 1981, p. 6.

25. Section 6 mobility rights are qualified by Section 6 (4), which sanctions "any law, program or activity that has as its object the amelioration in a province of conditions of individuals in that province who are socially or economically disadvantaged if the rate of employment in that province is below the rate of employment in Canada."

26. Scott, "The Canadian Constitutional Amendment Process," p. 96.

27. *Ibid.*, p. 98.

28. The best short discussion of the reaction of the Parti Québécois government and the Liberal opposition to the contents of the November 5, 1981, agreement is contained in Scott, "The Canadian Constitutional Amendment Process," pp. 94-105. See also Claude Morin, *Lendemains piégés: Du référendum à la nuit des longs couteaux* (Montréal, 1988), pp. 284-314.

29. Scott, "The Canadian Constitutional Amendment Process," p. 99.

30. *Ibid.*, pp. 104-05.

31. Donald Johnston, ed., *With a Bang, Not a Whimper: Pierre Trudeau Speaks Out* (Toronto, 1988), p. 95.

32. The Constitutional Committee of the Quebec Liberal Party, *A New Canadian Federation* (Montreal, 1980), pp. 31-33.

33. Rémillard, "L'Accord constitutionnel de 1987 et le rapatriement du Québec," p. 205.

34. "Notes for a briefing of the Select Committee on Constitutional Reform, Ministry of Intergovernmental Affairs (Ontario), February 2, 1988" (mimeo), p. 8.

35. Attorney General for Ontario, "Brief to the Select Committee of the Legislature on Constitutional Reform, May 4, 1988" (mimeo), p. 11.

36. For this view, see Rémillard, "L'Accord constitutionnel de 1987 et le rapatriement du Québec," p. 190; also Claude Morin, "Trudeau nous a légué un héritage empoisonné," in Johnston, ed., *Trudeau parle*, p. 136. On the other hand, one of Trudeau's critics, Marcel Adam, believes that those who were constitutionally sophisticated knew what Trudeau

had in mind. "La vraie question est: comment les Québécois ont-ils compris M. Trudeau?" in Johnston, ed., *Trudeau parle*, p. 130.

37. When the Parti Québécois government, nearly a month after the November 5 agreement, established its minimum conditions for accepting the patriation plan, the Charter's automatic application to Quebec was to be restricted to democratic rights. Charter provisions relating to sexual equality, fundamental freedoms, and minority-language guarantees in education were not to restrict the jurisdiction of the National Assembly in these matters. The use of French and English in federal government institutions and services was acceptable. Scott, "The Canadian Constitutional Amendment Process," p. 103. When the federal government refused to agree to these conditions, the Quebec government vigorously used the notwithstanding clause and thus significantly blunted the impact of the Charter on the civic consciousness of Québécois.

38. Johnston, ed., *With a Bang*, p. 58. See also the French version, Johnston, ed., *Trudeau parle*, for an appendix containing more of Trudeau's defence of his actions. Unfortunately, the appendix is not reproduced in the English version.

39. Pierre Trudeau réplique: "Ce n'est pas comme cela qu'il faut écrire l'histoire,'" in Johnston, ed., *Trudeau parle*, pp. 141-42.

40. David Milne, *The Canadian Constitution: From Patriation to Meech Lake* (Toronto, 1989), p. 167. Contradictory poll evidence is cited by political scientist Pierre Fournier and Trudeau in Johnston, ed., *Trudeau parle*, p. 148. Although Latouche described 1982 as "a significant turning point" and asserts that "Quebec's defeat . . . was perceived as serious by broad sections of the Quebec population," he adds: "Yet we must not exaggerate the extent or intensity of a dissatisfaction that was the prerogative of those who actively participated in the political process, and in Quebec, as elsewhere, this is always a minority.

"The passage of the *Constitution Act, 1982* did not send the citizens running into the streets. Nor was the government anticipating vast movements of civil disobedience. Quebec City quite simply chose not to sign the constitutional agreement, rejecting both its letter and its spirit." Daniel Latouche, *Canada and Quebec, Past and Future: An Essay*, Volume 70 of the Research Studies of the Royal Commission on the Economic Union and Development Prospects for Canada (Toronto, 1986), p. 97.

41. Marcel Adam, "Peut-on imaginer l'Ontario isolée?" in Johnston, ed., *Trudeau parle*, p. 133 (translation).

42. "This argument is plausible." Peter M. Leslie, "Submission to the Special Joint Committee of the Senate and the House of Commons on the 1987 Constitutional Accord," in Clive Thomson, ed., *Navigating Meech Lake: The 1987 Constitutional Accord* (Kingston, 1988), p. 9.

43. Milne, *The Canadian Constitution*, pp. 156-57; Scott, "The Canadian Constitutional Amendment Process," p. 102.

44. Jean Chrétien, "Bringing the Constitution Home," in Thomas S. Axworthy and Pierre Elliott Trudeau, eds., *Towards a Just Society: The Trudeau Years* (Markham, Ont., 1990), pp. 296, 394.

45. Morin, *Lendemains piégés*, pp. 282-83.

46. For a contrary opinion, see Latouche, *Canada and Quebec*, pp. 69-71.

47. Attorney General of Manitoba *et al.* v. Attorney General of Canada *et al.* (Patriation Reference) In the Supreme Court of Canada, September 28, 1981, reproduced in Peter H. Russell, Rainer Knopff, and Ted Morton, *Federalism and the Charter: Leading Constitutional Decisions*, new edition (Ottawa, 1989), pp. 711-59. This volume (pp. 762-70)

also includes "Re: Objection to a Resolution to Amend the Constitution (Quebec Veto Reference) in the Supreme Court of Canada (1982) 2 s.c.r. 793, in which the Supreme Court unanimously and anonymously denied that patriating the constitution without Quebec's consent was "unconstitutional in the conventional sense."

48. Rhéal Séguin, "PQ has reason to celebrate 10 years after losing referendum," *Globe and Mail*, May 19, 1990; Lise Bissonnette, "A sheep in Trudeau's clothing," *Globe and Mail*, January 20, 1990.

49. Marcel Adam, "Peut-on imaginer l'Ontario isolée?" in Johnston, ed., *Trudeau parle*, p. 133. He admitted, however, that this would hold little attraction for Trudeau because of the divergence between his and Ryan's views on the reform of Canadian federalism.

50. Laforest, "Ten Years Later," pp. 1, 25.

51. *Ibid.*, p. 24. This is also the opinion of Adam, "La vraie question est: comment les Québécois ont-ils compris M. Trudeau?" in Johnston, ed., *Trudeau parle*, p. 131, and of Morin, *Lendemains piégés*, p. 37. Laforest's paper has been very helpful in drawing these and other references to my attention.

52. See in particular Trudeau's contributions in Appendice A of Johnston, ed., *Trudeau parle*.

53. Premier Robert Bourassa, speeches to the Quebec National Assembly, June 18, 1987, and June 23, 1987, in Johnston, ed., *With a Bang*, pp. 142-43. See also Gil Rémillard's prediction of the tremendous gains that would flow to Quebec from the distinct society clause, as quoted in Denis Robert, "La signification de l'Accord du lac Meech au Canada anglais et au Québec francophone: un tour d'horizon du débat public," in Peter M. Leslie and Ronald L. Watts, eds., *Canada: The State of the Federation 1987-88* (Kingston, 1988), p. 150.

54. For example, two of Bourassa's speeches are included as Appendix B in Johnston, ed., *With a Bang*. Johnston made frequent use of these and similar statements in his many interventions against Meech Lake.

55. Attorney General for Ontario, "Brief to the Select Committee of the Legislature on Constitutional Reform, May 4, 1988" (mimeo), p. 3.

56. Denis Robert, "La signification de l'Accord du lac Meech au Canada anglais et au Quebec francophone," in Leslie and Watts, eds., *Canada: The State of the Federation 1987-88*, pp. 118, 140.

57. Attorney General for Ontario, "Brief to the Select Committee of the Legislature on Constitutional Reform, May 4, 1988" (mimeo), p. 5.

58. Canadians for a Unifying Constitution, *Meech Lake: Setting the Record Straight* (n.p., 1990), p. 3.

59. See Un Dossier du *Devoir, Le Québec et le Lac Meech*, pp. 314-15, 375-77, for Lévesque's ambivalence in May and June, 1987.

60. Brian Mulroney to Clyde Wells, November 2, 1989 (mimeo), p. 3.

61. Lowell Murray, "The Process of Constitutional Change in Canada: The Lessons of Meech Lake," *Choices* (Institute for Research on Public Policy, February, 1988).

62. "Carstairs storms out of *Le Devoir* office after failing to get apology for cartoon," *Globe and Mail*, October 28, 1989.

63. David Hatter, "Opposing premiers hold firm on Meech," *Financial Post*, November 10, 1989.

64. Rhéal Séguin, "No sellout of Quebec, Premier tells Parizeau," *Globe and Mail*, June 12, 1990. In the final round of bargaining on a companion resolution, Bourassa made certain minor concessions to get an agreement: "I showed my good faith and accepted to

discuss certain subjects, such as the Canada clause, which has been discussed for the last 30 years. I also committed myself to the amendment on the equality of sexes, and I also accepted the legal opinion on the distinct-society clause." However, he felt the legal opinion would be of little or no value in the courts.

For many Quebec critics of the Accord, its spending power provisions were viewed as an unacceptable compromise in that they recognized the federal government's right to make conditional grants in areas of provincial jurisdiction.

65. Lucien Bouchard to Prime Minister Mulroney, May 21, 1990 (released by the Prime Minister's Office, May 22, 1990), p. 2.

66. John D. Whyte, to the Special Joint Committee, *Minutes of Proceedings and Evidence of the Special Joint Committee of the Senate and of the House of Commons on the 1987 Constitutional Accord*, No. 10, August 20, 1987, p. 60.

67. Ramsay Cook, "Alice in Meechland or the Concept of Quebec as 'A Distinct Society,' " in Thomson, ed., *Navigating Meech Lake*.

68. John D. Whyte, "Memorandum concerning the meaning and potential impact of section 7 of the constitutional accord, 1987," to the Canadian Council on Social Development, August 13, 1987 (mimeo), p. 11.

69. Mr. Colling Irving, Legal Counsel, Quebec Association of Protestant School Boards (Montreal), *Debates of the Senate*, February 3, 1988, p. 2617.

70. Laurence Grafstein, "*Look Back in Anger*: The 1987 Constitutional Accord, Report of the Special Joint Committee of the Senate and the House of Commons," *University of Toronto Faculty of Law Review*, 46 (Winter, 1988), pp. 231-32. Even the Report of the Special Joint Committee agrees that the Accord "reflects a more decentralized view of Canada than does the Constitution Act, 1982." The 1987 Constitutional Accord, *Report* of the Special Joint Committee of the Senate and the House of Commons, *Minutes of Proceedings and Evidence of the Special Joint Committee of the Senate and of the House of Commons on the 1987 Constitutional Accord*, No. 17, September 9, 1987, p. 15.

71. Even restrained and shrewd observers, such as Gordon Robertson, wrote of the "unwillingness of English-speaking Canada," and of " 'English Canada's' apparent refusal," etc., thus imputing a corporate existence and capacity to act to English (-speaking) Canada that does not exist. Gordon Robertson, *A House Divided: Meech Lake, Senate Reform and the Canadian Union* (Halifax, 1989), p. 70.

72. Doug Ward and Keith Baldrey, "Socreds say Meech has to change," *Vancouver Sun*, October 28, 1989.

73. Geoffrey York, "Opposition to Meech Lake accord gathers force in rural Manitoba," *Globe and Mail*, January 22, 1988.

74. Peter O'Neil, "Resentment in West a block to Meech deal, Devine says," *Vancouver Sun*, August 22, 1989.

75. John Schreiner, "Filmon's stand on accord wins support," *Financial Post*, March 26, 1990.

76. Julian Beltrame, "Politicians seen as part of bilingualism problem," *Vancouver Sun*, February 24, 1990.

77. Graham Fraser, "Politicians grope awkwardly to respond to municipalities' English-only resolutions," *Globe and Mail*, February 9, 1990.

78. "Globe and Mail-CBC News/Poll," *Globe and Mail*, July 9, 1990. Five per cent were "Not sure/don't know." Among home-language French speakers, the approval rate was 12 per cent, the disapproval rate 86 per cent, and not sure/don't know 2 per cent.

79. Manitoba Task Force on Meech Lake, *Report on the 1987 Constitutional Accord* (Winnipeg, 1989), pp. 18-19.

80. Graham Fraser, "Federal Strategy on Meech coming to light," *Globe and Mail*, March 10, 1990.

81. Grafstein, "*Look Back in Anger*," p. 227.

82. Robert, "La signification de l'Accord du lac Meech," pp. 121, 141-42, 149, 153. This is an extremely valuable article on differences in attitudes in Francophone Quebec and English Canada to the constitution in general and the Charter in particular.

The views of the Charter as a threat and of the "distinct society" as a defence against its homogenizing pressures are recurring leitmotifs in a collection of Quebec documents on the Meech Lake debate. Un Dossier du *Devoir, Le Québec et le lac Meech*, pp. 109-10, 123, 152-54, 157, 158-61, 180-81, 196, 252, 256.

83. At least one Southam News-Angus Reid poll indicated that 62 per cent of Quebecers agreed with non-Quebec opinion that the Charter of Rights should take precedence over the distinct society provisions. Discussed in editorial, "The real voice of the people," *Financial Post*, November 15, 1989.

84. Rémillard, "L'Accord constitutionnel de 1987 et le rapatriement du Québec," in Forest, dir., *L'Adhésion du Québec*, pp. 193, 205.

85. Jeremy Webber *et al.*, Letter to Editor, November 2, 1989 (mimeo), p. 1.

86. Lise Bissonnette, "It's once more unto the Meech for Canadians," *Globe and Mail*, March 12, 1988; Lise Bissonnette, "Quebeckers muddled over Meech," *Globe and Mail*, October 28, 1989.

87. Un Dossier du *Devoir, Le Québec et le lac Meech*, pp. 169, 185, 195, 196, 205-06, 214, 322.

88. Webber *et al.*, Letter to Editor, November 2, 1989 (mimeo).

89. Graham Fraser, "Premiers who oppose accord 'desire a solution,' minister says," *Globe and Mail*, January 8, 1990.

90. "Meech discord report rouses PM," *Vancouver Sun*, March 8, 1988. Shortly after this, Mulroney commented: "I have a commitment from the premiers that this thing is going to pass. It's going to pass. We have the undertaking, and that's that." Graham Fraser, "PM says 1982 flaws removed 'flexibility' in Meech Lake talks," *Globe and Mail*, June 13, 1988.

91. Susan Delacourt and Graham Fraser, "Marathon talks were all part of plan, PM says," *Globe and Mail*, June 12, 1990. "Posing the question rhetorically to the three holdouts, he [Mulroney] said: 'How can we explain to you why certain things were done when you weren't there? And perhaps had you been there, we'd have done things differently. But you weren't there, you weren't elected, so you didn't have the right to be there."

92. "One of the most astonishing, and frightening, things about the Proceedings before the Joint Committee . . . has been that the defenders of the Accord seem to have made not the faintest attempt to analyze, and answer, the very specific, detailed adverse criticisms of one section after another, by people eminently qualified to speak." Eugene Forsey, "Submission on the Meech Lake Accord, to the NDP Public Hearing on that Subject, Calgary, September 22, 1987" (mimeo), p. 5.

Forsey was also extremely critical of the quality of the *Report of the Special Joint Committee of the Senate and the House of Commons on the Meech Lake Accord*, as was Laurence Grafstein. See Eugene Forsey, "Analysis of the Report of the Joint Committee on the Constitutional Accord, 1987," mimeo (n.d., n.p.); Grafstein, "*Look Back in Anger*."

93. "Notes for an Address to the House of Commons by the Right Honourable Brian Mulroney, Ottawa, March 27, 1990" (mimeo), p. 3.

94. Lynn Smith, "Could the Meech Lake Accord Affect the Protection of Equality Rights for Women and Minorities in Canada?" *Constitutional Forum*, 1 (Winter, 1990), p. 17.

95. See *Report* of the Special Joint Committee of the Senate and the House of Commons, September 9, 1987, pp. 129-36, for the argument that the Meech Lake process was justified by and should be limited to the unique Quebec situation to which it was a response, and pp. 142-43, for the argument that future processes of constitutional change must be more open. Also (Ontario) Select Committee on Constitutional Reform, *Report on the Constitution Amendment 1987* (Toronto, 1988), pp. 4-6, 42-45, 47-48. And *Report* of the Special Committee to Study the Proposed Companion Resolution to the Meech Lake Accord, *Minutes of Proceedings and Evidence of the Special Committee to Study the Proposed Companion Resolution to the Meech Lake Accord*, No. 21, May 8-15, 1990, p. 9, recommendation 13.

96. Manitoba Task Force, *Report on the 1987 Constitutional Accord*, pp. 69-71; Legislative Assembly of New Brunswick, Select Committee on the 1987 Constitutional Accord, *Final Report on the Constitutional Amendment 1987* (Fredericton, 1989), pp. 25-29.

97. Senate of Canada, "Committee of the Whole on the Meech Lake Constitutional Accord, Third Report, June 1988," pp. 23-27, with extensive citation from witnesses opposed to the process.

98. Premier Wells asserted that "perhaps the worst flaw in the Accord was the closed process which resulted in eleven first ministers telling the 26 million people of Canada how they will be governed in the future, instead of the 26 million people of Canada telling the eleven first ministers how they will govern." "The Meech Lake Accord, An Address to the Canadian Club of Montreal by Clyde Wells, 19 January 1990" (mimeo), p. 1. Newfoundland's proposals to open up the process are noted in "Constitutional Proposal: 'An Alternative to the Meech Lake Accord' Submitted by the Government of Newfoundland and Labrador to the First Ministers' Conference November 9th and 10th, 1989," p. 7.

99. Manitoba Task Force, *Report on the 1987 Constitutional Accord*, pp. 5, 70.

100. Cohen, "That Bastard Trudeau," *Saturday Night*, June, 1990, pp. 45-46. This view, of course, was central to Trudeau's criticisms. See Johnston, ed., *With a Bang*. See also Roger Gibbins for similar criticisms: "A Sense of Unease: The Meech Lake Accord and Constitution-Making in Canada," in Gibbins, ed., *Meech Lake and Canada: Perspectives from the West* (Edmonton, 1988), pp. 125-29.

101. Tony Hall, "Native People – A Search for Dignity," *Globe and Mail*, August 2, 1988.

102. Geoffrey York, "Meech faces rough ride in Manitoba Legislature," *Globe and Mail*, June 11, 1990. It is appropriate to put aboriginal "opposition to the Meech Lake Accord . . . into perspective. For aboriginal people the Accord, following as it did on the heels of the failed aboriginal summit of March 1987, is yet another instance in Canada's history where native interests have been ignored. To understand their fears one has to remember that since Confederation Canada has at one time or another made it impossible for Indians to become lawyers or doctors, required Indians on the prairies to have a pass to leave the reserve, outlawed the potlatch in B.C., forcibly relocated the Inuit in the early 1960s from Port Harrison (Inukjuak), Quebec to Resolute Bay and Grise Fjord, North West Territories, and has unilaterally taken land which has been reserved for Indians. The Meech Lake Accord is seen as part of the pattern by federal and provincial authorities to

42

deny aboriginal rights. For native people, the Accord is another nail in the coffin, burying native aspirations." Donald J. Purich, "The Meech Lake Accord and Canada's Aboriginal People," in John D. Whyte and Ian Peach, eds., *Re-Forming Canada? The Meaning of the Meech Lake Accord and the Free Trade Agreement for the Canadian State* (Kingston, 1989), pp. 78-79.

103. Section 16 of the Accord exempted the Section 27 multicultural clause of the Charter and various aboriginal constitutional clauses from the ambit of the Section 2 interpretation clause.

104. Beverly Baines, "The 1987 Constitutional Accord and Sexual Equality Rights," *CAUT Bulletin*, June, 1988, p. 11.

105. Manitoba Task Force, *Report on the 1987 Constitutional Accord*, p. 24.

106. Normally, according to Anthony Parel, multiculturalism makes it onto the constitutional agenda as an afterthought. "The Meech Lake Accord and Multiculturalism," in Gibbins, ed., *Meech Lake and Canada*, pp. 171-73. Lynn Smith, "Could the Meech Lake Accord Affect the Protection of Equality Rights?" is a good example of the generalized distrust of the first ministers in charge of the Meech Lake process.

107. To Mulroney, the first and "crystal clear lesson is . . . to ensure public involvement." Premier Wells said "never again" and referred to "the total unacceptability of this process." According to Filmon, no first minister "would ever participate [again] in [such] a process" devoid of public input. To McKenna, "the most important" concern was the unacceptability of the process. Peterson agreed that the process must become "more open . . . more sensitive and more responsive." *First Ministers' Conference on the Constitution*, verbatim transcript, Ottawa, Ontario, June 9-10, 1990 (Document: 800-029/004 Canadian Intergovernmental Conference Secretariat), pp. 3, 9, 24, 33, 44.

108. [Gang of Eight], "Amending Formula for the Constitution of Canada: Text and Explanatory Notes," Ottawa, April 16, 1981.

109. Paul M. Sniderman *et al.*, "Consensus and Dissensus: Mass and Elite Attitudes toward Language Rights in the Canadian Charter of Rights and Freedoms," revised version of a paper presented at the annual meeting of the American Political Science Association, mimeo, Chicago, 1987, p. 21.

110. Johnston, ed., *With a Bang*, pp. 94-95. See also pp. 46, 58.

111. John D. Whyte, "The 1987 Constitutional Accord and Ethnic Accommodation," in Katherine E. Swinton and Carol J. Rogerson, eds., *Competing Constitutional Visions: The Meech Lake Accord* (Toronto, 1988); Michael Behiels, "General Introduction," in Michael D. Behiels, ed., *The Meech Lake Primer: Conflicting Views of the 1987 Constitutional Accord* (Ottawa, 1989).

112. William Thorsell, "Canadians reclaim their many solitudes," *Globe and Mail*, September 23, 1989.

113. Bourassa responded to Mulroney's attacks on the notwithstanding clause as follows: "The leader of Quebec cannot abdicate his responsibility to protect the French culture to another government which is responsible to a majority of another culture." He described the clause as "not only useful to Quebec, but also necessary." Benoit Aubin, "Fight looms over opting-out clause," *Globe and Mail*, April 7, 1989.

114. Robert, "La signification de l'Accord du lac Meech," pp. 118, 140-41 (my translation).

115. Manitoba Task Force, *Report on the 1987 Constitutional Accord*, p. 25.

116. New Brunswick Select Committee, *Final Report on the Constitutional Amendment 1987*, p. 42.

117. New Brunswick Select Committee, *Final Report on the Constitutional Amendment 1987*, p. 44.

118. Samuel LaSelva, "Does the Canadian Charter of Rights and Freedoms Rest on a Mistake?" *Windsor Yearbook of Access to Justice*, 8 (1988), p. 223.

119. In a poll taken early in February, 1990, the following responses were given to the statement: "Quebec should have the right to pass laws affecting the distinctive culture and language of Quebec – even if those laws conflict with the Charter of Rights and Freedoms."

Strongly agree	8%
Agree	13%
Disagree	34%
Strongly disagree	37%
Not sure/don't know	8%

Globe and Mail, February 12, 1990. No breakdown was provided for French-English or Quebec/rest-of-Canada differences in responses.

120. Canadians for a Unifying Constitution, *Meech Lake: Setting the Record Straight*, p. 6. See also Stanfield and Pickersgill to Clyde Wells, January 10, 1990, mimeo (open letter), p. 3.

121. Susan Delacourt and Rhéal Séguin, "PM scrambling to save Meech accord," *Globe and Mail*, May 23, 1990. In the average three-year period within the past fifteen years there were nine federal or provincial elections, three of which resulted in a change of government, with obvious potential negative consequences for incomplete ratification processes under the three-year rule. "The opposition to Meech: The Recalcitrants or the Amending Formula?" *Language and Society*, 31 (Summer, 1990), p. 9.

122. Jean Chrétien, "A Challenge of Leadership, A Speech delivered . . . to the Faculty of Law, University of Ottawa, January 16, 1990" (mimeo), p. 11.

123. *Ibid.*

124. Daphne Bramham, "A 'Brooklyn Bridge' in Meech Proposal," *Vancouver Sun*, June 7, 1990.

125. Pauline Comeau, "The Man who Said No," *Canadian Forum*, LXVIV (July/August, 1990), p. 11.

126. J.A. Corry, "The Uses of a Constitution," in Law Society of Upper Canada, Special Lectures, *The Constitution and the Future of Canada* (Toronto, 1978), pp. 1-15.

127. Peter Russell, "The Supreme Court Proposals in the Meech Lake Accord," p. S104, and Richard Simeon, "Meech Lake and Shifting Conceptions of Canadian Federalism," p. S23, both in *Canadian Public Policy*, 14, Supplement (September, 1988).

128. "Globe and Mail-CBC News/Poll," *Globe and Mail*, July 9, 1990. In a slightly earlier poll, 71 per cent of Canadians supported having a referendum on Meech Lake, including 58 per cent Quebec support. Julian Beltrame, "Canadians want Meech referendum, poll finds," *Globe and Mail*, April 7, 1990.

Acknowledgements

Permission to reprint the following articles is gratefully acknowledged from: *Canadian Public Policy*: "Recent Federalist Constitutional Proposals," v, 3 (1979), and "Citizens (Outsiders) and Governments (Insiders) in Constitution-Making: The Case of Meech Lake," xiv, Supplement (1988);"An Overview of the Trudeau Constitutional Proposals," *Alberta Law Review*, xix, 3 (1981); "Federalism and the Provinces," Centre for Human Settlements, Faculty of Graduate Studies, University of British Columbia, and Hilda Symonds and H. Peter Oberlander, eds., *Meech Lake: From Centre to Periphery* (Vancouver, 1988); "Ottawa, the Provinces, and Meech Lake," Academic Printing & Publishing and Roger Gibbins, ed., with Howard Palmer, Brian Rusted, and David Taras, *Meech Lake and Canada: Perspectives from the West* (Edmonton, 1988); "The Politics of Constitutional Renewal in Canada," Keith G. Banting and Richard E. Simeon; "Political Science, Ethnicity, and the Canadian Constitution," from David Shugarman and Reg Whitaker, eds., *Federalism and Political Community: Essays in Honour of Donald Smiley* (Peterborough, Ont.: Broadview Press, 1989); "Ritual, Taboo, and Bias in Constitutional Controversies in Canada, or Constitutional Talk Canadian Style," *Saskatchewan Law Review*, 54 (1990).

We would also like to thank Thomas Courchene and the School of Policy Studies, Queen's University, for allowing us to publish the author's address to the School's Inaugural Conference, "Political Scientists and the Constitutional Crisis: The View from Outside Quebec," April 13–14, 1989.

The editor would also like to acknowledge the generous financial assistance of the Social Sciences and Humanities Research Council of Canada.